LIBRARY IN A BOOK

GAY RIGHTS

Rachel Kranz
Tim Cusick

Facts On File, Inc.

GAY RIGHTS

Facts On File, Inc.
11 Penn Plaza
New York NY 10001

Library of Congress Cataloging-in-Publication Data

Kranz, Rachel.
    Gay rights. / Rachel Kranz and Tim Cusick.
       p. cm.— (Library in a book)
    Includes bibliographical references and index.
    ISBN 0-8160-4235-7
      1. Gay rights—United States. I. Cusick, Tim. II. Title. III. Series.

HQ76.8.U5 K73 2000
305.9`0664—dc21

                                  00-035348

Facts On File books are available at special discounts when purchased in bulk quantities for businesses, associations, institutions or sales promotions. Please call our Special Sales Department in New York at 212/967-8800 or 800/322-8755.

You can find Facts On File on the World Wide Web at http://www.factsonfile.com.

Text design by Ron Monteleone

Printed in the United States of America.

MP Hermitage 10 9 8 7 6 5 4 3 2 1

This book is printed on acid-free paper.

CONTENTS

Acknowledgments

PART I
OVERVIEW OF THE TOPIC

Chapter 1
Introduction to Gay Rights   **3**

Chapter 2
The Law of Gay Rights   **70**

Chapter 3
Gay Rights and U.S. Culture   **101**

Chapter 4
Chronology   **122**

Chapter 5
Biographical Listing   **135**

Chapter 6
Glossary   **152**

PART II
GUIDE TO FURTHER RESEARCH

Chapter 7
How to Research Gay Rights   **161**

Chapter 8
Annotated Bibliography   **170**

Chapter 9
Organizations and Agencies   **243**

PART III
APPENDICES

Appendix A
Excerpts from Court Decisions   **253**

Appendix B
Excerpts from Statements of Government
Policy and Legislation   **272**

Appendix C
Excerpts from Historical Documents   **276**

Credits   **286**

Index   **287**

Acknowledgments

The authors wish to thank Jeff Domoto, for his tireless and invaluable help with databases and other computer-related problems; Paula Ettelbrick, for her cogent and generous explanations; and Terence Maikels, for his expert, patient work as editor.

For his invaluable web site, www.gayrightsinfo.com, the authors thank the anonymous but thorough site author.

For help with permissions, they also wish to thank Martha Shelley; Karla Jay; Nancy K. Bereano of Firebrand Books; and Urvashi Vaid.

Finally, Rachel Kranz wishes to thank Ellie Siegel for the conversations that began many years ago and that have borne fruit in the writing of this book.

PART I

OVERVIEW OF THE TOPIC

CHAPTER 1

INTRODUCTION TO GAY RIGHTS

One of the most astonishing social transformations of the past three decades has been the changes wrought by the gay rights movement in the United States. Homosexuality has gone from being a taboo subject that could barely be mentioned in public to a common topic of debate among politicians, voters, and the media. From being invisible, closeted, and fearful of persecution, gay men and lesbians have "come out" as politicians, TV stars, activists, and "the family next door." The notion of legally recognized gay marriage, once an unthinkable concept, has become a genuine possibility, as portrayed positively on popular TV shows like *Friends* and negatively acknowledged in the federal "Defense of Marriage Act," which was designed to keep any state from recognizing same-sex marriages. In many states and cities around the country, gay people have won an array of court, legislative, and cultural victories: the right to receive domestic partnership benefits, antidiscrimination laws in employment and housing, positive representation in school curricula, increased penalties for antigay violence that can be viewed as "hate crimes," and an unprecedented visibility in U.S. culture, from openly gay musicians (k.d. lang, Elton John, George Michael) to movie and TV stars (Anne Heche, Ellen DeGeneres, Rupert Everett) to politicians (Massachusetts representative Barney Frank; Maine state treasurer Dale McCormick; New York state senator Deborah Glick; Carrboro, North Carolina mayor Michael Nelson). Even the terminology has changed: from "homosexual," "invert," and "pervert" to "gay," "queer," and "out and proud."

Ironically, these very victories have brought with them a backlash. Many nationwide religious and political groups have made antigay activity a major item on their agenda, including a wide variety of legal and political efforts: electing antigay state and city legislators, working to repeal local gay rights ordinances, and organizing statewide referendums to overturn local antidiscrimination rules. Another recent trend is the growing number of boycotts of allegedly "gay-positive" TV shows and their corporate sponsors, as well as recent campaigns against "gay-friendly" companies—companies that advertise in gay publications, offer domestic partnership benefits to gay employees, and include antidiscrimination language in their personnel policies. Legal, political, and cultural battles are being fought over school curricula, public libraries, and the laws regulating adult sexual activity.

The contradictory situation for gay rights can be summed up by contrasting the long roster of corporations and city agencies that offer domestic partnership benefits with the almost 20 states in which gay sexual activity is explicitly illegal; by placing the dozens of openly gay politicians alongside the list of antigay resolutions taken in cities and states around the country; by turning from the new visibility of gay men and lesbians on prime-time TV to the escalating wave of nationwide antigay violence in places as diverse as Greenwich Village in New York City and Laramie, Wyoming.

Clearly, no one book can cover everything there is to know about gay rights. This book's goal is much more modest: to provide a sense of the major issues in this important movement, and to offer ways of finding out more information. To that end, this chapter provides an overview of the movement and its history. The next chapter focuses on gay legal issues and mentions important court cases and major developments in government policy. Chapter 3 discusses cultural issues: what's been going on in schools, the arts, popular culture, religion, and public opinion. A chronology outlines the political evolution of gay rights. A set of brief biographies of major figures in the area and a small glossary are also available for further reference.

Part 2 of this book offers a wide variety of suggestions for researching gay rights; provides a bibliography of recent articles and major books; and lists organizations—some in favor of gay rights and some opposed. Finally, the book concludes with some documents—articles, manifestos, speeches, laws, and court decisions—that convey key issues that have preoccupied the gay rights movement for the past 30 years.

It's important to remember that although there has been a powerful movement for gay and lesbian rights, there's no such thing as a single "gay rights movement." That is, while a number of people and organizations have fought many political, legal, and cultural battles, there is not necessarily widespread agreement on any side. Some gay activists have advocated working within the system; others have urged demonstrations and direct action. Some gay rights leaders argue that gay people are a distinct culture that ought to be respected; others insist that gay men and lesbians are exactly like their heterosexual counterparts except for their choice of a same-sex romantic partner. Some gay activists are deeply concerned with the rights of sexual minorities, among them transgendered people and people who practice sadomasochism and other unconventional sex acts. Other gay leaders fear that "those people give the rest of us a bad name." Over the past 30 years—since the modern gay rights movement began with the Stonewall uprising of 1969—gay rights activists have argued over sexual freedom, political strategy, and the very definition of gayness and lesbianism.

Meanwhile, many gay individuals do not even see themselves as supporting "gay rights," preferring to hide their homosexuality or play down its importance. Yet these same people might be moved by a political crisis, such as the spread of AIDS or a statewide referendum calling for the firing of any teacher suspected of being gay. Or they might be moved by a more personal matter—a longtime partner being excluded from a family event, the threat of losing custody of a child, the realization that their boss or colleagues regularly exclude them from the "social" luncheons and afterwork happy hours at which company business is often discussed. To all of these people, "gay rights" means something different and the impact of "the gay rights movement" has been experienced differently as well.

This chapter begins by listing a broad range of topics included in the term "gay rights." It then discusses some of the contradictions and splits within the movement and continues by offering a history of gay rights in the United States that shows some ways in which many of these contradictions and splits have played out. By the time this volume is published, the political climate may have changed yet again. The resources provided by the rest of this book will enable further investigative research to track the ever-changing condition of gay rights in the United States.

GAY RIGHTS:
A BROAD RANGE OF DEMANDS

The movement for gay rights has encompassed a broad range of demands— and a great deal of conflict. The following list gives a sense of the areas that concern the modern gay rights movement. Some of these issues are discussed in depth later in this chapter in the section "Legal Issues" or in Chapters 2 or 3. Many gay men and lesbians disagree strongly about various points on this list. However, here is a quick overview of the types of issues that currently concern many gay men and lesbians:

- *Basic legal rights:* As of press time, almost 20 states have enforceable "sodomy" laws—laws that outlaw certain sexual acts between consenting adults in private. Arkansas, Kansas, Maryland, Missouri, Oklahoma, and Texas outlaw these acts only between people of the same sex. Florida, Idaho, Louisiana, Massachusetts, Michigan, Minnesota, Mississippi,

North Carolina, South Carolina, Utah, and Virginia outlaw "sodomy" between any two adults, including legally married heterosexual couples. Alabama excludes married couples from its law but outlaws sodomy among all other consenting adults, gay and straight. (Georgia, New York, Pennsylvania, and Tennessee have sodomy laws on the books, but state supreme courts have ruled that they are not enforceable. Texas's law is also being challenged. For more information on sodomy laws, see Chapter 2.) Various members of the gay rights movement are working to overturn sodomy laws, state by state, so that gay sexual practices will not be against the law.

- *Employment rights:* Although 19 states, hundreds of local governments, and thousands of private employers have antidiscrimination laws or regulations, it is still widely possible for a person to be fired simply because an employer dislikes gay people. Ending employment discrimination is a major goal of one part of the gay rights movement. Since one of the major employers in the United States is the armed forces, the right of gay men and lesbians to participate in the military is another concern.

- *Recognition of families:* One of the more personal aspects of discrimination against gay people is a refusal to recognize the families they have created. Some gay activists are working to win legal recognition for gay marriage. Others are concerned about child custody—the likelihood that a lesbian or gay man will lose the right to raise her or his child. Still other gay people are working to win the right of a gay person or a gay couple to act as foster parents or to adopt a child. Benefits for domestic partners are another big area of concern. According to a 1997 study conducted by the Society for Human Resource Management and reported in *USA Today*, about 10 percent of all employers now recognize gay (and straight) unmarried partnerships and so award health insurance and other benefits to the unmarried partner. Compared with the situation even 10 years before that survey, 10 percent is an extraordinary number—but the overwhelming majority of gay and lesbian couples still cannot receive the financial advantages usually enjoyed by married straight couples.

- *Responses to violence:* As the brutal 1998 murder of Matthew Shepard demonstrated, it is still not physically safe to be a gay man or lesbian in the United States. Antigay violence is viewed by some as a *hate crime*— a type of crime motivated by prejudice against a certain social, ethnic, or religious group. In some parts of the country, hate crimes directed against African Americans, Jews, and other ethnic groups receive harsher penalties than crimes of violence judged not to be hate crimes. Many gay activists believe that giving hate-crime status to violence directed against gay men and lesbians would send a strong message for gay rights.

- *Religious recognition:* Groups like Dignity, a gay Catholic group, and Integrity, for gay Episcopalians, reflect the wishes of many gay people to be recognized by their religion of choice. Several Christian and Jewish denominations ordain gay and lesbian ministers and rabbis; there are also many gay and gay-friendly churches and synagogues around the country. However, most Western religions, as well as many individual congregations, are strongly resistant to the idea of accepting homosexuality, whether they view it as a sin or a psychological disorder. Hence, one part of the gay rights movement has focused on winning full religious recognition of gay men and lesbians.

- *Participation in society:* Many gay men and lesbians point out that they enjoy the same activities as heterosexuals and share many of the same identities. Gay boys might want to be Boy Scouts or Boy Scout leaders; gay and lesbian people of Irish descent would like to march in a St. Patrick's Day parade; and gay teachers wish to pursue their careers without having to lie about their private lives. Yet, when Eagle Scout and assistant scoutmaster James Dale of New Jersey was identified in a newspaper photograph in 1990 as the leader of a gay rights group, the Boy Scouts of America expelled him. The New Jersey Supreme Court ordered the Boy Scouts to restore his membership; the Scouts appealed the case to the Supreme Court, which ruled in the organization's favor. Meanwhile, St. Patrick's Day parade organizers in Boston and New York have successfully managed to forbid openly gay and lesbian groups from marching in their parades. And many court cases have supported a school district's right to fire a teacher for being gay, while referendums in various states—so far, all defeated—have sought to make "no gay teachers" into a statewide policy. In addition to fighting for the right to be in the classroom, many gay activists want what they call a "gay-friendly" or "gay-tolerant" curriculum: educational materials that present being gay as an acceptable way of life that deserves respect.

- *Cultural expression:* For many years, books and visual materials that portrayed gay relationships were considered obscene, and openly gay people were virtually absent from movies, television, popular music, advertisements, and other forms of popular culture. One part of the gay rights movement has focused on creating books, movies, music, and other forms of artistic and commercial expression that portray gay life and gay concerns. In some cases this has been an alternative movement, in which gay and lesbian presses and journals, performance artists and theater companies, music festivals and record companies have created new forms of writing, music, theater, and journalism. In other cases, cultural work takes place in the established worlds of popular and high culture, with gay novelists being

7

published by mainstream presses and gay TV writers creating their own network shows. Still another aspect of cultural expression has been "queer studies"—the efforts of academics of all different types of sexual orientation to challenge the very concept of gender and sexual preference and to interpret history, art, literature, and modern culture in new ways.

- *Political power:* This term means widely different things to different people. Some gay activists focus on electing gay men and lesbians to positions of power. Others are concerned with building broad-based organizations that can lobby politicians to win gay demands. Still other gay people focus on direct action—demonstrations and other types of public protest to draw attention to urgent issues. A significant number of gay rights activists are committed to building coalitions across political movements. Of course, these activities frequently overlap.

- *Sexual freedom:* Many gay men and lesbians became involved in various aspects of the gay rights movement because of their wish to express themselves sexually in ways that the larger society might not accept. The early gay liberation movement celebrated the freedom of gay men and lesbians to choose their partners and sexual arrangements, which often involved an interest in sexual experimentation. Some people claimed new identities: as transvestites, transsexuals, or as other types of transgendered individuals; as practitioners of S and M (sadomasochism); or as other types of so-called sexual minorities. Others insisted on their right to explore new types of relationships—such as various nonmonogamous arrangements or three-way relationships—or simply to enjoy the sexual opportunities available at discos, bathhouses, and clubs. For many gay men and lesbians, a commitment to sexual freedom and a respect for a variety of sexual identities is central to their vision of gay rights.

CONFLICTS AND CONTRADICTIONS

Virtually every item on the preceding list has been the cause of some controversy among those who identify themselves as supporters of gay rights. Debate and disagreement have marked the modern gay rights movement since the founding of the Mattachine Society in 1950. The following are some of the major conflicts that the movement struggles with today.

ASSIMILATIONISM VS. MAINTAINING A CULTURAL IDENTITY

Some activists, theorists, and commentators have argued that gay people are basically the same as their heterosexual counterparts. All they want is to be allowed to participate in their society on equal terms, or to be given "a place at the table," in the words of Bruce Bawer, whose 1993 book was so titled. Journalist Andrew Sullivan, former editor of the centrist journal the *New Republic*, has likewise argued in his 1995 book, *Virtually Normal*, that homosexuality is a purely personal quality, not a cultural category. In the same vein, the gay magazine *Out* has published editorials with a point of view identified as "postgay," meaning that gayness is no longer something to worry about or to be defined by.

Other gay activists and writers claim a more significant place for "gay culture," "lesbian perspectives," or a "queer outlook." Law professor and novelist Ruthann Robson, for example, has written eloquently about the need for lesbians to resist the pressure to fit into relationships and family patterns designed by and for heterosexuals. Playwright Tony Kushner has talked about developing a "Theater of the Fabulous," informed by (though not limited to) his special perceptions and cultural style as a gay man. Kushner has also written of a "socialism of the skin," a view of politics in which sexual orientation and experience are integral to a political vision—an outlook that he likewise relates to his experiences as a gay man.

Still others argue that "gay culture" only exists because of gay oppression. Daniel Harris, for example, in his book *The Rise and Fall of Gay Culture*, analyzes gay men's historic love of divas and movie stars as a kind of cultural code. Referring to certain movies and actresses, he argues, was a way for gay men to recognize themselves and each other in a world that made a more open acknowledgment of their sexual feelings very dangerous. Likewise, attending cultural events like Judy Garland concerts was a safe way to be with other gay men, while identifying with glamorous, cosmopolitan performers was one way for gay men to feel superior to the society that seemed to hold them in contempt.

According to Harris, much of gay male culture and identity grew out of a common response to oppression. Thus, in the 1950s and 1960s, he says, there was no "generation gap" in the white gay urban culture of cities like San Francisco and New York: men from age 20 through age 70 liked the same movies, the same music, and the same style of dress. Today, he says, young gay men have far more in common with young straight men than they do with gay men in their 40s and 50s, a sign of how far the mainstream culture has expanded to include gays. As the dominant culture becomes more gay-friendly, Harris believes, assimilation—the gradual blending of gay men into the larger culture—is inevitable. (Harris's analysis is only concerned with men. Analysts of lesbian culture tend to be more skeptical about the possibilities of assimilation.)

Clearly, the conflict between the drive to assimilate and the wish to maintain an identity is less a hard-and-fast division between two distinct points of view than a kind of creative tension that shapes various debates. Should gay men and lesbians pursue the legal option of marriage, for example, so that their relationships can be subject to the same laws and cultural expectations as those of straight couples; or should they celebrate their ability to create new kinds of arrangements? Do gay and lesbian politicians bring a unique and valuable perspective to the political arena, along with an important commitment to represent the interests of an ignored minority; or do they simply run as "the best candidates for the job"? Is there a way of claiming equal citizenship and of making a special cultural contribution at the same time? As gay men and lesbians become more visible in the larger society, winning both legal rights and cultural acceptance, these questions will continue to preoccupy people who identify as gay.

IS BEING GAY INHERITED, LEARNED, OR CHOSEN?

At first glance, this might appear to be a straightforward question, one that might be answered as a matter of fact by the disciplines of psychology, biology, or genetics. In fact, the question gives rise to an intensely political debate, and the search for an answer is as much driven by a particular agenda for gay politics as by an objective search for truth.

Both experts and the general public have put forth various theories of what makes people gay. Some religious traditions have viewed being gay as a choice, and therefore a sin. Other religious perspectives hold that while sexual *feelings* for people of the same sex may be inborn and therefore blameless, the choice to *act* upon those feelings is sinful. (Still other religious perspectives view homosexuality as simply another way of life and make no religious judgment on it one way or another.)

Psychological schools of thought are also contradictory. Sigmund Freud, the founder of modern psychology, held that homosexuality was not in itself a disorder but merely one of many sexual possibilities that a human being might be drawn to. Freud did attribute interest in same-sex relationships to early childhood events: generally speaking, he believed that men and women who made same-sex choices later in life had become overly attached to the opposite-sex parent by age five. Thus, a boy who had a deep emotional involvement with his mother might be unable to devote himself to other women as he grew older. He might also identify with his mother, so that, feeling like a woman, he would choose men for sexual partners. However, Freud offered a parallel set of early childhood experiences to explain heterosexuality. In his view, all sexual choices were molded during these years, with a wide variety of possible results.

Psychologists and psychiatrists working in the Freudian tradition have tended to maintain Freud's analysis while discarding his tolerance. For most of its history, Freudian analysis and other psychological approaches have viewed male and female homosexuality as a learned pattern of behavior—and as a sickness. Attempts to "cure" the sickness have included psychoanalysis, aversion therapy (for example, showing a man pictures of naked men while administering electric shock or nausea-inducing drugs), or even electroshock therapy. Among the early testimonies heard at gay consciousness-raising sessions in the 1970s were the stories of women and men who had tried to "overcome" their same-sex feelings through therapy or who had been committed to mental hospitals by their families for months or even years.

In the early days of the gay liberation movement, gay activists were less concerned with how gayness was created and more concerned with removing the stigma that made it a sin, a sickness, or a crime. Some gay activists turned the question around, asking hostile psychiatrists, "What made *you* heterosexual?" Others took comfort from the fact that some form of same-sex activity seemed to appear in virtually every human society, as evidenced by the reports of such anthropologists as Margaret Mead. A high point for the movement came in 1973, when, after months of work by gay activists, the American Psychiatric Society took homosexuality off its official list of mental disorders. Since then, homosexuality has not been considered a mental illness.

As the 1970s ended, though, a backlash developed. Religious organizations began to promote the vision of gay men and lesbians as making sinful choices. They also portrayed gayness as something that could be imposed upon an impressionable child. When singer and former beauty queen Anita Bryant began a 1977 campaign to revoke a gay rights ordinance in Dade County, Florida, she called her movement "Save Our Children," saying, ". . . since homosexuals cannot reproduce, they must recruit, must freshen their ranks. And who qualifies as a likely recruit: a 35-year-old father or mother of two . . . or a teenage boy or girl who is surging with sexual awareness?"

Gay rights activists denied this portrait of gay men and lesbians as child molesters, but the movement still included a wide range of opinions about the true causes and nature of homosexuality. Some argued that homosexuals were just "born that way," citing the accounts of those who have claimed they "just knew" that they were "different" than other kids by the age of four or five. Generally speaking, in the 1970s and early 1980s, gay men were more likely than women to argue this position. Thus, when Congresswoman Bella Abzug began introducing a federal gay rights bill to Congress, some gay male activists wanted the bill to refer to "sexual orientation," to express their view of homosexuality as something they were born with.

On the other hand, the lesbians lobbying Abzug preferred the term "sexual preference," to indicate that their lesbianism was an active choice. Theorist and poet Adrienne Rich wrote a famous article, "Compulsory

Heterosexuality and the Lesbian Continuum," in which she argued that both men and women were more likely to prefer women's bodies, since both genders were traditionally raised by women. Thus, while it might indeed be "natural" for most men to have sexual feelings about women, most women would also probably choose female sex partners—if society did not punish this choice so severely. Rich called on women to resist society's efforts to suppress their lesbianism, inviting them to recognize what she considered the lesbian component in their female friendships and work partnerships.

Many other lesbian-feminists of the 1970s and early 1980s took a similar position, arguing that women who were true to their natures and/or genuinely committed to the liberation of women would avoid "sleeping with the enemy" and would choose lesbianism as the deepest expression of their feminism. Slogans like "Feminism is the theory, lesbianism is the practice" and "A woman needs a man like a fish needs a bicycle" expressed this view.

Yet other lesbians responded to Rich with anger and dismay. They considered their erotic feelings for women as quite different from their friendships, and they accused Rich of downplaying the purely sexual component of lesbian relationships. They also argued that heterosexual feminists needed the support of the women's movement to intervene in *their* relationships; rather than being advised to sleep with women, they should be helped to change their relationships with men. Feminists who followed Rich were more likely to see lesbianism as a choice; feminists who saw lesbianism in more sexual terms were more likely to see their sexuality as inborn or determined early on. (Straight feminists had a wide range of responses to Rich, from agreeing that their relationships with women were essentially lesbian to resenting Rich's lack of concern for their own efforts to refashion their relationships with men. Some straight feminists admired what they saw as Rich's courage and clarity while still maintaining their interest in heterosexuality.)

Rich's debate with other lesbian feminists points to a larger difference between gay men and lesbians. Whereas lesbians—whether they agreed with Rich or not—tended to see their political constituency as women in general, working with the feminist movement in various ways and trying to attract a broad range of women to their events, gay men were more concerned with finding support among other gay men. They were far less interested in reaching out to straight men than in connecting with other gay men in a variety of ways—cultural, political, emotional, and sexual. To some extent, this was because many lesbians identified with women in general as an oppressed group, whereas many gay men did not see what they had in common with "oppressive" straight men. Likewise, many straight feminists had an interest in overcoming homophobia to reach "all women," particularly lesbians, who were often doing significant work in the women's movement, whereas straight men in general had no parallel interest in reaching out to gay men (although the straight men in the political organizations that recognized homosexuality as a category of oppression did feel such a concern and did reach out to some extent).

A new wrinkle in the debate was provided in 1991 by Simon LeVay, a biologist working at the Salk Institute for Biological Studies in La Jolla, California, who offered new support for the theory that homosexuality was somehow inborn. In the August 30, 1991 issue of *Science* magazine, LeVay published the results of a study in which he had found differences in the brains of gay and straight men. LeVay had performed autopsies on six women and 35 men. Eighteen of the men were gay men who had died of AIDS and one was a bisexual man who had also died of AIDS. According to LeVay, the hypothalamus—one tiny part of the brain—was twice as large in the gay men as in the heterosexual men he studied, while the hypothalamuses of the straight men were twice as large as those of the women.

The study provoked an immediate controversy among both scientists and activists. Initially, a spokesperson from the Lambda Legal Defense and Education Fund, the prominent gay rights legal organization, called LeVay's results "intriguing," pointing out that if homosexuality were indeed inborn, it could no longer be considered either a sin or a psychological disorder. Many activists seized on LeVay's findings with relief: now they could argue that discrimination against gay people was wrong because gayness was a biological condition that people could not control.

Other activists found this argument frightening. John DeCecco, a professor of psychology at San Francisco State University and the editor of *Journal of Homosexuality*, called LeVay's study "nineteenth-century nonsense" that could have "dangerous" political ramifications. (DeCecco's citing of the 19th century was a reference to a time when scientists sought a much more direct causal relationship between biology and behavior than is now accepted.) DeCecco pointed out that if people believed that gayness was inborn, they might begin trying to screen and abort "potentially homosexual" fetuses. He also argued that homosexuality was more complicated than a mere biological response: "Homosexuality is not one thing," he said. "It's had many, many different meanings over the centuries." Anne Fausto-Sterling, a professor of medical science at Brown University, agreed. LeVay's suggestion that homosexuality was somehow biological, she said, "takes a complicated, intricate gender system and reduces it to whom you want to screw."

Other people criticized LeVay from a scientific point of view. They said that a study comprised of only 41 subjects provided a sample far too small from which to draw conclusions, particularly since all the gay men in the study had died of AIDS, which is known to cause alterations in the brain.

LeVay has defended his work. He points out that he never claimed to offer a comprehensive theory of homosexuality; he was only suggesting that it might be possible to study sexual choices on a biological level. Two other highly publicized studies relating homosexuality to genetics seemed to promise a whole new body of work, but as of this writing little has appeared. Meanwhile, years after the initial studies, none of the results have ever been replicated. (*Replication*—conducting a similar experiment and obtaining similar results—is how the scientific community judges whether an experiment has delivered valid results or was merely a fluke.) "I think we're as much in the dark as we ever were," said biologist Evan Balaban, in an August 17, 1998 *Newsweek* article on the topic.

The question of what homosexuality "really" is seemed particularly important to gay men and lesbians who saw the process of "coming out"—publicly declaring one's homosexuality—as central to the building of a gay movement. Throughout the 1970s and 1980s, gay men and lesbians emphasized the need for their brothers and sisters to claim their gay identity. The notion of remaining "in the closet"—hiding one's sexuality from others, or even failing to admit it to oneself—was seen as the ultimate betrayal, so much so that some journalists—most notably Michelangelo Signorile—established the practice of "outing," or making public the sexuality of other people against their wishes.

The very notion of outing was based on the idea that coming out was a responsibility that gay people had to each other, as well as to themselves, and that coming out would inevitably lead both to a healthier personal life and to more political power for the gay community generally. After all, no other oppressed group—women, people of color, disabled people, people living in working-class communities or doing working-class jobs—was invisible. Only gay men and lesbians had the option of hiding their true identities. If straight people could believe they did not know any gay people, they would have a far easier time supporting discrimination; if gay people believed they were a tiny, isolated minority, they would have a far harder time standing up for their rights. In this context, the gay rights movement placed a great deal of importance on gayness or lesbianism as a *true* identity, one that a person had the responsibility to claim and even to celebrate—regardless of whether being gay was seen as learned, inborn, or too mysterious to analyze.

In the 1990s, a number of Christian antigay groups responded to the challenge posed by coming out with a challenge of their own: they called on gay men and lesbians to "convert." Whereas gay rights groups called on people to recognize their essential homosexuality, religious organizations like Exodus International and the Christian Coalition asked people to recognize their true *heterosexuality*.

14

Popularized by "ex-gays" John and Anne Paulk, who met at an Exodus counseling program and were married in 1992, the idea of conversion was brought to America's attention by a series of ads appearing in mainstream magazines and newspapers in 1998. Founded in 1976, Exodus now includes 83 chapters in 35 states and claims to have "touched" 200,000 lives.

Exodus's philosophy seems to draw on a version of classical Freudian theory: boys with absent fathers, girls with absent mothers, do not progress through the "proper" developmental stages, so they turn to people of the same sex to make up for the absent parent. Their treatment includes a combination of therapy, prayer, group support, and workshops to rediscover one's "inner heterosexual." Although it has allowed no long-term studies, the group claims a 30 percent success rate, with success being defined as abstinence from homosexual activity. Some members eventually marry, while others simply abstain from sexual actions that they believe are sinful. Still other veterans of Exodus avoid homosexuality and/or maintain heterosexuality for a time, and then "slip." For example, in 1979, two of the group's founders, Michael Bussee and Gary Cooper, fell in love and left the group.

In an ironic reversal for those who remember the lengthy battle to get the American Psychiatric Association to take homosexuality off its list of disorders, the American Psychological Association has strongly advised against "reparative therapy" of the kind offered by Exodus. In 1997, the group declared that such therapy was scientifically ineffective and possibly harmful. Most mainstream psychologists and psychiatrists now view Exodus's theory of childhood development as discredited—although a 1998 *Newsweek* poll found that 56 percent of the general public and 11 percent of the gay people polled *did* believe that gays could become straight.

Some observers believe the entire debate about what causes homosexuality—indeed, about the nature of "homosexuality" itself—is based on false assumptions. Although it is true that our genes determine a great deal of who we are, the relationship between genes and human behavior remains unclear. "People very much want to find simple answers," said Neil Risch, a professor of genetics at Stanford University, who was also quoted in the *Newsweek* article. "A gene for this, a gene for that . . . Human behavior is much more complicated than that." *Newsweek* reporters John Leland and Mark Miller went on to explain: "The existence of a genetic pattern among homosexuals doesn't mean people are born gay, any more than the genes for height, presumably common in NBA [National Basketball Association] players, indicate an inborn ability to play basketball."

Likewise, environmental factors—the conditions of a person's upbringing—may indeed affect a man's or woman's sexuality—but it is not clear how. If homosexuality were related to psychology, we ought to be able to use psychological testing to distinguish between gays and straights. Yet in blind psychological evaluations—tests in which the evaluator was not aware of the subject's sexual orientation—there was no way to tell who was gay and who was straight. No psychological pattern, problem, or tendency was associated with homosexuality; it seemed that the *only* way that gays differed from straights, as a group, was in their choice of sexual partner.

It does seem that sexuality is a great deal more mutable than the terms "homosexual" and "heterosexual" would suggest. After a 12-year partnership with a woman whose child they raised together, longtime lesbian-feminist author Jan Clausen became involved with a male partner. This transition became the topic of her 1999 book, *Apples and Oranges: My Journey to Sexual Identity.* Likewise, veteran gay male activist William "Bro" Broberg, began a relationship with bisexual lawyer and activist Lisa Kaplan that was reported in *Out* magazine. "I'm not an ex-gay," Broberg told reporter Sara Miles. "I'm still basically oriented towards men. . . ." In a similar vein, Clausen writes about colleagues who call her a "former lesbian," a label she rejects—as well as "bisexual"—in favor of the designation "floating woman," someone who refuses the rigid categories of "gay/straight," "masculine/feminine," "apples/oranges."

Clearly, neither Clausen nor Broberg was driven by the dislike of homosexuality that seems to motivate the "success stories" of Exodus. Nor was either reluctant to keep on living as a lesbian or gay man. On the contrary, each has eloquently described the same kind of self-questioning and fear of being condemned by their communities that have become virtual cliches for men and women who choose to be gay. "I would still like to be just gay," Broberg told *Out* magazine. "It just seems like a very bad idea to sell out true love because you don't ideologically understand how you can be feeling it."

Certainly, there are numerous examples of men and women who have considered themselves heterosexual all their lives suddenly discovering new sexual or romantic feelings for same-sex partners—or finally deciding to act upon feelings that they previously had ignored. While many gay men and lesbians tell the story of "always knowing" who they were and desperately seeking support from others like themselves, many others tell a different coming-out story, in which different stages of life called for different choices. New choices might be inspired by changing life circumstances, such as parents dying or children growing up; changing social circumstances, such as a move to a more gay-friendly area; changing cultural circumstances, such as society's greater tolerance of gay men and lesbians; or simply meeting a person who suddenly makes the idea of same-sex romance seem desirable.

The idea that someone must be identified as "really" gay or straight—essentially one thing or the other—is challenged by many so-called queer theorists, who argue that our whole system of gender and sexuality is far more mutable, far more susceptible to social influences, and far more complicated than the rigid categories of "gay," "straight," "bisexual," "male," and "female" would allow. The queer theory of the 1990s stands against the gay and lesbian movement's traditional mistrust of bisexuals (people who expressed sexual interest in both genders), who were often portrayed as trying to "have it both ways" or to deny their true homosexual natures. (Many lesbians and gay men felt that bisexuals were untrustworthy simply because they were able to return at a moment's notice to the world of heterosexual privilege, a choice unavailable to their "purely" gay or lesbian sexual partners.)

As science, politics, and culture progress, we can expect new answers to the old questions of what makes people gay and what "gayness" is. We can also expect new ways of asking the questions.

GAY MEN AND LESBIANS: ALLIES OR ENEMIES?

In a column in *Out* magazine, feminist and transgender activist Pat Califia (now Patrick Califia) explored the historic tensions between gay men and lesbians in the gay rights movement. Gay men, she wrote sardonically, tended to see lesbians as "ugly, brawling, manhating bull dykes in dungarees and crew cuts." Many lesbians, on the other hand, viewed men as "inherently more violent, misogynist, stupid, money grubbing, promiscuous, dirty, kinky, and diseased than women."

Although Califia was deliberately dealing in stereotypes, most observers of the modern gay rights movement would agree that the past 30 years have been marked by a certain amount of tension between lesbians and gay men. The first two modern gay rights groups were sex-segregated: the Mattachine Society, founded by three men in Los Angeles in 1950, was theoretically for both gay men and lesbians, but it had an overwhelmingly male membership; the Daughters of Bilitis, founded in San Francisco in 1955, was explicitly for women. From the beginning, lesbians and gay men faced different problems as well as common enemies. They also brought different resources and experiences to bear on their political involvement.

For many gay men in the 1950s and 1960s, a key political issue was their right to have sex. The police often raided gay bars and cruising areas (public areas such as parks, public restrooms, and the waterfront, where gay men could often go to have sex or to find sexual partners), putting men at risk of arrest, jail time, fines, and possibly publicity that might destroy marriages, careers, and social standing.

Although there was a lesbian bar culture in many cities, women's sexual activities tended to be more private—and less visible. To this day, each gender views its own situation as a mixed blessing: while men generally feel freer to enjoy their sexuality and are recognized as sexual beings, gay men are more often targets of violence directed at their very visible sexuality. Because women in our society are generally seen as less sexual, many straight people can't even imagine what two women could do with each other without the help of a man; "no man, no sex," the reasoning goes. Alternately, some straight men find the idea of two women together sexually exciting. Either way, women's sexuality is suppressed or trivialized—though women who are unmistakably sexual may face severe punishment in response.

Thus, while sodomy laws—laws that make homosexual sex illegal—affect both gay men and lesbians, they have, historically, affected them in different ways. Gay men have most often been the targets of police raids and harassment, particularly where public sexual activity is involved. Lesbians, on the other hand, suffer from sodomy laws when it comes to child custody: a mother who is a lesbian or is perceived as one is by legal definition a criminal, and so may be denied the right to raise her children. Lesbians—and straight women—who are known to have sexual partners to whom they are not married, are often penalized by the unwritten rule that says a mother is not allowed to be sexual. (Although gay fathers may also be penalized by sodomy laws, they are in any case less likely to be awarded child custody in a society that still tends to award custody to the mother.)

Men and women faced other conflicts as they tried to work together for gay rights. The modern gay rights movement began in 1969, a time when the second wave of feminism was just getting started. Initially, feminism seemed to hold promise for both women and men, particularly gay men, as women's liberation challenged the very notion of traditional male/female sex roles. Indeed, many of the early gay liberationists were men who challenged these roles as well, asserting that men could learn to knit and sew, to raise children, and to engage in other traditionally "female" activities, challenging the entire gender system as well as celebrating their own homosexuality.

Yet other men who happened to be gay longed for the prestige and recognition traditionally awarded to straight men. They saw gay activism as a way to become *more* "masculine," not less—that is, to claim the power that society gave straight men, even if some women complained that such power was being taken at their expense.

Thus, from the first days of the earliest post-Stonewall groups, women complained that men took up "too much space," and the men had predictably mixed reactions to the charge. For example, early dances held at New York City's "Firehouse," a gay social space sponsored by the Gay Activists Alliance, were overwhelmingly dominated by gay men, who, from the women's point of view, played the music too loud and created a hypersexual atmosphere in which conversation or more low-key encounters were impossible. The men were overjoyed to have a public space where they could finally express their sexuality and meet other men; the women felt excluded from a space that they thought was supposed to be theirs too.

Certainly, there were—and are—many lesbians who celebrated their right to be sexual, to enjoy multiple partners and a wide range of sexual practices, to reject monogamy and marriagelike arrangements, to claim the power and freedom of an openly sexual identity that has traditionally been reserved for men. But many other lesbians were shaped by a society that viewed sex as dangerous for women, particularly young women. Then-current feminist analysis also explored the ways in which male sexuality had oppressed women, from trapping women in inequitable marriages to judging women by their appearance to terrorizing women through rape and sexual violence. For lesbian women affected by these experiences and analyses, gay men's celebration of their newfound sexual freedom seemed insensitive at best, oppressive at worst.

Many gay men, on the other hand, felt that they had spent their whole lives being asked to suppress their sexuality and play by rules that were not theirs. What did liberation mean, if not the chance to finally enjoy sex openly, to speak and write openly about it, to enjoy the new power and pleasure that the gay rights movement seemed to offer?

Out for Good, a history of the gay rights movement, cites numerous examples of early, apparently trivial conflicts between gay men and lesbians over the place of public sexuality in what was supposed to be a common movement. For example, *Come Out!*, an early newspaper of the Gay Liberation Front, one of the first post-Stonewall groups, included a detailed description of fellatio. Men felt liberated by the chance to speak openly about something they had always been made to feel ashamed of and wanted the support of their movement in their search for sexual information and sexual pleasure. Women denounced the focus on male sex, which they felt excluded them.

Likewise, a playful representation of a giant penis, which its creators called a "Cock-a-pillar," was part of the 1971 "Christopher Street West" parade in Los Angeles (an early version of a Gay Pride parade). Many gay men loved the freedom and exuberance that the huge phallic symbol represented. But many lesbians felt that this overwhelming display of a male sex organ implicitly left them out. They did not see the gay rights movement in such overwhelmingly sexual terms, nor did they feel welcome in the presence of this reminder of male sexuality.

As both the gay rights and the women's movement continued, many lesbians came to see feminism—which called for the unity of all women—as their true political home. Why identify with gay rights, they asked, when the gay rights movement seemed to require an alliance with men who often seemed even less sympathetic to women than straight men, who at least had a built-in sexual incentive to get along with the opposite sex. As lesbian-feminism proceeded through the 1970s, an increasing number of women began to identify as *separatists*, lesbians who wished to live in exclusively female—or exclusively lesbian—communities, in which men were not allowed.

Even lesbians who had no interest in separatism felt a certain frustration in dealing with various gay rights groups, which were often dominated by men even as women did much of the organizational and clerical work. Throughout the 1970s, women frequently raised the issue of equal representation in the leadership of gay rights organizations. While some gay men were sympathetic to this demand, others resented it. If meetings attracted more men than women, they asked, whose fault was that? They believed that women need not feel excluded if they would only choose to participate. Likewise, if gay men were better fund-raisers and had far more access to wealth than lesbians because of the overall social trend to pay men higher salaries than women and the historical pattern that favored men in issues of inheritance and offered them greater access to family wealth—why shouldn't they continue to enjoy the political and social power that came with the money?

Then, in the 1980s, an easing of tension between male and female activists came from a most unlikely source: the AIDS epidemic. As each year brought new disastrous news of deaths within the gay male community, lesbians and gay men joined in new efforts to address the crisis. Although lesbians as a group were less affected by AIDS than either straight women or gay men, they saw the crisis as their issue, just as, in the 1970s, many of them had seen the pro-choice and battered women's movements as their issue. In the 1970s, they had identified broadly as women, and they fought for women's freedom even in areas that did not directly concern them. In the 1980s, as AIDS shaped the way mainstream America viewed homosexuality, lesbians fought for money for AIDS research, recognition of the rights of PWAs (people with AIDS), and a reasonable program of sex education and AIDS prevention.

It was not only political vision that motivated women to become involved in AIDS-related work. Many of them had always been close to gay men, whether as part of the gay rights movement or on a personal level. At the same time, AIDS raised questions for many gay men about the kind of public, no-holds-barred sexuality that they had thought was theirs by right. Many observers describe the late 1970s and early 1980s as "party time" for gay men—an era when discos and clubs were the center of gay male activity, when sex and drugs and all-night dancing were more compelling than any form of political action. The AIDS crisis both curtailed that version of sexual freedom and made politics seem more urgent.

In this new climate of political and personal urgency, gay men and lesbians were more able than before to find common ground. The new recognition of women's place in the movement was reflected in a variety of ways, both symbolic and real. For example, in 1986, the National Gay Task Force became the National Gay and Lesbian Task Force (NGLTF).

Another issue was generational. Many of the AIDS activists who started ACT UP (AIDS Coalition to Unleash Power), Queer Nation, the Lesbian Avengers, and other militant groups had grown up with mothers—and fathers—shaped by the feminist movement. While the first generation of gay activists grew up in a world in which middle-class mothers rarely worked outside the home and women politicians were virtually unknown, the ACT UP generation took it for granted that women could hold economic, social, and political power, at least to some extent. Politically active men and women in their 20s thus had different political resources than the generation that had come before.

As the urgency of the AIDS crisis recedes with the development of protease inhibitors (a treatment that seems to be able to halt the disease for at least some people), many observers are questioning how the differences between men and women will affect the future of the gay rights movement. Ironically, the very gains of the movement are producing greater splits. As AIDS becomes less of a threat, and as gay people in general become more accepted and visible in the larger society, gay men benefit disproportionately, for they now have access to the greater economic and social power that men in general have always had. Many gay male couples fall into the privileged category known as "DINKS"—dual income, no kids. Lesbian couples are, on average, at the bottom of the economic ladder, since women's earnings average only 64 percent of men's, and since lesbians are more likely to have children, either from a previous relationship or as part of their current partnership.

These conditions tend to give gay men and lesbians quite different perspectives on a wide range of social issues, particularly the feminist concerns of equal pay, child care, equal opportunity, and welfare rights. Although there are certainly many exceptions to the following generalization, it could be said that gay men have more often tended to see the issue of gay rights as specifically about gay issues, whereas lesbians—especially those from a lesbian-feminist tradition—have seen lesbian issues as inseparable from the larger issues of race and class, as well as issues that affect straight women, such as abortion and battering. (Lesbians have also demanded—with mixed success—that straight feminists recognize the centrality of lesbian rights to *their* concerns, arguing that if a woman, say, can lose custody of a child because of being a lesbian, every woman's right to raise her children is thereby threatened.)

Meanwhile, gay men are becoming ever more culturally visible—a combination of changing social attitudes and gay men's employment in television, film, journalism, and fashion. Yet lesbians are still generally treated as either nonexistent or a dirty joke. There have been some positive portrayals of lesbian characters on prime-time TV—Robin Bartlett's warm-hearted sister on *Mad About You*, the lesbian couple that got married and is raising a child on *Friends*, the similar lesbian couple on the police drama *NYPD Blue*. The cable special *If These Walls Could Talk 2* sympathetically portrayed sexual relationships between women, as did the Oscar-winning movie *Boys Don't Cry* (although in the Hollywood tradition, the penalty for such relationships in that film was a violent death). However, while there were several out gay male characters in the 1999 fall TV lineup, there were virtually no lesbians. Nor have there been any big-budget lesbian commercial films to parallel such movies as *The Bird Cage*, *In and Out*, and *The Talented Mr. Ripley*. The hour-long teen drama *Popular* features a sympathetic gay male teacher who talks persuasively about the importance of coming out, while the proto-lesbian science instructor is portrayed as an embarrassing joke who lives with her sister, cannot find a relationship, and is called "sir" by her students. (The show does occasionally feature a sympathetic lesbian mother, however.)

At the same time, lesbians' increased power and visibility within the gay rights movement has provoked resentment among some gay men. Pat Califia wrote, ". . . in an era when lesbians enjoy positions of unprecedented power in our national organizations and media, many gay men resent what they see as the ham-fisted enforcement of gender parity." She goes on to quote writer and activist Larry Kramer: "I guess what I resent now is how everything seems to be rammed down everybody's throat in an attempt to compromise and please each other. I've always thought that having to have gender parity [an equal number of men and women] on the board of an organization was not necessarily useful if it meant you could not use the best people. Quite often you don't have an equal number of smart whatevers who are willing to participate."

Kramer has frequently said that he does not believe lesbians can understand the issues that concern gay men. In an email to the former editor of *Out* magazine, and again in a telephone interview with Pat Califia, he proposed a three-part movement, one for men, one for women, one united.

Meanwhile, many lesbians still complain of not having full representation in the leadership and decision-making of various gay rights groups; of being treated disrespectfully by gay men; or of simply being ignored in discussions of gay rights. Many gay men would agree. Martin Duberman, in his review of *Out for Good* in the *Nation*, points out that relatively unknown gay male activists are profiled, while many better-known lesbian activists are ignored. Michelangelo Signorile, a well-known columnist and author of *Life Outside*, told Pat Califia, "[E]xcept for the core groups of activists, most gay men have not really worked on issues relating specifically to lesbians and don't know anything . . . about lesbian culture and sexuality. Gay men need to learn about sexism, and to me that has always just been part of the work."

CIVIL RIGHTS VS. GAY LIBERATION

As with the conflict between assimilation and maintaining a cultural identity, the tension between gay rights and gay liberation continues to shape gay and lesbian activism in profound and unexpected ways. Simply put, "gay liberation" implies the need to transform the entire society, while "civil rights" refers more narrowly to the notion of winning equal rights for gay men and lesbians within the existing society. But tempting as it is to discuss the two views as separate and distinct, in practice, they often overlap, blending into one another within a single organization—or a single individual.

In the early days after Stonewall, "gay liberation" was a term—and an ideology—that seemed to flow naturally out of the prevailing political atmosphere of the 1960s. African Americans, women, students, antiwar activists, hippies, and members of the New Left had mounted a broad political and cultural challenge to virtually every U.S. political and social institution: capitalism, the military-industrial complex, the university system, the family, the working world of nine-to-five jobs, patriarchy (some feminists' term for centuries of male domination), sexual repression, and conformity. The Black Panthers were an active, viable organization whose breakfast programs for poor children accompanied their slogan of "Black is Beautiful" and their challenge to white racism. The Vietnam War had radicalized many men and women with its view of the United States as aggressor, and of the American way of life as oppressive and dangerous to the rest of the world. The growing women's movement was challenging everything from unequal pay to the unequal use of pronouns (Why, asked some early feminists, should "he" be used generically to refer to both men and women?).

In this context, when gay patrons of the Stonewall Inn fought back against the police raids that many had come to take for granted, their action was seen as representing a greater refusal: they effectively declared a giant NO to the social, political, and economic system that supported only one, narrow view of human sexuality—that of monogamous, heterosexual marriage—and stood ready to violently punish anyone who transgressed. Early supporters of gay liberation could identify with the Black Panthers, New Leftists, feminists, and antiwar activists who also said "no," not to a specific law or situation, but to what they saw as a whole system of oppression and repression. The early slogan "Gay is Good" (see Appendix C), was a direct reference to the African-American insistence that "Black is Beautiful," while the very name "Gay Liberation Front"—an organization founded in the wake of the Stonewall uprising—drew on the National Liberation Front of the North Vietnamese.

Early manifestos of gay liberation explicitly said that without the abolition of capitalism and other repressive systems, gay people—indeed, no people—could ever be truly free. Thus early gay liberation meetings included discussion of the Vietnam War and voted to donate funds to the Black Panthers, not out of a sense of liberal guilt, but because these early activists genuinely saw their movement as part of a larger one.

"Social justice movements in this country are often started by radicals who are then, and usually in short order, repudiated and supplanted by liberals," wrote historian Martin Duberman in the June 14, 1999 edition of *The Nation.* Thus the Gay Liberation Front was soon joined by a new organization more specifically focused on achieving gay legal and civil rights: the Gay Activists Alliance. Later, gay men—and some lesbians—who saw themselves as more middle-class, more "respectable," and generally happier with mainstream society than the early "gay lib" radicals, founded the National Gay Task Force (now the National Gay and Lesbian Task Force) and the National Gay Rights Lobby (which eventually mutated into the Human Rights Campaign Fund, and then the Human Rights Campaign), organizations intended to lobby Congress and engage in other more conventional political activities.

The conflicts between conservative, liberal, and radical approaches to gay rights/liberation were also conflicts involving gender, race, and class. As we saw in the previous section, gay men and lesbians often had quite different visions of how much change was needed in the larger society to guarantee their own freedom. Middle- and upper-class gay men, who had amassed a great deal of power and privilege, were more likely to see gay rights in narrower terms. They often felt that the society as it was (the status quo) was working fine: however, *they* did not want to be excluded from it. This type of gay man tended to be white, as well, and less than sympathetic to demands from feminists or people of color that they broaden their approach or open their ranks. For example, the Municipal Elections Committee of Los Angeles (MECLA) was a group of wealthy gay men formed in 1977 to win more political power in Los Angeles elections. They continued for many years to raise funds with which they won electoral influence among the city's political elite. They saw no reason to include other "oppressed groups" in their ranks; their whole reason for being was to take advantage of their access to money and power.

While lesbian-feminists tended to be more explicitly preoccupied with power issues, they too faced troubling conflicts over race and class, conflicts which pointed to larger disagreements over how best to achieve lesbian rights. Initially, it seemed that the problems of power and oppression could be satisfied simply by becoming more inclusive. The history of lesbian-feminism in the 1970s is the story of one disempowered group after another challenging the leaders and members of the movement, on the grounds that women of color, Jewish women, the disabled, and working-class and poor women were being explicitly or implicitly excluded from activities that were open to the more privileged.

Lesbian-feminists often found creative ways of responding to these charges. Women's concerts, for example, an early cultural expression of the lesbian-feminist movement, frequently offered free child care, sliding-scale admissions, and signers for the hearing impaired, in their efforts to make sure that every member of the women's community was able to attend. Women's presses made efforts to include women of color and low-income women in their collectives and on their publications lists. The words *reproductive rights* were added to the term *pro-choice* or *abortion rights* to recognize that for many women on welfare, including African Americans, Latinas, and Native Americans, the problem of forced sterilization was of more concern than the legal right to terminate a pregnancy.

Despite these responses, the lesbian-feminist movement continued to struggle with the problems of social inequality, which often went beyond matters of inclusion and representation to more fundamental political issues. Many lesbian-feminists, for example, were committed to separatism, a vision of community in which only women, or only lesbians, would be allowed to participate. While these separatist communities were not by definition for whites only, many women of color, as well as many white women from poor and working-class backgrounds, found separatism problematic. These women saw their male counterparts as oppressed, too, and as potential allies. While they wanted a movement that would defend their right to be lesbians, they also wanted to fight for liberation on the grounds of race, class, and the broader issues of gender. Many of them charged that separatism was inherently elitist, that only privileged white women had the resources to cut men out of their lives—and that only privileged white women would feel comfortable ignoring the problems of their fathers, brothers, and sons.

Class, race, and political vision became issues once again during the AIDS crisis. The public image of a person with AIDS was that of a middle-class white gay man who was part of the "party" culture of gay, urban communities. Gay Men's Health Crisis (GMHC), founded in 1981, was the first organization created to deal with the crisis; it was overwhelmingly dominated by white, middle-class men and remained so for some time. Throughout the 1980s, however, and with increasing urgency in the 1990s, activists raised the problems of gay men of color, who were less likely to be "out" than their white counterparts, who might not speak English as a first language, who were more likely to have sex with other men without self-identifying as gay, and who therefore had different needs when it came to AIDS prevention, education, and treatment.

AIDS activists—both gay and straight—also pointed out the growing problem of AIDS among women, primarily women of color, who were sexually involved with gay/bisexual men and/or with intravenous (IV) drug users. The question of how responsible a group like GMHC ought to be for these other populations with AIDS speaks again to the movement's political self-definition. Is the goal specifically to improve the lives of white gay men, many of whom can now be helped by—and can afford—expensive protease inhibitors? Is the goal to help all people with AIDS, including those who cannot afford the new treatments? Would this require a simple increase in public funding or a broader challenge to the whole way health care is delivered, with a call for national health insurance or even socialized medicine? Is the movement stronger, or weaker, when it tries to speak for a broader constituency and to make more profound changes in the political and public health systems?

Differing visions of political activism also surfaced with the founding of ACT UP, a militant direct-action group that seemed to return to 1960s-style demonstrations and civil disobedience in its efforts to change the policies of corporations, the U.S. government, and the Catholic Church. Initially, at least, ACT UP seemed to represent an implicit challenge to the more mainstream, "within-the-system" approaches of the more established gay rights groups. Ironically, both Gay Men's Health Crisis—the first group ever founded to respond politically to AIDS—and ACT UP were co-founded by Larry Kramer. Kramer had a radical vision for both organizations and was deeply distressed when GMHC seemed to become more interested in social services than in political action. Eventually, GMHC forced Kramer to leave the organization he had helped to found—and so, eventually, did ACT UP.

The growth of queer theory, and the political activism that accompanies it, raised new questions about the direction the gay rights movement should take. Queer theorists even wondered if *gay rights* was the correct term by which the movement should define itself, as some queer theorists challenged the very notion of "gay" and "straight," or even of two genders. "Why not see humanity as including many genders?" these scholars ask. "Why not see sexuality as a continuum, or as an ever-changing field of play, rather than as a set of distinct categories?"

More traditional gay rights activists respond with concern. These activists assert that many gay men and lesbians do not *want* to change the entire gender system. They simply want to be left alone to form relationships, raise children, and pursue their careers. Won't they be frightened off by an approach that purports to challenge fundamental social arrangements? And what about support from the larger society? Straight people who agree that a gay man should not be fired from his job simply for being gay might be repelled by the notion that, for instance, he has the right to wear a dress to that job.

Yet another criticism of queer theory is that on some level, it works *against* taking political action or building a movement. Many lesbians and gay men are uneasy with a theory that denies the very existence of gay men and lesbians, of men and women, in the name of an ever-changing system of multiple genders and sexualities. People who are concerned with such issues as child custody and antigay violence are puzzled or even offended by a theory that allows a heterosexual married woman such as the scholar Eve Kosofsky Sedgwick to proclaim that she is "really" a gay man.

This discussion, which began with two clear categories—civil rights and gay liberation—has quickly dissolved into a multiplicity of political perspectives: queer theorists, lesbian feminists, separatists, conservatives, liberals, radicals, and many others. Each of those labels contains numerous perspectives as well, the definitions of which change as political conditions change. Some observers lament that the gay rights movement is at odds with itself. Others see the very diversity of gay rights as a source of strength, in that the many different kinds of gay men and lesbians can all be reached.

GAY MARRIAGE: PROBLEM OR SOLUTION?

Nowhere is this multiplicity more evident than in the current debate over gay marriage, an issue which raises virtually all of the contradictions considered so far in this chapter. The legal recognition of gay marriage has been of interest to the modern gay rights movement almost since its inception. In 1971, two African-American lesbians in Milwaukee went to city hall to get a marriage license—and their case eventually wound up in federal court. They were unsuccessful, but they were far from the last gay or lesbian couple to demand access to what many viewed as the seat of heterosexual privilege: the right to have one's relationship recognized by the state.

Over the past 30 years, gay men and lesbians have won various types of recognition for the relationships and families they have constructed (for more information, see "Legal Issues," later in this chapter). Yet the prospect of legally recognized, state-sanctioned marriage did not seem imminent until 1996, when it appeared as though the Hawaii Supreme Court might find that gay people's right to marriage was guaranteed under the state's equal-protection law.

Late in 1999, the Hawaii state legislature rewrote the state constitution, rendering moot whatever the state supreme court's ruling might have been. They had also passed a law specifying that marriage could only take place between one man and one woman. Yet also in late 1999, the Vermont Supreme Court ordered that state's legislature to come up with some arrangement under which gay Vermonters could have equal access to the legal and financial benefits of marriage. In response, the Vermont legislature created a new category for long-term relationships, called a "civil union." This legislation extends most marriage benefits available under Vermont state law, such as family leave, child custody, and worker compensation, to unmarried, committed couples. Because the new law stops short of actually granting same-sex couples a marriage license, however, the debate over gay marriage is likely to continue into the foreseeable future.

To some activists, the civil rights aspects are very clear. To them, same-sex couples should have the same rights to enjoy the benefits of marriage that are now the exclusive property of heterosexuals—the right to be covered by a partner's health insurance, to inherit property without paying an estate tax, to be able to visit a partner in a hospital or to care for a partner who is disabled, and to be recognized as taking part in a legitimate life partnership. They also believe that gay people should be able to adopt children as a couple, just as straight married people do, and they see gay marriage as a step in that direction.

Moreover, legalization of gay marriage would clear child custody issues. When a woman married to a man gives birth, her husband automatically assumes legal custody of the child, whether or not he is the biological father; it takes a paternity suit, custody battle, or some other legal effort to deprive him of that status. But when a woman in a lesbian partnership gives birth, her partner has no automatic legal rights. Even if she makes the effort to adopt the child as a second parent or to be awarded joint custody, she very often will not succeed. Likewise, in a heterosexual marriage where one partner already has children, the other partner may adopt as a second parent, if the missing parent is dead or makes no objection to giving up parental rights. This kind of second-parent adoption is far more difficult in a lesbian or gay relationship.

On one level, these are practical demands: people want access to the financial benefits that go with being married, they want to be able to raise children, and, in case of medical emergency or death, they want to be sure that parents or other family members do not have the right to bar access to a gay or lesbian spouse, or keep that spouse from making crucial decisions.

On another level, these are social demands: many gay men and lesbians want the emotional satisfaction that comes from being recognized as partners, from having a relationship taken seriously, from having the same societal support that heterosexual couples do when they face difficulties and challenges, and from being recognized as married by others in their religion. (In fact, many ministers and rabbis will marry same-sex couples, although, as described in Chapter 3, this has caused a great deal of controversy within many religious denominations. However, these ceremonies have no *legal* standing.)

Other gay activists have a different perspective. Some feminists—gay and straight—claim that heterosexual marriage is a property arrangement that oppresses women. Although many gay and lesbian feminists support legalizing gay marriage—E. J. Graff eloquently argues for this position in her 1999 book, *What Is Marriage For?*—many others see it as perpetuating the notion of women and children as property. Antimarriage feminists point out that marriage was originally a property relationship in which a man could control a woman—restricting the woman's sexual activities, depriving her of financial independence, even possessing the right to physically and sexually abuse her—and the children she bore. Moreover, marriage gives the state a say in how a personal relationship should be conducted. In many states, for example, adultery is grounds for divorce. Many feminists—and other gay rights activists—object to bringing gay relationships under the rubric of state-sanctioned monogamy.

Other feminists argue that if gay marriage becomes legal, lesbian mothers who marry other women will have improved standing in child custody matters, which traditionally penalize women—gay or straight—who engage in extramarital sex. These arguments are countered by those who claim that gay marriage will only serve to further marginalize and disempower those lesbians and gay men who do not choose to marry, effectively punishing those who claim the right to less conventional sexual relationships.

Many sexual liberationists in the gay rights movement join in the antimarriage chorus. Opponents of monogamy, for example, see marriage as an outmoded system that represses sexual freedom. They, too, argue that gay marriage will lead to even more intense discrimination against "unacceptable" unmarried gay men and lesbians. People who choose less conventional arrangements, such as three-way relationships, S and M, or transgendered identities, are also concerned about being marginalized should gay marriage become available. Certainly, these unconventional lifestyle choices do not necessarily imply that a relationship will not be committed, longlasting, or loving—in some cases, it may even be monogamous—but it may not fit within the bounds of a legally recognized marriage. Gay people whose lives do not seem to fit mainstream ideas worry about being split off from more "socially acceptable" gay men and lesbians.

Yet another section of the gay rights movement sees gay marriage as a profoundly revolutionary step. Since many people view marriage as the foundation of mainstream society, gay people's participation in it seems to transform both the nature of marriage and the nature of society itself. Certainly the fear that gay marriage would have this result seems to animate many religious and right-wing opponents of same-sex unions.

Lesbian marriage advocate E. J. Graff takes still a different position. Studying marriage throughout the centuries, Graff discovered that there is no single definition of marriage or the family. The idea that there is a "true" marriage that gay people could either participate in, reject, or transform is a myth, Graff argues, for marriage has meant so many different things in so many different societies that, in the larger scheme of things, enabling gay people to enter legal marriages would be just another in a long series of changes.

The current interest in gay marriage takes place against the backdrop of the AIDS crisis, which has caused many gay men to reconsider their traditional attachment to sexual liberation. Gabriel Rotello, for example, in his 1997 book, *Sexual Ecology: AIDS and the Destiny of Gay Men*, has taken the position that gay men need to develop "serial monogamous" relationships (being sexual with only one partner at a time), an arrangement that resembles marriage far more than the wide-ranging promiscuity that some gay men see as synonymous with liberation. Rotello's connection of monogamy and safer sex has enraged many gay men and lesbians. Some object to his characterization of lesbians as more monogamous: the so-called pro-pleasure lesbians, for example, have pointed out that many lesbians are also seeking sexual liberation, frequently rejecting monogamy and embracing a variety of unconventional sexual practices. Others object to his association of marriage and safety, claiming that many heterosexual married couples are not monogamous either—they are just not honest about it. Still others see Rotello as retreating from the gay liberationist view; even if AIDS requires new sexual ethics and arrangements, these critics say, there is no reason to adopt the outmoded and restrictive morality of the past.

Andrew Sullivan, whose experience as a person with AIDS is chronicled in his 1998 book, *Love Undetectable*, has long been a supporter of gay marriage. Opposing himself both to what he calls liberationists and to liberals, he argues for the narrowest possible definition of gay rights. In his 1995 book, *Virtually Normal*, Sullivan explicitly called for the gay rights movement to fight for gay rights—including marriage and military service—without insisting on the tolerance of the larger society.

By contrast, in *Sappho Goes to Law School*, legal scholar and novelist Ruthann Robson argues that legalizing lesbian marriage will put both cultural and legal pressure on lesbians—and, by implication, on gay men. "A landlord who refused to rent to a lesbian couple because they were unmarried or not in a registered domestic partnership (either because the landlord believes in the sanctity of marriage or simply prefers to rent to a 'stable couple') does not seem to me an improvement over a landlord who refused to rent to two women because they were lesbians," she comments. Robson also cites numerous examples of cases in which unmarried heterosexual couples were denied housing by landlords who successfully claimed a religious exemption to the fair housing laws—in other words, landlords whose religion led them to believe that unmarried cohabitation was wrong.

Why, asks Robson and other analysts, should lesbians and gay men seek state-sanctioned marriage, rather than trying to make marriage-related benefits available to *all* citizens, whether married or not? Why not insure housing rights for all, rather than allowing landlords to decide who has the right to live together? Why not extend health insurance to all U.S. residents, rather than simply extending a spouse's health insurance to his or her partner? Why not allow child custody, visitation, and other similar issues to depend on a person's contractually expressed wishes, so that friends, multiple sexual partners, and others might be accorded the same status as legal spouses, if the person so wishes?

These broader questions recall the early objections of antimarriage feminists, who pointed out that if women could earn as much money as men, could depend on affordable child care, could count on affordable housing, and could rely on national health insurance, there would no longer be any *economic* reason for women and men to live together. Challenging marriage became a much deeper challenge to the prevailing social system. Lesbian and gay theorists who oppose marriage likewise ask: "Why should the state recognize any one emotional arrangement between people, and reward it with legal, financial, and social benefits?"

Once again, a wide range of political perspectives comes into play, including those of the activists who support legalized gay marriage in the short run while advocating wider-ranging political transformation in the long term. (E. J. Graff, for example, supports both legalized gay marriage and a broader political agenda.) The question of gay marriage has now been raised in several courts and stage legislatures, as well as in Congress, even as many lesbians and gay men continue to have extralegal marriage ceremonies in religious or civil contexts. Gay and lesbian marriage will almost certainly continue as a major legal and social issue for quite some time.

A BRIEF HISTORY OF GAY RIGHTS

The following brief history is intended primarily as a reference point. Readers looking for more in-depth information on the history of the gay rights movement can look at a number of books, including John D'Emilio's *Sexual Politics, Sexual Communities: The Making of a Homosexual Minority in the*

Gay Rights

United States, 1940–1970 (1983); Jonathan Katz's *Gay/Lesbian Almanac: A New Documentary* (1983); Martin Duberman's *Stonewall* (1993); Martin Duberman, Martha Vicinus, and George Chauncey, Jr.'s *Hidden from History: Reclaiming the Gay and Lesbian Past* (1989); Molly McGarry and Fred Wasserman's *Becoming Visible, An Illustrated History of Lesbian and Gay Life in Twentieth-Century America* (1998); and Dudley Clendenin and Adam Nagourney's *Out for Good: The Struggle to Build a Gay Rights Movement in America* (1999).

Although this book discusses the modern gay rights movement as beginning in 1969, it is important to remember that homosexuality itself has a far more ancient history. Some form of same-sex involvement among both men and women seems to be present in virtually all societies, in virtually all eras, although, as John DeCecco, editor of *Journal of Homosexuality*, reminded us earlier, "Homosexuality is not one thing. It's had many, many different meanings over the centuries."

For example, the lesbian anthropologist Kendall (who uses only that name), writing in *Boy-Wives and Female Husbands: Studies of African Homosexualities*, edited by Stephen O. Murray and Will Roscoe, describes arrangements among women in the African nation of Lesotho that to her eye are lesbian: "From [university students and domestic workers] I learned of fairly common instances of tribadism or rubbing [two women rubbing their genital areas together], fondling, and cunnilingus between Bathoso women, with and without digital penetration [the penetration of fingers into the vagina]. This they initially described as 'loving each other,' 'staying together nicely,' 'holding each other,' or 'having a nice time together.'" But, Kendall stresses, because no male sexual organs were involved, the women were adamant in insisting that these relationships did not constitute "sex." Moreover, virtually all of the women who had such relationships were also married, for it was unthinkable for a woman in that society *not* to be married.

Likewise, John Boswell, in *Same-Sex Unions in Premodern Europe*, points out that modern definitions of homosexuality do not necessarily fit the lived experiences of people in other cultures and other times. Yet, he writes, "many cultures other than Western ones have recognized and institutionalized same-sex unions—Japanese warriors in early modern times, Chinese men and women under the Yuan and Ming dynasties, native Americans from a number of tribes (mostly before white domination), many African tribes well into the twentieth century, and residents (both male and female) of the Middle East, South-East Asia, Russia, other parts of Asia, and South America." Boswell also discusses same-sex unions in ancient Greece and Rome and medieval Europe.

In one of the first history books to emerge from the modern gay rights movement, *Gay American History*, a documentary history of U.S. lesbians and gay men, author Jonathan Katz describes the difficulty of identifying same-sex activity in other historical periods: "When simply working, living, and loving, homosexuals have been condemned to invisibility." Thus, Katz points out, many of our records concern gay men and women who have "made trouble"—molesting children, committing murder, and engaging in other crimes common to both heterosexual and homosexual citizens. At the very least, however, Katz's documents—dating back to 1566 and including the account of a Frenchman in Florida charged with sodomy and murdered in 1566 by the Spanish military authorities, an execution for sodomy in Virginia in 1624, and another in New Haven, Connecticut in 1646—indicate that homosexual activity existed in early America. Indeed, one of the earliest documents on record of a minister being separated from his church because of homosexual activity concerned the 1866 case of Horatio Alger, who went on to write the "rags to riches" stories that for some express the very essence of the American dream.

Historians and other scholars argue that although various types of same-sex *activity* have always taken place, the notion of same-sex *identity* is a relatively new one. For men and women to define themselves by their choice of sexual partner was not possible until they could live autonomous lives—that is, lives separate from the family structures that had organized the human economy from the beginning of human history until the 20th century. Not until the development of an urban culture could people afford to live apart from their families and define themselves by how they *chose* to live.

U.S. urban culture from the first included a gay and lesbian subculture, in the form of bars, nightlife, theatrical entertainment, and prostitution. In New York City, Greenwich Village soon became known as a center of gay nightlife. So did Harlem, reflecting the African-American community's traditional tendency to be more tolerant of gay and lesbian activity than was dominant white society.

However, if gay and lesbian life was in some sense tolerated—and certainly tolerated more in the 1920s, 1930s, and 1940s than in the 1950s and 1960s—it was also regulated. In 1933, for example, New York State's highest court upheld a regulation against gay men and lesbians congregating in bars, and the State Liquor Authority threatened to withdraw the license of anyone who served gay patrons or allowed them to congregate. Such laws drove gay and lesbian bar culture underground, into establishments run by organized crime.

Gay men, as we have seen, always had access to more public venues for their sexual activity, including such cruising areas as parks and waterfronts. Lesbians were more reluctant to engage in such public activity, and they were less likely to congregate in bars, although many predominantly working-class cities, such as Buffalo, New York, had an active lesbian bar scene.

There were also some lesbian clubs in various cities. Lesbians in New York City recalled the 1930s and 1940s, when they would buy three-piece suits—jacket, skirt, and pants. They would wear the skirt on the street and change into the pants when they got to the club.

Upper-class white men had their own gay bar scene—the bars or lounges of certain aristocratic hotels. These discreet establishments included the Oak Room at the Plaza and the King Cole Room at the St. Regis in New York City, the Top of the Mark at the Mark Hopkins in San Francisco, and the Biltmore Bar in Los Angeles.

World War II produced an even more open climate for gay men and lesbians, as servicemen from out of town flocked to gay and lesbian bars. "It was as open then, from about 1944 to 1947, as it is now," recalled New York resident Leo Adams in an interview with curator and historian Fred Wasserman, coauthor of *Becoming Visible*. "Anybody in uniform seemed to be available at that time."

Thus gay men and lesbians continued to face social isolation and legal restrictions. In 1934, for example, the Motion Picture Production Code officially banned all references to and depictions of homosexuality from Hollywood films. In the late 1940s and early 1950s, Senator Joseph McCarthy, known for his attacks upon communists—actual or suspected—in the U.S. government, was engaging in a similar attack upon homosexuals. And in the 1950s, despite a growing nightlife in cities throughout the nation—especially New York, Los Angeles, and San Francisco—police raids on gay bars and arrests of gay men rose sharply in cities as diverse as Washington, D.C.; New York; Miami; Memphis; Baltimore; Pittsburgh; Wichita, Kansas; Ann Arbor, Michigan; Minneapolis; Boise, Idaho; Seattle; and Pasadena, California. In 1959, New York City revoked the liquor licenses of virtually all gay bars.

EARLY ORGANIZING

In this climate, it was perhaps not surprising that the first gay rights organization in the United States should have been founded by a Communist, Harry Hay, who established the Mattachine Society in Los Angeles in 1950. (An interracial gay organization, Knights of the Clock, was also founded in Los Angeles in 1950, but its function was more social than political.) Hay called the Mattachine society a "homophile" movement, making a distinction between those who loved men and those who were explicitly sexual with them. He intended the term "homophile" to include supporters of homosexual rights as well as actual homosexuals.

Despite this apparent timidity, Hay's vision was actually quite radical, for he saw the possibility of homosexuals forming their own group to defend their own distinct culture, much as African Americans, Jews, and Mexican Americans had done. The Mattachine Society grew slowly, but, in a pattern that would be repeated throughout the 1990s, found itself energized by the very oppression it sought to end. When Mattachine Society member Dale Jennings was accused of "lewd and dissolute conduct" in a Los Angeles park, he decided to take the case to court. The first U.S. court case to raise the issue of gay rights ended in a deadlocked jury, and the case was dropped, but the Mattachine Society had made good use of the incident. Flyers distributed to various gay male venues—beaches, bars, parks, rest rooms—brought exposure, new members, and eventually, new chapters to the early gay rights group. In fact, in another common pattern of the movement, increased success led to a more conservative approach, and in 1953, the founders had to resign from the group because of their Communist ties, which made the new members uneasy. These new recruits rejected the founders' radical vision of a distinctive gay culture, claiming that they simply needed help adjusting to mainstream society. In 1954, they took up the slogan "Evolution, not Revolution," a position that would eventually lead to their demise soon after the Stonewall uprising had raised the possibility of a more militant gay liberationist approach.

The first U.S. lesbian rights group, the Daughters of Bilitis, was founded in 1955 in San Francisco. Although its political approach did not survive into the 1970s, its early membership certainly did. Founders Del Martin and Phyllis Lyon and member Barbara Gittings were gay rights activists who continued as leaders in the movement through Stonewall and for many years beyond.

From a 1970s radical perspective, though, the "DOB," as it was discreetly known ("Bilitis" was supposed to have been a lover of the allegedly lesbian poet Sappho of ancient Greece), was thoroughly middle-class, with an emphasis on respectability and no interest in the butch-femme working-class women who made up much of the lesbian bar scene. (The terms *butch* and *femme* refer to the masculine and feminine roles adopted by some men and women in gay and lesbian culture.) This ambivalent attitude toward lesbianism is reflected in the title of an article from the *Ladder*, the DOB's magazine: "Raising Children in a Deviant Relationship."

To people familiar with the gay club and bar scenes of the 1980s and 1990s, the climate of the 1950s and 1960s is almost unimaginable. Same-sex couples were not allowed to touch or even to dance together. In the gay male bars where dancing was allowed at all, at least one woman had to be found to get out on the dance floor—followed by two dozen or so men, all of whom could claim to be dancing with her. To avoid being harassed or even arrested, same-sex dance partners tried to dance side by side, rather than face to face. In some states, it was illegal for men to wear women's clothing and vice versa, making drag queens literally outlaws, not just socially or sexually, but also legally.

Novelist Leslie Feinberg recalls that in the mixed-sex gay bar she frequented in Niagara Falls, New York, lesbians and gay men danced in same-sex couples when they could—but switched to male-female couples whenever the cops appeared at the door. "We [lesbians] in our suits and ties paired off with our drag queen sisters in their dresses and pumps."

Although one middle-class gay man recalls that "few I knew were very conscious of needing liberation," for many others, the constant threat of exposure was a continual fact of life. Arrests made in gay bars might be published in the local newspaper, possibly putting an end to a person's marriage, job, and standing in the community, and bringing shame and ostracism to one's children and family. Even though gay bars became legal in New York after 1967, raids were common, and police violence was frequent, particularly against gay men. Some survivors of that time describe routine beatings inside the police wagons that took arrested gay men to the station.

THE STONEWALL UPRISING

Even before the event that simply became known as "Stonewall," there were already stirrings of a new political climate for gay men and lesbians. Early in 1969, for example, Carl Wittman, antiwar activist, leftist, and liberationist, had written a gay liberation manifesto that was to anticipate many of the political perspectives that marked the early 1970s. The *Advocate*, a gay newspaper, had been founded in Los Angeles in 1967. In New York City, Craig Rodwell had opened the Oscar Wilde Memorial Bookstore, which he intended less as a place to sell books than as a center for gay activity.

Ironically, when the uprising finally occurred, many people failed to recognize its significance. Looking back, however, there is no denying that what began as a skirmish at a Greenwich Village bar became the harbinger of a new movement for human rights. Detailed accounts of Stonewall have taken on the quality of myth, as more people remember being there than could possibly have fit in the tiny, grimy bar. It is generally accepted that a diverse group of bar patrons, led by the drag queens who were Stonewall regulars, spontaneously began to fight back during a police raid. The resistance turned into a riot, which lasted for several days.

Something about the least accepted, most marginalized segment of the gay male community—the men who dressed as women—engaging in physical combat with New York City cops captured the imagination of both gay and straight observers. Although initial press coverage of the event ranged from contemptuous to condescending, gay/lesbian political response was immediate and strong. The Gay Liberation Front (GLF) was founded in

July 1969, just weeks after the uprising. By 1970 the tiny New York group had grown to encompass 19 cells (their politically inflected word for "chapter"), 12 consciousness-raising groups, three households, a marxist study group, several political caucuses, and a newspaper called *Come Out!*.

Two months after its founding, in September 1969, the fledgling group held its first demonstration—at the alternative weekly paper, the *Village Voice*, which had refused to print the word "gay" on the grounds that it was obscene. Although groups of women and drag queens eventually left GLF to form other groups, including the Radicalesbians and the Street Transvestite Action Revolution (STAR), the GLF continued through the early 1970s.

The next major group to form was the Gay Activists Alliance (GAA). Whereas the GLF had seen itself as part of a larger movement, the GAA defined itself as exclusively gay. The GLF had operated on New Left principles: no formal structure, open meetings, free discussion. The GAA, by contrast, operated according to *Robert's Rules of Order* (the authoritative manual for parliamentary procedure), with a formal structure and even a constitution. Founders of the GAA, while sharing many of the GLF's radical sympathies, wanted a gay-specific organization that ran more efficiently than the GLF was able to do.

Even after Stonewall, police violence and fear of the consequences of an arrest continued to haunt many gay men and lesbians. In March 1970, the same police officer who had led the raid on the Stonewall Inn began arresting people at the Snake Pit, another Greenwich Village gay bar. More than 160 people were hustled outside and brought to the police station, including patrons, management, and bartenders. All were arrested and given summonses for disorderly conduct—charges that were eventually dismissed. But Argentine national Diego Vinales was in the United States on a visa. Since the Internal Security Act of 1950 (known as the McCarran Act) had made it illegal for homosexuals to enter the United States, Vinales feared being deported once his orientation was discovered. He hurled himself out of the second-story window at the police station and impaled himself on a 14-inch spike in the wrought-iron fence below. He was brought to the hospital in critical condition and was later charged with resisting arrest. The protest at St. Vincent's Hospital, where Vinales was held, featured a GAA flyer that read, "Any way you look at it—that boy was PUSHED!! We are All being pushed."

Meanwhile, lesbian feminists were exploring their position in the larger feminist movement, particularly in the National Organization for Women (NOW), the largest and most influential national feminist group. Although feminist leader Betty Friedan had called lesbians diversionary and had even accused them of being sent by the Central Intelligence Agency (CIA) to discredit the women's movement, other NOW leaders were more sympathetic to lesbian issues. After a number of battles within the organization, a resolution supporting lesbians passed at the 1971 NOW National Conference, and in 1975 NOW declared lesbian rights to be a national priority.

ELECTORAL VICTORIES AND DEFEATS

Much of the early gay rights movement was concerned with winning political power, through electing gay candidates, passing gay rights legislation, and gaining a voice in the Democratic Party. In 1974, the first two openly gay candidates were elected: Kathy Kozachenko and Elaine Noble. Kozachenko, a University of Michigan student, won a seat on the Ann Arbor City Council. The council was a liberal body that for years had included students elected from the wards dominated by the University of Michigan. Elaine Noble's 1974 election to the Massachusetts state legislature was considered far more significant. Noble consistently stressed that she was running to represent the working people of her district, whom she intended to support through a wide variety of progressive legislation; her lesbianism was openly discussed, but was not the centerpiece of her campaign. She got a great deal of media attention for her broad-based campaign, which made her the first openly gay state representative.

Noble was soon joined by other gay legislators, including Minnesota state senator Allan Spear, who came out after he was already in office—and who then went on to win reelection in 1976. Meanwhile, for the first time in history, the 1972 Democratic Party featured five openly gay and lesbian delegates and alternates. One of them, longtime activist Jim Foster, even made a speech from the floor calling for gay rights to be added to the party platform. Though Foster's speech was made late at night, when virtually no one was listening, and though the efforts to affect the platform were not successful, gay leaders still had hopes of having a voice in the Democratic Party. Indeed, by 1980, there were 77 gay and lesbian delegates to the Democratic Convention, and in 1984, gay rights became part of official party policy.

At the same time, throughout the 1970s, more and more communities across the country were passing antidiscrimination legislation to protect gay rights in employment, housing, and public accommodation. To both opponents and supporters, it seemed that the civil rights of gay men and lesbians were fast becoming accepted.

BACKLASH

The victories of the gay and lesbian rights movement brought with them a backlash—an effort to erase the gains and return homosexuality to its former status as unspeakable sin and unpardonable crime. In 1977, singer and former beauty queen Anita Bryant led a broad-based campaign that included many religious leaders in an effort to repeal a gay rights ordinance that had recently been passed in Dade County, Florida. Bryant, whose organization was called "Save Our Children," sought to portray gay men and lesbians as child molesters, "recruiters" of innocent young people into their sinful ranks. Bryant was joined by the Reverend Jerry Falwell, who two years later would found the New Right group, the Moral Majority; the National Association of Evangelicals; the Roman Catholic archdiocese of Miami; the president of the Miami Beach B'nai B'rith (a Jewish organization); both of Florida's senators and its liberal governor; and groups who opposed abortion rights and the Equal Rights Amendment (ERA), a proposed constitutional amendment guaranteeing equal rights to women. Bryant's referendum was successful by more than a 2-1 margin, and the measure was repealed, inspiring similar referendums in St. Paul, Minnesota; Wichita, Kansas; and Eugene, Oregon in 1978.

In what would become a familiar dialectic, defeat spurred the gay rights movement to new activism, and a record number of men and women turned out for gay rights events in the summer of 1977. Some 75,000 people marched in New York City's "Christopher Street Liberation Day March," five times as many as had marched in the previous year, while in San Francisco, 300,000 people turned out. And a nationwide orange juice boycott succeeded in convincing the Florida Citrus Commission to remove Bryant as their spokesperson.

But Bryant had also inspired California state senator John Briggs to put forward a new referendum in 1978, Proposition 6, popularly known as the Briggs Amendment, which would have banned all lesbians and gay men from working as public school teachers, while prohibiting any teacher or school employee from saying anything positive about homosexuality on school grounds. The Briggs Initiative was defeated 59 percent to 41 percent, in part because former California governor Ronald Reagan was convinced to come out against it, which influenced many voters to vote *no*. The defeat of the Briggs Amendment appeared to turn the tide of the backlash, especially since the people of Seattle also defeated an anti–gay rights referendum by a two to one margin.

Then, on November 27, 1978, a shocking event reminded Americans that it was still dangerous to be gay—or to support gay rights. Dan White, a right-wing former San Francisco supervisor (analogous to a city council position), enraged at what he saw as the progay direction of San Francisco politics, had resigned from the board of supervisors. A few days later, he changed his mind and asked Mayor George Moscone, who was known to be gay-friendly, for his job back. When Moscone refused, White walked into city hall with a gun and assassinated first Moscone, then Harvey Milk, another supervisor, who was openly gay. White's lawyer used a strategy that became known as the "Twinkie defense," arguing that White was suffering from intense depression brought on by an overindulgence in junk food, a depression that distorted his judgment in a kind of temporary insanity. Apparently, this approach worked, for White was charged, not with murder, but with manslaughter, for which he received a sentence of only 7 years and 8 months. The "White Night Riots" were the result, in which gay men and lesbians in San Francisco's Castro District caused some $1 million damage in their outrage.

Just as the early, heady days of gay liberation had drawn inspiration from the liberatory climate of the 1960s and 1970s, so was the backlash of the late 1970s and the 1980s shaped by the generally right-wing trend in the United States. When Ronald Reagan was elected president in 1980, he saw his victory as a mandate to turn back the social reforms of the New Deal. New Right groups also saw his election as a signal that their time had come. Anticommunist, antiunion, antifeminist, anti–affirmative action, and antiwelfare, these new groups were also decidedly antigay. And while many Americans were uneasy about the New Right's attacks on women and people of color—at least at first—gay men and lesbians seemed a safe target.

THE AIDS CRISIS

Once again, the gay rights movement was about to witness a dialectical process, in which its greatest defeats turned into its greatest strengths. AIDS first appeared on the scene as a barely understood disease mentioned briefly as a "rare cancer" in news reports in 1981. Later, the disease was dubbed Gay-Related Immune Deficiency (GRID) since it was clear that many gay men seemed susceptible to it. By 1982, scientists realized that anyone could be infected, and that, in addition to gay men, the most common victims seemed to be users of intravenous drugs, hemophiliacs (people whose blood does not clot properly, causing them to bleed profusely from even minor cuts), and the recipients of blood transfusions. The disease was renamed Acquired Immune Deficiency Syndrome, or AIDS.

It was clear that sexual activity had something to do with the transmission of the disease, but in those early years, no one knew exactly how or why. Still, scientists understood that having multiple sexual partners increased one's chances for the disease—and multiple sexual partners were what the gay bathhouses were all about. Gradually, the call came, from both inside and outside the gay community: close the bathhouses.

For many gay men, sexual liberation was synonymous with gay rights. The idea that sexual activity—which seemed such a hard-won freedom— might prove deadly was unthinkable. The notion that bathhouses should now be closed by the state—which so many gay men remembered as the force behind humiliating arrests and raids—seemed offensive at best and oppressive at worst, particularly in a hostile political climate. Conservative commentator William F. Buckley actually wrote a *New York Times* op-ed piece calling for people with AIDS (PWAs) to be tattooed for identification. Others called for PWAs to be quarantined.

Nevertheless, some gay activists strongly believed that the bathhouses had become, not a site of sexual freedom, but a danger to public health. Others, while opposing state regulation, wanted the bathhouses to close voluntarily—or at least to police themselves, to monitor group sex, conduct AIDS education, and offer free condoms. The controversy over the bathhouses continued throughout the mid-1980s. In some places, they were closed—and gay rights and civil liberties groups fought court cases to get them reopened. In other places, they closed of their own accord. Other bathhouses remained open or reopened. While some observers reported a drop in bathhouse business, others claimed that gay men continued to go to the baths—though perhaps they behaved somewhat differently once they got there.

Although the dangers of AIDS were suspected as early as 1981, President Ronald Reagan did not even mention the disease publicly until 1987 (though he did send a telegram of condolence to his old friend, movie star Rock Hudson, when it became known that Hudson had the disease in 1985). By the time Reagan addressed the issue, there were 36,000 reported AIDS cases in the United States alone (the disease was spreading even more rapidly in Africa, and cases had been reported in Europe and the Caribbean), and almost 21,000 Americans had died. A disproportionate number of the U.S. deaths were people of color.

Moreover, very little money, relatively speaking, was allocated for AIDS research. Congress did not even grant funds until 1983, when it budgeted only $33 million. A U.S. Department of Health and Human Services hot line created in 1983 was staffed with only six operators—who were expected to handle more than 10,000 calls each day. As of July 1983, some 90,000 calls had been left unanswered.

So the gay and lesbian community rallied in its own defense. In 1982, writer Larry Kramer cofounded Gay Men's Health Crisis (GMHC) in New York City. Other AIDS groups were quickly formed around the country, primarily to provide social services and support for people with AIDS. In 1987, the militant political action group, AIDS Coalition to Unleash Power (ACT UP) was formed in New York City. Soon there were ACT UP chapters elsewhere in the United States and in Paris, London, and Berlin. ACT UP protestors challenged the drug companies, the U.S. Food and Drug Administration, and the medical establishment, demanding more, better, and cheaper treatments, as well as fighting for AIDS education and prevention. In the words of sociologist Steven Epstein: "the AIDS movement [was] the first in the United States to accomplish the mass conversion of disease 'victims' into activist-experts."

As we have seen, the militancy of ACT UP and the rapprochement between gay men and lesbians were two unexpected results of the epidemic, which left thousands of people dead and devastated an entire community. Yet this tragic disease also brought a new visibility and, oddly, a new acceptability to gay life in America. Ironically, people with AIDS constituted the first class of gay men (and lesbians) to receive federal protection, when the civil rights protections afforded under the 1990 Americans with Disabilities Act were extended to people with AIDS in 1998. Because people with AIDS, or people infected with HIV (the virus that causes AIDS) were considered "disabled," AIDS or HIV status could no longer be a reason to fire someone from a job or deny a person housing or public accommodation. Also, ironically, the 1993 movie *Philadelphia*, starring Tom Hanks, Antonio Banderas, and Denzel Washington, documenting an early case of AIDS discrimination, was one of the first modern commercial movies to portray gay characters.

AIDS activism also brought the gay rights movement closer to other activist communities. The tenants' movement in New York City, for example, had traditionally resented gay men, both because of homophobia and because gay men were frequently willing to buy apartments in newly gentrifying neighborhoods, thus displacing previous tenants—poor and working-class people who were often people of color as well. Yet when landlords began evicting the surviving partners of men who had died of AIDS, the gay rights movement and tenant activists were able to unite around a common cause. (For more on AIDS and housing rights, see the discussion of *Braschi v. Stahl Associates Co.* in Chapter 2.) In New York City, this coalition led to the election of several gay leaders, including State Senator Deborah Glick, the first open lesbian to be elected to the New York State Assembly (1990), and City Councilman Tom Duane, the first openly gay man to hold that office. (Duane later became the first openly HIV-positive person to be elected to public office in New York as well. He is now a state representative.)

THE NINETIES AND BEYOND

In the 1990s, a generation of activists appeared who had been born after Stonewall and who had a whole new set of assumptions about what being gay or lesbian in America might mean. Early in the decade, meanwhile, gay activists faced challenges in Oregon and Colorado, where statewide antigay referendums were proposed in 1992. In Oregon, the measure was defeated, although local antigay ordinances began to appear the following year. In Colorado, the infamous Amendment 2 nullified gay rights legislation elsewhere in the state and banned local governments from implementing new gay rights measures. Ironically, *Romer v. Evans*, the 1996 Supreme Court ruling that overturned Amendment 2, is considered by many to be one of the most important progay court rulings in U.S. history, although it is still too early to assess *Romer's* actual implications.

Throughout much of the 1990s, the Republican Party continued to position itself as deeply opposed to gay rights, particularly at its 1992 convention, where Patrick Buchanan called for "cultural war" against homosexuals. However, the 1990s were also the decade that saw the founding of the Log Cabin Republicans, a group of gay Republicans committed both to their party and to gay rights.

In 1992, Democratic presidential candidate Bill Clinton promised he would overturn the ban on gays and lesbians in the military if he were elected—and then went on to implement a far weaker policy, popularly known as "don't ask, don't tell." In yet another irony, more gay men and lesbians have been discharged under this policy than under the previous blanket prohibition against gay or lesbian sexual activity. (For more on military policy, see Chapter 2.)

Even in the face of escalating attacks from the religious right, gay and lesbian family arrangements received more recognition in the 1990s than in any other previous decade. By 1997, more than two dozen cities had domestic partnership registries, through which gay men and lesbians could receive some measure of legal recognition for their relationships, if not full-fledged marriage. (For more on gay marriage, see Chapter 2.) More than 50 cities offered domestic partnership benefits to their municipal employees, while numerous colleges, universities, labor unions, and corporations extended such benefits as well, in a de facto recognition of gay/lesbian marriage. Indeed, by 1997, half of the Fortune 1000 companies offered domestic partners health and other benefits, as did 10 percent of the nation's employers.

Perhaps the most profound shift of the 1990s, a transition that is discussed more fully in Chapter 3, was the move from invisibility to visibility. When the decade began, gay men and lesbians were still marginalized, still invisible, still outside the frame of reference of most of American culture. Even if gay men and lesbians had won some rights, achieved political office, and created a margin of safety for their sexual and emotional lives, they were not seriously taken into account as a political or cultural force that had to be seen as part of the national life.

Now, even if religious right organizations continue to demonize gay men and lesbians, the fact that gay people exist and the assumption that they should be treated with respect has been brought to the attention of the American public in a way that cannot be ignored. Although discrimination, exclusion, and even violence against gay men and lesbians is still common, there now exists a cultural and political framework to name those problems and object to them. What use gay men, lesbians, and their allies will make of this framework in the decades to come remains to be seen.

LEGAL ISSUES

Legal battles have been a major aspect of the modern gay rights movement. Yet it is important to specify the limits as well as the significance of the legal aspects of gay rights. As discussed earlier, different activists hold different visions for the gay rights movement. Some define their goal quite narrowly—no laws should exist barring gay people from having the same rights as their heterosexual counterparts. Conservative journalist Andrew Sullivan, for example, calls for marriage and military service to be legally opened to gay people, because getting married and serving in the armed forces are rights that heterosexuals have always enjoyed. Unlike those whom he calls "liberals," however, Sullivan is not interested in using the law to "impose tolerance." He defends the right of private organizations to treat gay men and lesbians differently from straight people.

Other activists want full participation of gay people in every aspect of society. Their vision includes total acceptance of gay men and lesbians in religious, civic, educational, and cultural institutions. Gay-friendly school curricula; the ordination of gay and lesbian ministers, priests, and rabbis; the rights of gay men and lesbians to march under their own banner in a St. Patrick's Day parade; the elimination of negative stereotyping in television, movies, and the news media—these are the kinds of goals favored by more liberal gay rights organizations.

Yet even these goals occupy an uneasy space that is sometimes within the realm of law and sometimes beyond the law's reach. The right of a teacher to be openly gay, for example, might be framed as a legal issue—but what about that teacher's right to talk openly about his or her personal life in the classroom, to take part in gay political activities in the community, or to teach a gay-friendly curriculum? Likewise, a lesbian or gay student might conceivably be able to seek legal protection if she or he is being harassed—but what about the student's opportunity to speak to a gay-friendly counselor, form a gay student group, or bring a same-sex date to a school event? It is not clear where legality ends and the place for political organizing, consciousness-raising, and other extralegal activities begins. (*Note:* An *illegal* activity is *against* the law; an *extralegal* activity is simply *outside* the law. Breaking a window on school property would be *illegal.* Convincing the principal to hold a school assembly on gay and lesbian issues might be *ex-*

tralegal, if there were no existing law to regulate the matter.) Certainly, this was the case when Aaron Fricke, a gay high school student in Providence, Rhode Island, went to the courts and won the right to bring a male date to his school prom. If students at Fricke's school hadn't been ready to accept him and his date, his legal right would have meant very little indeed. Later students found other ways to convince schools to change their policies than by taking them to court.

As early as 1975, gay activist John D'Emilio was warning the gay rights movement to beware of depending too heavily on either court cases or legislation. While these are important tools, he argued, they are not necessarily the most profound or lasting ways of effecting change—although they may be necessary preconditions before other kinds of work can be done. Also, the effort to win a court case, elect an official, or pass a law may itself be a larger exercise in political organizing. A campaign to elect a gay politician, change school policy, or convince a city council to pass a nondiscrimination ordinance might offer the chance to mobilize gay and lesbian supporters, speak to straight people about gay issues, work with a variety of political allies, and generally change the political and cultural climate in a community. But it can also, as D'Emilio warned, be a kind a trap: an organization's resources can become entirely focused on a few politicians or judges, while the larger community continues in ignorance or apathy.

Contrasting the case of gay men and lesbians who seek to march in their local St. Patrick's Day parades with the ability of an openly gay contingent to march in New York City's Puerto Rican Day parade reveals both the strengths and the limits of the legal approach. So far, although gay and lesbian groups in New York and Boston have sought various legal means to win their right to march under a gay Irish banner in their local parades, they have not been successful—and they have won few friends in the Irish-American community in the process. Why then have gay Puerto Ricans won more acceptance?

The answer lies not in legal rulings, but in politics. The St. Patrick's Day parade is the creation of Irish community groups in which few if any gay men or lesbians openly participate. Most mainstream Irish organizations could well believe that the role of gay people in their community is negligible, not least because Irish-American gays and lesbians who are active in political or community affairs tend not to work specifically with Irish groups. Rather, they are active with gay and lesbian organizations, or in other contexts: a multiethnic neighborhood organization, a labor union, or a women's group. As such, they have developed little credibility with the mainstream Irish community. If they want to participate in an Irish parade, their best option may indeed be a legal battle—though even a victory might serve only to convince other Irish people that gays and lesbians are truly outsiders trying to force their way in.

Puerto Rican gay men and lesbians, on the other hand, have been active in the mainland Puerto Rican community in a number of ways. Take the example of Margarita Lopez, an open lesbian who has recently won a seat on the New York City Council representing a predominantly Latino neighborhood. Lopez is known for her commitment to gay and lesbian rights—but she has also won a reputation as a tireless fighter for tenants' rights, low-income housing, and a variety of other issues of concern to the Puerto Rican community—and to poor and working-class people generally. When she and others like her come looking for a place in the larger community's celebration, a foundation of respect and political affiliation has already been laid.

Another limit of legal approaches is the tendency to fit gay and lesbian issues into the sometimes restrictive structures already established by society and the law. Legal scholar and law professor Ruthann Robson describes this problem in her book *Sappho Goes to Law School*, where she analyzes the contradictions between winning rights for lesbians and what she considers the distortion of lesbian lives and relationships to fit inappropriate heterosexual models. Like many other gay liberationists, Robson wonders to what extent legal battles can make more space for the gay and lesbian community, and to what extent working within the law only serves to restrict gay men and women. The rest of this chapter looks at a few of these battles. Specific laws and cases are discussed in depth in Chapter 2, while Chapter 3 discusses legal battles pertaining to culture.

SODOMY LAWS

As of early 2000, almost 20 states made homosexual sex illegal under sodomy laws. These laws serve as a constant threat in the lives of many gay men and women. Besides posing the literal threat of arrest, they affect people's lives in a myriad of ways, especially in child custody battles. Gay rights activists also argue that sodomy laws represent society's way of equating gay men and lesbians with criminals, while anti–gay rights activists claim that they represent society's assertion that homosexuality is indeed immoral. Clearly, the ways that straight people view gay men and lesbians, and the ways in which gay people view themselves, cannot help but be affected by the legal climate, even if individuals are not consciously aware of specific laws.

The Background of Sodomy Law

Although sodomy laws claim a religious basis in the Judeo-Christian tradition—the name comes from the biblical community of Sodom, where sodomy was presumably practiced—there is relatively little in either the Old or the New Testament on homosexual practices. Although the story of Sodom appears in Genesis, there is actually no reference to any specific sexual act that was practiced there. The story in the Old Testament says that God heard rumors of Sodom's sinfulness and sent two male angels to find out more. The angels arrive at the house of a man called Lot and are immediately besieged by men of Sodom. Lot offers the men his daughters to keep them from attacking the visitors; they refuse the daughters and leave. God decides that Sodom is so sinful that it must be destroyed, but the nature of the sin is never specified.

Scholars have long debated the correct interpretation of the story of Sodom. According to John Boswell, in his book *Christianity, Social Tolerance, and Homosexuality*, many biblical scholars believe that what angered God was Sodom's lack of hospitality to visitors, a serious crime in an ancient world where the lack of welcome might expose a visitor to starvation or death by exposure. Boswell also points out that the only place in the Old Testament where homosexual acts are explicitly mentioned is in Leviticus:

Thou shalt not lie with mankind as with womankind: it is abomination. (18:22)

If a man also lie with mankind, as he lieth with a woman, both of them have commited an abomination: they shall surely be put to death; their blood shall be upon them. (20:13)

Boswell argues that the Hebrew word "toevah," translated in the King James Version of the Bible as "abomination,"

> *does not usually signify something intrinsically evil, like rape or theft (discussed elsewhere in Leviticus), but something which is ritually unclean for Jews, like eating pork or engaging in intercourse during menstruation, both of which are prohibited in these same chapters. . . . [T]he prohibition of homosexual acts follows immediately upon a prohibition of idolatrous sexuality (also "toevah"). . . .*
>
> *The distinction between intrinsic wrong and ritual impurity is even more finely drawn by the Greek translation, which distinguishes in "toevah" itself the separate categories of violations of law or justice . . . and infringements of ritual purity or monotheistic worship. . . . The Levitical proscriptions of homosexual behavior fall in the latter category.*

Other progay biblical scholars point out that Jews, at whom the injunctions of the Old Testament are directed, are also charged with following the 613 commandments listed in Deuteronomy, which were meant to distinguish them from other tribes who did not share their religion. These practices include not eating pork or shellfish; praying in the morning, evening, and before meals; posting the words of the Lord on the doorpost of one's house; men not using a razor on their beards; and other specific customs. Today, some Orthodox Jews consider themselves obliged to follow all 613 commandments; other followers of the Judeo-Christian tradition tend to focus on the Ten Commandments, in which the only forbidden sexual practice to be named is adultery (when a married person has sex outside his or her marriage).

Some anthropologists have another interpretation of the Old Testament passages: they point to them as an early society's way of preventing sexual acts that would not lead to procreation (conceiving children). The need for population was a major feature of rural societies, so that masturbation, homosexuality, and other practices would likely be discouraged.

Fundamentalists, on the other hand, have indicated these passages as evidence of the specific sinfulness of homosexuality. Seeing the Bible as the literal word of God, they argue that homosexuality is explicitly condemned, and is therefore immoral—indeed, abominable.

One of the few New Testament references to sodomy comes in St. Paul's Epistle to the Romans, in which Paul wrote

For this cause God gave them up unto vile affections: for even their women did change the natural use into that which is against nature: And likewise also the men, leaving the natural use of the woman, burned in their lust toward another; men with men working that which is unseemly, and receiving in themselves that recompense of their error which was met. (1:26–27)

Progay scholars have argued that this passage, like the ones in the Old Testament, reflects not so much a central theological principle as a religion's wish to distinguish itself from a surrounding culture, in which homosexuality was accepted. They point out that neither Jesus Christ nor his disciples ever made mention of homosexuality.

Many antigay Christians, on the other hand, believe that Paul's words, in conjunction with the passages quoted from the Old Testament, constitute a ringing denunciation of homosexuality. Seeing the entire Bible as the word of God, they are less interested in making a distinction between Jesus' and Paul's words than in interpreting what they believe God has ordained.

According to Boswell, the actual Christian tradition varied greatly with regard to homosexuality. In some cases, same-sex marriage ceremonies took place in Catholic churches; in other cases, homosexuality was uneasily tolerated; in still other cases, it was condemned. By the late Middle Ages, canon (church) law forbade same-sex practices, a teaching that was reflected in many civil (nonchurch) legal codes, which forbade various types of sex that did not lead to procreation. In other words, the sodomy law existed as part of a larger prohibition against any kind of sexual activity that did not lead directly to conceiving a child, including masturbation, oral-genital contact, and oral-anal contact. Early sodomy laws did not distinguish between homosexuals and heterosexuals; they were simply intended to restrict sexual activity to that which resulted in procreation.

University of Denver historian Arthur Gilbert argues that Christianity's interest in focusing on the "spirit" as "higher" than the body is related to the religious opposition to anal sex in particular. Philosopher and theologian Thomas Aquinas condemned male-male anal sex more severely than other types of nonprocreative sex, such as masturbation and fellatio. Indeed, Aquinas found anal sex more sinful than either rape or incest, whether the practice was conducted between two men or between a man and a woman. Church punishment was traditionally more severe for anal sex than for oral-genital contact and extended even to married heterosexual couples. The sexual practice, not a same-sex relationship, was what was being condemned.

Again, fundamentalists disagree. They tend to see the Christian tradition as uniform and unchanging—and as unqualifiedly opposed to homosexuality in any form. "[T]he homosexual agenda . . . I believe, not only counters the Bible, but also contradicts the Judeo-Christian values set forth by our nation's Founding Fathers," the Reverend Jerry Falwell has said. "I believe the Bible—God's infallible Word—prohibits all sexual activity outside the traditional bonds of marriage between a man and a woman."

Sodomy Laws in America

English common law (law handed down by tradition, rather than passed by a legislative body) is the basis for the American legal tradition in sodomy law as in other matters. The first appearance of sodomy in English common law was in 1533, under the rule of Henry VIII, when a statute found that the "detestable and abominable vice of buggery committed with mankind or beast" was a felony punishable by death. "Buggery" was a catchall term that encompassed a range of sexual acts, including heterosexual, homosexual, and human-animal activity. Laws against buggery were rarely applied against two women—as in much of Western culture, it was difficult for legal authorities to envision that two women could be sexual without the presence of a man—but women were sometimes found guilty under that law.

The British North American colonies followed English common law in sodomy statutes as in other areas, so each of the 13 original colonies either had its own specific sodomy law or was governed by default under the English statute of 1533. The official penalty for sodomy, in both the United States and England, was death, as shown in the death penalty cases cited by historian Jonathan Katz. (Some 105 men were hanged for sodomy in Britain between 1703 and 1829; in the U.S. colonies, at least two men, and possibly five, were killed under antisodomy laws that quoted directly from Leviticus.) Until 1961, all 50 U.S. states continued to have sodomy laws on their books.

The trend against sodomy laws in the United States began in 1961, when Illinois became the first state to decriminalize sodomy. In the 1960s and early 1970s, a number of other states repealed their sodomy laws. Then, in 1976, the gay rights movement experienced its first major legal setback in this area. The U.S. Supreme Court upheld Virginia's right to make private, consensual sodomy a felony. The Virginia law applies to people of all sexual orientation, with a maximum penalty of 20 years—and is still on the books.

Although anti–gay rights activists were pleased, gay rights advocates were disappointed in the Virginia ruling. The Supreme Court had generally sought to avoid ruling on gay and lesbian issues for most of the 1970s and early 1980s, and its Virginia ruling was terse and uninformative. A U.S. district court panel composed of three judges had ruled that Virginia's law was constitutional, and by a 6-3 vote, without explanation, the Supreme Court agreed.

The trend toward repealing sodomy laws continued. Then, in 1986, the Supreme Court handed down *Bowers v. Hardwick*, upholding the rights of states to make sodomy laws. (For more on this case, see Chapter 2.) Yet despite the fears of many in the gay rights movement and the hopes of many who opposed gay rights, *Bowers v. Hardwick* did not actually lead to the reinstatement of any sodomy laws. Rather, states continued to repeal their sodomy laws, even as many state supreme courts found unenforceable or unconstitutional some sodomy laws that remained on the books.

Sodomy Laws Today

Although the Supreme Court has remained largely silent on the subject since *Bowers v. Hardwick*, state courts continue to rule on the constitutionality of sodomy law. In Michigan in 1990, a circuit court judge ruled that the state's sodomy law was prohibited by the state constitution. However, the attorney general decided not to appeal the ruling—some say, because he knew he would lose. Although Michigan law makes the ruling binding on all state prosecutors, the door remains open for future litigation that might attempt to resuscitate the statute.

In Louisiana in 1994, a lawsuit resulted in a prohibition against enforcing the state's 1805 "crimes against nature" law in every parish except Jefferson (where New Orleans is located). (In Louisiana, the term *parish* is synonymous with *county* and is not exclusively suggestive of a church parish.) In 1998, a district judge ordered Jefferson Parish to stop enforcing the law as well, protecting noncommercial, private oral and anal sex between consenting adults. Finally, in February 1999, a state appeals court unanimously struck down the law, saying, "There can be no doubt that the right of consenting adults to engage in private non-commercial sexual activity, free from governmental interference, is protected by the privacy clause of the Louisiana Constitution." However, state prosecutor Tim McElroy appealed this decision to the Louisiana Supreme Court, which on July 6, 2000 upheld the law and its felony penalty of up to five years imprisonment for oral or anal sex between consenting adults.

The Louisiana decision, interestingly enough, was not in response to a gay activist case but rather one involving alleged heterosexual rape. Prosecutors who have trouble proving rape have historically turned to sodomy statutes—which involve consensual acts—in an effort to convict the supposed rapist of *something*. This was the case in Louisiana, where an alleged rapist had been charged under the state's old laws against oral and anal sex.

The 1998 Georgia state supreme court ruling, *Powell v. State of Georgia*, involved a similar situation: the case of Anthony Powell, a straight man charged with forcing his wife's 17-year-old niece to engage in anal sex. Powell admitted to the sex but claimed it was consensual. He was consequently charged not under the rape law, but under the sodomy law, which prohibits even consensual anal sex and other sexual acts considered to constitute sodomy. Powell's case eventually led to the state high court overturning the Georgia sodomy law—the same law that had been upheld by the U.S. Supreme Court in *Bowers v. Hardwick*. While many gay rights advocates found the *Powell* case distasteful, they appreciated the symbolic value inherent in the fact that the state involved in *Hardwick* was finally forced to throw out its law.

Maryland still has a sodomy law on the books, but a circuit court judge ruled on October 23, 1998 that residents of that state could legally engage in same-sex oral sex. Same-sex anal sex and solicitation (inviting someone to have sex) are still against the law. However, on January 14, 1999 the Maryland attorney general's office agreed to stop enforcing state laws against consensual oral and anal sex conducted in private. This ruling was the result of a compromise reached with the American Civil Liberties Union (ACLU), which had been challenging the state's law against same-sex oral sex.

In Massachusetts, the legal situation is rather complicated. A state supreme court ruling on another law seemed to suggest that the court would also strike down the sodomy law, at least as it applies to consensual sex conducted in private. However, the Massachusetts sodomy law has not been formally challenged and still remains on the books.

In Texas, the situation is even more complicated. In 1993, the Texas Court of Appeals ruled that the state's sodomy laws were unconstitutional in the case of *City of Dallas and Mack Vines v. Mica England.* England, a lesbian, had sued the state of Texas, the city of Dallas, and Mack Vines of the Dallas police force when she was refused the right to apply for a job with the police department on the grounds that she was a lesbian. In the process of upholding England's employment claim, the court found that the state's sodomy laws were unconstitutional, but since England's case did not directly challenge that law, the state could not rule directly on it.

Another Texas case began on September 17, 1998 when John Lawrence, 55, and Tyrone Garner, 31, were arrested for having anal sex in their home. Houston police had entered the men's home after receiving a call from a third man claiming to have seen a man with a gun, a report that later turned out to be bogus. Some observers believe that this case might be the challenge that leads to the final dismantling of Texas's law, which applies only to homosexuals. Indeed, on June 8, 2000, Texas's 14th Court of Appeals found that the sodomy statute violated the state constitution's equal rights protections. Appeals as of July 2000 were still in process, however, and the ultimate effect on the state's sodomy law is unclear.

Meanwhile, challenge cases in Mississippi, Arkansas, and Puerto Rico are under way. And in Minnesota, a case in which a male bartender was arrested for engaging in oral sex with a woman in the bar after closing time—an act that violated the state's sodomy law—has also led to a challenge. However, the Minnesota case concerns a more public act, one recorded on the bar's security camera and viewed in an unrelated investigation, so it does not raise privacy issues in the same way as the Lawrence-Garner case.

"We still live under *Bowers v. Hardwick*," states Paula Ettelbrick, a law professor at New York University and the University of Michigan, and the family policy director at the National Gay and Lesbian Task Force. Ettelbrick argues that in *Bowers v. Hardwick* the Supreme Court managed to conflate homosexual *behavior*—the commission of certain acts—with homosexual *identity*, so that "behavior has come to be equated with identity for gay men and lesbians, but not for straight people."

Ettelbrick acknowledges that fewer states criminalize sodomy now than they did when *Bowers v. Hardwick* first came to the forefront, and that no state chose to recriminalize the act as a result of the Supreme Court case. "Most states don't criminalize sodomy at this point," she says. "However, they have carte blanche to do so. For lesbians and gay men, it's a continual threat."

Anti–gay rights activists see the matter a little differently. They view *Bowers v. Hardwick* as evidence that mainstream society still considers homosexuality unnatural and immoral—and deserving of punishment by law.

EMPLOYMENT ISSUES

Although workplace issues are a central concern of the gay rights movement, most of the significant activity in this regard has been in the form of employee agitation, rather than court cases or legislation. (For more detail on pending legislation, see Chapter 2.) The gay/lesbian employee action group People of Diversity, for example, has been recognized by Chrysler, while Ford recognizes a similar group and added sexual orientation to its antidiscrimination bylaws in 1996. The gay/lesbian employee group GM PLUS is agitating for similar results at General Motors. The efforts of Ron Woods, a Chrysler worker and activist in the United Auto Workers (UAW) labor union, have made an enormous difference in the treatment of gay auto workers while gaining national attention through an extensive profile in the July 21, 1997 edition of the *New Yorker.* And beginning August 1, 2000, the Big Three automakers extended domestic partner benefits to the same-sex partners of more than half a million gay and lesbian employees.

The Employment Non-Discrimination Act (ENDA), first introduced in 1994, was intended to offer gay men and women federal protection against antigay discrimination on the job. However, ENDA has still not been passed by Congress. Meanwhile, gay rights activists often turn to other solutions when they believe workplace discrimination has occurred.

Harassment on the Job

A more cloudy area of employment rights for gay men and lesbians concerns on-the-job harassment. Until recently, such harassment was frequently thought of as *sexual harassment*—the creation of an unpleasant work climate for women by men who resented their presence or who wanted them to offer sexual favors. Sexual harassment—long considered a subset of discrimination against women—has been illegal for some time, and a growing cultural awareness of this problem has encouraged many employers to set up internal provisions for preventing it, educating employees about it, and, when necessary, punishing it.

But for gay men and lesbians, on-the-job harassment may not fall under federal protection. Take the case of James Quinn, a Nassau County, New York police officer who describes years of torment by colleagues who objected to his sexual orientation. Quinn endured being shown pornographic pictures and was subjected to a wide variety of pranks, including colleagues putting rocks in the hubcaps of his car so that criminals could hear his car coming. Quinn's supervisors not only failed to stop the harassment, they also occasionally joined in, leading Quinn to sue for discrimination under federal civil rights law. Even though the law did not specifically apply to sexual orientation, a jury awarded the police officer $380,000, an amount upheld on appeal by a federal judge, who found that the department's conduct had been "motivated by irrational fear and prejudice toward homosexuals."

The case of *Oncale v. Sundowner Offshore Services Inc.* shows that even straight men and women might benefit from expanded on-the-job protection for gay men and lesbians. Joseph Oncale, a roustabout on an offshore oil drilling rig, claimed to be sexually harassed by his boss and the other men he worked with. Apparently, Oncale's coworkers believed that he was gay, even though Oncale—as well as all of his coworkers—claimed to be straight. In his suit, Oncale described mistreatment that included being pinned to the wall by fellow workers as his boss put his genitals on Oncale's head and performed a mock rape on him.

Traditionally, the courts have had difficulty dealing with same-sex harassment, and at first Oncale's case seemed to be no exception. The Fifth Circuit Court of Appeals, for example, threw out the suit on the grounds that federal law simply did not apply. Federal law has found sexual harassment to be illegal because it violates existing provisions against discrimination on the basis of sex. In other words, women have the right to be treated just as well as men. So if a man is harassing a woman by putting up pornographic images in her work space, making repeated sexual overtures, or otherwise creating a hostile climate, the woman is being discriminated against on the basis of sex—she is being asked to endure treatment that a man in her position would not have to endure. But given that both Oncale and his harassers are male, in what sense can Oncale's harassment be considered sex discrimination? And, if it's not sex discrimination, in what sense is it against the law?

ENDA, of course, would explicitly outlaw discrimination on the basis of sexual orientation. But if ENDA is not passed, what protection do gay workers have against harassment perpetrated by members of their own sex?

Lawyer, legal scholar, and law professor Paula Ettelbrick suggests that gay legal strategists might look for some relief in federal laws against sexual discrimination. But they would have to offer a new interpretation of those laws, arguing that they are not limited to sex—the biological state of being male or female—but also involve gender, the behaviors considered appropriate to males and females in our society. If only sex discrimination is outlawed, a woman who behaved in ways considered "unfeminine"—for example, wearing pants to work—might be fired with impunity. Her employer could simply demonstrate that it was not *women* that he objected to— just women who do not "act like" or "look like" women.

Likewise, if sex discrimination concerns only a person's biological status, there's nothing to stop men from harassing another man. The pending case of Joseph Oncale, for example, concerns a straight man harassed by male coworkers and a supervisor who believed Oncale was gay. Since many other men worked for the Sundowner company without incident, Oncale clearly was not being singled out on the basis of sex. He was being harassed on the basis of gender—not for being a man, but for being a *kind* of man his boss and his colleagues disapproved of.

Thus, gay legal strategists are asking just how far federal provisions against discrimination on the basis of sex are supposed to go. Do they simply safeguard the right of a woman—or a man—to *be* at a particular workplace, so that a construction site must hire qualified women and a day-care center must hire qualified men? Or do the laws protect the right of people to act in ways that are traditionally reserved for the other gender—for women to wear pants, have loud voices, seem "tough"; for men to act gentle, have soft voices, seem "effeminate"? Clearly, both gay and straight people cross these gender lines, so the questions raised by *Oncale v. Sundowner* are not limited to protection for gay men and lesbians; they concern all people who want the freedom to choose their own behavior without being limited by rigid ideas of gender.

It therefore seemed significant that when the Supreme Court heard oral arguments in *Oncale* in 1997, the justices seemed quite receptive to discussing both same-sex harassment and the broader issues of gender. Chief Justice William Rehnquist asked whether it might be possible for a woman to sexually harass another woman, while Justice Ruth Bader Ginsburg expressed her concern about the treatment of a worker not perceived to be "made of sterner stuff." "In oral arguments in *Oncale* . . ." *Detroit News* columnist Deb Price wrote in 1997, "even the most conservative justices' questions seemed to suggest they believe that whether the victim and the aggressor [in sexual harassment cases] are the same or opposite genders is irrelevant."

Although the Court eventually sent *Oncale* back to trial (as of mid-2000, the case was still undecided), many observers found its respectful hearing of the issues to be a hopeful sign for gay rights. In the past, Rehnquist and Justice Antonin Scalia have made strong antigay statements, including Scalia's minority opinion on Colorado's Amendment 2 in *Romer v. Evans* (see Chapter 2). Yet both Scalia and Rehnquist seemed able to treat *Oncale* more dispassionately. As Price wrote, "A court that can—at least momentarily—stop treating gay issues as dynamite is well on its way to seeing that all laws should apply equally to everyone, regardless of sexual orientation."

Life on the Job

On-the-job harassment of lesbians and gay men may be one of those issues where a combination of legal and political strategies are needed to win gay rights—and where changes in the culture happen at widely varying rates. For example, a study published in the October 6, 1999 edition of the *Medical*

Student Journal of the American Medical Association found that lesbian physicians were more than four times more likely to be harassed on the basis of their sexual orientation than were heterosexual women doctors, both during training and in medical practice. The survey, conducted by the Women's Physician's Health Study, included responses from 4,501 physicians nationwide between the ages of 30 and 70. Some 18.2 percent of all lesbian doctors said they had experienced harassment because of their sexual orientation during medical school, compared to 3.6 percent of heterosexual women doctors. The harassment apparently worsened after medical school: some 32.6 percent of lesbian doctors reported sexual orientation–based harassment in a work setting, compared to 7.7 percent of heterosexual women doctors.

The situation for gay men and lesbians working in finance and on Wall Street is even more grim, according to an article by Michelangelo Signorile in the October 1998 issue of *Out* magazine. The only openly gay member of the New York Stock Exchange is Walter Schubert, president and CEO of the brokerage firm Schubert Group International, LLC, a well-known financier whose family has held a seat on the stock exchange for at least two generations. Meanwhile, in a high-profile 1996 case, employee Joseph Daniel filed a $75 million lawsuit against Dresdner Bank A.G., charging that the German institution had failed to follow through on an announced promotion to vice presidency and eventually fired him after learning he was gay.

Daniel explains that in the summer of 1996, he reluctantly responded to a colleague's questions by admitting that he had gone on vacation to the Fire Island Pines, a well-known gay resort area near New York City. In September 1996, Daniel's promotion to vice president—supposedly effective July 1, 1996, and already announced by letter to bank employees and clients—was revoked. Daniel responded by writing a memo requesting domestic partner benefits for himself and his partner, both as a way of complaining about the discrimination and to remind the company that San Francisco, where Dresdner Bank does business, has outlawed city contracts with any firm that does not offer domestic partners and married couples the same benefits.

Less than two weeks after Daniel wrote his memo, he was dismissed. He claims it was because of his sexual orientation; the company says it was simply corporate downsizing. Daniel's case continues in the courts—the first such case to involve a Wall Street firm.

Federal Employment

One of the largest employers in the United States is the federal government, and civil service jobs have long represented some of the most stable and secure employment available. So the government's employment policies with regard to gay men and lesbians carry particular weight. And the decision, made at the beginning of the cold war, to prohibit gay people from any kind of federal employment, sent a clear signal to society that gay men and lesbians were not acceptable employees.

The official reason given for keeping gay people out of civil service jobs was that their homosexuality made them security risks. In an era when fear of communism and anxiety about Soviet spies was running high, antigay government officials like Senator Joseph McCarthy could argue that gay and lesbian federal employees, fearful of having their sexual activities made public, were vulnerable to blackmail by "foreign powers." The image of homosexuals and communists stealing state secrets and selling them to the Soviets was one that alarmed many Americans—though some political commentators at the time and many historians since have believed the claims of espionage and sabotage to have been exaggerated, if not entirely fabricated.

The Red Scare and the antihomosexual panic that accompanied it led the Civil Service Commission and the Federal Bureau of Investigation to develop procedures to identify homosexual job applicants and keep them from being hired, as well as to discover and fire gay people already working for the government. This antigay climate continued well into the early 1970s—but it was countered somewhat by the famous case of *Norton v. Macy*, in which the Supreme Court found that a gay man could not be fired for illegal sexual conduct if that conduct did not specifically affect the performance of his duties as a federal employee. (For more on *Norton v. Macy*, see Chapter 2.)

Another landmark for gay rights activists came in 1973, when the U.S. Civil Service Commission dropped its ban on hiring gay people. In 1978, another Supreme Court ruling suggested that openly gay federal employees had the right to keep their jobs. And in 1980, the Office of Personnel Management actively banned discrimination on the basis of sexual orientation in all federal service jobs.

FREE SPEECH AND ASSEMBLY

As discussed earlier, gays and lesbians have not only had to battle for individual liberties (i.e., the right to engage in private, consensual sexual behavior and not be discriminated against for doing so), they have also had to fight for the right to congregate with others who share their sexual orientation. The harassment visited upon the patrons of the Stonewall Inn by the police was a way for society to discourage gays and lesbians from meeting with each other openly. In a way, the issue of open association was the spark that ignited the modern gay rights movement.

School Organizations and the Right to Assemble

The major assembly issue for gay rights activists, however, has been fought on college campuses. The landmark case is considered *Gay Students*

Gay Rights

Organization of the University of New Hampshire v. Bonner, a 1974 New Hampshire Supreme Court case ruling that a gay student group had the same rights to a state college's facilities as any other student organization. A similar case was fought at Georgetown University, a private institution that in 1980 had expelled its gay student group from campus. Eight years later, a court case finally affirmed the right of the Georgetown gay and lesbian students to have access to campus facilities.

Controversy over gay student groups continued throughout the 1980s. In 1981, for example, Florida's legislature passed the Trask Amendment, withholding funds from any state institution that recognized a gay student group. Eventually, the state supreme court found that law unconstitutional. And in 1983, in an echo of *Bonner*, the Fourth Circuit Court of Appeals ordered the University of South Carolina to reinstate a gay and lesbian student group that had been prohibited from meeting on campus.

In 1998, a high school group began to fight a similar battle. The group was known as Homosexual-Heterosexual Alliance Reaching for Tolerance (HHART), a gathering of about 25 students meeting at Smoky Hill High School in Aurora (near Denver). HHART sued the Cherry Creek School District for equal representation at their school, charging that it had been left out of lists of high school clubs, omitted from the "club" section of the student-parent handbook, and excluded from listings in the school's multicultural events calendar.

The group had been permitted to put up posters at their high school, showing a cartoon character literally coming out of a closet (a reference to the slang term for gay people being open about their sexuality). But the suit contended that certain words and phrases had been censored from the signs: "homosexual," "lesbian," "gay," and a quote from *Hamlet*, "To thine own self be true." The suit also claimed that one student had been ordered to take a button with a gay slogan off his backpack, and that the group's adviser, teacher Linda Harmon, was refused supplemental pay for her after-hours work with the club. Not only was Harmon refused pay, but the school decided to assign a counselor to the group, suggesting that members were in need of psychological help.

Smoky Hill school officials were puzzled by the suit, while district officials, approached for a January 23, 1998 article in the *Denver Post*, declined to comment, explaining that they had not yet seen a copy of the legal documents involved. Interestingly, HHART was formed in response to Colorado's Amendment 2, the statewide referendum that abolished a gay rights ordinance in Denver, and that was later overturned by *Romer v. Evans*. (Denver has since reinstituted its gay rights provision.) The HHART suit seems to be the first effort to claim that a gay high school club has constitutional rights. As of mid-2000, it had not yet been decided.

Introduction to Gay Rights

Free Speech and the U.S. Post Office

In the days before Stonewall, many gay people relied on the U.S. mail for their contact with a larger homosexual world. Men in particular sought to receive magazines, postcards, and photographs with images of male bodies in varying stages of nudity. For the many men who were terrified of revealing their gay identities in their own communities, these homoerotic images were a lifeline to a world in which their sexuality could be affirmed.

One common form of gay male erotica was the so-called physique magazines, featuring bodybuilders who were nude except for their underwear or "posing straps" (a piece of cloth that covered only the genitals). Although bodybuilding magazines were often sold in regular newsstands and were frequently available in public places such as barbershops, many gay men treated them as a mild form of pornography. Gay men also used the mail to order more explicit homoerotic materials.

However, until 1965, everything that traveled by post was regulated by the 1873 Comstock Law, which prohibited the mailing of "obscene, lewd, or lascivious" materials. The Comstock Law had been most notoriously used to prevent birth-control pioneer Margaret Sanger from mailing out information about family planning. In the 1940s, it also began to be used against bodybuilding magazines, which were warned to "police their contents, even their ads" for homosexual material—or risk being unable to use the U.S. mail. And in 1954, the homophile magazine *One* was seized by the Los Angeles postmaster, who had refused to mail the magazine on the grounds that it was obscene and filthy. Although, like most homophile publications, *One* was more text- than image-oriented, printing mainly nonsexual articles and stories about gay life, the mere mention of homosexuality was apparently enough to qualify as obscene.

Of course, the definition of "obscene" was open to interpretation by a court, but few small publishers could afford legal battles, whether they published bodybuilding magazines, homophile publications, or actual pornography. Both the receivers and the senders of gay male images were taking enormous risks, as were those involved with homophile magazines. Many subscribers to any type of gay-related publication got their materials at post office boxes, which they held anonymously or under false names. Publishers were also creative. Because it was illegal to mail fully nude photographs, one publisher began covering male genitals with fig leaves painted in washable ink. Customers could simply rinse the ink off after they received the photos.

Despite all this caution, the first big crackdown against bodybuilding magazines occurred in 1960. Physique magazine publisher Herbert Womack was selling 40,000 copies a month when his stock was seized by the postal authorities. His case was heard by the Supreme Court in 1965, in a case known as *Manual Enterprises v. Day.* "[E]ven though the material appealed to the prurient taste of male homosexuals and was 'dismally unpleasant, uncouth, and tawdry,' it lacked 'patent offensiveness' and therefore should not be considered obscene," the Court ruled.

The sexual revolution brought further court cases that eroded the authority of the Comstock Law. In December 1965, the first full frontal male nude appeared in a publication: the homophile *Drum* magazine. *Drum* was a departure from the earlier, more staid homophile publications like *One* and the *Ladder* (published by the lesbian group Daughters of Bilitis). As Molly McGarry and Fred Wasserman explain in *Becoming Visible,* "[Due to] the lead of publications like *Drum,* it became increasingly clear to many in the gay community that homosexual liberation and a larger sexual liberation could never be separated." A quote from an early ad for *Drum* makes this clear:

> *DRUM stands for a realistic approach to sexuality in general and homosexuality in particular. DRUM stands for sex in perspective, sex with insight and, above all, sex with humor. DRUM presents news for "queers," and fiction for "perverts." Photo essays for "fairies," and laughs for "faggots."*

FAMILY ISSUES

Because the families formed by lesbians and gay men are by definition unconventional, a key area in gay legal activism has been the attempt to win recognition for lesbian and family units, whether these involve couples, parents and children, or both. One of the most famous controversies in this field arose with the case of Sharon Kowalski. In November 1983, Kowalski was injured in a car accident that left her with extensive physical and neurological damage, limiting her ability to move and to communicate. At the time of the accident, Kowalski had been living with her lover, Karen Thompson, in a house they were buying together in Minnesota. Thompson wanted to continue to care for Kowalski, whom she considered her life partner, but legally speaking, Kowalski's parents had responsibility for Sharon—Thompson had no legal standing whatsoever—and Kowalski's parents were unable to believe that their daughter had been involved in a lesbian relationship.

Thompson faced the prospect of not even being allowed to visit Kowalski, whom her parents took to their northern Minnesota home. Thompson turned to the courts for help, in a complicated legal process that lasted some eight years. A doctor testifying on the parents' behalf averred that "visits by Karen Thompson would expose Sharon Kowalski to a high risk of sexual abuse."

Eventually, Kowalski's parents withdrew their claim to be Sharon's guardian—but the trial judge still refused to award guardianship to

Karen Thompson. The judge pointed out that the Kowalski parents objected to Thompson, in part because she was a lesbian. He was also concerned that Thompson had been involved with at least one other woman since the accident. He further cited the fact that Thompson had taken Kowalski, after the accident, to lesbian and gay gatherings and had revealed her sexual orientation to her parents, thus invading her privacy. He therefore awarded guardianship to a supposedly neutral third party.

In 1991, a Minnesota appellate court awarded Thompson guardianship, relying on uncontroverted medical testimony that Kowalski, while unable to speak, did indeed have the capacity to choose her guardian and to indicate—as she did repeatedly—that Thompson was her choice. The decision also emphasized that Thompson was "the only person willing to take care of Sharon Kowalski outside of an institution," and called Thompson and Kowalski "a family of affinity which should be accorded respect." Regarding Thompson's involvement with other women, the court noted her testimony that "anyone who is involved in her life understands that she and Sharon are 'a package deal,'" and pointed out that "it is not uncommon for *spouses* to make changes in their personal lives while maintaining their commitment to the injured person."

Cases like Kowalski's led some gay rights advocates to argue for the legalization of gay marriage, which would have offered legal protection to the Thompson-Kowalski relationship. But some gay liberationists do not draw that conclusion. Legal scholar Ruthann Robson agrees that "if Sharon and Karen had been legally married rather than simply 'exchanging rings' in an extralegal ceremony Karen Thompson would have been Sharon Kowalski's legal guardian absent unusual circumstances." Yet, Robson points out, other legal models than the family might be available to acknowledge a relationship like Thompson's and Kowalski's: "caretaker" and "dependent," for example, an arrangement that implies greater sexual freedom for Thompson than the image of faithfully married spouse.

State and Federal Actions on Gay Marriage

As discussed previously in this chapter, gay men and lesbians have been trying to obtain legal recognition for their marriages almost since the beginning of the modern gay rights movement. The first indication that success was possible, however, did not come until 1993, when the Hawaii Supreme Court ruled in *Baehr v. Lewin* that forbidding same-sex marriage might be unconstitutional under the state's constitutional provision against sex discrimination. The court found that a Hawaii statute requiring couples to be of opposite sex in order to obtain a marriage license discriminated against people on the basis of sex—though the court made explicit the distinction between "discrimination on the basis of sex" and "discrimination on the basis of sexual orientation":

> *"Homosexual" and "same-sex" marriages are not synonymous; by the same token, a "heterosexual" same-sex marriage is, in theory, not oxymoronic [contradictory of itself]. A "homosexual" person is defined as "[o]ne sexually attracted to another of the same sex." Taber's* Cyclopedic Medical Dictionary *839 (16th ed. 1989). "Homosexuality" is "sexual desire or behavior directed toward a person or persons of one's own sex." Webster's* Encyclopedic Unabridged Dictionary of the English Language *680 (1989). Conversely, "heterosexuality" is "[s]exual attraction for one of the opposite sex," Taber's Cyclopedic Medical Dictionary at 827, or "sexual feeling or behavior directed toward a person of persons of the opposite sex." Webster's* Encyclopedic Unabridged Dictionary of the English Language *at 667. Parties to "a union between a man and a woman" may or may not be homosexuals. Parties to a same-sex marriage could theoretically be either homosexuals or heterosexuals.*

In other words, a straight person might want to marry another straight person of the same sex—and not to allow him or her to do so would be sex discrimination. Both "Jane" and "John" should have the same right to marry "Jill"; to deny "Jane" that right simply because she is a woman is to discriminate against her on the grounds of sex.

This reasoning somewhat disingenuously assumes that neither "Jane" nor "Jill" is necessarily homosexual. The court has thus affirmed their right to marry without affirming *homosexuals'* right to marry. As Ruthann Robson put it in *Sappho Goes to Law School,*

> *Even the Hawai'i Supreme Court in* Baehr v. Lewin *fails to accord full respect to gay and lesbian persons. The Hawai'i Supreme Court acknowledged that although there is a fundamental right to marry, this right does not extend to same-sex couples. . . . [In a] footnote [the court] accused the state attorney general of injecting the issue of homosexuality into a case in which it would be otherwise absent.*

Despite the court's wish to distance itself from homosexuality, both gay rights and antigay organizations seized upon *Baehr* as evidence that gay men and women would soon be allowed to marry in the state of Hawaii. And, according to our federal system, legalizing gay marriage in Hawaii—or in any other state—seemed to mean that gay couples who married there would be recognized as married in the other 49 states.

How does this work? Traditionally, under the U.S. Constitution, marriage has been considered a state matter—each state decides who is allowed to marry, at what age, under what circumstances, and so on. And, under the "full faith and credit" clause of the Constitution, whatever contract is entered into in one state must be recognized by another state—unless the second state has explicitly made a policy against it. Thus, all things being equal, if one state allows marriage at age 14 and another sets the marriage age at 16, the 14-year-old's marriage would be fully recognized in the second state—unless a law specifically identified such marriages as against state policy.

To guard against the prospect of a state legalizing gay marriages that would then have to be recognized in other states, right-wing groups at both the federal and the state level sprang into action. The Defense of Marriage Act (DOMA), explicitly making same-sex marriage a violation of federal policy, was passed in 1994. For many, DOMA was a shock, for the federal government had never before attempted to usurp the states' prerogative to define marriage. Meanwhile, some 32 states successfully passed laws preventing the recognition of same-sex marriage, while Hawaii itself passed a new law asserting that marriage could include only one man and one woman. (See Chapter 2 for specific state laws.) (Under the full faith and credit clause of the U.S. Constitution, each state is supposed to honor contracts made in other states. However, these laws meant that the states did not have to recognize homosexual marriage contracts that could be potentially entered into in other states and could presumably refuse recognition to legal gay marriages made in Sweden, Denmark, Iceland, and other foreign jurisdictions.)

Thus, late in 1999, the Hawaii Supreme Court ruled that *Baehr* was moot: same-sex couples did not have the right to marry in Hawaii. At the same time, though, the Vermont Supreme Court found that same-sex couples had the right to all the benefits of marriage available in their state to straight married couples. Whether or not marriage per se was available to gay couples, the Vermont high court ruled that the state legislature had to allow them some legal means to obtain those benefits. The legislature responded by creating a legal category of partnership called a "civil union," which extends most marriage benefits to same-sex couples.

Domestic Partnerships

Although until recently the possibility of legally recognized same-sex marriage seemed remote, lesbian and gay couples have fought for legal and economic equality by means of establishing the notion of domestic partnership. As the result of gay rights agitation, many cities and states now allow same-sex couples to register for domestic partnership, which, depending on the locale, might entitle them to some—though never all—of the rights of marriage, such as being listed as next of kin on various legal documents or enjoying visitation rights in case of medical emergencies.

Likewise, domestic partnership has been recognized by a wide variety of public and private employers, so that many same-sex couples now enjoy family health insurance and other benefits that are accorded to heterosexual married couples. In many cases, unmarried straight couples can also avail themselves of the benefits of domestic partnership.

Child Custody

Recognition of gay and lesbian families goes one step further when children are involved. A major gay rights issue has traditionally been the custody of children who live within a gay or lesbian family, whether from a previous heterosexual relationship or by virtue of one partner's giving birth. In this context, sodomy laws are frequently used as evidence that gay—and, more often, lesbian—parents are criminals who ought not to be allowed custody of their children. Whether or not sodomy laws are invoked, gay custody cases are often ruled by the notion that "good" homosexuals should hide their relationships from their children, and that good parents should either be celibate or should be engaged in long-term monogamous relationships that resemble the ideal of heterosexual marriage.

The case of *White v. Thompson* in Mississippi shows that as recently as 1990, lesbian mothers' custody of their children could be challenged not only by the children's fathers, but by relatives further removed. In *White*, the father's parents sought custody of their grandchildren on the grounds that the mother was unfit, primarily because she was a lesbian. The Mississippi trial court agreed that the mother was "unfit, morally and otherwise, to have custody of her children."

The mother appealed the case to the Mississippi Supreme Court, arguing that the trial court had erred in basing its decision solely on the fact that she was gay. The state supreme court agreed that lesbianism could not be the *sole* issue in a judgment of fitness, but ruled that it could indeed be a major issue:

> *Although the predominant issue in this case seems to have been Mrs. White's lesbianism, and the chancellor may have relied entirely upon this, we find that a review of the entire record and circumstances present . . . shows that the chancellor's decision that Mrs. White was an unfit mother, morally and otherwise, was not against the substantial weight of the evidence.*

The circumstances also included some testimony that the children had not been properly supervised, clothed, or fed, but the extent of the problem was left vague in the final ruling. In that ruling, the judge also referred to

White's class status, finding that the neglect of the children was "no more than one would expect to find in any case where a twenty-four-year-old mother with but a high school diploma and no independent means" was attempting to support her children. Yet a dissenting justice found that ". . . most of An's [the mother's] neglect is attributable to the employment she has been forced to pursue because of David's [her ex-husband and the children's father] irresponsibility." Given that Mississippi's standard practice is to automatically award custody to the biological parent, especially the mother, it seems unlikely that a heterosexual in An White's place would lose custody of her children to their father's parents without more striking evidence of her lack of fitness.

Not only did White lose custody of her children to her ex-husband's mother and stepfather (the ex-husband himself had severe financial problems, a history of alcoholism, and no interest in custody), she was also denied the opportunity to visit her children in the presence of her lover. Even if her lesbianism was not the only standard of her "unfitness," it seemed to play a key role in the custody decision.

The case of *Chicoine v. Chicoine*, a South Dakota Supreme Court ruling of 1992, also concerns restrictions of visitation for a lesbian mother. The initial case involved Lisa Chicoine, a divorced mother who sought custody of her two children, James, age 6, and Tyler, age 5. At the trial level, the children's father won custody, with Lisa being allowed unsupervised overnight visits every other weekend, as long as "no unrelated female or homosexual male [were] present during the children's visit."

The case proceeded up to the state Supreme Court, where an opinion written by Justice Henderson cited both Leviticus and the Egyptian Book of the Dead to justify the presumption against homosexuality:

> *Lesbian mother has harmed these children forever. To give her rights of reasonable visitation so that she can teach them to be homosexuals, would be the zenith of poor judgment for the judiciary of this state. Until such time as she can establish, after years of therapy and demonstrated conduct, that she is no longer living a life of abomination (see Leviticus 18:22), she should be totally estopped [sic, a legal term] from contaminating these children. After years of treatment, she could then petition for rights of visitation. . . .*
>
> *There appears to be a transitory phenomenon on the American scene that homosexuality is okay. Not so. The Bible decries it. Even the pagan "Egyptian Book of the Dead" bespoke against it [citation omitted]. Kings could not become heavenly beings if they had lain with men. In other words, even the pagans, centuries ago, before the birth of Jesus Christ, looked upon it as total defilement.*

Although Justice Henderson's opinion was not shared by the entire court, the majority opinion did reverse the trial court's decision and terminated Lisa Chicoine's unsupervised visits. The court pointed out that "Lisa admits that it is inappropriate to hold hands, kiss and show affection to her lesbian partners in front of her children"—yet she had engaged in these open displays of affection.

The criminalizing of lesbianism—and, by implication, male homosexuality—is evidenced in the story of Sharon Bottoms, the lesbian mother who in *Bottoms v. Bottoms* fought her own mother for custody of her child. Pamela Kay Bottoms challenged her daughter Sharon's custody in Virginia in the early 1990s, claiming that her daughter's lesbianism made her an unfit mother. The trial judge pointed out that

> *[Sharon Bottoms] readily admits her behavior in open affection shown to April Wade in front of the child. She further admits consenting that the child referred to April Wade, her lover, as to quote the words "Da Da."*

By having a lesbian partner, the judge ruled, Sharon Bottoms's conduct was "illegal," and her "circumstances of unfitness" were thus of "such an extraordinary nature" that they should disqualify her from custody. Sharon Bottoms was then denied overnight visits with her child, as well as any visits in the presence of her lover.

Sharon Bottoms appealed the case as far as the Virginia Supreme Court. But the state's high court upheld the trial decision, which relied upon a previous Virginia Supreme Court ruling that had found a lesbian mother per se unfit to raise her child.

The denial of custody to a parent is particularly noteworthy in Virginia, considering the extent of that state's efforts to uphold parental custody. For example, in one Virginia case not involving homosexuality, a grandmother was denied custody of her grandchild, in favor of leaving the child with her one surviving parent—even though that parent was sharing a household with the person who had killed the child's other parent.

Although it is usually lesbian mothers who are denied child custody, sometimes gay fathers are also deprived. In a Mississippi case, David Wiegand, a California resident, sought custody of his 15-year-old son after learning that the boy's stepfather had been arrested twice and convicted of physically assaulting the boy's mother. For eight years, Wiegand had lived in a monogamous relationship with a male partner, with whom he had entered into a domestic partnership agreement and living trust arrangement. The court agreed that the boy's father would probably offer his son a more stable home. Yet Wiegand was denied custody, a decision upheld on February 4, 1999 by the Mississippi Supreme Court. Unlike the women in

Introduction to Gay Rights

Chicoine and *Bottoms*, Wiegand had refrained from open displays of affection in front of his son, admitting, in the words of the high court, "that an open sign of affection between homosexual partners is not proper for the child at this age. . . . [Y]et despite refraining from that activity, he merely retreats behind closed and locked doors, hiding and secreting his own sexuality from [his son]." Therefore, custody was to remain with the mother (and her abusive husband), although Wiegand was granted visitation rights in the presence of his partner. As the court said:

> *even if [the son] is embarrassed, or does not like the living arrangement of his father, this is not the type of harm that rises to the level necessary to place such restrictions on [the father's] visitation with his son.*

Lisa Keen, covering the decision in the February 19, 1999, edition of the gay newspaper *New York Blade*, pointed out that the court discussed Wiegand's sexual practices to an extent that would probably never appear in a similar opinion involving heterosexual parents. As the court wrote:

> *According to David, [he and his male partner] regularly engage in homosexual activities which include both oral and anal intercourse. However, they described their sexual relations, as well as their open affections between each other, at least in the presence of the child, to be discreet and performed only behind closed and locked doors.*

In some cases, family recognition for gay and lesbian families cuts both ways, for there are times when gay fathers and lesbian mothers may not wish to share custody of their children with their former partners—yet would have to do so if their de facto families were truly recognized. In the case of *Alison D. v. Virginia M.* (1991), one member of a lesbian couple in New York gave birth to a child by means of artificial insemination. When the couple separated, the biological mother refused to let her former partner visit the child, and the New York state court likewise refused to acknowledge the rights of the nonbiological mother. Only one dissenting judge, the feminist jurist Judith Kaye, believed that the lesbian ex-partner had a claim to the child she had helped to raise, pointing out that "more than 15.5 million children do not live with two biological parents, and that as many as 8 to 10 million children are born into families with a gay or lesbian parent."

A few months after *Alison D.*, a similar case came up in Wisconsin's Supreme Court, *In re ZJH (Sporleder v. Hermes)*. In this case, two women had lived together as lovers for about eight years. When Sporleder had tried, and failed, to conceive a child through artificial insemination, the couple decided that Hermes would adopt a child. (As discussed in Chapter 2, two-parent adoption has been extremely difficult for gay couples.) The couple separated, the adoption was finalized, and Hermes decided not to allow her former partner to visit the child. Sporleder was then not able to win custody or visitation rights. A number of courts in other states have made similar rulings.

Although custody fights between two gay people may at first seem like a less pressing issue than the specter of heterosexual parents denying gay biological parents their rights, all of the custody cases discussed in this section refer to the same three problems: 1) what is the definition of a gay or lesbian family? 2) what rights do the adults in those families have?—and, perhaps most importantly, 3) what is in the best interests of the child? Formerly, family courts tended to rule that being gay or lesbian itself rendered a parent unfit—much as being gay or lesbian formerly disqualified employees from the civil service. In family law as in civil service policy, the courts are coming to embrace instead the idea of a *rational nexus*—an interconnected set of reasons that determine a parent's fitness. Being gay or lesbian might or might not be part of that nexus, depending on the personal opinions of the judge. But the focus in family law is coming to be less on the specific fitness of the parent as determined by his or her sexual practices, and more on the rational nexus of factors that determine the best interests of the child.

Since the rational nexus test allows courts to take the focus off lesbianism or male homosexuality as the key criterion for fitness, advocates for gay/lesbian rights hope that this new approach will make it easier for gay and lesbian parents to keep their children. However, unless social attitudes toward homosexuality continue to change, it's likely that the "rational nexus" test will continue to work against homosexual parents in general and lesbian parents in particular. Besides the general prejudice against lesbian sexuality, lesbians are likely to have lower incomes than their ex-husbands, which seems to make them less desirable parents in the eyes of many courts. And if the ex-husband seeking custody is married in an apparently stable heterosexual relationship, courts may view this with more favor than either an extralegal lesbian marriage or a more unconventional lesbian relationship.

Although gay fathers are more likely to have higher incomes than lesbian mothers, they face similar types of social prejudice, as the David Wiegand case made clear. Both gay men and lesbians, though, also face the risk that a court will prefer the heterosexual parent—or even the child's grandparents.

Adoption

Until the late 1970s, the notion that an open lesbian or gay man might be allowed to adopt a child was virtually unthinkable—as was the idea that a single person should be allowed to adopt. However, gay rights groups in many states fought for the right of gay adoption—and gradually, gay adoptions became accepted, at least in some parts of the United States.

Although gay individuals were sometimes allowed to adopt, the concept of a gay couple adopting a child still seemed beyond the pale throughout the 1980s and most of the 1990s. A gay man or lesbian who was in a relationship with a biological or adoptive parent might eventually be allowed to adopt the partner's child. But for an adoption agency to grant parental rights to two same-sex parents was relatively rare.

Then, in December 1997, a New Jersey lawsuit forced that state to allow gay, lesbian, and unmarried heterosexual couples to adopt children on an equal basis with married couples. The decision came in the form of a consent decree with state authorities, the final outcome of a class-action lawsuit brought by gay and lesbian couples and by the American Civil Liberties Union. The decision did not technically affect private adoption agencies, but many observers believed that the ruling would widen the chances of gay couples adopting jointly.

The case also resulted in New Jersey residents Jon Holden and Michael Galluccio being able to adopt their foster son, Adam, in December 1997. Though the Holden-Galluccio adoption produced its share of controversy, the political climate was changing quickly. By the time the couple tried to adopt Adam's sister, two years later, they found the process, once so arduous, was now virtually routine. Although gay adoption remains out of the question in many states, other states are beginning to accept the concept of two same-sex parents who act as a couple to adopt one or more children.

Currently, about half the states allow individuals in a gay or unmarried straight relationship to adopt a child. But the "second-parent" adoption requires an additional petition, which can make the adoption far more problematic. Moreover, four states—Arkansas, Florida, Mississippi, and Utah—have banned gay/lesbian adoption illegal. In California, social workers are required to recommend against adoption by unmarried couples—gay or straight—but judges have the discretion to ignore the recommendation.

CHAPTER 2

THE LAW OF GAY RIGHTS

LEGISLATION AND LEGAL BATTLES

This section summarizes the major legislation and legal battles in the field of gay rights, specifically with regard to sodomy; federal employment; gays in the military; AIDS and disability law; state, city, and private employment; marriage; domestic partnerships; adoption; hate crimes; and immigration.

Those trying to arrive at a clear sense of gay legal rights must remember that these rights are often carved out piecemeal in response to court cases, legislation, and custom. Anti–gay rights activists have added a new category to the list: initiatives and referendums. A major tactic of the anti–gay rights movement of the 1990s was to introduce statewide referendums overturning existing local antidiscrimination laws and banning new ones. Likewise, the question of gay marriage has been dealt with in the courts, in the legislatures—and via referendum, such as the recent voter approval in California of Proposition 22 (the Knight Initiative), which declares that "only marriage between a man and a woman is valid or recognized" in that state. Without such an initiative, California would have been legally obligated to recognize homosexual marriages contracted in another state. Such initiatives often come in response to legislation and are often challenged in the courts, so that understanding legislation and legal battles is only part of a very complicated story.

SODOMY LAWS

Sodomy laws are state laws that outlaw specific sexual practices. Usually these laws are directed at all adults; sometimes they are directed specifically at homosexuals; occasionally they are directed at unmarried people, whether they are straight or gay.

The first state to decriminalize sodomy was Illinois, which adopted a "model penal code" in 1961. Illinois's action was part of a larger decision to legalize all adult, private, consensual sex, on the theory that it was not the state's business to enforce a particular type of sexuality or morality. (*Private* sex takes place in a private venue, such as a home, as opposed to a public place, such as a bar, park, public restroom, or street. *Consensual* sex has been freely agreed to by all parties involved, as opposed to rape or sexual harassment. *Adult* sex refers to all parties being above the age of consent specified in a state law. For more on age of consent, see Chapter 6.)

In 1967, the American Civil Liberties Union (ACLU) reversed its previous position and opposed sodomy laws. In 1971, the Idaho legislature first repealed and then reinstated its sodomy statute, making sodomy for both straight and gay couples a felony potentially punishable by a life sentence.

Three factors helped speed up the movement to remove sodomy laws from the books: the Stonewall uprising of 1969 and the gay rights movement that grew out of it; the general loosening of sexual prohibitions that resulted from both the "sexual revolution" of the 1960s and the women's movement of the 1970s; and a variety of Supreme Court cases upholding the right to various kinds of sexual privacy. In 1965, for example, in *Griswold v. Connecticut*, the Supreme Court overturned prohibitions on the use of birth control by married couples, which they saw as violating the privacy of a marriage bond that should be considered sacred. Although *Griswold* referred specifically to marriage, the notion that the state had no business in an adult couple's bedroom was thus established.

In fact, in the early 1970s, several states did repeal their sodomy laws: Connecticut (1971), Colorado (1972), Oregon (1972), Delaware (1973), Hawaii (1973), North Dakota (1973), and Ohio (1974). However, although sodomy itself is legal in Ohio, a man asking another man to have sex ("seeking consent") is a first-degree misdemeanor under the "importuning statute," a law otherwise used to criminalize prostitution. Conviction of the charge carries a fine and six months in prison, or a seven-month prison term if the person convicted cannot pay the fine. Heterosexual and lesbian couples are not criminalized under Ohio law, revealing once again how lesbian sexuality is often far less visible than its gay male counterpart.

Although Massachusetts has a sodomy law on the books to this day— under which sodomy between consenting gay or straight adults is a felony carrying a sentence of up to 20 years—the Massachusetts Supreme Court ruled in 1974 that the law's prohibition of "unnatural and lascivious acts" did not apply to private, consensual adult behavior.

In 1975, two more states, New Hampshire and New Mexico, repealed their sodomy laws. In 1976, California, Maine, Washington, and West Virginia followed suit, meaning that about one-third of all U.S. gay men and lesbians were now "decriminalized."

The trend toward repealing sodomy laws continued, not least because the supporters of gay rights were pushing for this particular legal reform.

Gay Rights

Despite the backlash resulting from Anita Byrant's Dade County, Florida campaign in 1977 and the Briggs Initiative in California in 1978 (see Chapters 1 and 4), Indiana, South Dakota, Vermont, and Wyoming repealed their old laws in 1977. In 1978 they were joined by Iowa and Nebraska; in 1979 by New Jersey; in 1980 by Alaska; and in 1983 by Wisconsin. Two other states later took their sodomy laws off the books: Nevada (1993) and Rhode Island (1998).

Court decisions vitiated other sodomy laws. Although sodomy laws remain on the books to this day in New York and Pennsylvania, supreme courts in both states ruled in 1980 that the laws were not enforceable under the state constitutions.

In 1981, the District of Columbia voted to nullify its sodomy law. But the Moral Majority—a right-wing group that often opposed the gay rights movement, led by Reverend Jerry Falwell—lobbied hard against the move in the House of Representatives, which, under U.S. law, has final legal jurisdiction over the nation's capital. The House of Representatives overruled the decision, reinstating the district's sodomy laws by a vote of 219–199, evidence of a growing backlash against gay rights that was not to be reversed until 1992. As journalist Debbie Nathan put it in her *Nation* article, "until 1992 it was illegal in the District of Columbia to copulate in any orifice except the vagina."

Rulings in Kentucky (1992), Tennessee (1996), Montana (1997), and Georgia (1998) found state sodomy laws unconstitutional. The Kentucky decision was particularly noteworthy because that law had applied only to homosexuals.

U.S. states that still have enforceable sodomy laws include Alabama (misdemeanor; law does not apply to married couples), Arkansas (misdemeanor), Kansas (misdemeanor), Maryland (felony), Missouri (misdemeanor), Oklahoma (felony), and Texas (misdemeanor; laws apply to homosexuals only; however, the Texas law is currently being challenged in a court case that at press time had reached the state court of appeals). States in which sodomy laws apply to everyone—gay, straight, married, and unmarried—include Arizona (misdemeanor), Florida (misdemeanor), Idaho (felony), Louisiana (felony), Massachusetts (felony), Michigan (felony), Minnesota (misdemeanor), Mississippi (felony), North Carolina (felony), South Carolina (felony), Utah (misdemeanor), and Virginia (felony).

FEDERAL EMPLOYMENT

For many years, homosexuality was banned by federal civil service regulations. Due in part to the landmark case of *Norton v. Macy* (see Court Cases), homosexuality gradually became tolerated in federal employment, despite regulations in force against it.

The Law of Gay Rights

A class action suit in 1973, *Society for Individual Rights* [a gay organization] *v. Hampton,* created a definitive change in civil service policy. A supply clerk was fired when his army discharge papers revealed his homosexuality. He brought suit against the government's antigay policy, and a federal court, using *Norton v. Macy* as its guide, ordered the Civil Service Commission to

> *forthwith cease excluding or discharging from government service any homosexual person whom the Commission would deem unfit for government employment solely because the employment of such a person in the government service might bring that service into contempt.*

In other words, the fear that having gay employees would cause the public to lose respect—to have "contempt"—for an agency was no longer a reason to fire or refuse to hire gay men and lesbians.

Accordingly, in 1975, the U.S. Civil Service Commission announced that it had dropped its ban on hiring gay people—except for the FBI and the intelligence agencies, where the fear that homosexuals could be more easily blackmailed (and were more personally unstable) continued to operate.

Then, in 1977, a federal court upheld the firing of a gay clerk who "flaunted" his homosexuality by kissing a man in public, being active in the gay rights movement, and applying for a license to marry another man. When the Supreme Court vacated the lower court's decision in 1978, it suggested that openly gay employees had the right to keep their jobs. Although the court offered no explanation in its 1978 ruling, later cases, especially *Van Ooteghem v. Gray* (1980) suggest that the free speech rights of gay civil servants are indeed protected.

So in 1980, the government took another step: the Office of Personnel Management (OPM) actively prohibited employment discrimination on the basis of sexual orientation in all federal civil service jobs. And throughout the 1980s and 1990s, groups such as Federal Lesbians and Gays (FLAG) and Federal GLOBE (Gay, Lesbian, Bisexual Employees) continued to push for better conditions for gay, lesbian, and bisexual civil servants.

Their efforts have been largely successful. A number of agencies now have nondiscrimination policies, including many cabinet departments—Agriculture, Commerce, Education, Energy, Health and Human Services, Housing and Urban Development, Interior, Justice, Labor, State, Transportation, Treasury, and Veterans Affairs—as well as the Departments of the Air Force, Army, and Navy (which supervises the U.S. Marines), though these rules apply to civilian employees only. Many other government agencies have similar antidiscrimination policies, including the offices of the president and vice president, the CIA, Environmental Protection Agency, Equal Employment Opportunity Commission (EEOC), Federal Trade Commission, Library of

Gay Rights

Congress, NASA, and the U.S. Postal Service. And on May 29, 1998, President Bill Clinton issued an executive order prohibiting discrimination against federal workers on the basis of sexual orientation. However, Clinton's order carried no enforcement measures, and it failed to include the nation's largest employer, the U.S. military—one of the last government employers with an explicit policy of antigay discrimination.

GAYS IN THE MILITARY

From World War II through 1994, the military's policy on gay men and lesbians was quite clear: homosexuality was considered "incompatible with military service." As discussed in Chapter 1, President Bill Clinton pledged during his 1992 campaign to eliminate this half-century ban and welcome gay men and lesbians as members of the U.S. Armed Forces.

Certainly, many in the gay rights movement were of two minds about welcoming gays into the military. For many, the military was seen as an evil to be avoided, particularly for those who remembered an era when the draft had brought thousands of unwilling young men to serve in a war that many regarded as unjust. On the other hand, as with gay marriage, the immediate civil rights issue seemed to many activists more pressing than the larger questions of political principle. If straight people were allowed—or drafted—into the army, then, they believed, gay people ought to have the same right. Besides the symbolic effects of military service—its suggestion that gay men and women were indeed full-fledged members of society—allowing gays into the military would give young men and women access to training, education, veterans' benefits, and other opportunities open to heterosexual youth.

Supporters of gays and lesbians in the military argued that there had always been homosexual soldiers, many of whom had received the military's highest awards. Speaking both to the gay rights movement and to society at large, they urged legal recognition for what they claimed was a long-standing situation.

Opponents of gays in the military argued that the open presence of homosexuals would weaken the morale and cohesiveness of fighting units, make straight soldiers uncomfortable about sharing quarters and showering with lesbian and gay soldiers, and run counter to the U.S. military tradition. Some opponents also said or suggested that gay men and women were less fit morally and/or physically and could not fight as well as or as bravely as their heterosexual counterparts. Many opponents of gay and lesbian soldiers did not believe that there were already many lesbians and gay men serving—with varying degrees of openness—in all branches of the military; that indeed, all fighting forces throughout history had included gay men (and, in some cases, lesbians).

In any case, Clinton's promise was not fulfilled. Georgia senator Sam Nunn of the Armed Service Committee and U.S. Army general Colin Powell were both strong opponents of the open participation of gay men and women in the military. Under pressure from them, losing the public relations battle, and fearful of his waning influence in Congress, Clinton retreated from his promise of an executive order lifting the ban on gays and instead instituted a policy commonly known as "don't ask, don't tell," wherein gay men and women were not allowed to make their homosexuality public, but neither could they be asked by recruiters what their sexuality was.

As it turned out, Clinton's policy was probably worse for gay servicemen and women than the previous regulations had been. The new policy prohibited gay soldiers from engaging in any homosexual conduct, in or out of uniform, and actually criminalized a gay *identity*: soldiers could be discharged just for being identified as gay or lesbian, whether or not they committed any specific acts.

As a result, more gay soldiers were discharged under "don't ask, don't tell" than under the previous ban on homosexual soldiers. An increase in attacks on and harassment of gay and lesbian soldiers was also noticed. Nor did the policy win Clinton any political points. The right wing attacked Clinton for being "soft on homosexuality," while gay rights activists and their allies accused him of reneging on his promise.

Reports of antigay harassment provoked such widespread concern that in August 1999 the Pentagon issued new guidelines that prohibited commanders from investigating the sexual orientation of service members who reported antigay harassment or threats. Rather, commanders were directed to investigate the threat itself.

Criticism of the policy continued, and in December 1999 Clinton finally decided to bring his policy under review, largely because of continued concern over the death of Barry Winchell, a gay soldier who had been bludgeoned to death in his Fort Campbell, Kentucky barracks. Winchell had reportedly been harassed repeatedly by the fellow private who eventually killed him. However, because of "don't ask, don't tell," Winchell was allegedly afraid to report the harassment for fear of being discharged. Winchell's mother later sued the military for $1.8 million, a case that had not yet been decided as this book went to press.

First Lady Hillary Clinton denounced the current policy, while Vice President Al Gore, in the midst of his own presidential campaign, said bluntly, "Gays and lesbians should be allowed to serve their country without discrimination." Clinton himself, in a televised weekend interview on CBS News, said that the policy he had once championed was "out of whack." On the following Monday, December 13, 1999, Defense Secretary William Cohen announced an intensive 90-day review of the policy. As of the start of the new millennium, the future of gays in the military was still unclear.

Gay Rights

AIDS and Disability Law

As stated in Chapter 1, there is one specific provision that protects the rights of some gay and lesbian employees: the extension of the 1990 Americans with Disabilities Act (ADA) to cover people with AIDS and HIV. (Although most gay men and lesbians do not have AIDS or HIV, and although many people with AIDS and HIV are not gay, the ruling does affect many gay men in particular.) In a 1998 decision, *Bragdon v. Abbott*, the Supreme Court ruled 5-4 in favor of Sidney Abbott, an HIV-positive Maine woman filing suit against Randon Bragdon, a dentist who had refused to fill a cavity for her in his Bangor office. Bragdon had insisted on treating Abbott in a hospital, where he said he could take greater precautions against infecting himself or his staff.

Abbott argued that as a person with HIV, she was entitled to the same protection against discrimination as other disabled Americans. The Court agreed that people with AIDS and HIV did indeed come under the 1990 act's definition of the disabled—that is, people who were unable to engage in a "major life activity." Since children of people with AIDS or HIV might be born infected, people with AIDS or HIV cannot freely engage in reproduction, which the court agreed was clearly a major life activity. As a result of the 1998 decision, people with AIDS or HIV now have protection from discrimination in employment, housing, and public accommodations (i.e., restaurants, hotels, and other public places).

Gay rights groups and AIDS organizations hailed the decision, as did the American Civil Liberties Union. "It sends a message to a lot of people beyond those with HIV that they shouldn't be denied the opportunity to work or receive services because people are uncomfortable with their condition," said Gary Buseck, executive director of Gay and Lesbian Advocates and Defenders.

However, the Court did not rule on the specific question of whether Abbott had the right to be treated in Bragdon's office, as she had claimed. The ADA does allow disabled people to be treated differently if they pose a "direct threat to the health or safety of others." Therefore, the Court sent the question of where Abbott should have been treated back to federal appeals court, where, as of early 2000, Bragdon still hoped to win.

State, City, and Private Employment

Interestingly, the public's attitude toward homosexuality in general, and its attitude toward antigay employment discrimination in particular, are widely divergent. A 1998 *Washington Post*/Harvard University poll found that 57 percent of the respondents thought that homosexuality itself was "unacceptable." Yet 87 percent believed that gay men and lesbians should have equal rights when it came to employment. Clearly, many people who do not approve of homosexuality per se still think gay men and lesbians should be given equal treatment at work.

According to gay rights lawyer and activist Paula Ettelbrick, that is largely because people view workplace discrimination very differently now than they used to. In her view, the civil rights movement has helped many Americans to see *any* kind of on-the-job discrimination as simply unfair. Even when an employer is not legally required to avoid antigay discrimination in particular, Ettelbrick sees a kind of cultural attitude that suggests that such discrimination is wrong. Ironically, says Ettelbrick, this very improvement makes it somewhat more difficult to pass antidiscrimination legislation. Precisely because fewer employers now feel comfortable in telling a gay man or lesbian, "I'm firing you because you're gay," it is hard to find examples of the most egregious types of discrimination. And those who do experience such treatment are often afraid to testify about it, especially if they're living fearful and closeted lives.

Incidents of discrimination still exist, however, in the subtle guise of being excessively criticized by a supervisor or excluded from key meetings, as well as in more overt forms. In 1991, for example, Robin Shahar, a lawyer, took a job in the office of Georgia attorney general Michael Bowers (the same public official involved in *Bowers v. Hardwick*). But when Shahar and her lover held a private commitment ceremony, Bowers withdrew the job offer: According to the Supreme Court case *Bowers v. Hardwick*, Bowers pointed out, Shahar was a felon. Thus he could explain his action not as discrimination but rather as the wish to hire only law-abiding citizens. Shahar's case made it all the way to the Supreme Court—which in 1998 refused to hear it. (Ironically, that was the same year that the Georgia Supreme Court overturned the state's sodomy law.)

Despite cases like Shahar's, it's clear that gay men and lesbians have won more on-the-job rights. As of mid-2000, the following states had prohibited sexual-orientation discrimination in public and private employment: California, Connecticut, Hawaii, Massachusetts, Minnesota, Nevada, New Hampshire, New Jersey, Oregon, Rhode Island, Vermont, and Wisconsin. Another seven states had prohibited such discrimination in public employment only: Illinois, Iowa, Maryland, New York, New Mexico, Pennsylvania, and Washington. Maine passed a statewide antidiscrimination law in 1997, but it was repealed by a statewide referendum.

Dozens of local laws also prohibit on-the-job discrimination against gay men and lesbians. Some of these ordinances apply to all employers; others concern only city or local governments; still others apply exclusively to private employers doing business with the city. Redress might come through a lawsuit, an appeal to a human rights commission or equivalent body, or both. Many private companies also have nondiscrimination policies, and a number of labor unions have won nondiscrimination clauses in their contracts.

EMPLOYMENT NON-DISCRIMINATION ACT (ENDA)

Beyond these piecemeal local victories, national gay rights groups have sought federal protection against employment discrimination. The Employment Non-Discrimination Act (ENDA) was first introduced into Congress in 1994 as a way of separating employment rights for gay men and lesbians out of a more broadly conceived gay rights bill. As discussed in Chapter 1, Congresswoman Bella Abzug first began introducing federal gay rights legislation in 1974; 25 years later, no such bill has become law.

Gay rights groups thought that the employment part of the bill might have a better chance of success if it were detached from the more controversial provisions against discrimination in housing and public accommodations. Thus ENDA would extend to gay men and lesbians only the protection of Title VII, the federal law that prohibits employment discrimination on the basis of race, religion, national origin, and sex. Under Title VII, people who believe they have suffered from discrimination have the right to sue their employers.

Initially, wrote *Detroit News* columnist Deb Price in a May 30, 1997 column, ENDA "was widely perceived on Capitol Hill as a liberal Democratic pipe dream." Gradually, though, members of Congress began to realize "that neither their institution nor our nation is as homophobic as they'd assumed."

"Employment protections [for gay workers] have really emerged as a mainstream, bipartisan issue," Human Rights Campaign legislative director Winnie Stachelberg told Price at that time. As evidence of this, Price cited the fact that when ENDA came up for a vote in September 1996, the Republican-controlled Senate nearly passed it, with a vote of 49-50.

Support for ENDA seemed to transcend national and partisan boundaries. According to an April 1997 survey conducted by Tarrance Group and Lake Sosin Snell Perry & Associates, 68 percent of all Americans supported ENDA, a figure that remained relatively stable when broken down by region (77 percent in the Northeast, 71 percent in the Midwest, 68 percent in the West, and 62 percent in the South) and party (79 percent of Democrats favored the bill; 69 percent of independents; and 59 percent of Republicans).

However, when the bill came up before the House of Representatives in 1997, the House failed to act. The bill had been consistently supported by President Clinton since 1995, a move lauded by Elizabeth Birch, the executive director of the Human Rights Campaign, which had made ENDA a major focus of its lobbying efforts. "ENDA is the watershed event that history will record 50 or 100 years in the future," Birch was quoted as saying in a November 7, 1997 *Christian Science Monitor* article by Skip Thurman. "There is a transformation going on . . . [Through his support of ENDA,] the President has absolutely altered the air we breathe."

Still, ENDA seems to be stalled in Congress. As of mid-2000, the federal antidiscrimination measure had not yet been passed—even though polls continue to show widespread support for the protection of gay employment rights. "Legislators at every level don't really want to expand the protection of civil rights laws," Paula Ettelbrick comments. "We might be able to keep local legislators from repealing the civil rights and affirmative action laws that already exist—but it's extremely difficult to expand them to include sexual orientation along with race and gender."

MARRIAGE

In 1993, in *Baehr v. Lewin*, Hawaii's high court ruled that same-sex couples had the same right to marry as straight couples, although it made an explicit distinction between "same-sex" and "homosexual," suggesting that, for example, two straight women might wish to marry one another, and that to forbid such a marriage would constitute discrimination on the basis of sex.

The Hawaii case was appealed, but there seemed to be a distinct possibility that Hawaii would legalize same-sex marriage. In response, some 28 states passed laws preventing the recognition of same-sex marriage: in 1995, Utah; in 1996, Arizona, Delaware, Georgia, Idaho, Illinois, Kansas, Michigan, North Carolina, Oklahoma, Pennsylvania, South Carolina, South Dakota, and Tennessee; in 1997, Arkansas, Florida, Indiana, Maine, Minnesota, Mississippi, Montana, North Dakota, and Virginia; and in 1998, Alabama, Alaska (in the form of a constitutional amendment passed by popular vote), Iowa, Kentucky, and Washington. Hawaii, the state considered most likely to legalize same-sex marriage, passed a constitutional amendment in 1998 restricting the marriage contract to heterosexual couples.

Missouri attempted to pass a gay marriage recognition ban, but the state supreme court overturned it because of bad legislative procedure. The remaining 19 states without an explicit ban on same-sex marriage at the start of 2000 were Colorado, Connecticut, Louisiana, Maryland, Massachusetts, Nebraska, Nevada, New Hampshire, New Jersey, New Mexico, New York, Ohio, Oregon, Rhode Island, Texas, Vermont, West Virginia, Wisconsin, and Wyoming. However, same-sex marriage is not legal in any of those states—it simply has not been explicitly prohibited.

California is off that list largely through the efforts of Republican state senator Pete Knight. On March 7, 2000, Californians voted to approve Proposition 22, commonly referred to as the Knight Initiative (since Senator

Knight had been instrumental in placing it on the ballot), by a 25 percent margin. This statewide referendum added language to the state's Family Code ensuring that marriage is defined as taking place only between a man and a woman—and preventing the state from recognizing same-sex marriages contracted in any other state.

Meanwhile, on December 11, 1999 Hawaii's Supreme Court ruled that the state's new constitutional amendment did indeed make same-sex marriage illegal in that state. At the same time, a lawsuit in Vermont, brought by a couple who were denied a marriage license, led to a December 20, 1999 Vermont Supreme Court decision that making a distinction between heterosexual and homosexual couples was prohibited by state antidiscrimination law. The state high court ordered the legislature to come up with some arrangement that would allow same-sex couples access to all the legal and financial benefits enjoyed by heterosexual couples. In response, the state legislature created a new category of legally recognized affectional partnership called a "civil union." Couples who enter into civil unions will enjoy most, but not all, of the benefits that the state extends to married couples. Lawsuits in other states, particularly those with liberal courts, seem likely.

DOMESTIC PARTNERSHIPS

Whether or not they support legalized gay marriage, many activists have suggested an alternate strategy: working for the de facto recognition of gay families, particularly through the extension of domestic partnership benefits to gay couples. Heterosexual senior citizens and the disabled, who are often unwilling to marry for fear of reductions in their Social Security or other government benefits, have been the unlikely allies of the gay movement in the fight for the recognition of domestic partnerships. Many feminists, straight as well as gay, have also supported domestic partnerships in their efforts to create for women other partnership options than traditional forms of marriage.

As of mid-2000, seven states had some kind of statewide provision for domestic partners of government employees: California (health care facility visitation rights); Connecticut (health benefits); Hawaii; Massachusetts (bereavement leave, health care facility visitation rights); New York (health benefits); Oregon (family leave, sick leave, dental benefits, health benefits); and Vermont (civil union legislation). Washington passed a bill effective in 2001 that will grant gay and lesbian government employees health benefits for their domestic partners. California and Massachusetts also offer domestic partnership registry, whereby either straight or gay couples can register as domestic partners in a kind of legal alternative to marriage.

Counties in Arizona, California, Florida, Illinois, Michigan, New Jersey, Oregon, Texas, Washington, and Wisconsin all offer government employees some form of benefit. So, too, do cities and towns across the nation. Besides municipalities in the counties just mentioned, towns in Colorado, Connecticut, Georgia, Indiana, Iowa, Louisiana, Maine, Maryland, Massachusetts, Minnesota, Missouri, New York, North Carolina, Ohio, Pennsylvania, and Vermont have offered their employees some form of domestic partnership recognition. Cities that have recognized domestic partnerships include some of the nation's major urban centers: San Francisco; Boulder and Denver, Colorado; Atlanta; Chicago; New Orleans; Portland, Maine; Boston and Cambridge, Massachusetts; Ann Arbor and Detroit, Michigan; St. Paul, Minnesota; St. Louis, Missouri; New York City; Chapel Hill, North Carolina; Philadelphia and Pittsburgh, Pennsylvania; Olympia and Seattle, Washington; Madison and Milwaukee, Wisconsin; and the District of Columbia. San Francisco's domestic partnership law is one of the strongest in the nation: It requires any company doing business with the city to offer equal benefits to married couples and domestic partners.

Although not as volatile a topic as same-sex marriage, domestic partnership benefits have caused their share of controversy. Some state legislatures have banned the extension of various types of partnership benefits, as in Pennsylvania, where state-funded schools are prohibited from offering domestic partnership benefits to gay employees.

Sometimes benefits will be challenged after they are made available. Arlington County, Virginia, for example, had offered health and dental benefits to domestic partners. But on March 4, 1999, on narrow technical grounds, Circuit Court Judge Benjamin Kendrick ruled that this was illegal. Seeking a more lasting precedent, he urged the county to appeal his ruling to the state supreme court and stayed (delayed) his decision until the county should appeal. The Virginia attorney general sided with those seeking to overturn the law, as did the Virginia Supreme Court. Thus, Arlington County no longer offers domestic partnership benefits.

Likewise, on July 8, 1999 in *Connors v. City of Boston*, the Massachusetts Supreme Court ruled that Boston had overstepped its bounds when it extended spousal health benefits to the domestic partners of its unmarried employees. Relying on the Home Rule Amendment to the state constitution, a law that had been virtually ignored for the past 35 years, the Supreme Court ruled that the state legislature, rather than local municipalities, had jurisdiction over decisions involving health benefits. Although *Connors* has not yet been applied statewide, it would seem to overturn benefits being offered elsewhere in Massachusetts.

The *Connors* case was the result of a suit brought by the American Center for Law and Justice (ACLJ), a Virginia-based conservative law firm allied with the antigay Christian Coalition. ACLJ had also brought suit against New York City's domestic partnership benefits, which were signed into law on July 7, 1998. On that date, New York City established a domestic partner registry for all citizens, bereavement leave for city employees, visitation rights for all domestic partners in city-run facilities, and succession rights to apartments owned by the city (that is, a domestic partner would have the right to continue residence on the lease of a deceased partner).

Two weeks after the bill was signed, the ACLJ filed a challenge, which a Manhattan supreme court judge threw out in February 1999. ACLJ attorney and regional director Vincent McCarthy says he plans to appeal the decision, claiming that the law is "an end run around the marital statute and is one step closer to legitimizing homosexual marriages, which we don't want." The ACLJ has filed similar cases in San Francisco (pending) and Santa Barbara, California (thrown out December 17, 1998). After its success in Boston, it seems likely to continue this strategy around the country.

Nevertheless, gay rights activists remain hopeful about the survival of domestic partnership benefits. "The ACLJ is pursuing a losing strategy," said Suzanne Goldberg, a staff attorney for the Lambda Legal Defense and Education Fund, as quoted in the February 19, 1999 issue of the *New York Blade* (a gay weekly newspaper). Openly gay New York state senator Tom Duane agrees. "In fact," he said in the same article, "most of us have gone on to the next battle, which is expanding domestic partnership across state lines and to companies that contract with the city. . . . We would like to be able to get married. But in the meantime, we'd like to get as close to full and equal rights as possible."

Meanwhile, across the country, thousands of private institutions offer some version of domestic partnership benefits. Many of these benefits are available to unmarried heterosexual partners as well as to gay couples. As stated in Chapter 1, one estimate has it that 10 percent of all U.S. employers offer some kind of benefits to domestic partners.

GAY ADOPTION

Precisely because of the widespread social stereotype that gay men and lesbians ought not to come in contact with children, the notion of gay adoption and gay foster parenting has had a difficult time winning acceptance. Yet remarkably few states forbid it outright. Florida has a 1977 law on the books prohibiting gay individuals from adopting children either privately or publicly. In 1999, Arkansas established state agency rules that would prevent homosexuals from adopting, and in the same year, Utah banned unmarried couples of any kind from providing state-sponsored adoption and foster care. However, these rules do not affect Utah's private adoption and foster care agencies, which are responsible for the overwhelming majority of children who are placed with adoptive or foster parents. In California, social workers are required to recommend against adoption by unmarried couples, but judges are allowed to ignore these recommendations. In 2000, the state of Mississippi also banned gay/lesbian adoptions.

Even if lesbians and gay men are not forbidden to adopt, however, the procedure in most states is far from easy. In practice, about half of all U.S. states allow individuals in gay or unmarried relationships to adopt children. According to Kate Kendell, director of the National Center for Lesbian Rights, some 8 million to 13 million children are being raised by gay and lesbian parents nationwide. However, most of these children are not adopted.

New Jersey made U.S. history in December 1997 by becoming the first state in the nation to allow both gay and heterosexual unmarried couples to adopt children on the same basis as married couples. Lawyers had argued that state policy against gay adoptions violated the equal protection rights of lesbian and gay couples. Moreover, the lawyers claimed, as in custody cases, the best interests of the child should take precedence.

"This is a complete and total victory for gay families, equal rights and thousands of children in the state waiting to be adopted," said Lenora M. Lapidus in an interview with the *Los Angeles Times* published December 18, 1997. Lapidus is the legal director of the New Jersey chapter of the ACLU, which had helped to bring the class action lawsuit on behalf of gay and lesbian couples seeking to adopt. "This settlement guarantees that all couples seeking adoptions will be judged only by their ability to love and support a child." The Christian Coalition and other conservative organizations were predictably dismayed. "Our position is that adoption should be something that is within the framework of a family, and a family is defined as a husband and wife," said Arne Owens, the Christian Coalition's communications director, in the same article.

The New Jersey couple in question was Jon Holden and Michael Galluccio, who adopted their son, Adam, when he was two years old. The couple had begun caring for Adam when he was three months old, a drug-addicted baby who had been exposed to—but not infected with—HIV. Under previous policy, Holden or Galluccio might have been able to adopt separately—as in the cases discussed in the custody section. By adopting as a couple, however, they were assured that both would have rights to the child.

A December 20, 1997 editorial in the *Washington Post* pointed out that the New Jersey decision was actually only "an incremental development in the debate" over gay adoption. As the editorial explained, many states already permitted gay men and lesbians in relationships to adopt children, and many others allowed a gay man or lesbian to adopt a partner's child later on. Some gay couples had even adopted children *as* couples—but only because of court decisions. The new achievement in the New Jersey case was to "remove as a matter of state policy the fiction that the state is dealing with individuals rather than with a couple. More than anything else, the settlement is an acknowledgment of the current reality."

Although the *Post* editorial urged caution in the matter of adoption policy, Holden and Galluccio found quite a different reception when they adopted a second child in 1999. Their first adoption effort "took a battery of lawyers, a court ruling, and a landmark change in New Jersey policy," according to an article by Joan Biskupic in the November 5, 1999 edition of the *Washington Post*. Yet when the two men adopted their second child, "it took them only a few months of the usual paperwork that any couple might face."

Galluccio says that it is not just the rules that are changing. "In 1997, when we finally got Adam, our family was an oddity to people," he told Biskupic. "There was a look of bewilderment in people's eyes. But now, we've become more ordinary."

Like many gay activists who fall into the "gay liberationist" rather than the "civil rights" camps, legal scholar and professor Ruthann Robson supports the growing acceptance of lesbian families—but cautions against too great an eagerness to fit lesbian (and, by implication, gay male) arrangements into the traditional patterns of heterosexual family life. Like many gay liberationists, she wonders why only two lesbians are allowed to co-adopt a child, and why they must be involved in a monogamous, long-term relationship that looks as much as possible like heterosexual marriage. Why, she wonders, could not three or more people agree to raise a child? Why could not people who engage in a variety of sexual arrangements still not offer a stable, loving home to a child? Moreover, like others who hold her view, Robson worries that the kinds of lesbian (and, by extension, gay male) families that are accepted by the courts are the ones in which upper-class incomes and trust funds help to erase the courts' traditional reluctance to recognize same-sex couples. In their gratitude for court approval, Robson warns, lesbians (and gay men) risk reinforcing the oppressive restrictions of class and heterosexual marriage.

HATE CRIMES

The notion of "hate crimes"—crimes that include an element of bias, or hate, against a particular group—has become widely understood in the 1990s, as gays and lesbians, people of color, and other oppressed groups have sought to increase the penalties for bias crimes and bias-related violence. The first instance of gay men and lesbians receiving any kind of federal protection was their inclusion in the 1990 Hate Crimes Statistics Act, which requires the U.S. Department of Justice to collect, maintain, and report statistics on criminal acts that are motivated by race, religion, national origin, or sexual orientation. Although Senator Jesse Helms of North Carolina called the act part of a conspiracy by "the radical elements of the homosexual movement," the Senate passed the law by a 92-4 vote, and the bill passed the House by a similar margin.

The federal law does not allow for any specific actions to be taken by the federal government, nor does it increase criminal penalties for any type of crime. Moreover, in order to win the sexual orientation provision of the law, the following text had to be included:

> *the American family life is the foundation of American society; federal policy should encourage the well-being, financial security, and health of the American family; and schools should not de-emphasize the critical value of American family life. . . . Nothing in this Act shall be construed, nor shall any funds be appropriated to carry out the purpose of the Act be used, to promote or encourage homosexuality. . . . Nothing in this section creates a right to bring action, including an action based on discrimination due to sexual orientation.*

Indeed, during the first few months after the Hate Crimes Statistics Act was enacted, the justice department refused to accept complaints of violence against gay men and lesbians on its Hate Crimes Hotline.

On October 6, 1999, President Clinton signed an executive order amending the U.S. military's criminal code to impose harsher penalties when bias against sexual orientation was involved in violent crime. The executive order also allowed for confidentiality for soldiers and officers who consulted privately with therapists, in an apparent effort to allow the victims of antigay crime to receive therapy without opening themselves to nonconfidential administrative proceedings that would dismiss them from the service on the basis of their homosexuality. (As stated earlier, federal policy on gays in the military is currently under review.)

Meanwhile, a new federal law, the Hate Crimes Prevention Act (HCPA), would increase penalties for hate crimes. The HCPA gained political currency in the wake of the brutal murder of Matthew Shepard, a 20-year-old college student beaten and left for dead in Laramie, Wyoming, a killing that seemed motivated at least in part by homophobia. Despite the more than 200 sponsors of the HCPA in 1999, however, it remains stalled in Congress.

Besides federal law, 23 states offer extra penalties for crimes that include bias on the basis of sexual orientation: California, Connecticut, Delaware, Florida, Illinois, Iowa, Kentucky, Louisiana, Maine, Massachusetts, Minnesota, Missouri, Nebraska, Nevada, New Hampshire, New Jersey, New York, Oregon, Rhode Island, Tennessee, Vermont, Washington, and Wisconsin. Arizona, Indiana, and Maryland each have laws allowing for the collection of hate crime statistics regarding crimes in which sexual orientation is an element, but do not impose greater penalties for hate crimes. (Another 20 states have hate crimes legislation without reference to sexual orientation.) Some cities and counties, among them St. Louis County, Missouri; the District of Columbia; Chicago; Wichita, Kansas; Louisville, Kentucky; Albuquerque, New Mexico; Buffalo, New York; and Toledo, Ohio, all have some form of hate crimes law covering sexual orientation.

A number of questions have arisen, however, as to the usefulness of hate crimes law to gay rights activism. The Gay and Lesbian Alliance Against Defamation (GLAAD), the Human Rights Campaign (HRC), the National Gay and Lesbian Task Force (NGLTF), and Parents, Families and Friends of Lesbians and Gays (PFLAG), along with many other religious, ethnic, feminist, and civil rights groups, have all supported the notion of hate crimes legislation. But a number of observers have questioned whether such laws will in fact reduce the amount of bias crime that actually takes place, or whether it will simply add to the current climate of fighting crime with harsher sentencing rather than education and organizing.

"Even as national lesbian and gay organizations pursue hate crimes laws with single-minded fervor, concentrating precious resources and energy on these campaigns, there is no evidence that such laws actually prevent hate crimes," writes Richard Kim, assistant director of the Nation Institute, in the July 12, 1999 edition of the *Nation*. Kim quotes HRC political director Winnie Stachelberg as admitting that "local law enforcement agencies are often reluctant to report [such] crimes."

Moreover, bias crimes against gay men and lesbians can also be committed by law enforcement officers—the very people charged under the law with reporting antigay violence. According to Shawna Virago, for example, a male-to-female transexual activist with the San Francisco–based Community United Against Violence (CUAV), some 50 percent of reported incidents of violence against transgendered people in the San Francisco Bay area in 1998 were committed by law enforcement officials.

"[H]ate crimes laws are aimed at lengthening prison sentences, not creating safer community spaces," argues Kim, who calls for local organizing rather than increased prison sentences as a response to escalating violence against gays and lesbians.

Other opponents of hate crimes laws—both inside and outside the gay rights movement—object to them on civil liberties grounds. They argue that violent actions should be punished, but that penalties for what a criminal might have been thinking should not be added.

But many gay rights advocates continue to push for hate crimes law as a way to communicate to society that antigay violence is not acceptable. In a climate where gay existence is still rendered illegal—or potentially illegal—by *Bowers v. Hardwick*, local sodomy laws, and military policy, these gay activists look to federal and local hate crimes legislation as a way to redress the balance. Whether hate crimes laws, community organizing, or some combination of the two is the most effective way to address antigay violence continues to be debated.

IMMIGRATION

Immigration law for gay men and lesbians has been influenced by three other legal situations. One is sodomy law, which criminalizes homosexual sex. The second is the anticommunist hysteria of the 1940s and 1950s, which led to the passage of the McCarran-Walters Act of 1950, banning both Communists and "sexual deviates" from entering the United States. (In 1967, the Supreme Court ruled that this definition applied to lesbians and gay men.) And the third is the failure to recognize gay relationships, which means that foreign-born gay and lesbian partners of U.S. citizens cannot obtain visas and other immigration assistance as they could if they were legally married.

Thus, in 1985, an official of the U.S. Immigration and Naturalization Service (INS) ruled that "a bona fide marital relationship cannot exist" between two gay men or women. The case involved a U.S. citizen and his partner, a native Australian, who had been involved in a monogamous relationship lasting more than 11 years, at least 10 of which had been spent in the United States. On appeal, the INS ruling was upheld by a federal court, and the native Australian was deported.

A contrasting case occurred in 1993, when the INS granted political asylum to a gay Mexican citizen who claimed that his life would be in jeopardy were he returned to his native Mexico. The landmark case seemed to be the first time that the INS recognized sexual orientation as a valid claim for asylum under the 1980 Refugee Act. Although Congress did finally remove the specific barriers to gay men and lesbians entering the United States, gay and lesbian relationships are still not recognized as part of immigration law.

INTRODUCTION TO MAJOR COURT CASES

The rest of this chapter summarizes the landmark court cases in the field of gay rights that currently have the most relevance for the legal battles likely to occur over the next several decades. Key federal and state cases in the area of sodomy law, legal protection, federal employment, free speech and assembly, family recognition, and housing rights are summarized, and their impact on the gay rights movement is explained.

Although each of the cases profiled remains extremely important for both pro– and anti–gay rights activists, it is important to note that none of these cases stands as the last word on any issue. *Bowers v. Hardwick*, for example, the 1986 U.S. Supreme Court ruling that upheld Georgia's sodomy law, would seem to have established the principle that the highest court in the land looked kindly on state laws prohibiting certain types of sexual activity. Yet several states—including Georgia—went on to overturn their own sodomy laws, either via legislative action or through court decisions. Likewise, in *Braschi v. Stahl Associates Co.*, the New York Supreme Court found that a longstanding domestic partnership of two men constituted a de facto family that ought to receive the same recognition in housing matters as a legally married heterosexual couple. Yet the same court later ruled against a lesbian who sued her former partner for visitation rights to a child the two had long cared for together, seeming to contradict its earlier recognition of lesbian and gay families. Students of the legal side of gay rights, then, must know about relevant court decisions, but must not mistake them for absolute guides to future trends in either legislative or legal arenas.

SUPREME COURT CASES

Sodomy

BOWERS V. HARDWICK (1986)

Background

Michael Hardwick, a 29-year-old man, had been issued a summons for drinking a can of beer from a paper bag outside the Atlanta gay bar where he worked. Since he had not yet paid his fine for "public drunkenness," a police officer went to his home to serve him a warrant. A houseguest answered the door and allowed the officer in to see whether Hardwick was home. The officer found Hardwick's bedroom, opened the door, and saw Hardwick and another man having oral sex on the bed. "What are you doing in my bedroom?" asked Hardwick when he saw the officer, who eventually arrested Hardwick under an 1816 statute prohibiting oral and anal sex by either homosexuals or heterosexuals, punishable by one to 20 years in prison.

Legal Issues

If it had been up to the state of Georgia, Michael Hardwick would only have spent one night in jail, for the prosecutor declined to press charges after that.

But Hardwick decided to challenge the law by bringing suit against state attorney general Michael J. Bowers. Hardwick and his supporters hoped to bring into question the entire notion of sodomy laws. Hardwick and his partner were both consenting adults having sex in the privacy of their bedroom. The law under which they were convicted would have applied equally to a married heterosexual couple and suggested a degree of invaded privacy that gay rights activists believed would horrify the American public.

Indeed, the U.S. Court of Appeals for the Eleventh Circuit upheld Hardwick's position with enthusiasm, "The activity [Hardwick] hopes to engage in is quintessentially private and lies at the heart of an intimate association beyond the proper reach of state regulation," ruled the lower court. If the state wanted to regulate such private activity, it would have to prove a "compelling interest" to do so, an interest that Hardwick and his lawyer, Hardvard law professor Laurence Tribe, believed did not exist.

The Georgia state attorneys saw it differently. For them, what was at stake was the legality of homosexuality itself. As Bowers wrote in his brief:

> *In Georgia it is the very act of homosexual sodomy that epitomizes moral delinquency. . . . [Homosexuality] leads to other deviate practices, such as sadomasochism, group orgies, or transvestitism, to name only a few. . . . [Homosexual sodomy is often committed in] parks, rest rooms, "gay baths," and "gay bars," and is marked by the multiplicity and anonymity of sexual partners, a disproportionate involvement with adolescents and indeed, a possible relationship to crimes of violence. Similarly, the legislature should be permitted to draw conclusions concerning the relationship of homosexual sodomy in the transmission of AIDS. But perhaps the most profound legislative finding that can be made is that homosexual sodomy is the anathema of the basic units of our society—marriage and the family. To decriminalize or artificially withdraw the public's expression of its disdain for this conduct does not uplift sodomy, but rather demotes those sacred institutions to merely other alternative lifestyles.*

Decision

On June 30, 1986 the Supreme Court handed down its ruling. According to a *New York Times* headline, "High Court, 5-4, Says States Have the Right to Outlaw Private Homosexual Acts." The Court's decision upheld the sodomy law, which itself referred only to "any sexual act involving the sex organs of one person and the mouth or anus of another." But the justices ignored the heterosexual implications of that language and noted particularly that gay men and lesbians had no particular right to engage in *homosexual* sodomy.

Gay Rights

"The issue presented is whether the Federal Constitution confers a fundamental right upon homosexuals to engage in sodomy and hence invalidates the laws of the many states that still make such conduct illegal and have done so for a very long time," wrote Justice Byron R. White in the majority opinion. Michael Hardwick was asking the Court to establish "a fundamental right to engage in homosexual sodomy. This we are quite unwilling to do." As for the argument that the privacy of one's home should offer some protection, White wrote, that would be like saying that it would be permissible to harbor stolen goods or narcotics at home.

The Court's dissenting opinion, written by Justice Harry A. Blackmun, was more supportive of gay rights: "I can only hope," Blackmun wrote, "that the court will reconsider its analysis and conclude that depriving individuals of the right to choose for themselves how to conduct their intimate relationships poses a far greater threat to the values most deeply rooted in our nation's history than the tolerance of nonconformity could ever do."

Impact

Both gay rights activists and those who opposed gay rights noted the significance of the date that *Hardwick* was handed down: the day after the 17th anniversary of the Stonewall uprising. Yet "[i]t was not the ruling itself that angered [gay legal activists] so much," wrote Dave Walter in the August 5, 1986 issue of the *Advocate*, a gay paper. "[R]ather, it was the blatantly homophobic opinion that accompanied the decision."

To gay rights activists, singling out gay sex was bad enough. The justices in the majority had gone further, comparing gay sex to "adultery, incest, and other sexual crimes," and citing the biblical roots of social prohibitions against same-sex practices.

There was another important legal implication to the ruling. Previously, U.S. law had referred only to particular acts. But in the *Hardwick* case, "homosexuals" were defined as people who performed certain acts. Gay men and lesbians had become a criminal class under a decision that supported the right of heterosexuals to perform the very same acts.

The decision provoked immediate protest. Thousands of gay men and lesbians in New York City took to the streets in two demonstrations that were the biggest in New York since the 1970s: One thousand men and women sat in at Sheridan Square in Greenwich Village, stopping traffic at several intersections. And a protest march disrupted the July Fourth "Liberty Weekend" at the Statue of Liberty that was being attended by President Ronald Reagan and Chief Justice Warren Burger. The news also sparked protests in Washington, D.C.; San Francisco; Cincinnati; and Dallas.

Both gay rights supporters and anti–gay rights politicians agreed that sodomy laws spoke to the fundamental question of whether or not society could accept homosexuals. "Sodomy laws have a much broader impact and scope than making gays *sexual* criminals," lawyer Arthur S. Leonard had written earlier that year in the *New York Native*, a gay paper. "In the judicial sphere, they have provided justification for denying child custody and visitation rights, licenses to engage in the professions, naturalization as American citizens, and a host of other civil and human rights that most people take for granted."

Noach Dear, an Orthodox Jewish New York City councilmember who had led a fight against a local gay rights bill, also viewed the ruling as significant. "The court has interpreted that a homosexual lifestyle is not a civil right and should not be exempted," Dear said in the July 1, 1986 edition of the *New York Times*. "It said they are not equal to heterosexuals." Or, as Moral Majority leader Jerry Falwell put it, the Court had held that "perverted moral behavior is not accepted practice in this country."

"The time for gay rage is now," the *Advocate* concluded in an editorial. The usually moderate newspaper went on to say, "The time has come for gays to use massive, widespread, creative acts of civil disobedience to help win fair treatment and equal rights." Indeed, besides the immediate local protests, gay activists responded by planning a march on Washington.

Those who opposed gay rights believed that *Hardwick* reinstated society's opposition to the "homosexual lifestyle," as Dear put it. But, perhaps ironically, *Hardwick* turned out to have little actual impact on U.S. sodomy law. Although the door seemed wide open to do so, no state ever reinstated a sodomy law in response to the decision, and two other states later took their sodomy laws off the books: Nevada (1993) and Rhode Island (1998). Moreover, the supreme courts of Kentucky (1992), Tennessee (1996), Montana (1997), and Georgia (1998) overturned their states' sodomy laws.

"Byron White had framed [*Bowers v. Hardwick*] as an appeal by homosexuals for special protections under the Constitution," explain gay rights chroniclers Clendenin and Nagourney in *Out for Good*. "But the public perception was that the nation's highest court had condoned the most far-fetched kind of government intrusion into private life. It was so shocking, and so reinforced the stereotypes that homosexuals had created of their opponents—sexual puritans peeping in through bedroom keyholes—that it produced a mocking defiance of the court that swept up newspaper editorialists, legal commentators, cartoonists, and talk show hosts."

Indeed, a Gallup poll for *Newsweek* found that Americans disapproved of the decision by 47 percent to 41 percent, and opposed by 57 percent to 34 percent the logical conclusion that "states should have the right to prohibit sexual practices conducted in private between consenting homosexual adults." (The poll was conducted on July 1 and 2, 1986 by telephone, of 611 adults, with a 5 percent margin of error.) It seemed that many Americans, gay and straight, agreed with the words of gay rights lawyer Tom Stoddard, writing in the *University of Chicago Law Review*, who commented, "The critical constitutional question in *Hardwick* was not what Michael Hardwick was doing in his bedroom, but rather what the state of Georgia was doing there."

Legal Protection

ROMER V. EVANS (1996)

Background

The story of *Romer v. Evans* begins in Colorado in 1992. The right-wing backlash that had swept the nation throughout the late 1970s and 1980s made itself felt in statewide referendums in Oregon and Colorado. Each vote would have overturned all local gay rights legislation in their respective states while prohibiting the further passage of antidiscrimination laws.

The Oregon measure, known as Proposition 9, called gay people "abnormal" and "perverse." It was defeated 57 percent to 43 percent. The following year, however antigay activists took the fight to a local level, and passed more than a dozen antigay initiatives in cities, towns, and counties.

Meanwhile, in Colorado, the antigay Amendment 2 passed 53 percent to 47 percent. The measure, which nullified existing gay rights laws in Denver, Boulder, and Aspen, provided that

> *Neither the State of Colorado . . . nor any of its agencies, political subdivisions, municipalities, or school districts, shall enact, adopt, or enforce any statute, regulation, ordinance or policy whereby homosexual, lesbian or bisexual orientation, conduct, practices or relationships shall constitute or otherwise be the basis of, or entitle any person or class or persons to have or claim any minority status, quota preferences, protected status or claim of discrimination. . . .*

After Colorado voters approved the referendum, a coalition of gay rights activists sued the state in 1996 as an effort to block the referendum from taking effect. The title of the case (*Romer v. Evans*) is actually misleading. Richard G. Evans, a civil servant in the Denver mayor's office, was a member of the gay rights coalition. Colorado governor Richard Romer was named as the defendant in the case as he was the chief executive of the state even though he personally opposed the referendum. After the initial court case ruled to overturn the referendum, the state appealed the case to the Supreme Court, thus making Romer the plaintiff in the Supreme Court case by name only.

The Law of Gay Rights

Legal Issues

Were gay people a privileged group using the law to win special rights, or were they a persecuted minority that had the right to seek necessary protection under the law? Right-wing organizations took the former position, which led them to sponsor Colorado's Amendment 2 as well as Oregon's Proposition 9. Under the Colorado amendment, gay men, lesbians, and bisexuals were a priori prevented from claiming discrimination or seeking protection under the law.

Gay rights groups took the second position—and objected strongly to a law that prevented them from seeking legal protection anywhere in the state of Colorado. NGLTF family policy director Paula Ettelbrick called the law "particularly vicious."

Decision

The U.S. Supreme Court struck Amendment 2 down. In his majority opinion, Justice Anthony M. Kennedy wrote a ringing denunciation of the amendment:

> *Amendment 2 classifies homosexuals not to further a proper legislative end but to make them unequal to everyone else. This Colorado cannot do. A state cannot so deem a class of person a stranger to its laws.*

In other words, the Court found that no state can simply rule against a group of people, denying them equal protection under the law. If *anyone* was allowed to seek legislative protection against discrimination under Colorado state law, gay men, lesbians, and bisexuals ought to be able to do so as well. For the first time, the highest court in the land had explicitly ruled that gay men and lesbians were entitled to the right of "equal protection under the law," which is guaranteed under the Fourteenth Amendment to the Constitution.

Justices Antonin Scalia, Clarence Thomas, and William Rehnquist dissented, in a minority opinion written by Scalia. First, Scalia took issue with the majority's opinion that "homosexuals" were a politically unpopular group that required the Court's protection. He found that notion "nothing short of preposterous" given their "enormous influence in American politics" and the fact that they composed "no more than 4% of the population [yet] had the support of 46% of the voters on Amendment 2."

Scalia also berated the court for "tak[ing] sides in the culture wars":

> *When the Court takes sides in the culture wars, it tends to . . . [reflect] the views and values of the lawyer class from which the Court's Members are drawn. How that class feels about homosexuality will be evident to anyone who wishes to interview applicants at virtually any of the Nation's law schools. The interviewer may refuse to offer a job because the applicant is a*

Republican; because he [sic] is an adulterer; because he went to the wrong prep school or belongs to the wrong country club; because he eats snails; because he is a womanizer; because she wears real-animal fur; or even because he hates the Chicago Cubs. But if the interviewer should wish not to be an associate or partner of an applicant because he disapproves of the applicant's homosexuality; then he will have violated the pledge which the Association of American Law Schools requires all its member-schools to exact from job interviewers: "assurance of the employers's willingness" to hire homosexuals.

In other words, Scalia did see "homosexuals" as a protected class with special rights—rights presumably not available to people who ate snails, wore real fur, had gone to the wrong prep school, or belonged to the Republican Party. He and his fellow signers of the minority opinion partook of the conservative view that sees gay rights not as "leveling the playing field" in a world where gay men and lesbians still face violence, loss of child custody, loss of jobs and housing, and other forms of discrimination; but rather as giving special protection to people who do not really need it.

Impact

Despite the minority opinion, most observers saw *Romer v. Evans* as an enormous victory for the gay rights movement—even if its implications have not yet become clear. Ettelbrick points out that the decision very specifically referred to laws that intentionally exclude gay men and lesbians from the state's protection. However, she explains, laws that were on the books from the years before the gay rights movement could not possibly be interpreted as intended to frustrate gay rights. A state law passed in 1932, for instance, that defines marriage as between a man and a woman would not necessarily come under *Romer* as making a class of people, such as gay men and lesbians, "stranger[s] to its laws." Rather, it would simply be seen as a law of its time, defining marriage as the people of the state saw fit.

"In *Romer*, the court turned an important corner and recognized that gay men and lesbians in this country have legitimate claims for equality," argues Mary Bonauto, civil rights director of the Boston-based Gay and Lesbian Advocates and Defenders. "That's an important tone to set for the Congress, state legislatures, and courts around the country."

Yet there are limits to *Romer* as a tool for gay rights. *Romer* extends the Constitution's equal protection to people targeted on hostile grounds, but it does not necessarily wipe out longstanding refusals of state and federal governments to recognize gay and lesbian rights. Nor does it necessarily prevent future anti–gay rights legislation from passing.

Reporter Joan Biskupic also wrote about the limits of *Romer* in the November 5, 1999 edition of the *Washington Post*: ". . . while [*Romer*] had an impact on some discrimination cases—particularly in the workplace—its actual legal reasoning was narrow and its influence, ultimately, limited. . . . As a result, changes in laws affecting gays have already responded to the shift in public attitudes rather than driving it. For example, despite major shifts in areas such as employment, custody and domestic partnership, there have been fewer gains in other areas where gay rights advocates had hoped to make substantial progress, particularly after the *Romer* ruling." Biskupic cites military policy and same-sex marriage as areas where *Romer* has ultimately had little effect.

"In urban America, particularly the Northeast, there have been enormous strides toward equality," says Yale University law professor William Eskridge, an authority on gay law. "But in a big chunk of the country, particularly the Deep South and West, people can still label us 'degenerates' and 'sex perverts.'"

Still, the effects of *Romer* have certainly been felt, if only in subtle ways. For example, on August 4, 1999 the New Jersey Supreme Court became the first state high court to rule against discrimination based on sexual orientation among the Boy Scouts of America. In *Dale v. Boy Scouts of America*, the court found that the organization's refusal to accept gay and bisexual men as members violates New Jersey's antidiscrimination law. Although there was no direct reference to *Romer*, echoes of the 1996 case could be heard in their ruling:

> . . . *a lesbian or gay person, merely because he or she is homosexual, is not more or less likely to be moral than a person who is heterosexual.*

The U.S. Supreme Court reversed this decision, though, on June 28, 2000.

FEDERAL COURT CASES

Federal Employment

NORTON V. MACY (1969)

Background

Early on the morning of October 22, 1963 a budget analyst at the National Aeronautics and Space Administration (NASA) was driving his car around Lafayette Square, a well-known gay cruising area in Washington, D.C. The driver picked up another man, drove once around the square, and dropped his passenger off where he had found him. This behavior was observed by two police officers in the morals squad, a special unit charged with watching out for acts considered immoral, such as prostitution, drug dealing, and homosexual behavior. The driver was arrested, as was the passenger, Madison Monroe Proctor, who said that the driver had felt his leg and invited him up for a drink. The men were taken to the morals office, while the head of the morals squad called the driver's boss, NASA's chief of security. The employee, Norton, was fired, because, in the words of the eventual federal court ruling:

> *NASA concluded that appellant [Norton] did in fact make a homosexual advance on October 22, and that this act amounted to "immoral, indecent, and disgraceful conduct." It also determined that, on the basis of his own admissions to [the NASA Security Chief] . . . appellant possesses "traits of character and personality which render [him] unsuitable for further Government employment."*

This judgment was upheld by various levels of the civil service, so Norton appealed his case to the Supreme Court.

Legal Issues

At stake in *Norton v. Macy* was the extent to which immoral or illegal behavior should disqualify a person from holding a federal job. At the time of the case, there was no question that Norton had admitted to certain acts that were illegal in the District of Columbia—and generally regarded as immoral by mainstream society. Yet should such illegal and apparently immoral behavior constitute a reason for firing a federal employee?

Decision

The court took no exception to Norton's arrest, or to the law under which he was arrested. But, the court ruled, even if Norton *had* been guilty of "immoral, indecent, and disgraceful conduct," it was not the government's business to police the private behavior of its employees:

> *. . . the notion that it could be an appropriate function of the federal bureaucracy to enforce the majority's conventional codes of conduct in the private lives of its employees is at war with elementary concepts of liberty, privacy, and diversity.*

The only way a person's immorality could be of concern to a federal employer, said the court, was if that immorality specifically impinged upon the person's ability to perform his or her duties.

The court was at pains to specify that homosexuality might indeed be an impediment to performing some federal jobs. The risk of blackmail, the possibility of personal instability, the prospect of offensive overtures to others in the workplace, and the dangers of conduct that might bring embarrassment to the agency were all acceptable reasons to fire a gay person or to refuse to hire one. However, to fire someone for being gay, a federal employer had to establish the connection between being gay and being unfit for a particular job. It could not justify a firing "merely by turning its head and crying 'shame,'" to quote the circuit court ruling.

Impact

Norton v. Macy established what came to be known as the "rational nexus" test—the notion that being gay did not per se make a person unfit for employment. Rather, there had to be a *rational nexus* (a set of interconnected reasons) to believe that the person would be unfit. Since Norton was a competent employee, did not have access to classified documents, had kept his coworkers unaware of his conduct, and did not have contact with the public, there were no rational grounds for firing him.

Although in later cases the courts were able to find a rational nexus between homosexuality and unfitness based on what gay rights advocates considered extremely weak criteria, the changing attitudes of the 1970s began to have their effect. Moreover, the fact that so many gay men and lesbians were now open about their sexuality meant that their sexual lives could no longer be a cause for blackmail. In 1971, in a kind of legacy of *Norton v. Macy*, the *Washington Post* actually criticized the Civil Service Commission for its blanket prohibition against homosexuals, claiming that gay employees' "private sexual behavior is their own business."

STATE COURT CASES

Free Speech and Assembly

GAY STUDENTS ORGANIZATION OF THE UNIVERSITY OF NEW HAMPSHIRE V. BONNER (1974)

Background

This case involved the Gay Students Organization (GSO), which on November 9, 1973 sponsored a dance on the University of New Hampshire campus. "After the dance," according to the state supreme court's ruling, "there was criticism by the Governor of New Hampshire, who complained to the University about the propriety of allowing such a 'spectacle.'"

Then the GSO sponsored a play, which was presented on December 7, 1973. "Although the play itself caused little comment," the court decision explained, "there was some reaction to 'Fag Rag Five' and 'Fag Rag VI,' two 'extremist homosexual' publications which were distributed sometime during the evening." (*Fag Rag* was a Boston-based gay newspaper, known for its provocative writing on sexuality.) As a result, the governor of New Hampshire wrote an open letter to the university's board of trustees, in which he stated that "indecency and moral filth will no longer be allowed on our campuses. Either you take firm, fair and positive action to rid your campuses of socially abhorrent activities or I, as governor, will stand solidly against the expenditure of one more cent of taxpayers' money for your institutions." In other words, stop gay activity on campus or risk losing funding.

Legal Issues

From the point of view of gay rights supporters, the issue was the right of gay students to assemble freely, as guaranteed under the First Amendment. From the point of view of gay rights opponents, the matter concerned the right of a public university to determine what kinds of activities were appropriate for its campus.

Decision

The supreme court found for the GSO. "[T]his case is quite simple," the decision read. "The First Amendment guarantees all individuals, including university students, the right to organize and associate 'to further their personal beliefs.'" Unless the university could show compelling reason not to do so, it was required to recognize any "bona fide student organization and grant to that organization the rights and privileges which normally flow from such recognition."

Impact

Bonner established the right of gay students to form organizations at public universities and colleges. The case was important to gay student groups fighting for the right to form clubs at private universities in the 1980s and at high schools in the 1990s.

Family Recognition/Housing

BRASCHI V. STAHL ASSOCIATES CO. (1989)

Background

Miguel Braschi and Leslie Blanchard were two men who had lived together in a rent-controlled Manhattan apartment for nearly a decade. When Blanchard died, the building owner threatened to evict Braschi, since only Blanchard's name was on the lease. Had Blanchard and Braschi been a heterosexual married couple, Braschi would have had the right to retain the lease; as the survivor in a gay couple, Braschi seemed to have no rights. He took the landlord to the highest court in the state of New York, referring to the New York City rent-control regulation forbidding eviction of "either the surviving spouse of the deceased tenant or some other member of the deceased tenant's family."

Legal Issues

At stake in *Braschi* was the legal recognition of a gay domestic partnership. Since U.S. lesbians and gay men cannot get married, gay rights activists and opponents are both keenly interested in the various ways in which legal recognition can be accorded to their de facto arrangements.

Decision

The court found for Braschi, ruling that he was a surviving spouse or member of Blanchard's family and therefore entitled to a share in Blanchard's lease:

> . . . we conclude that the term family, as used in [the regulation], should not be rigidly restricted to those people who have formalized their relationship by obtaining, for instance, a marriage certificate or an adoption order. The intended protection against sudden eviction should not rest on fictitious legal distinctions or genetic history, but instead should find its foundation in the reality of family life. In the context of eviction, a more realistic, and certainly equally valid, view of a family includes two adult lifetime partners whose relationship is long-term and characterized by an emotional and financial commitment and interdependence. This view comports both with our society's traditional concept of "family" and with the expectations of individuals who live in such nuclear units. . . .

In its consideration of Braschi and Blanchard's family life, the court noted approvingly that the two men had lived together as permanent life partners for more than 10 years, regarding each other and being regarded by others, as spouses:

> The two men's families were aware of the nature of the relationship, and they regularly visited each other's families and attended family functions together, as a couple. Even today, appellant [Braschi] continues to maintain a relationship with Blanchard's niece, who considers him an uncle.

The court went on to cite the financial involvement of the two men—Blanchard had given Braschi power of attorney, left him his estate, and named him beneficiary of his life insurance policy; the two men shared checking and savings accounts and credit cards. "Hence," the ruling concluded, "a court examining these facts could reasonably conclude that these men were much more than mere roommates."

Impact

As the result of the *Braschi* ruling, the New York State Housing Agency went on to announce a broader definition of family that explicity included same-sex couples. In a community decimated by AIDS, in which many surviving partners were not named on the leases of their own homes, this had enormous significance for both the gay rights and the tenants movement.

CHAPTER 3

GAY RIGHTS AND U.S. CULTURE

As discussed in previous chapters, the term "gay rights" has many different senses. It can indicate a political movement, whose expression is found in the growing number of gay and lesbian politicians, and in the increasing prevalence of gay rights legislation: antidiscrimination measures, domestic partnership benefits, and hate crimes legislation. It might indicate a legal status: whether or not homosexuality is criminalized via sodomy laws, whether gay and lesbian parents are considered unfit by the courts in child custody cases, or whether gay student groups have the right to meet on public and private campuses.

"Gay rights" may also be used in a more general sense, to express the place of gay men and lesbians in U.S. culture. Students of the issue might ask whether gay rights has progressed to the point where Americans take for granted the representation of gay men and lesbians in popular culture, as characters on TV shows and in movies, as figures in advertising, and as popular musicians. Or they might look at the extent to which gay people feel safe coming out in various occupations. They could look at the way gay issues are represented in the news media. Or they could examine the extent to which gay men and lesbians have won full participation in religion, education, and civic organizations, such as the Boy Scouts of America. All of these areas of inquiry would reveal something about the kinds of rights enjoyed by gay men and lesbians in the United States at this point in history.

As with the study of political, historical, and legal views of gay rights, examining gays' place in the culture is rife with contradiction. A lesbian mother in Mississippi may lose custody of her child to her husband's parents even as the coming-out episode of *Ellen* wins millions of viewers and sympathetic media coverage. A gay autoworker at Chrysler faces harassment and physical attack, while a gay stockbroker brings the first gay rights suit on Wall Street, even as the tiny Republican town of Plattsburgh in upstate New York elects its first gay mayor, or as a regional board of the Presbyterian Church votes to allow ministers in 95 churches to perform same-sex commitment ceremonies (though not gay marriages). On the one hand, gay

101

men and lesbians are visible and empowered in our culture as never before; on the other hand, gay people still face physical, emotional, and economic abuse that ranges from losing a job to being denied membership in a church to being attacked or even murdered for their sexual orientation.

Most observers of the gay rights movement note its contradictory nature—the remarkably swift progress accompanied by the extremely violent backlash.

And, as with all historically oppressed groups, the mainstream society's view of gay men and lesbians—and many gay people's view of themselves—is complicated by stereotypes and misinformation. In a column in the November 1999 issue of *Out* magazine, Pat Califia takes issue with the prevailing image of gay people as more affluent than the rest of the society. She reports on the 1996 study by the Simmons Market Research Bureau, conducted in conjunction with the Mulryan/Nash advertising agency, which found that 21 percent of all gay people live in households with incomes over $100,000, while 22 percent hold graduate degrees. But, Califia points out, the study was "hardly representative": it was based on a sample taken from the mailing lists of political groups, mail-order firms, and credit card companies, and so was skewed to higher incomes.

Califia cites a more accurate study, conducted by University of Massachusetts economist M. V. Lee Badgett, which relied on figures from six different random samples that included information on sexual orientation, along with the 1990 U.S. Census. Badgett's study painted a far different picture than that of the "affluent DINKS" (dual income, no kids) frequently referred to in both mainstream and gay media. "When the data were adjusted for variables such as education, location, occupation, experience, and race," Califia reports, "Badgett found that gay men who worked full time earned as much as 27 percent less than similar straight men. No income disparity between lesbians and straight women was found, but it's well documented that all women's earnings lag behind those of men."

A comprehensive assessment of gay men and lesbians in U.S. culture is clearly beyond the scope of this book. This chapter highlights some of the key areas for gay rights that seem to go beyond strictly legal rights (although courts and legislatures may be involved), specifically discussing gay activity in culture, education, and religion.

FREE SPEECH AND COMMERCIAL SUCCESS: GAY CULTURE IN THE 1990s

The 1990s began in the wake of a major cultural battle for supporters of gay rights. In 1989, the work of the late gay photographer Robert Mapplethorpe, which included homoerotic images of nude men, was featured in a traveling exhibit that appeared in a number of museums around the country, including the Contemporary Arts Center of Cincinnati. Mapplethorpe's more controversial images featured sadomasochistic imagery, including a self-portrait of himself naked except for a leather cap and jacket with a bullwhip inserted in his anus. Also in the exhibit was a photograph of a man's torso in a three-piece suit, with a large black penis sticking out of the unzipped pants.

Recognizing the potentially volatile nature of the exhibition, officials restricted access to the museum to those over the age of 18, and even removed images felt to be disturbing or explicit to a special, isolated room. Nevertheless, a local sheriff raided the exhibit and eventually obtained a grand jury indictment against museum director Dennis Barrie on obscenity charges. Although he was eventually acquitted, Barrie left the museum.

Meanwhile, the exhibit had been funded by the National Endowment for the Arts (NEA) to travel around the country and was slated to go on to a museum in Washington, D.C. In response, Senator Jesse Helms and the religious right charged that public funds should not be used to support "pornography," particularly in the nation's capital.

Attacks on the NEA continued. In 1990, NEA head John Frohnmayer, fearing further obscenity charges, withdrew grants that had been made to four performance artists—Karen Finley, Holly Hughes, Tim Miller, and John Fleck. Hughes, Miller, and Fleck were leading figures in gay culture, while Finley, publicly identified as straight, was known for the way her work challenged narrow ideas of gender and criticized the sexual and social repression of women. Each of the "NEA Four" had already been approved by an independent panel of artists, so Frohnmayer's action struck many as, if not outright censorship, a high-handed government intervention to curtail artistic freedom. Moreover, under pressure from the religious right, the NEA went on to include a "decency clause" in all of its grants: to get public money, recipients had to promise not to do "obscene" work.

Public outrage at gay culture continued in various forms throughout the 1990s. In Charlotte, North Carolina, for example, a progressive city known as "the showplace of the South," the Mecklenburg County Commission voted to stop funding organizations that exposed the public to "perverted forms of sexuality." The commission's action was inspired by a local production of *Angels in America*, the Pulitzer Prize–winning play by Tony Kushner featuring several gay characters. *Angels* had won several awards on Broadway, where it had played for several months, and the show soon became a favorite of regional theaters around the United States. Since the local production was presented by the Charlotte Repertory Theater, which received some funding from the county, county commissioners felt justified in cutting funds to the arts council that had funded the theater, to prevent further support for images of "deviant sex." Although to gay rights sup-

porters, the play merely presented recognizable portraits of gay men, opponents were outraged by the play's matter-of-fact acceptance of homosexuality and its images of (fully clothed) men embracing as a prelude to having
sex.

The commission's action drew fire from local gay and lesbian activists—
and from the local business community, which feared that the antigay and
anti-art activity would make Charlotte look provincial and unfit to host the
many banks and corporate headquarters it was courting. A mere week after
the county commissioners voted, executives from a wide variety of groups—
including the Charlotte-based NationsBank Corporation, First Union Corporation, Duke Power Company, and the local Urban League—announced
a campaign directed against the offending politicians, who were facing reelection the following year.

The leader of the county commission's action was Hoyle Martin, an
African American originally from New York City who voted with socially
conservative white Republicans to get his measure passed. Martin admitted
that these politicians did not usually represent the interests of his inner-city
constituents. But he was willing to make common cause with them against
the more liberal elements on the commission in order to discourage homosexuality, which he considered one of America's greatest threats.

The actions of Helms, Frohnmayer, and Martin took place against a
growing visibility of gay culture in America, most notably on television, but
also in movies, theater, popular music, and the literary world. When both
TV comedian Ellen DeGeneres and her character came out as lesbians in
the spring of 1997, the move caused both more and less furor than anyone
expected. On the one hand, advertisers such as the Chrysler Corporation
pulled their commercials from *Ellen*'s "coming out" episode, and individual
stations, like one in Birmingham, Alabama refused to air the April 30
episode. When a Birmingham gay comedian tried to rent a theater to show
the episode, the theater owner refused, saying that the issue was "too controversial." (The comedian was eventually able to rent a city-owned theater.)

Moreover, millions of people watched Ellen come out on Disney-owned
ABC-TV, and the show was renewed for the following season. When *Ellen*
was finally pulled from the air, it was not due to any political controversy,
but rather because of low ratings. The openly gay DeGeneres has gone on
to appear in such mainstream movies as *EdTV,* a 1999 comedy directed by
Ron Howard, while her former lover, Anne Heche, starred in a variety of
big-budget films with big-name costars like Harrison Ford.

In March 1999, the conservative Christian Action Network tried to stem
the tide of gay themes and characters on television by calling for an "HC"—
"homosexual content"—rating to be attached to every TV show with a gay

character. Max Mutchnick, openly gay cocreator of the show *Will & Grace*, which features two openly gay characters, responded calmly: "[HC is] totally offensive, but it adds up to nothing. The numbers are telling us everything." Indeed, according to Scott Seomin, entertainment media director of the Gay and Lesbian Alliance Against Defamation (GLAAD), the spring 1999 TV season featured more than 25 gay or bisexual characters on network series, with more new gay characters featured on shows the following fall. If anything, the trend is for even more openly gay characters to populate the small screen.

The big screen has not been as inclusive. Although big-budget Hollywood movies like *In and Out* and *The Birdcage* have drawn a certain amount of attention, most of the increased attention to gay culture in the movies has come from independent filmmakers, such as lesbian filmmaker Rose Troche (*Bedrooms and Hallways*, 1999) or first-time director Don Roos (*The Opposite of Sex*, 1997). Gay characters are also coming to populate the margins of otherwise "straight" films, such as *Happy, Texas* (1999), which features a gay sheriff who becomes involved in a larger comic mix-up in which two straight men must pretend to be gay.

More striking is the new openness of mainstream publishers to gay and lesbian authors. The *New York Blade*, a gay newspaper, publishes its own best-seller list, made up of the top-selling books at a number of gay and women's bookstores nationwide. Their November 1999 list included a number of books published by mainstream presses, including Penguin (Jaye Zimet's *Strange Sisters: The Art of Lesbian Pulp Fiction, 1949–1969*), St. Martin's (Paul Russell's novel *The Coming Storm*), Simon and Schuster (Brad Gooch's memoir and self-help book, *Finding the Boyfriend Within*), Consortium (Rik Isenee's celebration of gay midlife, *Are You Ready?*; Michael Thomas Ford's memoir, *That's Mr. Faggot to You: Further Trials From My Queer Life;* Dan Woog's *Friends and Family: True Stories of Gay America's Straight Allies*); Dutton (Dan Savage's *The Kid: What Happened After My Boyfriend and I Decided to Go Get Pregnant: An Adoption Story*); and J.P. Tarcher (Christian de la Huerta's *Coming Out Spiritually*). For anyone who remembers the time when homophile magazines had to be sent to anonymous post office boxes in brown paper wrappers, this list is truly remarkable.

On the other hand, it is not insignificant that the *Blade*'s best-seller list is divided into "Women's books," "Men's books," and "General Interest"—and that four of the five women's best-sellers are published by the veteran lesbian/gay presses Naiad and Alyson. With some notable exceptions—Dorothy Allison, Sarah Schulman, Sapphire, Adrienne Rich—it has been far harder for lesbian writers and poets to be published than for gay men.

In response to the extreme difficulty of being accepted into the mainstream, as well as from a genuine commitment to alternatives, lesbian cultural institutions flourished in the 1970s. Kitchen Table Press, for women of color; Crossing Press's feminist series; Spinsters Ink; Firebrand; Aunt Lute; and Diana Press were only some of the women's publishers that released lesbian novels and poetry, self-help books, anthologies, and political analyses, publishing authors like Jewelle Gomez, Sally Gearheart, Adrienne Rich, Audre Lorde, Jane Rule, Cherrie Moraga, and Barbara Smith. Yet, the same cultural acceptance that has enabled lesbian novelist Dorothy Allison (*Bastard Out of Carolina, Cavedweller*) to find a home with a commercial press, has also helped drive many alternative publishers out of business.

The 1970s and 1980s were also a time of "women's music," with events like the annual Michigan Womyn's Festival, and with performers like Holly Near, Meg Christian, Cris Williamson, Margie Adam, and Alix Dobkin as regular fixtures on the women's concert circuit. Many of these women recorded with Olivia, a women's record company that for a time expanded into a virtual network of women's businesses, including a travel agency. Partly driven by a separatist ideal and partly inspired by a utopian image of women's community, lesbian feminists and other women ran a wide range of businesses, from bookstores to coffeehouses to vegetarian restaurants. Observers who remember the 1970s and 1980s applaud women's new ability to reach a wider audience, even as they lament the growing commercialization, standardization, and depoliticization of lesbian culture. This commodification of lesbian culture reached a peak in May 1993 with a *New York* magazine cover article declaring the advent of "lesbian chic," which presented female same-sex relationships as glamorous, slightly exotic alternatives to heterosexual relationships. For many lesbians, this image of them as sexy, urbane women was a welcome relief from the popular stereotype that portrays them as mannish, unattractive asexuals. Many others, though, were disturbed by the implication that lesbianism was merely a set of lifestyle poses that could be put on and discarded at will.

Meanwhile, gay and lesbian voices are heard in the mainstream music world to an extent unimaginable only 20 years ago. Throughout the 1990s, many world-famous musicians openly declared their homosexuality, with little or no impact on their commercial popularity. One of the first to do so was 1970s British rock star, and now Broadway composer, Elton John, who has gone on to be a major celebrity advocate for gay rights and AIDS research and prevention. Other British pop stars to come out of the closet include Boy George, who had early in his career used his sexual ambiguity as a way to distinguish himself from other singers, and George Michael, who was unwillingly outed when he was arrested in April 1998 for indecently exposing himself to a male undercover police officer in a Beverly Hills, California public restroom. Both have since become vocal supporters of gay rights, as has the Irish singer Sinead O'Connor, who came out in the spring of 2000.

As of this writing, no significant American male pop star has openly identified himself as gay; however, several prominent North American women musicians have chosen to make their sexuality public. Among them are k.d. lang who, in 1992, became the first major lesbian singer to come out. She chose to make her announcement in the pages of *Vanity Fair* magazine, which posed her and model Cindy Crawford in a very provocative cover photo: lang is in a barber chair, her face lathered in shaving cream, while Crawford pretends to shave her—a scenario that lang describes in the article's interview as a fantasy of hers. Such an unambiguous representation of lesbian sexual fantasy in a mainstream publication had been unheard of until then and was an indication of how far the culture had come in tolerating depictions of same-sex desire. On the other hand, the Indigo Girls (Amy Ray and Emily Saliers), also openly lesbian, faced discrimination in May 1998, when they gave a series of free concerts at high schools in three Southern states. Parents in South Carolina and Tennessee objected to their presence at the schools because of their sexual orientation, forcing the duo to cancel three concerts. Another prominent lesbian entertainer, Melissa Etheridge, along with her partner Julie Cypher, has become a vocal spokesperson for gay parents. When Cypher was pregnant with their first child, she and Etheridge posed for the cover of *Newsweek* magazine because, as they told *Rolling Stone* in February 2000, they felt "it meant something to the (gay and lesbian) community." Given how little coming out has hurt these musicians' careers, it is likely that this trend will continue into the future.

The gay and lesbian magazine world faces many of the same issues as the alternative press. Many of the early gay and lesbian publications identified deeply with gay rights, feminism, sexual liberation, and/or gay liberation. Journals like *Fag Rag*, *Gay Sunshine*, and *Come Out!* celebrated the exciting new post-Stonewall gay identity, while newspapers like *The New York Native* and the California-based *The Advocate* were considered political vehicles as much as sources of information. One short-lived but extremely influential publication was *Outweek*, which was produced in New York from June 1989 to June 1991. Among other things, *Outweek* served as an important voice of the AIDS activist community; was instrumental in the promotion of the term "queer" as a replacement for the words "gay" and "lesbian"; and introduced the concept of "outing" (the practice of publically disclosing a celebrity's or politician's sexual orientation, usually against his or her wishes) through the weekly column of staff writer Michelangelo Signorile. Many members of the gay and lesbian community, though, found *Outweek*'s politics to be too radical and its attitude toward straight people too hostile. As a result, it never found a wide, national readership or large companies willing to buy ad space in its pages. Today, glossy publications like *Out* and *POZ* (for people with HIV/AIDS) feature ads from Fortune 500 companies and profiles of heterosexual movie stars along with their coverage of gay politics and culture. Furthering the trend to a more mainstream, "corporate" model of gay and lesbian publishing, in February 2000 *Out* announced that it had been acquired by Liberation Publications, the company that publishes the *Advocate*. Liberation now controls the two magazines with the widest specifically homosexual readership. What this bodes for the future of gay and lesbian journalism nationally remains to be seen.

The dilemma in gay and lesbian culture parallels the larger tensions in gay and lesbian politics: accessibility versus political clarity; assimilation versus the maintenance of a unique identity; commercialization versus an alternative vision. Some might find a mainstream publisher's release of a gay male self-help book revolutionary, or at least a sign that gay men have finally been accepted into the culture at large. Others see the event as symbolic of cooptation, the loss of a uniquely gay perspective in the face of mass cultural homogenization. And the extent to which lesbian culture remains more marginalized and less commercial than gay male culture is suggested by the fact that, despite the hundreds of self-help books available to straight women, no commercial publisher has yet brought out an equivalent volume for lesbians.

EDUCATION

There are three major issues in education for gay men and lesbians: the rights of gay and lesbian teachers, the rights—and safety—of gay/lesbian students, and the nature of school curriculum. As with other issues we have examined, there is quite a bit of overlap between legal issues—court cases, referendums, legislation—and cultural issues—the general level of acceptance for lesbians and gay men in our society.

GAY TEACHERS' RIGHTS

One of the first incidents involving a gay teacher's right to be politically active was the case of John Gish, a high school teacher in Paramus, New Jersey, who was fired in 1972 for accepting the presidency of the local Gay Activists Alliance. The case continued through 1980, when Gish's firing was upheld by New Jersey State Education Commissioner Fred G. Burke, who called Gish's activism "conduct unbecoming to a teacher."

Another turning point for gay teachers' rights came in 1977, when the Oklahoma state legislature unanimously passed a law requiring gay and lesbian teachers to be dismissed and banning the favorable mention of homosexuality in the public schools. The legislation was challenged in a case that went to the Supreme Court in 1985. The Court invalidated the law by a tie vote of 4-4, giving many unwarranted optimism when *Bowers v. Hardwick* came before the Court the following year.

As discussed in Chapter 1, the 1978 Briggs Initiative sought to achieve a similar goal via referendum in the state of California. Proposition 6 would also have removed all gay teachers from the school system, as well as banning positive references to "homosexual" behavior. The initiative, however, was defeated, which seemed to many to be an affirmation, albeit backhanded, of gay and lesbian teachers' right to teach.

Throughout the 1970s, 1980s, and 1990s, gay and lesbian teachers fought a number of battles across the nation. In 1993, for example, the Tenth Circuit Court of Appeals ruled that school officials in Kansas could legally refuse to hire a teacher who was suspected of being gay. Even though the applicant in question was heterosexual, the court upheld the district's right not to hire him.

In the more gay-positive atmosphere of the 1990s, teachers have tended to fight back more often than before—and, occasionally, they win. Wendy Weaver, for example, was a teacher and volleyball coach in Spanish Fork, Utah. After acknowledging to a student that she was a lesbian, she was fired from the coaching part of her job and put under a gag order: she was told that if she discussed her sexual orientation with "students, staff members or parents of students," she would be fired. In December 1998, Weaver won a suit overturning the gag order. She says she has felt no retaliation from the school district, which did not appeal the decision and which obeyed the court's order to offer her the coaching job again. Weaver has declined the coaching job but says she has a new principal who is supportive—and her classes are filled. However, a group of right-wing parents have filed their own lawsuit, seeking Weaver's removal from the classroom.

In some cases, gay and lesbian teachers have been able to turn to their communities or their unions. The California Teachers Association (CTA), for example, took up the case of Jim Merrick, a 40-year classroom veteran and winner of the 1996 Chamber of Commerce Teacher of the Year Award in a rural district outside Bakersfield, California. Merrick spoke out anonymously against a local politician who called gay people "sick." Somehow, his own sexuality became known to parents, who began to remove their children from his classroom. Merrick and his union fought the administration's concession to the transfer requests, which they claimed violated the state Labor Code's provisions against job discrimination on the basis of "actual or perceived sexual orientation." Merrick also filed a complaint with the state and took medical leave due to job-related stress.

But Merrick intends to return and fight. Alluding to the 1998 case in Wyoming in which a gay college student was murdered, Merrick said, "I don't want another Matthew Shepard to happen, if I can help in any way. I've got lots of gay and lesbian kids in that school who are . . . getting the wrong message. We need to send them a different message."

"Gay teachers realize they have more resources than before," says Jim Anderson, communications director for the Gay, Lesbian, Straight Education Network (GLSEN), a national organization devoted to fighting homophobia in the schools. "We have bigger organizations, like GLSEN, like Lambda [Legal Defense and Education Fund], to help gay and lesbian teachers come out of the closet and fight for their rights."

Many gay and lesbian teachers are still in the closet, according to GLSEN executive director Kevin Jennings, because of the "unwritten contract that gay teachers have been given for eternity: 'You can keep your job, as long as you keep your mouth shut forever.'" But Jennings looks for change as teachers fight back.

Both opponents and supporters of gay rights have raised another issue: the right of parents to determine who shall—or shall not—be allowed to teach their child. Do teachers have rights that outweigh a parent's right to have a child moved to another classroom? Should groups that protect the rights of teachers also show concern for parents' legitimate concerns about what kind of classroom environment they want for their children? Some teachers argue that their districts would oppose a parent's move to transfer a child to avoid a teacher on the grounds of race, age, or physical handicap, while allowing parents to transfer students away from lesbian and gay teachers. But what about a parent's wish to have a teacher that is simply "more compatible" with the child, or one who shares the parent's own political, philosophic, or moral views? How should parents' rights be balanced with a school district's commitment to diversity and tolerance? These are questions that may be raised more often as gay and lesbian educators receive more recognition.

STUDENT RIGHTS

In 1980, a Providence, Rhode Island gay teenager named Aaron Fricke made history when he sued for the right to bring a male date to his high school prom. Fricke's 1995 memoir of the incident, *Reflections of a Rock Lobster*, introduced much of the United States to the existence of "out and proud" gay teenagers.

The 1982 establishment of Philadelphia's Byton High, the nation's first high school for gays and lesbians, likewise affirmed that young gay men and women had the right to receive support as they claimed their identities. In 1985, the New York City Board of Education followed suit by establishing the Harvey Milk School for gays and lesbians.

More than ever before, gay and straight students are now working together to overcome homophobia and promote awareness of gay issues. (In Chapter 2, for example, the efforts of HHART, a gay-straight student alliance at Smoky Hill High School outside Denver, was discussed.)

Aaron Fricke described a remarkably tolerant climate for himself and his date in 1980. Many other gay and lesbian teenagers, however, have suffered from teasing, harassment, and outright physical danger in school districts across the nation. Jamie Nobozny, a Wisconsin teenager, made history in 1996 when he became the first student to bring a successful suit against the school authorities that had failed to protect the young man from harassment that occurred beginning in the seventh grade and continuing through eleventh grade, including beatings that required hospitalization. As of early 2000, nine similar suits were pending, including cases in California, Illinois, Minnesota, Missouri, New Jersey, and Washington.

In Doug Ireland's January 31, 2000 *Nation* article, "Gay Teens Fight Back," California student Jared Nayfack described an incident on a trip sponsored by his Catholic high school, during which he was beaten to "a bloody mess" by a bigger student who, he said, "could have killed [him]." The other student was not punished; instead, Jared was put on academic and behavioral probation and was told by the dean that "I was at fault because I'd 'threatened the masculinity' of the kid who'd beat me up."

"Five or ten years ago, kids would go to a youth service agency and say, 'I need help because I think I'm gay,'" says Rea Carey, quoted in the same article. Carey is the executive director of the National Youth Advocacy Coalition (NYAC), a coalition of various service agencies that supports gay youth. "Today, more and more they say, 'I'm gay and so what? . . .' Being gay is not their problem, it's their strength. These kids are coming out at 13, 14, 15. . . . But they are experiencing more violence because of that."

A number of studies support the perception that gay and lesbian youth are at risk of violence, even in their own schools. A study of some 4,000 high school students conducted by the Massachusetts Department of Education found that 22.2 percent of students who identified themselves as gay, lesbian, or bisexual were likely to skip school because of feeling unsafe, as opposed to only 3.3 percent of other students. A 1997 study conducted by the Vermont Department of Health discovered that 24 percent of gay students had been threatened or injured with a weapon at school, as opposed to 8 percent of straight students. Moreover, a November 1998 poll conducted by *Who's Who Among American High School Students*—focusing on some 3,000 high school students considered "America's brightest"—found that 48 percent considered themselves prejudiced against homosexuals, up 19 percent from the previous year.

A number of states have responded by making efforts to pass safe-school legislation. Yet Republican parties in a number of states—including California, Colorado, Delaware, Illinois, New York, Texas, and Washington— have opposed such legislation. The California bill eventually passed, and the New York bill is still in committee as of this writing.

Meanwhile, Massachusetts has had a strong anti–gay harassment law in place since 1993 (supported by then-governor William Weld, a Republican). And on February 4, 1999 the Hawaii Board of Education voted to add sexual orientation as a protected category in the student misconduct and discipline code, which would enable students to be punished for antigay actions. The board was responding to testimony by gay and lesbian students who said they had been teased, chased, and beaten in school because they were gay or perceived to be gay.

SCHOOL CURRICULUM

If the "unwritten contract" that Jennings spoke of requires gay and lesbian teachers to remain silent about their sexual identities, it also requires teachers of all orientations to abstain from talking about gay and lesbian issues in a positive or even-handed way. As we have seen, many efforts to ban gay teachers have also been attempts to ban gay curriculum—or even the mere mention of homosexuality within school walls.

The debate about curriculum is taking place in a climate in which the religious right is trying to ban any kind of sex education in the schools and/or ensure that sexual abstinence is presented as the best option for teenagers. Given the antisex and antigay climate of many school districts, teachers' efforts to establish that there are indeed "many different kinds of families," and that some major historical and literary figures were gay, is an uphill battle.

One of the most famous curriculum battles took place in the New York City school system in 1993, when the so-called Rainbow Curriculum was adopted by schools chancellor Joseph Fernandez. The Rainbow Curriculum stressed cultural and ethnic diversity, and included materials about the positive contributions of African Americans, Latinos, women, and other groups ignored or undervalued by more traditional curricula. Fewer than five pages out of several dozen were devoted to gay men and lesbians, but the curriculum did recommend the children's book *Heather Has Two Mommies*, by Lesléa Newman, which presents a positive portrayal of a girl who lives with a lesbian couple.

The "gay portion" of the curriculum came under particular attack from five school districts in the conservative New York City borough of Queens, which saw the positive portrayal of homosexuality as an affront to their religious freedom and their right to consider homosexuality a sin. Also, many African-American parents and educators were distressed at the Rainbow Curriculum's gay-positive slant, and what had been a vital coalition of a broad range of progressive groups fell apart over the issue of homophobia. Fernandez had to resign as a result of the incident; *Heather* as well as its male counterpart, *Daddy's Roommate*, still remain controversial books in many school districts and public libraries.

On the other hand, a growing number of young adult books are being published every year, on topics ranging from sexually transmitted diseases to coming out to one's parents to learning how to get along with many different types of people. In a climate where openly gay people appear on MTV's reality-based show *The Real World* and where teenagers can watch the troubles of a fictitious gay high school student on a popular TV serial (*Dawson's Creek*), many high schools, middle schools, and even grade schools are taking a more open attitude toward presenting—or at least allowing— gay and lesbian images within school walls. This tolerance varies widely, however, depending on the larger community's tolerance, and on whether an organized antigay group has decided to focus on school curriculum.

RELIGION

One of the greatest challenges to organized religion in the 1990s has been the demand of gay men and lesbians to be welcomed fully into various denominations—to be given the right to join the church, marry, and become ordained. These demands have been posed in various ways—gay Catholics have formed Dignity; gay Episcopalians, Integrity; many gay Jews and Christians have founded their own synagogues and churches. And churches have responded in various ways—some denominations or movements have fully welcomed gay men and lesbians, some have allowed gay members but not gay religious leaders, some have welcomed gay people while abhorring the idea of homosexuality, and some have refused to accept gay men and women altogether. It is safe to say that no religious group in the United States has remained entirely untouched by the new religious presence of gay men and lesbians, however they have chosen to respond. Even conservative evangelist Jerry Falwell, whose Moral Majority has long been a mainstay of antigay activism, recently apologized to gay men and lesbians "for not always loving homosexuals," as he was quoted by Caryle Murphy in "Mutual Apology for Hateful Speech; Christian Right Leader Falwell, Gay Rights Activist Talk Tolerance," an October 24, 1999 article in the *Washington Post.*

Falwell's apology came in the wake of his meeting with a gay evangelical group led by his former ghostwriter, the Reverend Mel White. "My ultimate goal, I'll make no bones about it, is to bring them out of the lifestyle and to the Lord," Falwell told reporters in Lynchburg, Virginia, following his October 23, 1999 meeting with the gay activist group, as quoted in the October 24, 1999 *Washington Post* article (see Appendix C). White initially stressed that he and Falwell had remained friends, even after White declared his own homosexuality six years ago. At the meeting, according to Falwell spokesman March DeMoss, as cited in the *Washington Post*, White also apologized for hateful speech directed at Falwell and other antigay Christians. "When the gay community tries to demonize Jerry Falwell, I'm not going to let them get away with it," DeMoss quoted White as having said. (DeMoss's remarks were in turn quoted by the *Washington Post*.) Nevertheless, despite earlier plans, food was not served at the meeting—Falwell had been reprimanded by some evangelicals who believe that the Bible forbids Christians to share food with those who are "sexually immoral." And in the July 18, 2000 issue of the *Advocate*, White was quoted as saying, "We feel that the devastation has to end. We have been polite for too long," in response to Falwell's continued opposition to what Falwell refers to as the "gay lifestyle." White's group is currently organizing protests against the Presbyterian and Episcopal Churches after protesting the Southern Baptist Convention in June 2000.

CATHOLIC CHURCH

Churches have been split by varying views on homosexuality. Sister Jeannine Grannick and the Reverend Robert Nugent are a Catholic nun and priest who have traveled around the United States, trying to get Catholic parishes to fully accept homosexuals into the church. On July 13, 1999, the Vatican ordered them to end their 30-year ministry, placing a gag order on them after an investigation found that they had not complied with the church doctrine proclaiming the "intrinsic evil of homosexual acts." According to an article in the November 1999 issue of *Out* magazine, the two are confident that their case will be heard again.

EPISCOPAL CHURCH

Although there is no official policy banning gay unions, the church does believe that homosexuality is incompatible with church teachings. In 1996, however, a church court ruled that there was "no core doctrine prohibiting the ordination of a noncelibate homosexual person living in a faithful and committed relationship with a person of the same sex." Some 2.4 million people belong to the Episcopal Church USA; millions more belong to churches around the world which often tend to be less liberal on homosexuality than the U.S. and British churches.

UNITED METHODIST CHURCH

The United Methodist Church is also divided over gay rights—specifically over the right of gay men and lesbians to marry in holy union within the church. As of early 2000, Reverend Jimmy Creech faces sanctions for insisting on marrying gay couples in religious ceremonies. Creech married his first gay couple in Omaha, Nebraska on September 14, 1997, setting the stage for what *Out* reporter Lisa Kennedy calls "the first major rift in the nation's second largest Protestant denomination (there are 8.5 million members) since 1844. The issue then—slavery."

Creech was brought up on charges by the church leadership after the Omaha ceremony but managed to evade them through a technicality: he claimed that the church's prohibition against gay marriage was advisory only, without the force of law. He has since been warned that the ban is indeed a church law, and that if he breaks it, he faces the loss of his ministerial credentials. Yet he proceeded to officiate at the marriage of Larry Ellis and Jim Raymer in April 1999 in North Carolina.

Creech is not the only United Methodist minister to mutiny: in January 1999, 68 United Methodist ministers from the California-Nevada conference celebrated the marriage of Ellie Charlton and Jeanne Barnett in Sacramento. They, too, face loss of credentials, or, for the retired among them, the loss of health benefits and perhaps also their pensions. Reverend Greg Dell, who celebrated a gay marriage in 1998, has already been tried by the church, found guilty, and suspended from service. The only way he could reverse the suspension was to sign a pledge to uphold church law in future—so he chose to leave the ministry.

Not all denominations have faced such dramatic internal debates as the United Methodists or such explicit challenges as the Catholics. But none has remained untouched by gay and lesbian activism.

LUTHERANS

The largest Lutheran denomination in the United States is the Evangelical Lutheran Church in America (ECLA), with more than 5 million members. Recently, the ECLA has been wracked with conflict over gay issues. In February, the synod (local branch) in St. Paul, Minnesota asked the national church to end its ban on gay ministers. In April, Bishop Robert Mattheis threatened to expel a Berkeley, California congregation for having hired a gay pastor. In May, a synod in Milwaukee endorsed same-sex unions, even though these are not recognized by the national church. Currently, the church considers homosexuality a "departure from the heterosexual structure of God's creation" and requires that gay clergy remain celibate.

JUDAISM

Within modern Judaism, there are four major movements. *Reconstructionists*, the most liberal strand, allows gay men and lesbians both to marry within the religion and to become ordained as rabbis. *Reform Judaism*, historically known for its liberal views, supports gay people's legal right to marry and on March 29, 2000 its governing body, the Central Conference of American Rabbis, voted to allow members to officiate at same-sex commitment ceremonies. A 1998 poll found more than 500 Reform rabbis willing to officiate at such unions. According to a 1998 report by the Human Rights Commission, the *Conservative* movement no longer considers homosexuality an "abomination" and continues to debate whether it is a "sin." *Orthodox Judaism* stands firmly against homosexuality, based on the Book of Leviticus; however, Orthodox Jews also believe in upholding the other 612 commandments specified for Jews in the Torah (Old Testament).

ISLAM

Homosexual acts are a capital (death penalty) crime in such conservative Muslim countries as Saudi Arabia, Iran, and Afghanistan, whereas homosexuality is widely accepted, with varying legal status, in many liberal Muslim nations in Africa. Muslims in the United States have generally been unsympathetic to gay men and lesbians, but in 1998, Pakistani immigrant Faisal Alam founded Al-Fatiha, a group for gay, lesbian, bisexual, transgendered, and "questioning" Muslims. The group met at a May 1999 conference in New York City at which many of the 60 attendees registered under false names. Alam expected a larger showing at the group's June 2000 international retreat in London. "For many people, being gay and Muslim is an oxymoron," Alam said in a November 1999 article in *Out* magazine. "People have been living with separate identities for so long that for us to say, 'you can be gay and Muslim' really scares them."

CHURCH OF JESUS CHRIST OF LATTER-DAY SAINTS (MORMONS)

Mormons not only consider homosexuality a sin, they have consistently urged church members to oppose gay rights. (Southern Baptists have done the same; see below.) During the 1996 campaign to win same-sex marriage rights in Hawaii, for example, the church donated more than $600,000 to defeat the effort; in 1998, it made a $500,000 donation to the Alaska Family Coalition, which was working to enact a constitutional amendment that would ban same-sex marriages in that state. Some 740,000 Mormons living in California had been asked to vote for Proposition 22 (the Knight Initiative) in March 2000 (it has since passed, see Chapter 2). The church's tax-exempt status has been challenged as a result of its political activities.

SOUTHERN BAPTIST CONVENTION (SBC)

The nearly 16 million Southern Baptists in the United States make that church the largest U.S. Protestant denomination—and one of the most antigay, so much so that the leadership amended the Convention's constitution in early 2000 to make support for homosexuality the sole disqualifier for membership. And on June 14, 2000, the church made its anitgay stance part of its Faith and Message statement, which is considered second only to Scripture by the SBC.

The SBC's antigay position has often led to activism. When American Airlines became known for donating money to PFLAG, HRC, and GLAAD, the Southern Baptist Convention dropped them as a carrier, stating that the company supported movements that were "destructive of the family and society." It also rebuked President Clinton—himself a Southern Baptist—for making June 1999 Gay Pride Month; called for the recall of James Hormel, a gay man who is ambassador to Luxembourg; and re-asserted the belief that gay people can be "made heterosexual" through religious faith.

One of the group's most publicized acts was its boycott of the movies, television shows, and theme parks associated with the Walt Disney Corporation. For many years, Disney had found allies, and therefore loyal consumers, within the ranks of religious conservatives, who viewed the company as producing "pro-family" entertainment products. However, several changes within the corporation in the 1990s led many on the religious right to view the company with increased hostility. Disney's decision to extend medical benefits to the same-sex partners of employees and its tolerance of an annual "Gay Day" staged at Walt Disney World, in Florida, were cause for concern among many Southern Baptists and led the convention to threaten a boycott of the company in June 1996. But it was the Disney-affiliated ABC network sitcom *Ellen* that most rankled the conservative members of the church and pushed them to take action. When Ellen DeGeneres chose to come out of the closet, both as a celebrity and as a character on the show, in April 1997, the SBC's response was swift and unambiguous. In June of that year, the membership voted to boycott all Disney-related merchandise and entertainment. In an August 14, 1997 interview with the *Atlanta Journal-Constitution*, Richard Land, head of the Ethics and Religious Liberty Commission of the SBC, accused Disney of having a "Christian-bashing, family-bashing, pro-homosexual, morally challenged agenda." "Disney will remain in our prayers, but won't get in our pocket-books," he was quoted as saying. However, in a March 7, 1998 article in the same publication, only 30 percent of SBC members polled said they were honoring the action, and Disney corporate communications spokesman John Dreyer was quoted as saying that the boycott had had no discernible impact on corporate profits. But in April 1998, the company did cancel *Ellen* because of poor ratings, leading some in the gay community to speculate that the boycott had discouraged the company from supporting a failing show. As of early 2000, the SBC boycott against Disney is officially still in effect.

UNITED CHURCH OF CHRIST

One of the smallest (1.4 million members) and newest (founded in 1957) Protestant denominations in the United States is also one of the most pro-gay. In a November 1999 article in *Out* magazine, Lisa Kennedy and Michele James called the UCC "by far the most welcoming mainline denomination for gay men and lesbians." They pointed out that the group has ordained openly gay ministers since 1972 and remains the only Christian denomination to recognize same-sex marriages. The church has spoken out against sodomy laws and for equal gay participation in the military. Moreover, the UCC's highest body, the General Synod, has actively called on its congregations to study homosexuality and declare that they are "open and affirming."

PRESBYTERIAN CHURCH

The general assembly of this 2.6 million–member denomination has allowed noncelibate gay men and lesbians to apply for the ministry but insists that ordained ministers should be celibate. The church also won disfavor with gay rights activists when OneByOne, an official Presbyterian ministry for those dealing with "sexual brokenness," met with Exodus International, a Christian ministry dedicated to "converting" gay people to heterosexuality. (For more on Exodus, see Chapter 1.) As part of the church's annual general assembly meeting in 1999, OneByOne and Exodus discussed what they view as the problematic nature of "progay" theology, that is, any theology that does not condemn homosexuality as sinful. Yet also in 1999, a regional board of this church voted to allow 95 ministers to perform same-sex commitment ceremonies (though explicitly disallowing marriages).

THE RELIGIOUS SOCIETY OF FRIENDS (QUAKERS)

The Religious Society of Friends is a loosely organized denomination with no church hierarchy. Questions of policy are decided by each meeting, or church, and there are no ministers among Friends, so ordination is not an issue. Thus, the Quakers as a body cannot be said to have any particular stance on gay rights. However, traditionally, Quakers have tended to be supportive of movements for social change, such as civil rights and gay rights, and many Quaker meetings do recognize gay and lesbian marriages.

UNITARIAN UNIVERSALIST ASSOCIATION (UUA)

Unitarians have always been one of the most liberal of all denominations—they do not even consider themselves Christian, strictly speaking, favoring a more eclectic theology to go with their humanist views. Known for its support of gay rights, the UUA incurred the wrath of the Boy Scouts of America in 1998, when the BSA ordered the Unitarians to stop giving out religious awards to Unitarian scouts. The Boy Scouts consider homosexuality immoral and have tried to exclude gay members, a position that has attracted criticism from various liberal groups. The Unitarians actively condemned the scouts' position—and the scouts retaliated by asking the church to stop giving out the badges of honor that it, like many religious groups, awards to its member scouts. Hundreds of such awards are given out by the Unitarians every year—and UUA president John Buehrens said his group had no intention of abiding by the scouts' "outrageous" demand. With 250,000 members, the UUA is hardly a widespread organization, but it has long been known for taking the lead on civil rights and related issues.

GAY RIGHTS IN THE FUTURE?

What has the gay rights movement accomplished in the past 30 years, and what might be expected in the future? Not surprisingly, the answers are contradictory.

For example, despite the enormous changes made in the treatment of gay and lesbian youth—programs at lesbian and gay community centers, gay/lesbian high schools, even two fledgling group homes for gay youth—disproportionate numbers of young gay people continue to commit suicide, as do a very high number of gay male adults. A study in the April 2000 issue of the *American Journal of Public Health*, coauthored by psychologists Vickie Mays and Susan Cochran, found that 19 percent of men who reported having sex with other men had attempted suicide at least once in their lives versus only 3.6 percent of exclusively heterosexual men—this out of a sampling of 3,503 men. An article by B. Bower in *Science News* on October 23, 1999 reported on a study of 103 pairs of male/male twins aged

35 to 53. In each set of twins, one man had had sex only with females, while the other reported at least one male sex partner after age 18. (The men were taken from a larger study of 3,400 twin pairs who had served in the U.S. military between 1965 and 1975.) Nearly 15 percent of the participants with male sex partners had tried to commit suicide, compared to only 4 percent of the strictly heterosexual twins. Bower reports that "Homosexual twins also reported substantially more periods of contemplating their own death or the demise of others, wanting to die, and thinking about committing suicide."

The same article cites a study by psychologist David M. Fergusson of New Zealand's Christchurch School of Medicine, in which 1,265 New Zealand children were tracked from birth to age 21. Fergusson found that "suicide attempts and a variety of mental disorders—including major depression and substance abuse—occur particularly frequently in homosexual and bisexual young adults."

"Taken together with earlier studies, there can be little doubt . . . that homosexual orientation is associated with suicidality, at least among young men," said Gary Remafedi, a psychiatrist with the University of Minnesota Youth and AIDS Projects in Minneapolis, who published comments on the two studies.

For another indication of problems facing the gay community, we might look at the increasing rates of HIV infection among young men. According to a New York City Department of Health study, 18 percent of all African-American gay men aged 15 to 22 are infected with HIV, along with some 9 percent of young Latinos and 3 percent of young whites. The same study found that nearly 46 percent of all young gay men had engaged in unprotected anal sex in the past six months, according to a February 19, 1999 article by Mark Sullivan in the *New York Blade*. "Activists said the study confirms what they already suspected," Sullivan wrote, "that prevention messages haven't gotten through to minorities. Officials at Gay Men's Health Crisis said that anecdotal information prompted that organization to put programs in place—programs such as Peer 2000 and Soul Food, which are specifically geared toward young Black and Latino men."

Sullivan went on to cite a San Francisco study that found similar results: for gay men aged 26 to 29, only 58 percent reported consistent condom use in 1997, down from 62.2 percent in 1994; the proportion of gay men who said they never use a condom during anal sex rose from 30 percent in 1994 to 38 percent in 1997. And of that latter figure, 68 percent said they did not know the HIV status of all of their sex partners of the past six months.

Another sign of difficult times is the antigay actions of various U.S. corporations and institutions. For example, the bookstore chain Barnes and Noble has removed *POZ*, a magazine for people with AIDS/HIV, from several of its locations after receiving various conservative complaints. Also, FedEx Corporation has sued San Francisco because of the city's requirement that companies doing business with it must offer domestic partnership benefits.

Yet despite the continued setbacks and the issues on which very little progress has been made, "the gay rights movement continually passes small mileposts even when more major markers aren't in sight," as journalist Deb Price contends:

> *Much like driving across a prairie state, there's a sameness to the gay rights landscape now that creates the illusion of standing still.* . . . *In reality, we're part of the fastest-moving civil rights struggle in U.S. history, as attorney Evan Wolfson of Lambda Legal Defense and Education Fund always enjoys pointing out.* "*Compared to the past great struggles for equality,*" *he notes,* "*ours is moving at Internet speed.*"

Those who oppose gay rights present an oddly similar view: on the one hand, they contend that the majority of Americans opposes "the immoral lifestyle" of homosexuality; on the other hand, they find ever more arenas in which lesbian and gay cultural and political power can be felt. From images on television to elected public officials, from state supreme courts' apparent recognition of domestic partnership to churches that perform gay marriages, from antidiscrimination laws to corporate benefits for same-sex couples, the landscape for gay rights has markedly changed—even while some things apparently remain the same. What kinds of changes may take place in the new millennium, and how quickly these changes will be felt, remains to be seen.

CHAPTER 4

CHRONOLOGY

1869

- The word *homosexual* is created by Hungarian physician Karoly Maria Benkert (writing under the pseudonym K. M. Kertbeny).

1896

- The world's first periodical dealing with homosexuality—*Der Eigene* ("The Community of the Special")—is published in Germany.

1897

- Perhaps the first homosexual rights group, the Scientific Humanitarian Committee, is formed in Germany by Magnus Hirschfeld, Max Sporh, and Erick Oberg.
- British sexologist Havelock Ellis publishes *Sexual Inversion*, which is considered the first book in English to treat homosexual behavior as neither illness, sin, nor crime.

1924

- The first U.S. gay rights group, the Society for Human Rights, is founded in Chicago, but is soon disbanded when the wife of one of the members reports the group to the police.

1948

- U.S. sexologist Alfred Kinsey publishes his report *Sexual Behavior in the Human Male*, in which he puts forth the famous figure that 10 percent of all U.S. males may be homosexual.

Chronology of Gay Rights

1950–1954

- The nationwide hunt to expose homosexuals in U.S. government, the military, and other public realms, led by Senator Joseph McCarthy, leads to thousands of men and women losing their jobs for being either actual or suspected homosexuals. This political development is closely linked to McCarthy's hunt for actual or suspected Communists.

1950

- The McCarran Act is passed, excluding both Communists and "sexual deviates" from immigrating to the United States.

1951

- *The Homosexual in America*—one of the earliest arguments for tolerance of gay life—is published by Edward Sagarin, under the pseudonym of Donald Webster Cory.
- In Los Angeles, the Mattachine Society is founded by Harry Hay, Bob Hull, and Chuck Rowland to support gay men and lesbians and to educate the public on gay issues.

1955

- The first U.S. lesbian organization, Daughters of Bilitis (DOB), is founded in San Francisco by Del Martin and Phyllis Lyon, who also publish DOB's journal, the *Ladder*, until 1972.

1961

- Illinois becomes the first state to decriminalize private homosexual acts between consenting adults.

1964

- The Society for Individual Rights, a social and political club for gay men and lesbians, is founded in San Francisco.

1965

- Seven gay men and three lesbians picket the White House in the first gay rights protest in U.S. history. However, the protest is dwarfed by the 20,000 antiwar protestors gathered that same day at the Washington Monument.

1966

- The North American Conference of Homophile Organizations (NACHO) is founded to coordinate protests against antigay actions by the federal government.

1967

- The Supreme Court rules that the McCarran Act's ban on "sexual deviates" applies to lesbians and gay men.

1968

- Reverend Troy Perry founds the Metropolitan Community Church in Los Angeles. It is the first "gay church" in the United States and will go on to found branches in many other U.S. cities.

1969

- Carl Wittman's pre-Stonewall "Gay Manifesto" anticipates many of the goals of the early gay liberation movement.
- *June 27*: The day of entertainer Judy Garland's funeral also marks the beginning of the riots at the Stonewall Inn. Today these riots are generally understood as the beginning of the modern gay liberation/gay rights movement.

1970

- The Lutheran Church comes out against state sodomy laws and for anti-discrimination legislation to protect gay men and lesbians—although it maintains the right to exclude gay people from its own clergy.
- *June 28*: In a forerunner of modern Gay Pride events, 10,000 people commemorate the Stonewall uprising by marching in "Christopher Street Liberation Day" in New York City.

1971

- The National Organization for Women, perhaps the largest and best-known U.S. feminist group, adopts a policy making the oppression of lesbians "a legitimate concern for feminism."
- A recommendation for the repeal of all sodomy laws is adopted by President Richard Nixon's National Commission on Reform of Federal Criminal Laws.

- Idaho first repeals, then reinstates, the state's sodomy laws, which make homosexual acts a felony carrying a sentence of five years in prison.

1972

- East Lansing, Michigan adopts the first ordinance outlawing discrimination against gay men and lesbians in city hiring.

1973

- Rita Mae Brown's *Rubyfruit Jungle*, a groundbreaking autobiographical novel about growing up lesbian, is published.
- American Psychiatric Association removes homosexuality from its list of mental disorders in the *Diagnostic and Statistical Manual II*, its official catalog of mental and psychological problems.
- Lambda Legal Defense and Education Fund—one of the first organizations devoted specifically to gay legal rights—is founded in New York City.

1974

- New York City congresswoman Bella Abzug introduces the first federal Gay and Lesbian Civil Rights Bill.
- *January*: The Combahee River Collective, a feminist group led by African-American lesbians, holds its first meeting, in Roxbury, Massachusetts. Their publications would become pioneering documents in the development of lesbian feminism, bringing together an antiracist and a gay liberation critique.
- *November*: Openly gay candidates win their first U.S. elections: Kathy Kozachenko to the Ann Arbor, Michigan city council, and Elaine Noble to the Massachusetts house of representatives.

1975

- Despite his consistently superior ratings, the U.S. Air Force discharges Sergeant Leonard Matlovich on the grounds of his sexual orientation, as armed forces regulations require. Matlovich begins a long court battle to protest his discharge. On September 8, Matlovich becomes the first openly gay man to appear on the cover of *Time* magazine.

1976

- The U.S. Supreme Court upholds the state of Virginia's sodomy laws by a 6-3 vote.

Gay Rights

1977

- Billy Crystal plays the first gay character on a successful TV series: Jodie Dallas on the sitcom *Soap*.
- The State Department ends a decades-long policy when it announces that it will no longer consider sexual orientation as a reason to deny employment.
- *January*: Florida's Dade County passes an ordinance forbidding discrimination based on sexual identity. The official who introduces the ordinance, Ruth Shack, had featured a commercial sung by Anita Bryant as part of her campaign.
- *June*: In a campaign led by Bryant, voters repeal Dade County's ordinance, setting off a nationwide backlash against gay rights. Following the Dade County repeal, gay rights ordinances are overturned by referendums in St. Paul, Minnesota; Eugene, Oregon; and Wichita, Kansas. A gay rights ordinance in Seattle is upheld.
- *November*: After many unsuccessful campaigns, San Francisco activist Harvey Milk finally wins a seat on the San Francisco board of supervisors, becoming the first openly gay person to be elected to the government of a large U.S. city.

1978

- California voters defeat the Briggs Initiative, which would have allowed for the firing of all gay and lesbian teachers and of all teachers who refer positively to homosexuals in the classroom.
- San Francisco adopts its first gay rights ordinance.
- San Francisco has the largest Gay Pride parade in history—250,000 to 300,000 marchers—at least partly in response to the Briggs Initiative.
- *November* 27: Former San Francisco supervisor Dan White kills his fellow supervisor, the openly gay Harvey Milk, along with San Francisco mayor George Moscone in their city hall offices.

1979

- The Moral Majority, a right-wing group opposed to gay rights, among other causes, is founded by Reverend Jerry Falwell.
- Stephen M. Lachs, the nation's first openly gay judge, is appointed to the bench by California governor Jerry Brown.
- *May* 2: A San Francisco jury convicts Dan White of the lesser charge of manslaughter. The verdict enrages that city's gay population, which erupts in what has come to be known as the White Night riots.

- *October*: The first national gay and lesbian civil rights march on Washington draws more than 100,000 participants.

1980

- The Human Rights Campaign Fund, a gay lobbying organization, is founded.
- Six blind lesbians found the Womyn's Braille Press, dedicated to making lesbian and feminist literature available on tape and in Braille.
- A federal judge orders the U.S. Air Force to allow Sergeant Leonard Matlovich—who was discharged for being gay—to reenlist. Instead, the air force offers Matlovich a $160,000 settlement, which he accepts.
- Gay teenager Aaron Fricke wins a lawsuit in Providence, Rhode Island that enables him to bring a male date to his high school prom.
- Director William Friedkin's efforts to make *Cruising*, a movie about the "underside" of New York City gay life that starred Al Pacino, are frustrated by local gay protests, which object to the movie as homophobic and as encouraging violence against gays. Nonetheless, the film is completed and released.

1981

- Congressman Roger Jepsen introduces the "Family Protection Act," which, among other issues, would deny Social Security, welfare, and veterans' benefits to gay people as well as to those who propose that homosexuality is acceptable.
- *June*: The Centers for Disease Control report a rare form of pneumonia contracted by five gay men in Los Angeles; they believe the disease is linked to "some aspect of homosexual lifestyle." The disease, then called GRID (gay-related immune deficiency), will later be known as AIDS.
- *August*: Larry Kramer and a group of activists begin meetings that will lead to the founding of Gay Men's Health Crisis (GMHC), the first group to respond to AIDS.

1982

- The first statewide gay and lesbian civil rights bill, with provisions for employment, housing, and public accommodations, goes into effect in Wisconsin.
- Philadelphia's Board of Education establishes the nation's first high school for gays and lesbians, Byton High. In 1985, New York City will establish the Harvey Milk School for gay and lesbian students.

- *August*: The first Gay Games are held in San Francisco after a battle with the U.S. Olympic Committee, which will not allow the event to be called the "Gay Olympics."

1983

- *Torch Song Trilogy*, Harvey Fierstein's play about gay identity, wins the Tony Award for Best Play on Broadway; Fierstein wins the Best Actor award for starring in his own work.

1984

- Scientists at the Pasteur Institute in France, led by Luc Montagnier, announce the discovery of the virus that causes AIDS.
- The city of Berkeley, California extends domestic partnership benefits to gay and lesbian employees—the first time gay and lesbian partners have been recognized for benefits.
- *Labor Day*: Wigstock—an annual drag festival—is first held in New York City.
- *Election Day*: The 20,000 voters of West Hollywood, a Los Angeles neighborhood, vote to establish themselves as a new city; the five-person city council of this famously gay area includes a homosexual majority of two gay men and a lesbian.

1985

- Former city supervisor Dan White, released from jail after the murder of Mayor George Moscone and fellow supervisor Harvey Milk, commits suicide.
- Fourteen years after it is first introduced, a gay rights bill passes in New York City.
- *October 2*: Movie star Rock Hudson dies of AIDS, helping to raise the national consciousness of how widespread and deadly the disease is.

1986

- New Right spokesman Terry Dolan, who has long opposed "homosexual lifestyles," dies of HIV-related illness; after his death, many acquaintances assert that he was gay.
- *June*: In *Bowers v. Hardwick*, the U.S. Supreme Court upholds the right of states to make laws prohibiting sodomy and other private sexual acts between consenting adults. Meanwhile, the supreme court of Nevada—

the only state where heterosexual prostitution is legal—upholds that state's sodomy law.

1987

- U.S. congressman Barney Frank announces that he is gay, the first congressman to do so voluntarily (Representative Gerry Studds had earlier admitted he was gay in response to a scandal involving an alleged affair with a page).
- *March 24*: ACT UP (the AIDS Coalition to Unleash Power) protests against the cost of AIDS drugs by shutting down Wall Street; 17 people are arrested for civil disobedience. This is the beginning of a new, more militant approach in AIDS activism that will also energize the gay rights movement.
- *July 15*: For the first time, the *New York Times* uses the word "gay," rather than "homosexual."
- *October 11*: Almost 650,000 lesbians and gay men participate in the second March on Washington, where the quilt of the Names Project—memorializing people who have died of AIDS—is displayed for the first time.

1988

- Oregon voters repeal an executive order of the state's governor prohibiting discrimination in the employment of gay men and lesbians.
- Although the District of Columbia has passed a gay rights ordinance, the U.S. Congress votes to deny the district funding unless the measure is revoked.
- Raleigh, North Carolina adopts a gay rights ordinance.

1989

- In *Braschi v. Stahl Associates Co.*, a New York Court of Appeals rules that a gay male couple can be considered a "family" where housing rules are concerned, allowing surviving spouse Miguel Braschi to continue to enjoy his partner's lease.
- A Cincinnati jury trial rules that homoerotic portraits of men by the late gay photographer Robert Mapplethorpe violates a local obscenity law and shuts down the Mapplethorpe show at a local museum. Senator Jesse Helms and others use the controversy to attack the National Endowment for the Arts (NEA), which they claim supports "obscene" work with public funds.

- *Spring*: The first university or college department of lesbian and gay studies in the United States is established at San Francisco City College.

1990

- Largely as a result of the Mapplethorpe controversy, the NEA withdraws funds from performance artists Karen Finley, John Fleck, Holly Hughes, and Tim Miller. Three of the so-called NEA 4 are gay; all four speak out against the action as a homophobic infringement of free speech.
- A new generation of activists forms Queer Nation in New York City.
- In Polk County, Florida, officials agree to cease requiring gay prisoners to wear pink bracelets, a practice supposedly intended to reduce the spread of HIV, the virus that causes AIDS, by helping to distinguish gay from nongay prisoners.
- Congress ends a decades-long policy of using sexual orientation as a basis for denying immigration; however, a visitor's HIV-positive status is still grounds for denying a visa.
- President George Bush signs the Hate Crime Statistics Act, which requires the U.S. Department of Justice to collect statistics on criminal acts motivated by race, religion, national origin, or sexual orientation—the first time sexual orientation is included as a protected category in federal legislation.
- The Americans with Disabilities Act extends civil rights protection to disabled Americans—including people with AIDS. (Since 1998 it is no longer legal to discriminate against people with AIDS in housing, employment, or public accommodations.)

1991

- In Dallas, the First International Deaf Gay and Lesbian Conference is held.
- Amnesty International, a group that protects political prisoners, decides to extend its campaigns to include gay men and lesbians imprisoned on account of their sexual orientation or activities.
- Washington, D.C. and Baltimore each hold their first Black Gay Pride Day.

1992

- Navy airman apprentice Terry Helvey is sentenced to life imprisonment for the deadly beating of fellow sailor Allen Schindler, who is so badly disfigured that his mother has difficulty identifying him; Helvey is quoted as saying, "I'd do it again."

- Colorado passes Amendment 2, a referendum prohibiting gay rights legislation statewide and overturning gay rights ordinances in Boulder, Denver, and Aspen. A similar referendum in Oregon, Proposition 9, is defeated.
- *May 28*: The Lesbian Avengers, a direct action activist group of mainly young women, holds its first meeting in New York City; the group will later be instrumental in preventing an antigay referendum from being passed in Idaho.

1993

- Although one of President Bill Clinton's election promises was to lift the ban on gays in the military, his executive order instead establishes the policy known as "don't ask, don't tell," a policy that will lead to an increased rate of gay and lesbian discharges from the armed forces.
- A group of gay Republicans known as Log Cabin Republicans is founded in Washington, D.C.
- *The New York Times* reports that some 1,100,000 participants join in the March on Washington for Lesbian, Gay, and Bi [bisexual] Equal Rights and Liberation—while President Clinton and most legislators leave town for the weekend.
- The supreme court of Hawaii reverses a lower court's decision against same-sex marriage, raising the possibility that gay marriage might become legal in Hawaii.
- The Oregon Citizens Alliance—responsible for the defeated Proposition 9—joins with other antigay groups to target 11 states for antigay referendums over the next two years: California, Georgia, Idaho, Iowa, Maine, Minnesota, Missouri, Montana, and Washington.
- Although New York City public schools have adopted "Children of the Rainbow," an inclusive curriculum focusing on cultural diversity and including some gay-positive materials, five of 32 local school boards refuse to teach the curriculum, largely because of its tolerance for "gay lifestyles."
- *April 25*: Some 20,000 women march in the Dyke March on Washington, D.C.

1994

- At the fourth annual Gay Games in New York City, Olympic gold medalist Greg Louganis announces that he is gay.
- Massachusetts becomes the first state to outlaw discrimination against gay and lesbian students in the public schools.

- The Hawaii state senate adopts a bill outlawing same-sex marriage in an effort to preclude the possibility of court decisions allowing for such marriage.

- The U.S. Congress passes the Defense of Marriage Act (DOMA), which defines marriage as taking place only between a man and a woman. DOMA, which passes overwhelmingly, represents the first federal effort to define marriage, which had previously been a state matter.

- The Employment Non-Discrimination Act (ENDA) is introduced into Congress. ENDA would add sexual orientation as a category in the Title VII protections against workplace discrimination. As of early 2000, the bill has still not been passed.

1995

- A court ruling holds that Irish gays and lesbians cannot join in the St. Patrick's Day parade in Boston if the parade committee wishes to keep them out.

1996

- *January*: Protease inhibitors—a new treatment for AIDS—are introduced, and AIDS deaths fall by 47 percent.

- *May*: In *Romer v. Evans*, the U.S. Supreme Court overturns Colorado's Amendment 2, ruling that states may not target specific groups, including lesbians, gay men, and bisexuals, and forbid them from seeking civil rights.

1997

- *April 14*: Ellen DeGeneres, star of the ABC sitcom *Ellen*, announces that she is a lesbian and appears on the cover of *Time* magazine; her TV character will come out later that spring, making *Ellen* the first successful network sitcom whose main character is openly gay.

- *December*: The New Jersey Supreme Court rules that gay couples must be treated with the same procedures as straight couples when it comes to adopting a child; they are responding to efforts by Jon Holden and Michael Galluccio to adopt a child as a couple.

1998

- *February*: In a statewide referendum, Maine becomes the first state to nullify a statewide gay rights law. Activists claim that part of the problem was the timing of the election, an off-season when no other matters were on the ballot, prompting voters in 1999 to approve a constitutional amendment ensuring that referendums are introduced as part of general elections.

- *June 25*: The protections of the Americans with Disabilities Act are extended to include people with AIDS/HIV.
- *September*: State Senator William J. "Pete" Knight introduces Proposition 22, popularly known as the Knight Initiative, a statewide referendum that would keep same-sex marriage from being recognized in California, including gay marriages recognized by other states.
- *October 6*: College student Matthew Shepard is brutally beaten and left to die in Laramie, Wyoming; his death galvanizes gay protest and mainstream media outrage across the nation.
- *Election Day*: Hawaii adopts a provision in its state constitution forbidding same-sex marriage.
- *Election Day:* The first openly lesbian member of Congress—Tammy Baldwin, of Madison, Wisconsin—is elected.
- *November 22*: The sodomy law contested in *Bowers v. Hardwick* is struck down by Georgia's own supreme court.
- *December*: Dade County, Florida, the area where the backlash against gay rights began in 1977, passes another gay rights ordinance.

1999

- *Memorial Day Weekend*: President Bill Clinton appoints James Hormel ambassador to Luxembourg. Hormel is the first openly gay ambassador to represent the United States. Clinton makes the appointment on a holiday weekend, when Congress is not in session, to circumvent Mississippi senator Trent Lott's determination not to let Hormel's nomination come to the Senate floor for a vote.
- *August*: The New Jersey Supreme Court rules that James Dale, an Eagle Scout and assistant scoutmaster expelled from the Boy Scouts of America in 1990, must be reinstated. Dale was expelled after the scouts had learned he was gay; the state high court dismissed the scout's ban on homosexual and bisexual men as "bigotry," finding that the scouts were subject to the same antidiscrimination laws that governed restaurants or any other public accommodation.
- *December*: Hawaii's Supreme Court rules that the state's new constitutional amendment now precludes same-sex marriage; meanwhile, Vermont's Supreme Court orders the state legislature to find a way to offer same-sex couples the same legal and financial benefits as heterosexual couples, whether via marriage or some other arrangement.

133

- In the wake of the murder of U.S. Army private Barry Winchell, who was killed by associates who suspected him of being gay, President Clinton asks defense secretary William Cohen to review the "don't ask, don't tell" policy under pressure from many others. Vice President—and presidential candidate—Al Gore comments that gay people should be able to serve in the military without discrimination.

2000

- *March 7:* California voters overwhelmingly approve Proposition 22 (the Knight Initiative), which defines marriage as exclusively between one man and one woman, and which forbids the state from extending legal recognition to same-sex marriages contracted outside of its borders.
- *March 29:* The Central Conference of American Rabbis, the governing body of Reform Judaism, votes to allow its members to officiate at same-sex commitment rituals.
- *April:* Vermont's House of Representitives passes a historic law granting homosexual couples all of the legal rights accorded to heterosexual couples. Nationwide debates on the so-called civil union begin.
- *June:* New York's state legislature passes a hate crimes bill that includes sexual orientation among its protected categories. The vote comes after an 11-year effort by Republicans in the state senate to block passage of the bill.
- *June:* A Texas appeals court strikes down a law making homosexual sodomy illegal, on the grounds that since heterosexual sodomy has been legal since 1973, the law violates the state Equal Rights Amendment. Although the case's application in unclear, gay rights advocates consider this a victory.
- *June 28:* The U.S. Supreme Court supports the Boy Scouts of America's right to ban gay scoutmasters, on the grounds that First Amendment protection of freedom of association outweighs New Jersey's law against discrimination in public accommodations.
- *July 1:* The Vermont law on civil unions, having passed the state senate and been signed by the governor, goes into effect.

CHAPTER 5

BIOGRAPHICAL LISTING

Sidney Abbot and **Barbara Love,** partners and pioneering lesbians in the early feminist movement. They were among the organizers of a group of lesbians who attended the Second Congress to Unite Women in May 1970, arranged for the lights to be turned off, and then appeared on stage in lavender T-shirts stenciled with the slogan Lavender Menace, the phrase that feminist leader Betty Friedan had used to describe the "lesbian threat" to the women's movement. They were also early founders of the Radicalesbians, an offshoot of the Gay Liberation Front, and together coedited *Sappho Was a Right-On Woman* (1972), one of the first U.S. collections of lesbian literature.

Bella Abzug, New York congresswoman who introduced the first gay rights legislation in 1974—and continued to campaign for legislation for many years thereafter, known for her devotion to gay rights, particularly after she campaigned in gay male bathhouses.

Dorothy Allison, writer and activist. Allison is the author of *The Women Who Hate Me* (a collection of poems), *Trash* (a collection of short stories), *Bastard Out of Carolina* (a novel that was a finalist for the National Book Award), *Skin* (a collection of essays), and *Cavedweller* (a novel).

Sheldon Andelson, major fund-raiser behind the Municipal Elections Committee of Los Angeles (MECLA), one of the first gay efforts to use fund-raising as a way to attain behind-the-scenes political power. Andelson was influential in California and national politics for many years and was appointed to the California Board of Regents by Governor Jerry Brown in the late 1970s.

Gloria Anzaldúa, coeditor, with Cherríe Moraga, of *This Bridge Called My Back: Writings by Radical Women of Color,* a pioneering anthology of works by African-American, Latina, and other feminists. Moraga and Anzaldúa were also coeditors of *Compañeras.* When *This Bridge* was published in 1981, very few works by women of color had appeared, and Anzaldúa and Moraga helped to establish that lesbian-feminism could be a multiracial movement representing women from a wide range of economic backgrounds. Anzaldúa is also the author of *Borderland/La Frontera*, among other works.

Virginia Apuzzo, activist and politician. At the 1980 Democratic National Convention, she coauthored the first lesbian and gay civil rights plank ever adopted by a major U.S. political party. She is the former executive deputy commissioner of the New York State Division of Housing and Community Renewal, former commissioner of the New York State Civil Service, and a former executive director of the National Gay Task Force (since renamed the National Lesbian and Gay Task Force).

Jack Baker, the first openly gay person to be elected president of the University of Minnesota student body. This pioneering gay activist was featured in *Life* magazine with his lover, Mike McConnell, whom he married in a public (extralegal) ceremony.

Tammy Baldwin, Madison, Wisconsin woman who in 1998 became the nation's first lesbian congresswoman.

Robert Bauman, former Republican U.S. representative from Maryland who was known for his antigay role in Congress in the 1970s—and for the 1980 scandal surrounding the revelation that he had been buying sex from male prostitutes in Washington, D.C. After the incident, Bauman, who was married, apologized publicly to his wife and stepped down; the revelations hurt the conservative cause by making antigay leaders seem like hypocrites.

Arthur Bell, former *Village Voice* columnist. His position at the radical New York City newspaper enabled him to play a prominent role in the early gay rights movement of the 1970s. Bell was also an early member of the Gay Activists Alliance.

Lisa Ben, activist, singer, and writer who published the first known U.S. publication by and for lesbians, *Vice Versa*, a hand-typed and privately circulated periodical of the late 1940s.

Elizabeth Birch, executive director of the Human Rights Campaign (HRC), a position she held when HRC became the first gay rights organization to host a sitting U.S. president—Bill Clinton, who attended an HRC awards dinner in 1997. Birch also gained a certain notoriety when HRC endorsed right-wing New York senator Al D'Amato over liberal opponent Charles Schumer, in gratitude for D'Amato's votes on certain key congressional issues.

Melvin Boozer, the first openly gay person to be among the nominees for vice president; Boozer was nominated at the 1980 Democratic convention, which eventually chose Walter Mondale as its vice presidential nominee. In his convention speech, Boozer spoke of the similarities between the oppression he had experienced as an African American and as a gay man. President of the District of Columbia's Gay Activists Alliance, Boozer served for a short time as the Washington representative of the National Gay Task Force (which has since been renamed National Gay and Lesbian Task Force).

Ivy Bottini, activist who helped found the first local (New York) chapter of the National Organization for Women (NOW) but was forced out of NOW in 1970, as part of that organization's internal fight over the extent to which lesbians should be part of the women's movement. Bottini is widely credited with having developed the idea of feminist consciousness-raising, in which women shared personal stories in a noncritical, supportive environment in an effort to discover the political dimensions of their lives—a technique that has been widely used by feminist and lesbian-feminist groups, as well as by early gay liberation groups.

Michael J. Bowers, Georgia attorney general. Bowers is noted for prosecuting Michael Hardwick in the 1986 Supreme Court case that became known as *Bowers v. Hardwick* and for withdrawing a job in his office promised to lawyer Robin Shahar when he discovered she was a lesbian.

John Briggs, California state senator who introduced the 1978 referendum, Proposition 6, which is also known as the Briggs Initiative and which would have banned gay and lesbian teachers from the public schools and prohibited any positive mention of homosexuality on school grounds.

Howard Brown, former head of the Health Services Administration. Appointed in 1965 by New York City mayor John V. Lindsay, Brown was used to working behind the scenes for gay causes—but caused quite a stir when he came out as gay in a front-page *New York Times* story on October 3, 1973. Brown's prominence led him to be chosen first chair of the National Gay Task Force (later renamed the National Gay and Lesbian Task Force).

Rita Mae Brown, writer. Her 1973 autobiographical novel, *Rubyfruit Jungle*, is known as a classic lesbian coming-of-age story, and was one of the first lesbian novels to achieve commercial success. Brown's other novels include *Six of One, In Her Day, Venus Envy, High Hearts,* and a series of mysteries that she "coauthored" with her cat, Sneaky Pie Brown. She also won notoriety for her affair with the then-closeted tennis champion Martina Navratilova, on which *Six of One* was based.

Anita Bryant, singer and former beauty queen who led the first successful antigay backlash, the 1977 effort to repeal the Dade County, Florida gay rights ordinance. Bryant rose to fame very quickly with her organization, "Save Our Children," as she charged that lesbians and gay men were looking to "recruit" young people since, she contended, they could not "reproduce." Bryant's successful campaign against the Dade County ordinance galvanized a response from the gay community—but it also inspired more successful anti–gay rights activity throughout the nation. Her popularity dropped sharply in the 1980s, however, and she ceased to be a symbol of the anti–gay rights movement.

Patrick Califia, formerly Pat Califia, transgendered writer and former columnist for *Out* magazine. Califia is known for his commitment to working-class issues, his activism on behalf of the transgendered movement, and his open championing of sadomasochistic relationships as deserving of inclusion in a larger gay and lesbian community. As Pat Califia, she was the author of *Sapphistry, The Lesbian S/M Safety Manual, The Advocate Advisor, Doc and Fluff* (a novel), *Macho Sluts* (a novel), *Public Sex*, and *Sex Changes.*

Michael Callen, one of the earliest AIDS activists, who caused a stir in 1982 when he publicly made a connection between his sexually promiscuous life and his infection with the disease. Previously, leaders who called for gay men to change their sexual habits had been seen as suspect, but Callen had been known for championing sexual freedom, so his call for restraint had enormous impact during the early days of the crisis.

Margarethe Cammermeyer, recipient of the Bronze Star, a medal awarded for meritorious achievement, who was discharged from the Army National Guard after coming out as a lesbian. She went on to become an activist for lesbian and gay rights. Cammermeyer was portrayed by actress Glenn Close in a TV movie about her life.

Jack Campbell, the first major financial supporter of the gay rights movement and the founder of Club Baths, a chain of gay male bathhouses.

Jimmy Carter, president of the United States (1977–81). The first U.S. presidential candidate to acknowledge gay rights as an issue. Thanks to his aide, Midge Costanza, gay rights activists met with government officials in the White House for the first time.

Madolin Cervantes, heterosexual woman who served as treasurer of the Mattachine Society at the time of the 1969 Stonewall uprising. Her presence was yet another cause of dissension between the old-line homophile group and the new militant gay activism.

Karen Clark, a Minnesota state representative who was elected in 1980. She is the longest-serving openly gay public official in the United States.

Michelle Cliff, Jamaican-born writer and editor who, with poet/activist and partner Adrienne Rich, was coeditor of *Sinister Wisdom*, one of the most influential feminist magazines of the 1980s. Her books include a volume of poetry, *Claiming an Identity They Taught Me to Despise*, and the novels *Abeng, No Telephone to Heaven*, and *Free Enterprise.*

Bill Clinton, president of the United States (1993–2001). Clinton is noted for his 1992 campaign pledge to end the ban on gays in the military and for his 1993 executive order establishing "don't ask, don't tell," a policy whereby gay servicemen and women would be dishonorably discharged for disclosing their sexual orientation—but whereby recruiters and superiors were forbidden to ask whether someone was gay as a means of keeping or getting them out of the service. Clinton was also the first sitting U.S. president to attend a gay rights event, a fund-raiser held by the Human Rights Campaign in 1997, and he has consistently supported various gay rights bills, including the Employment Non-Discrimination Act (ENDA), the 1994 measure (which remains unpassed) to outlaw employment discrimination on the basis of sexual orientation. He is also known for signing the Defense of Marriage Act (DOMA), the first federal attempt to regulate marriage contracts in an effort to prevent same-sex marriage nationwide.

Roy Cohn, lawyer known for his involvement in the right-wing, anticommunist activities of the 1950s, particularly in the trial that led to the execution of Julius and Ethel Rosenberg. In the 1970s, he was a leading figure in the Republican Party and spoke out frequently against gay rights. He was later revealed to be gay and died of an AIDS-related illness, an irony that playwright Tony Kushner explored in his Broadway hit, *Angels in America*, which features Cohn as a major character.

Jeanne Cordova, well-known leader in 1970s and 1980s gay politics in Los Angeles. She was also hired for a time to write a column for the *Advocate*. Cordova was one of the organizers of the 1973 West Coast Lesbian Conference and a member of the collective that published *Lesbian Tide*, a lesbian newspaper.

Reverend Jimmy Creech, United Methodist Church minister known for performing marriage ceremonies for gay men and lesbians in direct opposition to the wishes of his church.

James Dale, openly gay assistant scoutmaster and Eagle Scout who was expelled from the Boy Scouts of America when his sexual orientation was revealed via a photograph showing him as the leader of a Rutgers University gay rights group. Dale's lawsuit over his expulsion from the Boy Scouts reached the New Jersey Supreme Court in 1999, when the state high court ruled unanimously that the Boy Scouts' ban on gay and bisexual men was unconstitutional under New Jersey's antidiscrimination law. The U.S. Supreme Court overturned the state decision in 2000.

Jo Daly, an early organizer of the Alice B. Toklas Club, an influential lesbian and gay Democratic club in San Francisco; one of the few openly gay delegates to the 1976 Democratic convention, and the first full-time paid liaison between San Francisco's Human Rights Commission and the gay community.

Gray Davis, California governor, 1999– . In his first two years of his governorship, he signed three new gay rights bills: one establishing an antidiscrimination provision, another outlawing discrimination against gay/lesbian students and teachers, and the third criminalizing housing and job discrimination against gay men and lesbians.

Madeline Davis, with Jim Foster, the first openly gay person to address a national political convention—the Democratic Convention of 1972.

Ellen DeGeneres, lesbian comedian and actress who came out publicly in 1997, and whose character on the network sitcom *Ellen* also came out. DeGeneres was featured on the cover of *Time* magazine, saying "Yep, I'm Gay!"—an indication of how much national attention the event had drawn.

Terry Dolan, a New Right activist known for his pioneering use of direct mail to raise funds for the right wing. Although Dolan lobbied strongly against gay rights, it was discovered that he himself was gay when he died of an AIDS-related illness.

Tom Duane, first openly gay New York City Council member; first openly HIV-positive elected official in the United States (New York state senator, 1999–   ). Duane is known both for his gay rights leadership and for his strong ties to the tenants and community movements of his district.

Martin Duberman, scholar and historian; professor of history at the Lehman Graduate Center of the City University of New York, where he directs the Center for Lesbian and Gay Studies; and a founder of the Gay Academic Union. His pioneering work on gay history includes *About Time: Exploring the Gay Past*; *Cures: A Gay Man's Odyssey*; and *Stonewall*. With Martha Vicinus and George Chauncey, he is the coeditor of *Hidden from History: Reclaiming the Gay and Lesbian Past*. He has also written eloquently on race, notably *In White America*, and is the author of *Paul Robeson*, considered the definitive biography of the singer and activist. His latest book is *Left Out: The Politics of Exclusion: Essays, 1964–1999*.

Stephen Endean, executive director of the Gay Rights National Lobby, and a national lobbyist for gay rights; founder of the Human Rights Campaign Fund, considered by many to be the major U.S. gay lobbying group. Endean's background was as a Minneapolis activist who lobbied his state legislature to pass a gay rights bill; although his efforts during the 1970s were unsuccessful, a statewide bill finally passed in 1993.

Lillian Faderman, scholar and teacher whose book *Surpassing the Love of Men: Romantic Friendship and Love Between Women from the Renaissance to the Present* established the existence of protolesbian "romantic friendships" among many women previously believed to be heterosexual; Faderman is especially well-known for her thesis that 19th-century poet Emily Dickinson could be said to be in love with her sister-in-law, Sue Gilbert. Faderman's work established the widespread existence of romantic friendship, suggesting that some version of lesbianism was far more widespread than previously believed. She is also the author of *Scotch Verdict; Odd Girls and Twilight Lovers: A History of Lesbian Life in Twentieth-*

Century America; and *To Believe in Women: What Lesbians Have Done for America—A History.*

Nathan Fain, one of the founders of Gay Men's Health Crisis (GMHC) and a pioneering journalist who covered the AIDS epidemic for *The Advocate* during the early years of the crisis.

Reverend Jerry Falwell, minister and televangelist, founder of the Moral Majority, one of the nation's first and most powerful New Right/religious right organizations and renamed the Liberty Federation in 1999. Falwell is also the founder of Liberty University, in Lynchburg, Virginia and the host of the religious TV program *Old-Time Gospel Hour.* He is the author of *Listen, America!, The Fundamentalist Phenomenon, Champions of God,* and an autobiography, *Strength for the Journey.*

Jim Foster, founder of the Alice B. Toklas Club, the first gay Democratic political club in the nation. He and Madeleine Davis were the first openly gay people to address a national political convention—the Democratic Convention of 1972.

Jim Fouratt, founder of the Gay Liberation Front and a major gay leader in the post-Stonewall period. Fouratt was an early member of the Gay Activists Alliance and ACT UP and is a sometime writer for the *Village Voice.*

Barney Frank, Democratic representative from Massachusetts; first U.S. member of Congress to voluntarily announce that he is gay. Frank has been a staunch supporter of gay rights and other progressive causes during his many years of service in the House.

Betty Friedan, feminist leader of the 1970s, notorious for claiming that lesbians were being sent by the CIA to discredit the feminist movement and for calling lesbians "the lavender menace." Friedan is also known for helping to inspire the second wave of U.S. feminism with her book *The Feminine Mystique,* in which she identified "the problem that has no name"—the unnamed but powerful malaise of middle-class American women who were restricted to domestic lives, a condition that Friedan considered unfulfilling.

Barbara Gittings, with her partner, Kay Tobin Lahusen, a leading spirit in the homophile and modern gay rights movement, leader in the Daughters of Bilitis, and a key figure in the efforts to convince the American Psychiatric Association to remove homosexuality from its list of disorders.

Barry Goldwater, right-wing Republican who surprised many by coming out strongly in favor of gay rights, not least because he has a gay grandson. Goldwater was also an explicit supporter of lifting the ban on gays in the military.

Jewelle Gomez, poet, novelist, essayist, and a former editor of *conditions,* a feminist magazine. *Conditions* was part of the widespread efforts of the early lesbian-feminist movement to establish a forum where women—especially lesbians—could express themselves, which was especially important in a time when mainstream magazines and book publishers all but ignored both lesbians and radical feminists. Poetry was an important aspect of the cultural battle of lesbian-feminism, and writing poetry was seen as a political act, especially for women of color like Gomez. Her poetry collections include *Flamingoes and Bears* and *The Lipstick Papers*. She is also the author of the novel *The Gilda Stories* and the essay collection *Forty-Three Septembers.*

David Goodstein, the controversial publisher of the influential Los Angeles–based gay newspaper the *Advocate* (January 1, 1975–June 22, 1985). In addition to running one of the two major U.S. gay newspapers for over a decade (the other paper was the *New York Native*), Goodstein played a key role in gay politics, helping to found the National Gay Rights Lobby (although he then refused to give the group his financial support), and influencing popular responses to many issues through his editorial policy. He is also somewhat notorious for having been extremely slow to recognize the AIDS crisis in the early 1980s, as his commitment to sexual freedom led him to see the dangers of the sexually transmitted disease as overrated; for some time, he viewed those who advised sexual restraint as homophobic.

Jeannine Grannick, a Catholic nun, who, with Robert Nugent, traveled around the United States, trying to get Catholic parishes to fully accept homosexuals into the church. On July 13, 1999, the Vatican ordered them to end their 30-year ministry and placed a gag order on them.

Barbara Grier, cofounder, with Donna McBride, of Naiad Press, the oldest existing lesbian publishing company in the United States.

Harry Hay, cofounder of the first U.S. gay rights group, the Mattachine Society. Hay was forced out of his own group in 1953 by new, more conservative members who feared repercussions of his Communist past.

Jesse Helms, right-wing U.S. senator from North Carolina. He is a leading figure in antigay legislation and is noted for his attempts to strip funding from the National Endowment of the Arts for its alleged support of obscene material as well as homosexuality. Helms is also known for his opposition to affirmative action, feminism, and a host of other progressive causes.

Jon Holden and **Michael Galluccio,** New Jersey couple that sought to adopt a son *as* a couple. Their suit led to the New Jersey Supreme Court ruling that stated gay couples had to be accorded the same rights in an adoption procedure as heterosexual couples.

Amber Hollibaugh, writer, filmmaker, and activist. She is known for her theoretical writings defending lesbian butch-femme culture, and for her film *The Heart of the Matter*, about women and AIDS. Hollibaugh is also the former head of the Lesbian AIDS project of GMHC.

James Hormel, businessman who became the first gay ambassador when President Clinton nominated him in 1998 to serve in Luxembourg. Because of Senator Trent Lott's unwillingness to let the vote on Hormel come to the Senate floor, Hormel's ambassadorship (awarded in 1999) relied solely on Clinton's appointment.

Reverend Jesse Jackson, the first U.S. presidential candidate to make support for gay rights a central part of his program in his 1984 campaign. Although Jackson and gay rights groups have quarreled over various issues, he is generally considered a strong supporter who has done much to link gay and lesbian issues with civil rights for people of color.

Jill Johnston, former *Village Voice* columnist who wrote the classic books *Lesbian Nation*, as well as *Marmalade Me*. *Lesbian Nation* was one of the first books by a mainstream publisher—or indeed, by any publisher—to acknowledge the existence of lesbian-feminism and to explain its significance to a wider world beyond the political circles within which the movement had begun.

Dr. Franklin Kameny, a Harvard-trained astronomer who was the first openly gay person to bring suit against the federal government. In 1953, he was arrested for stopping to watch the arrest of another gay man, and he took the matter to court. Kameny was also the first openly gay person to run for federal office—he ran for Congress from the District of Columbia in 1972. He was the founder of the Washington chapter of the Mattachine Society and a leader in organizing repeated demonstrations for gay rights.

Morris Kight, a Los Angeles leader who helped found the Gay Liberation Front and the Los Angeles Gay Community Services Center.

Edward Koch, controversial former New York City mayor and congressman, with a long and complicated relationship to gay rights. As a congressman, Koch helped fellow New York representative Bella Abzug sponsor gay rights legislation in the mid-1970s; as mayor, he tried to extend civil rights protections to lesbians and gay men, but faced opposition from the Catholic Church that ultimately defeated him. He was accused of being unresponsive to AIDS activists, not least because he had been insulted by Larry Kramer, founder of Gay Men's Health Crisis, the major AIDS activist group of the 1980s.

Larry Kramer, screenwriter, novelist, playwright, and activist. Kramer cofounded—but then was expelled from—the Gay Men's Health Crisis (GMHC), the first major AIDS activist group. He later cofounded—and was also expelled from—ACT UP, a major AIDS activist group of the 1990s. Kramer also won notoriety with *Faggots*, his 1978 novel decrying promiscuity in the gay community, and with *The Normal Heart*, a successful off-Broadway play about the founding of GMHC.

Tony Kushner, Pulitzer Prize–winning and Tony Award–winning playwright whose major work, *Angels in America: A Gay Fantasia on National Themes*, brought gay issues into the mainstream of American theater. Kushner followed the two-part, six-hour play (dubbed separately as *Millennium Approaches* and *Perestroika*) with *Slavs*, an exploration of the former Soviet Union, and *A Dybbuk*, an adaptation of an earlier play set in Russia at the dawn of the 20th century (in Kushner's version, the Holocaust is also evoked). He has also taken an active role in speaking out on gay issues and on politics in general, publishing most frequently in *The Nation*. One of his most controversial statements was made after the death of Matthew Shepard, when Kushner accused any church that had expressed antigay bias of being responsible for Shephard's murder. (He also accused himself and others who had not worked hard enough for gay rights of being similarly to blame.)

Dick Leitsch, leader of the New York Mattachine Society during the days of Stonewall. To the new generation of gay activists, he quickly became a symbol of what they viewed as the ineffectual old homophile movement.

Audre Lorde, poet and writer, who cofounded Kitchen Table: Women of Color Press with Barbara Smith, a strikingly important act at a time when much of the visible work of the lesbian-feminist movement was dominated by white women. Lorde also published numerous volumes of poetry, including *The Marvelous Arithmetic of Distance*; memoirs, including *The Cancer Journals* and *Zami: A New Spelling of My Name* (which she called a "mythobiography"); and essays, including *Sister Outsider*. Whether she was writing poems about racism, discussing her journeys through racial and sexual politics, or sharing the intimate details of her battle with breast cancer, Lorde raised new political issues and made new connections between areas of life that had previously been seen as separate. Thus she helped make the fight against breast cancer into a feminist issue, and she raised the importance of the lesbian/gay rights movement in fighting racism and sexism as well as homophobia.

Trent Lott, Republican senator from Mississippi. Lott compared homosexuality to kleptomania during a 1999 congressional debate and refused to let the ambassadorial nomination of gay businessman James Hormel to come to the Senate floor for a vote.

Phyllis Lyon and **Del Martin,** cofounders in 1953 of the first U.S. lesbian organization, Daughters of Bilitis. The couple also coauthored *Lesbian/Woman*, a classic memoir about growing up lesbian and beginning their partnership. Lyon and Martin continued as leading lesbian activists well into the 1970s and 1980s.

Robert Mapplethorpe, openly gay photographer. His homoerotic work was the subject of a great deal of controversy, particularly after a posthumous exhibit of his pictures led a local sheriff to obtain a grand jury indictment for obscenity against the director of the Contemporary Arts Center of Cincinnati. The Mapplethorpe exhibit featured sadomasochistic imagery, including a self-portrait of Mapplethorpe naked in a leather jacket and cap with a bullwhip inserted in his anus; there was also a photo of a man's torso in a three-piece suit, with a large black penis sticking out of the unzipped pants. The director was eventually acquitted, but Mapplethorpe's name has come to symbolize allegedly obscene, homoerotic, and publicly funded art (money for the exhibit to tour had come partly from the National Endowment for the Arts [NEA]), and the controversial artist was invoked by right-wing senator Jesse Helms and others in their battle to eliminate funding for the NEA.

Leonard Matlovich, U.S. Air Force sergeant discharged in 1975 after admitting his homosexuality. Although Matlovich had consistently been awarded high ratings for his service, armed forces regulations required that he be discharged once his sexual orientation was discovered. Matlovich considered his discharge unfair and continued to fight it for five years, until finally, in 1980, a federal judge ordered the air force to allow him to reenlist. The air force also offered Matlovich another choice—a $160,000 settlement—which the former sergeant accepted. Because Matlovich had been seen as such an outstanding soldier, he helped to raise the issue of gays in the military, particularly after he became the first openly gay man to appear on the cover of *Time* magazine in 1975.

Joseph McCarthy, right-wing U.S. senator who won political fame by crusading against communists and homosexuals, both of whom he claimed were corrupting the U.S. government. He is largely responsible for the U.S. Civil Service's ban on gay men and lesbians, maintained from the late 1940s through the mid-1970s.

James Michael "Mike" McConnell, gay rights activist. McConnell is also the lover of Jack Baker, whom he married in a public—though extralegal—ceremony in the early days of gay liberation. McConnell was fired from his job with the University of Minnesota when his homosexuality—and his activism—became public; he brought an unsuccessful suit claiming discrimination.

Norma McCorvey, gay, pseudonymous plaintiff in *Roe v. Wade*, the 1973 Supreme Court case that led to the legalization of abortion. She is the author of *I Am Roe*, a memoir about that experience. Later, McCorvey became disillusioned with feminists, whom she said "used" her, and she turned to antiabortion religious right groups, for whom she became a spokeswoman.

Harvey Milk, the first openly gay San Francisco supervisor, known for his tireless dedication to gay rights—and for his assassination at the hands of fellow supervisor Dan White, along with gay-friendly mayor George Moscone. Many gay rights advocates see him as a martyr to the movement. He is the subject of a famous biography by well-known, openly gay reporter Randy Shilts titled *The Mayor of Castro Street*, which later was adopted into a film documentary as well as an opera.

Kate Millett, feminist theorist, writer, and sculptor whose gradual admission of bisexuality in the early 1970s helped raise the issue within the feminist movement. Some leaders of the National Organization for Women, including Gloria Steinem, rallied around her; others, notably Betty Friedan, felt that open lesbians would discredit the feminist cause.

David Mixner, Los Angeles gay rights leader who helped found the Municipal Elections Committee of Los Angeles (MECLA), a group of wealthy gay men (later joined by some gay women) who became extremely influential in local and national politics. Mixner also had a certain amount of influence as a friend and early supporter of President Bill Clinton.

Cherríe Moraga, coeditor with Gloria Anzaldúa of *This Bridge Called My Back: Writings by Radical Women of Color*, a pioneering anthology of political works by African-American, Latina, and other feminists. When this collection first came out, very few works by women of color had appeared, and the two editors helped to establish that lesbian-feminism could be a multiracial movement representing women from a wide range of economic backgrounds. Moraga is also a playwright and essayist whose work includes *Loving in the War Zone*.

Robin Morgan, editor of the pioneering anthology *Sisterhood Is Powerful*, as well as a collection of essays entitled *Sisterhood Is Global*. Until 1993, she was the longtime editor of *Ms.* magazine, the first feminist publication to reach a broad, nationwide audience. In the 1970s, Morgan was known for helping to establish connections between lesbianism and feminism.

George Moscone, gay-friendly mayor of San Francisco who was assassinated along with supervisor Harvey Milk at the hands of ex-supervisor Dan White. White had resigned from the board of supervisors because it seemed to him too liberal and too supportive of gay rights; when he changed his mind and asked Moscone to reinstate him, Moscone refused. White then shot and killed Moscone and Milk in their offices at city hall.

Jamie Nabozny, gay Wisconsin teenager who, in November 1996, became the first student to successfully bring a suit against a school and school district for failure to protect him from antigay violence and harassment. A federal jury found that school officials had violated his constitutional right to equal protection when they dismissed his requests for help during five years of escalating attacks from other students that eventually led to injuries requiring surgery.

Holly Near, singer and songwriter who alerted many women to the links between feminism and lesbianism when she came out as a lesbian in the 1970s. She is also known for her musical partnership with folksinger Ronnie Gilbert of the Weavers. Near's pioneering lesbian-feminist album was *Imagine My Surprise.* Her other albums include *Hang in There, Fire in the Rain,* and *Don't Hold Back.*

Joan Nestle, cofounder, with Deborah Edel, of the Lesbian Herstory Archives in New York City and prominent editor whose anthologies include *The Persistent Desire: A Butch-Femme Reader,* the *Women on Women* series (with Naomi Holoch), and *Sister and Brother* (with John Preston). She is also the author of *A Restricted Country.*

Elaine Noble, a Massachusetts state representative and the first openly gay candidate elected to state office in the United States. She was an important grassroots leader in Boston politics who established that gay candidates could offer leadership on a broad range of issues.

Robert Nugent, a Catholic priest who, with Jeannine Grannick, traveled around the United States, trying to get Catholic parishes to fully accept homosexuals into the church. On July 13, 1999, the Vatican ordered them to end their 30-year ministry and placed a gag order on them.

Sam Nunn, Georgia senator, head of the Armed Services Committee, who strongly opposed President Clinton's efforts to lift the ban on gay men and lesbians in the military. As a result of his pressure, Clinton instituted the famous "Don't Ask, Don't Tell" policy.

John J. Cardinal O'Connor, Catholic leader who presided over the archdiocese of New York during the height of gay activism. O'Connor was known for his opposition to homosexuality and for his concern about sex education and the distribution of condoms, which gay rights activists saw as a necessary measure to combat the spread of HIV/AIDS. As a result, the militant gay rights group ACT UP sponsored a controversial protest in St. Patrick's Cathedral during a Sunday mass as a way of bringing its opposition to the cardinal's home ground. In 1995 on Gay Pride Day, O'Connor made a strong statement condemning antigay violence and opposing those who believed that Christianity required hatred of homosexuals. However, to many in the gay rights and AIDS activist communities, he remains a symbol of the institutional power wielded by those who oppose gay rights.

Jean O'Leary, a leading figure in lesbian-feminist separatist politics in New York and Los Angeles. She was also a cochair of the National Gay Task Force (NGTF) and a close friend of Midge Costanza, former aide to President Jimmy Carter. With Bruce Voeller, she established the importance of female leadership of the NGTF, which has since changed its name to the National Gay and Lesbian Task Force.

Reverend Troy Perry, founder of the Metropolitan Community Church, a church dedicated to supporting gay and lesbian members, which he began in Los Angeles in 1968 and which today has branches all over the United States. Perry had been an ordained charismatic preacher thrown out of his own church for homosexuality.

Reverend Fred Phelps Southern Baptist minister and pastor of the Westboro Baptist Church in Topeka, Kansas, whose opposition to gay rights and to homosexuality in general has led him to found the "God Hates Fags" web site and to organize protests against homosexuality at the funerals of those who have died from AIDS. Phelps gained national attention when he organized a demonstration at the funeral of Matthew Shepard, the gay youth who was murdered in Laramie, Wyoming in 1998. Phelps's militant antigay stance prompted another anti–gay rights leader, Reverend Jerry Falwell, to condemn him and other Christians who, in Falwell's view, preached hate rather than love.

Ronald Reagan, president of the United States (1980–88). Under his presidency, most of the New Deal federal programs established by Franklin D. Roosevelt in the 1930s were abolished. Reagan's presidency coincided with the AIDS crisis; most AIDS activists considered that he failed to address the issue early enough and was never willing to allocate sufficient funds for it. He was also seen as creating a climate under which the New Right and religious right could flourish.

Adrienne Rich, lesbian-feminist poet, essayist, and theorist. She wrote the influential essay, "Compulsory Heterosexuality and the Lesbian Continuum," arguing for the notion that there was a continuum between female friendship and lesbian relationships and that most women would probably choose lesbian relationships if society would not violently punish them for it and/or propagandize against them. Her feminist essay collections, *Of Woman Born* and *On Lies, Secrets, and Silences,* have been widely read and cited by other feminists; her volumes of poetry include *A Change of the World, Diving into the Wreck, Dream of a Common Language,* and *A Wild Patience Has Taken Me This Far.*

Sylvia Rivera, militant drag queen who broke away from the Gay Activists Alliance (GAA) to found Street Transvestites Action Revolution (STAR). A participant in the Stonewall riot, she gained notoriety within the gay community in 1970 while working as a prostitute, she simultaneously circulated a GAA petition demanding a New York City Council bill barring antigay discrimination.

Craig Rodwell, founder of the Oscar Wilde Memorial Bookstore in New York City, a pre-Stonewall center for gay culture. He was also the organizer of the first New York City Gay Rights parade.

Jose Sarria, the first openly gay person in the United States to run for public office. Sarria, a waiter and cabaret performer at San Francisco's Black Cat, ran for the office of city supervisor in 1961.

Antonin Scalia, Supreme Court justice known for his deep opposition to gay rights, particularly as expressed in his minority opinion in *Romer v. Evans,* the decision that overturned Colorado's Amendment 2. The Colorado law, passed by referendum, itself overturned all gay rights measures in the state while banning any future legislation that would have outlawed discrimination on the basis of sexual preference. Scalia's minority opinion defended Amendment 2, arguing that gay men and women were not a minority that needed the Supreme Court's protection, but a powerful political lobby that could legitimately be restrained by a law like the one passed in Colorado.

Robin Shahar, lawyer who had been offered a job in the office of Georgia attorney general Michael J. Bowers. When Shahar had a private commitment ceremony with her lover, Bowers discovered her sexual orientation and withdrew the job offer, citing the Georgia sodomy law that technically made Shahar a felon.

Judy Shepard, mother of murdered youth Matthew Shepard who gained national attention in the wake of her son's death. Although Judy Shepard had been relatively obscure and apolitical before the murder, she gradually became a spokesperson for gay rights and continues to fight for legislation that would increase the penalties for hate crimes against lesbians and gay men.

Matthew Shepard, college student whose brutal murder in Laramie, Wyoming provoked a nationwide outcry over antigay violence and led to support for hate crimes legislation around the nation.

Randy Shilts, influential author and journalist who covered many gay rights issues, most notably the AIDS crisis. He is author of *And the Band Played On,* an important account of that crisis; *The Mayor of Castro Street: The Life and Times of Harvey Milk;* and *Conduct Unbecoming: Gays and Lesbians in the U.S. Military.*

Barbara Smith, editor, theorist, writer, and publisher. Barbara Smith has been one of the major voices to articulate an African-American lesbian-feminist-socialist position and has long been recognized as one of the major African-American theorists and activists in the gay rights movement. With the Combahee River Collective, a group formed in 1973 as the Boston chapter of the National Black Feminist Organization, Smith helped write "The Black Feminist Statement," which was deeply influential in the feminist movement and beyond. Smith also wrote and coedited several books that were central in articulating an African-American viewpoint in the feminist and lesbian movements. With Gloria T. Hull and

Patricia B. Scott, she edited *All the Women Are White, All the Blacks Are Men, But Some of Us Are Brave,* the first black women's studies anthology. With Lorraine Bethal, she edited *Conditions: Five, The Black Women's Issue,* a highly influential issue of a major lesbian-feminist magazine. She also edited *Home Girls, A Black Feminist Anthology,* and, with Elly Bulkin and Minnie Bruce Pratt, wrote *Yours in Struggle: Three Feminist Perspectives on Anti-Semitism and Racism,* which played a significant role in the lesbian-feminist and feminist movements' debates on anti-Semitism and racism in the late 1970s. Her 1974 essay, "Towards a Black Feminist Criticism," was one of the first to argue that a black women's literary tradition existed and should be studied. With Audre Lorde, she was cofounder of Kitchen Table: Women of Color Press, which insured that women of color would have a voice in the feminist movement of the 1970s and 1980. Her latest publication is *The Truth That Never Hurts: Writings on Race, Gender and Freedom* (1998), a collection of her essays and speeches.

Charles Socarides, psychiatrist who held the theory that homosexuality was a disease therapy could cure. He was a major opponent of gay objectives in the 1973 fight to remove homosexuality from the American Psychiatric Association's list of disorders. Ironically, his son proved to be gay, and a gay rights activist.

Gerry Studds, first openly gay U.S. congressman, though not willingly— Studds came out when a scandal involving sex with congressional pages revealed his homosexuality. He was otherwise known as a liberal congressman active on a variety of issues.

Andrew Sullivan, one of the best-known gay conservatives. Sullivan is the former editor of the *New Republic* who became known for his books *Virtually Normal: An Argument About Homosexuality; Love Undetectable: Notes on Friendship, Sex, and Survival;* and *Same-Sex Marriage: Pro and Con,* which he edited. Sullivan has argued vehemently for same-sex marriage and for the rights of gays to serve in the military, both of which he sees as basic acknowledgment of gay people's citizenship and humanity. However, he opposes the more liberal and radical segments of the gay rights movement, which in his view constrain the liberties of other segments of society by imposing upon them a tolerance they do not feel and an acceptance of gay men and women that is not their own choice.

Brandon Teena, transgendered victim of a fatal gay bashing. Born Teena Brandon but able to pass successfully as a young man, Brandon Teena achieved notoriety when he was brutally murdered in a small Nebraska town. His story was later told in a documentary, *The Brandon Teena Story,* and in an award-winning feature film, *Boys Don't Cry.*

Robin Tyler, lesbian-feminist comedian and speaker who conceived the idea of the first National March on Washington for Lesbian and Gay

Rights. The 1979 event grew out of a joking remark that Tyler had made in response to a local defeat for gay rights in St. Paul.

Urvashi Vaid, former executive director of the National Gay and Lesbian Task Force, one of the major national gay rights groups in the United States. Her 1995 book, *Virtual Equality: The Mainstreaming of Gay and Lesbian Liberation,* is a major document of the transformation of the gay/lesbian rights movement from invisibility to political prominence. However, Vaid points out, "virtual" equality means that in many ways gay and lesbian rights are illusory, for while gay people have become more visible and politically active, they are still subject to violence and discrimination. Vaid was named by *Time* magazine in 1994 as one of "Fifty for the Future," that is, one of the 50 most promising U.S. leaders under the age of 40. Vaid was formerly a member of the feminist collective that published the journal *Sister Courage* in Boston. (See Appendix C.)

Bruce Voeller, founder of the National Gay Task Force, an organization he went on to create after his experience as third president of the Gay Activists Alliance. Voeller wanted to create a more middle-class, middle-of-the-road organization that would focus on lobbying and achieving concrete results, rather than on seeking a broader definition of gay rights.

Byron White, Supreme Court justice who wrote the *Bowers v. Hardwick* decision, reaffirming states' rights to pass sodomy laws, including versions of such laws that were specifically antigay.

Dan White, former San Francisco supervisor who assassinated Supervisor Harvey Milk and Mayor George Moscone. At his trial, White claimed that he was suffering from depression brought on by eating too much junk food, a gambit that became known as the "Twinkie defense." White received less than eight years for voluntary manslaughter but was released from prison early. He killed himself in 1985.

Mel White, gay evangelist and former speechwriter for Jerry Falwell, who broke away from Falwell to found Soulforce, a gay evangelical group. Falwell met with White and a group of 200 of his followers and apologized for his antigay remarks in the past.

Barry Winchell, U.S. Army private first class who was killed at Fort Campbell, Kentucky. His death eventually caused President Clinton to order a review of his "don't ask, don't tell" policy, which many believed contributed to the murder. Winchell had apparently been harassed by his assailant before the murder, but was afraid to report it for fear of revealing his sexual orientation.

CHAPTER 6

GLOSSARY

a priori A legal term, meaning "before the fact." A lawyer might say, for example, that in a state where sodomy is illegal, a sexually active lesbian seeking custody of her child is a priori a criminal; that is, she has been established as a criminal before the custody proceedings have even begun.

ACT UP (AIDS Coalition to Unleash Power) A militant group founded in New York City in 1987 that favored demonstrations and direct action to protest inadequate AIDS research and discrimination against people with AIDS; chapters soon spread all over the United States. Frequent targets included drug companies that refused to make treatments available at reasonable prices; the Food and Drug Administration, for refusing to speed up the availability of new treatments; the federal government, for allocating insufficient funds and attention to the epidemic; and the Catholic Church, for opposing widespread AIDS education and the distribution of condoms, which were known to help prevent the spread of the disease.

age of consent The age at which state law considers a person old enough to consent to a sexual act, usually 16 or 18. Sex with a person below the age of consent is considered *statutory rape*, that is, rape by definition. In many countries, the age of consent is older for homosexual than for heterosexual sex.

AIDS (Acquired Immune Deficiency Syndrome) A term used to describe the many diseases caused by *HIV*, the human immunodeficiency virus. AIDS was formerly known as GRID (Gay-Related Immune Deficiency) because the syndrome was first identified among gay men in the United States. Gay activists Bruce Voeller and Virginia Apuzzo pressed the U.S. Centers for Disease Control for a name change as it became clear that anyone, gay or straight, could succumb to the disease.

Amendment 2 Successful 1992 statewide referendum that outlawed gay rights legislation in Colorado. Until Amendment 2 was overturned by the U.S. Supreme Court in *Romer v. Evans* (1996), this law superseded the antidiscrimination ordinances in the Colorado cities of Aspen, Boulder, and Denver.

American Center for Law and Justice (ACLJ) A conservative legal group affiliated with the right-wing Christian Coalition that has recently brought suit against several cities who offer domestic partnership benefits to same-sex couples.

American Civil Liberties Union (ACLU) An organization devoted to *civil liberties*, the rights and freedoms guaranteed under the Constitution. In recent years, the ACLU has worked with many gay rights groups to support the right to sexual privacy and the abolishment of sodomy laws; same-sex marriage; and gay people's right to freedom of speech and free expression.

bisexual A term that describes sexual actions or feelings that involve people of either sex; people who call themselves bisexual are expressing their ability to be sexually interested in either men or women, though not necessarily to the same extent.

bottom A slang term used to refer to the submissive or more passive partner in a lesbian/gay relationship or in a sadomasochistic relationship. It also refers to the receptive partner in specific sexual acts.

Briggs Initiative A referendum unsuccessfully introduced to California voters in 1978 by State Senator John V. Briggs that would have barred gay men and women from teaching in the public schools.

butch A slang term meaning "masculine" or "the masculine one" that can be used to refer to either gay men or lesbians. In lesbian relationships, gender roles are sometimes divided, with one woman being the "butch" and the other the "femme."

Christian right, *also known as* **religious right** A term used to refer to the portion of the right wing that specifically identifies itself with Christianity, basing its politics on a fundamentalist reading of the Bible and a wish to enforce Christian morality in the political arena. More specifically, the term refers to such leaders as Reverends Jerry Falwell and Pat Robertson and their hundreds of thousands of followers in Falwell's Liberty Alliance and Robertson's 700 Club.

coming out The process by which a gay man or lesbian declares his or her sexual orientation to herself/himself and/or others. People may speak of being "out" to their parents but not "out" at work, for example.

consenting adults A term used to describe people whom state law recognizes as old enough to consent to sexual acts.

custody The right and responsibility to care for a child, often in dispute after a divorce when parents go to live in separate households. Historically, lesbian mothers (and, less frequently, gay fathers) have been denied custody of their children on the grounds of their homosexuality.

de facto A legal term meaning "in fact." Legal advocates of gay rights often speak of de facto recognition of same-sex relationships; that is, even though a relationship is not recognized in law by a marriage contract, it may be recognized in fact, by the extension of domestic partnership benefits, custody rights, and so on. Another example of a de facto relationship is the parental status of a same-sex partner who helps to raise a child; such a person might have no legal standing, but might be recognized as "in fact" acting as the child's parent.

The Defense of Marriage Act (DOMA) A 1994 bill passed overwhelmingly by Congress in response to the possibility that same-sex marriage might be recognized in Hawaii. Because our federal system requires each state to recognize contracts—including marriage contracts—established by one another, in the absence of specific contravening policy, conservatives pushed for a federal policy that would prohibit same-sex marriage in all 50 states. Many gay rights advocates believe that DOMA is an unconstitutional usurpation by the federal government of power that has traditionally belonged to the states.

de jure A legal term meaning "in law," to be contrasted with de facto, which means "in fact." Legal advocates of gay rights often contrast the de facto recognition of same-sex partnerships—through, for instance, the extension of domestic partnership benefits—with the de jure recognition of marriage, through the actual laws governing the marriage contract.

domestic partnership Relationship between an unmarried couple who share the financial responsibilities of a household. Although the term can be used to refer to unmarried heterosexual couples, it is most often used in discussions of same-sex couples to indicate a marriagelike relationship. Some states and cities have registries where same-sex couples can legally establish their domestic partnerships.

domestic partnership benefits The economic benefits that would normally go to married couples—insurance, pension, and other financial benefits—extended to domestic partners. While partnership benefits may be extended to both heterosexual and homosexual couples, the term is most often used in discussions of same-sex couples, who are thereby allowed to enjoy the financial benefits of marriage if not the full legal recognition of that state.

Employment Non-Discrimination Act (ENDA) A bill introduced to Congress in 1994 that would extend federal protection against employment discrimination under Title VII to discrimination on the basis of sexual orientation. As of this writing, the bill had not yet passed.

ex-gay movement A movement that gained national attention in the late 1990s, as members of the Christian Right promoted Exodus International and other organizations that claimed to be able to "convert" homosexuals to heterosexuality through a combination of prayer, counseling, and group support. The ex-gay movement held out the possibility that gay people could stop engaging in homosexual activity and that some could even enter full-fledged heterosexual relationships, including marriage.

femme A slang term meaning "feminine" or "the feminine one" that can be used to refer to either gay men or lesbians. In lesbian relationships, gender roles are sometimes divided, with one woman being the "butch" and the other the "femme."

GMHC Originally Gay Men's Health Crisis, the organization is now known by its initials to suggest a broader range of AIDS activism than the group's initial focus, which was on gay men with AIDS. GMHC was co-founded in August 1981, just months after the first AIDS cases were identified, by writer and activist Larry Kramer, who was soon expelled; its founding and subsequent history are the subject of Kramer's successful off-Broadway play, *The Normal Heart*.

hate crimes Criminal acts based primarily on prejudice against a particular group of people; the 1990 Hate Crimes Statistics Act recognizes race, religion, national origin, and sexual orientation as categories of people against whom hate crimes might occur. In some states, hate crimes carry harsher penalties than other criminal acts.

heterosexism Acts, words, or thoughts suggesting that heterosexuals are in any way superior to homosexuals; modeled on the terms *sexism* (commonly understood as the idea that men are superior to women) and *racism* (the idea that one race is superior to another).

HIV The human immunodeficiency virus; generally accepted as the cause of AIDS in humans.

homoerotic Having or expressing sexual feelings for people of the same sex.

homophile A 1950s and 1960s term that literally means "lover of men"; it was used by early gay rights organizations to indicate those who supported "homosexual" men; thus, members of homophile organizations such as the Mattachine Society were not necessarily admitting to being homosexual.

homophobia Literally, the irrational fear of homosexuals; used more widely to denote hatred for gay men and lesbians and the view that they are somehow inferior to heterosexuals.

Human Rights Campaign The major national gay rights lobbying organization, which focuses on influencing Washington politics through seeking influence among politicians and attempting to elect gay or gay-friendly political leaders. The group and its leader, Elizabeth Birch, became controversial in the gay rights movement when it endorsed right-wing New York senator Al D'Amato to reward him for some gay-friendly stands he had taken; many gay men and women perceived that his liberal opponent, Charles Schumer, was more generally supportive of gay people and their allies.

in the closet   Slang term for hiding one's gay or lesbian identity, feelings, or practices. A gay man or woman who is "in the closet" might have an active gay or lesbian life that he or she hides from others. The term also refers to people who are unaware of their own gay or lesbian feelings. This is also referred to as "closeted."

Knight Initiative   Known officially as Proposition 22, a referendum sponsored by California state senator Pete Knight and subsequently approved by that state's voters, legally defining marriage as being only between a man and a woman and requiring the state to deny recognition to same-sex marriages contracted in other states.

Mattachine Society   The first gay rights group in the United States. It was founded by Harry Hay in 1950.

Moral Majority   The name of a group once led by Reverend Jerry Falwell, now known as the Liberty Alliance. Falwell took the name from a remark of former President Richard Nixon, who claimed that there was a "silent majority" that did not agree with the more visible actions of radicals.

National Gay and Lesbian Task Force (NGLTF)   Formerly known as the National Gay Task Force, one of the major national gay rights organizations. Its activities range from national lobbying and educational efforts to grassroots organizing and legal work.

outing   A term made popular by gay journalist Michelangelo Signorile that means making someone's homosexuality public against the person's wishes. Outing was justified on the grounds that a public figure who could help other gay men and lesbians by revealing the truth had no right to hide this information, particularly if the person in question had opposed gay rights or made homophobic statements.

passing   The attempt to be viewed as belonging to another, preferred category; the word may indicate gay people who pass as straight, Jews who pass as gentile, or people of color who pass as white. In some contexts, the word also refers to men or women, including transsexuals and transgendered people, who pass as people of the opposite sex.

postgay   A term popularized by *Out* magazine, among others, meant to indicate that the time for gay rights activism is over and that gay people are now free to live their lives simply as human beings, not limited to the category of gay human beings.

queer   A relatively new term used to indicate both homosexuals and heterosexuals who do not accept mainstream society's definitions of gender and sexuality. It became popular in the 1990s as the gay rights movement became both broader and more militant.

Glossary

Queer Nation   A militant branch of ACT UP that became popular during the early 1990s, and was known for developing the term *queer* as a protest against the old categories of "homosexual" and "heterosexual." Rather than winning more rights within the existing system of gender and sexuality, Queer Nation wanted to challenge the system itself.

sadomasochism   The term for a variety of sexual practices and relationships, characterized by one dominant partner (a sadist, or in slang terms, the "top") and one submissive or passive one (a masochist, or in slang terms, the "bottom"). Sometimes sadomasochistic relationships involve the dominant partner inflicting physical or psychological pain on the submissive one; sometimes the relationship simply involves giving orders. Those who practice "S and M" stress that these are consensual relationships, wherein many provisions are made for the submissive partner to stop the pain or punishment at will.

separatism   A theory, popular among many lesbian-feminists of the 1970s, that a persecuted group of people should live as separately as possible in its own community.

sexual minorities   A catchall term for those whose sexual practices are unusual; generally used to refer to people who practice sadomasochism, as well as transvestites and transgendered people, as opposed to "maintream" gay men and lesbians (and heterosexuals).

sodomy   Originally, any sexual practice that involved the insertion of one male's penis into another male's anus; however, the legal use of the term varies widely. In some states it refers to other homosexual acts, such as one man's penis making contact with another man's mouth; in yet other states it refers to any contact between penis and anus or penis and mouth, whether homosexual or heterosexual. Sodomy laws can also be used to criminalize sexual acts among women, even though the original definition of the word could not be used that way.

top   A slang term used to refer to the dominant partner in a lesbian or gay relationship and/or to the dominant partner in a sadomasochistic relationship. It also refers to the insertive partner in specific sexual acts.

transgendered   A general term suggesting that a person has been born into a body of the "wrong" gender; that is, the person feels herself to be a woman, but has been born into a man's body; or feels himself to be a man, but has been born into a woman's body. Some transgendered people choose to dress as the gender they feel they "really" are; others may choose to have an operation and/or take hormones to change to their "true" gender. Some transgendered people identify as gay men or lesbians; others feel they are straight men or women born into the "wrong" bodies.

transsexual   A person who has changed from one gender to another, usually by means of an operation and/or hormone treatments.

transvestite   A person who dresses as a member of the opposite sex; although popular stereotypes suggest that transvestites are gay, people of any sexual orientation may be transvestites. Although some transvestites may feel that they are "really" of the opposite sex, many simply enjoy a permanent or temporary change of costume.

visitation rights   **(a)** The right to visit one's child, often an issue when child custody is in dispute. Historically, lesbian mothers (and, less frequently, gay fathers) have seen their visitation rights restricted on the grounds of their homosexuality; for example, they might not be allowed to see their children alone or might be forbidden to see them in the presence of their lesbian or gay partners. **(b)** The right to visit another family member when that person is ill and unable to make his or her wishes known; a right automatically granted to married heterosexuals who wish to see their spouses, but usually denied to gay men and women who wish to visit their partners.

PART II

GUIDE TO FURTHER RESEARCH

CHAPTER 7

HOW TO RESEARCH
GAY RIGHTS

One of the biggest difficulties confronted by the researcher of gay rights is the overwhelming amount of available material. As discussed earlier, the term *gay rights* can be used to refer variously to legal, political, cultural, social, and economic issues. Moreover, the gay rights movement has been moving, in the words of Evan Wolfson of the Lambda Legal Defense Fund, "at Internet speed," implying that researchers may be overwhelmed by the vast number of books, articles, magazines, web sites, and other sources of information on everything from Supreme Court decisions to commitment ceremonies.

Further complicating the problem is the uneven nature of the information: There is a great deal of information on some topics, very little on others. Some political, cultural, and legal arenas have been transformed at dizzying speed (even as this book was being prepared, for example, major developments were occurring regarding gay marriage and gays in the military), while others have changed very little after certain landmark events. (As of this writing, for example, it is possible to look back at the U.S. Supreme Court's 1993 *Romer v. Evans* decision, overturning Colorado's Amendment 2, and say that the apparent movement towards anti–gay rights legislation on a statewide level was slowed, although antigay initiatives continue on a local level.) In still other cases, the developments themselves have been uneven or wildly contradictory: custody battles are still difficult for lesbian mothers, even as more states have allowed gay couples to adopt; the U.S. Supreme Court's 1986 *Bowers v. Hardwick* decision upheld states' rights to maintain sodomy laws—yet no state recriminalized sodomy after that decision and the trend to overturn sodomy laws continued steadily into the 1990s.

How, then, can researchers proceed? Here are some general suggestions, followed by more specific advice about where to find material.

161

TIPS FOR RESEARCHING GAY RIGHTS

- *Define the topic as specifically as possible.* Whether surfing the Net, checking out a bookstore, exploring a library, or doing a database search, one is likely to run into an overwhelming amount of material even on an apparently narrowly defined topic. The more specifically a researcher has decided what aspects of gay rights are of interest and how much needs to be known, the easier it will be to find what he/she wants. For suggestions on particular categories that can help define a topic, see the subheads used in the periodicals section of Chapter 8.

- *Be aware of the key historical landmarks.* As discussed in Chapter 3, much of the gay rights movement has proceeded in leaps and bounds, defined by certain key historical moments. Among the most important are the Stonewall uprising of 1969; the beginning of the antigay backlash in 1977; the beginning of the AIDS crisis in 1981; the founding of ACT UP in 1987; and the election of President Clinton in 1992, which ushered in an era of major developments regarding gays in the military, gay marriage, and gay adoption, as well as an unprecedented welcoming of gay culture into the mainstream, along with the introduction of new medications that transformed the nature of the AIDS crisis. Obviously, the landmarks are different for various issues—we have tried to suggest the most important turning points in Part I of this book—so the researcher must have key dates firmly in mind to evaluate the usefulness of any published source.

- *Know the sources.* As we have also seen, there is no such thing as a monolithic "gay rights movement" or "anti–gay rights movement." Both supporters and opponents of gay rights have widely varying opinions; indeed, little agreement exists on what "gay rights" means. To some, it signifies sexual freedom; to others, it is defined by Supreme Court cases and lower court rulings; to still others, it refers to the growing political power of gay and gay-friendly politicians; to yet more others, it concerns such civil rights as adoption, child custody, marriage, employment, and housing. Thus the researcher looking for overviews or evaluations, or seeking commentators to help explain the significance of a particular event, has to be especially aware of a source's potential bias. To many people on both sides of the issue, Ellen DeGeneres's coming out on television seemed to have enormous significance; to others, the event meant relatively little. A new researcher would do well to remember the widely varying opinions and intense disagreements on this issue.

GETTING STARTED:
SOME HELPFUL SOURCES

BOOKS

This volume attempts to provide a comprehensive overview of the modern gay rights movement from 1969–2000. Another very useful overview, covering the period from 1900–1997, is *Becoming Visible: An Illustrated History of Lesbian and Gay Life in Twentieth-Century America*, by Molly McGarry and Fred Wasserman (New York: New York Public Library, Penguin Studio, 1998), which is based on an exhibit curated at the New York Public Library by Fred Wasserman, Molly McGarry, and Mimi Bowling. Drawing from the most extensive display of lesbian and gay history ever mounted in a museum or gallery space, the book covers gay history, politics, and culture. The book focuses on material concerning New York City, but is probably the single best overview of the gay rights movement currently available.

Another helpful source is *Out for Good: The Struggle to Build a Gay Rights Movement in America*, by Dudley Clendinen and Adam Nagourney (Simon & Schuster, 1999). Beginning with the Stonewall uprising in 1969 and proceeding to the height of the AIDS crisis in 1988, *Out for Good* is a thoroughly detailed chronicle of political events and organizations, with extensive coverage of New York City, Los Angeles, and San Francisco, and a great deal of information about other centers of lesbian and gay activity, such as Minneapolis, New Orleans, Atlanta, and Washington, D.C. *Out for Good* tends to focus on political and electoral events, offering profiles of people and organizations committed to working within the system; its information is far less comprehensive concerning radical politics, cultural activity, and developments in lesbian and gay theory. It also tends to cover gay men far more than lesbians. However, no other book includes such a wealth of information about the events of those two decades.

Witness to Revolution, The Advocate *Reports on Gay and Lesbian Politics, 1967–1999*, edited by Chris Bull (Alyson Books, 1999), is an anthology of major articles on gay rights from one of the nation's major national gay publications. Although this book is no substitute for an actual history, it does touch on many of the major issues of the past three decades, with particular focus on the gay conservatives who came out in the 1990s.

The books section of the following chapter includes information on a large number of books, but here, for your convenience, are some key historical and political texts (see individual listings in the following chapter for specific publication information):

163

- **Profiles of Key People and Events:** Martin Duberman's *Stonewall*; Kay Tobin and Randy Wicker's *The Gay Crusaders* (profiles of pre-Stonewall gay activists); Eric Marcus's *Making History* (a collection of oral histories); John D'Emilio's *Sexual Politics, Sexual Communities: The Making of a Homosexual Minority in the United States, 1940–1970*; Randy Shilts's *The Mayor of Castro Street: The Life and Times of Harvey Milk*.

- **Landmark Personal Accounts and Opinions:** Martin Duberman's *Cures: A Gay Man's Odyssey*; Robin Morgan's *Going Too Far: The Personal Chronicle of a Feminist*; Joan Nestle's *A Restricted Country*; Gore Vidal's *United States: Essays, 1952–1992*; Edmund White's *States of Desire: Travels in Gay America*.

- **Anthologies of Gay History:** Jonathan Ned Katz's *Gay American History: Lesbians and Gay Men in the U.S.A.*; Karla Jay and Allen Young's *Out of the Closets, Voices of Gay Liberation* (an anthology of the first post-Stonewall gay liberation writings in America, compiled in 1972); Mark Blasius and Shane Phelan's *We Are Everywhere, A Historical Sourcebook of Gay and Lesbian Politics* (including international material, with a focus on the United States, from 1754 to 1994).

- **Key Works of Lesbian Feminism:** Sidney Abbott and Barbara Love's *Sappho Was a Right-On Woman* (a 1972 exploration of lesbian issues); Del Martin and Phyllis Lynon's *lesbian/woman* (a cultural analysis); Kate Millett's *Sexual Politics: The Classic Analysis of the Interplay Between Man, Women, and Culture; Building Feminist Theory: Essays from* Quest, *a Feminist Quarterly*; Lillian Faderman's *Surpassing the Love of Men* (an analysis of early "romantic friendships" between women in 18th-, 19th-, and 20th-century America and Europe) and *To Believe in Women: What Lesbians Have Done for America—A History*.

- **Coverage of the AIDS Crisis:** Paul Monette's *Borrowed Time: An AIDS Memoir* and *Becoming a Man: Half a Life Story* (memoirs); Randy Shilts's *And the Band Played On* (a history of the crisis from the first appearance of the virus to the discovery of how it was spread); Larry Kramer's *Reports from the Holocaust: The Making of an AIDS Activist* (focusing on Kramer's key role in AIDS activism, 1981–1988).

- **Gay Urban Life:** Frances FitzGerald's *Cities on a Hill: A Journey Through Contemporary American Cultures*; George Chauncey's *Gay New York: Gender, Urban Culture, and the Making of the Gay Male World, 1890–1940*; Charles Kaiser's *The Gay Metropolis*.

- **Key Cultural Works:** Rita Mae Brown's *Rubyfruit Jungle* (a coming-of-age lesbian novel); Andrew Holleran's *Dancer from the Dance* (a portrait of pre-AIDS sexual liberation in New York City); Armistead Maupin's *Tales* *from the City* and *More Tales from the City* (a fictional chronicle of gay life in San Francisco throughout the 1970s and 1980s); Harvey Fierstein's *Torch Song Trilogy* (a Tony Award–winning play about 1970s gay life in New York—also available as a movie); Larry's Kramer's *The Normal Heart* (a play about the founding of Gay Men's Health Crisis at the beginning of the AIDS epidemic); Tony Kushner's *Angels in America* (a Pulitzer Prize–winning play about gay politics and the beginning of the AIDS crisis); Adrienne Rich's *The Dream of a Common Language: Poems, 1974–1978*; Judy Grahn's *The Work of a Common Woman* (a 1978 poetry collection); Rosa Guy's *Ruby* (a 1976 novel about a lesbian relationship in New York City's West Indian community); Audre Lorde's *Zami: A New Spelling of My Name* (a "biomythography" in which Lorde explores the interrelationships between her sexual and racial identities).

Two excellent reference works are *The Gay Almanac* and *The Lesbian Almanac*, both compiled by the National Museum and Archive of Gay and Lesbian History. Although their 1996 publication date means that contemporary readers may need to update some major facts, both books provide a wealth of useful information, such as lists of key authors, historical highlights and lowlights, brief biographies of major figures, statistics, and coverage of everything from culture and art to sports, religion, travel, and the media.

Another useful reference work is *The Gay and Lesbian Movement: References and Resources*, by Robert B. Marks Ridinger (G.K. Hall & Company), an annotated bibliography covering the U.S. gay liberation movement from the middle of the 19th century through 1993. Since the focus is specifically on the movement for social change, rather than on gay history in general, researchers looking for material on gay rights will find this volume particularly helpful.

NEWSPAPERS

One excellent way to research gay rights is to pick a narrowly defined topic and do a database search. In preparing this book, ProQuest, the database used by the New York Public Library, was very helpful, but many others are available. Most databases will provide both an abstract and the full article; however, because of a recently settled lawsuit, the *New York Times* provides only abstracts free of charge for anything published before December 1999. Other newspaper archives have followed the *New York Times*'s example and have begun instituting a fee for examining or printing a full article.

Even a narrowly defined topic can yield an overwhelming plethora of articles. For researchers trying to grasp an issue quickly, it might be useful to focus on one or two major newspapers. The *New York Times* and the *San*

Francisco Chronicle have the well-deserved reputations of never missing a major event related to gay rights; of the two, the *Chronicle* offers the most supportive coverage, as well as being readily available by database. The *Atlanta Journal-Constitution, Detroit News, Denver Post, Houston Chronicle, Los Angeles Times*, and *Washington Post* are also good sources for coverage, whereas the *Boston Globe's* coverage tends to be somewhat less exhaustive. The *Christian Science Monitor* offers a more skeptical view of the gay rights movement. The *Wall Street Journal's* coverage is the most critical, and that paper offers the most frequent expression of antigay opinion.

Reporters who regularly cover gay rights issues, and whose work tends to feature useful overviews and analyses, include Adam Nagourney of the *New York Times*, Deb Price of the *Detroit News*, and Joan Biskupic of the *Washington Post*. A search for articles by these writers is one good way to quickly spot key trends and events for a given period.

MAGAZINES

A second type of database is usually required for periodicals other than newspapers, particularly for scholarly journals and more specialized publications. For this book, the university database from Yale University, specifically its lesbian and gay abstracts section, was very helpful. Many universities have a similar database, although, as with Yale, they often require either an institutional affiliation or a fee. Scholarly journals that are particularly useful for researching lesbian and gay issues include the *Journal of Homosexuality*, the *Gay and Lesbian Review* (formerly the *Harvard Gay and Lesbian Review*), the *Gay and Lesbian Quarterly, Signs*, and *Choice*.

Specialized lesbian and gay periodicals are another key source of information. The best national sources of information are the weeklies the *Advocate* (which is based in Los Angeles) and the *Village Voice* (which is based in New York and is not specifically a gay/lesbian publication, but has excellent coverage and analysis and is also available online). *Gay Community News*, based in Massachusetts, is inclusive but published irregularly and has better coverage of radical politics and more extensive information about lesbian issues than the *Advocate*. *Off our backs* is a national monthly with a radical feminist perspective that offers frequent coverage of lesbian issues. *POZ* is a monthly magazine targeted toward the HIV/AIDS community. It is an excellent source for the latest information on treatment, activism, and legal cases involving HIV/AIDS.

Other key gay publications are the *Washington* [D.C.] *Blade, New York Blade, LGNY* (New York), *L.A. Gay Times*, and *Bay Windows* (San Francisco). *Sojourner*, in the Boston/Cambridge area, is a feminist journal with extensive coverage of lesbian issues and culture. Other local lesbian and gay publications usually include coverage of national events and trends.

One useful way of following lesbian and gay issues is to look for the work of particular columnists and journalists known for their investigative reporting and/or analysis. Hard-hitting journalist Michelangelo Signorile won fame (some would call it notoriety) for "outing" nationally known gay figures in his weekly column for *Outweek* magazine, but his work also includes extensive coverage of the gay marriage issue, sexism among gay men, trends regarding safe-sex practices, and other cutting-edge issues in the gay community. Signorile is also the author of *Queer in America: Sex, Media and the Closets of Power* (New York: Random House, 1993) and *Life Outside, The Signorile Report on Gay Men: Sex, Drugs, Muscles, and the Passages of Life* (New York: HarperCollins, 1997).

Richard Goldstein, a columnist and editor at the *Village Voice*, offers wide-ranging cultural and political analysis on a variety of topics, including gay issues, as do his fellow reporters Alisa Solomon, Lisa Kennedy, Donna Minkowitz, Guy Trebay, and Stacey d'Erasmo, all of whom write extensively for a number of other publications as well, including the *Nation*, a national political journal whose coverage of progressive politics includes frequent articles on gay rights. Doug Ireland is a regular *Nation* contributor who often writes about gay political issues. Mark Schoofs's Pulitzer Prize–winning AIDS coverage—primarily published in the *Village Voice*—includes both political developments and the latest scientific discoveries.

Dan Savage was a regular columnist for *Out* magazine. Savage also writes "Savage Love," a nationally syndicated sexual advice column, and is the author of *The Kid, An Adoption Story: How My Boyfriend and I Decided to Get Pregnant*. Elise Harris is a journalist whose work appeared in *Out* and elsewhere.

Major cultural and political commentators include Tony Kushner, author of the Pulitzer Prize–winning play *Angels in America* and a frequent contributor to the *Nation*; former *New Republic* editor Andrew Sullivan, whose conservative, Catholic perspective informs his books *Virtually Normal* and *Love Undetectable: Notes on Friendship, Sex, and Survival*; conservative writer Bruce Bawer, author of *A Place at the Table* (1993), a formulation of gay rights that stressed acceptance into mainstream society; and Gabriel Rotello, who won fame for his 1997 book, *Sexual Ecology: AIDS and the Destiny of Gay Men*, in which he argued that gay men needed to develop serially monogamous relationships to combat the spread of AIDS.

RESEARCH AND THE INTERNET

The Internet can also be a rich source of data. Again, researchers should be aware that they will encounter an overwhelming amount of information of widely varying quality if they simply enter "gay rights" or "gay legal rights" in a search engine (although this also can be a surprisingly effective way of finding good information quickly). Otherwise, there are two choices: to approach the issue from the "legal" side or to approach it from the "gay rights" side.

An outstanding source of gay legal rights information on the web is http://www.gayrightsinfo.com, which lists the latest on congressional voting records, federal departmental policy, state and local legislation, Supreme Court decisions, sodomy laws, antidiscrimination law, domestic partnership, hate crime/bias crime law, and corporate policy on gays and lesbians. The gay directory "gayscape," at http://www.gayscape.com, has a subcategory called "Pride," whose listings in turn include "gay rights," "activist groups," "anti-violence," "gays and lesbians in the military," and "gay, lesbian and bisexual youth."

A less user-friendly but still useful source is Queer Resources Directory, http://www.qrd.org, which has links to business, legal, and workplace issues. Information on court cases and legislation is also available through the web sites for the National Gay and Lesbian Task Force (http://ngltf.org), Human Rights Campaign (http://hrc.org), National Committee on Lesbian Rights (http://nclrights.org), and National Organization for Women (information on lesbian rights; http://now.org/now/issues/lgbi/lgbi.html). (For more detailed information, see the bibliography.)

Researchers looking for specific court cases and legislation can turn to one of the many free sources for legal information on the web. Check out http://legal.conline.com for a directory that offers you links to information on the U.S. Supreme Court, other federal courts, state courts, and electronic law libraries. Unfortunately, electronic law libraries—including Westlaw and Lexis-Nexis—all cost money to use, either via subscription or on a per-use basis, and they really are the only way to get comprehensive access to any court cases before 1990 with the exception of Supreme Court cases, which are available through http://findlaw.com. Findlaw.com also offers a comprehensive directory of various Internet legal resources, including a state-by-state guide, but many states do not offer online texts of court cases; many others go back only a few years or, at most, to 1990.

Another useful Internet resource is the Meta-Index for U.S. Legal Research, a service of Georgia State University's College of Law: http://gsu-law.gus.edu/metaindex. You can access Supreme Court cases, circuit court cases, federal legislation, and federal regulations, as well as find links to other online law resources.

Cornell Law School also offers its Legal Information Institute (http://law.cornell.edu), which makes available a variety of legal resources. For anything other than New York State law, however, researchers would do better to use one of the other sources.

Finally, for a wide range of information on international, federal, and state courts, Northwestern University offers government publications and maps at http://www.library.nwu.edu/govpub/resource/legal/courts.html.

ANTI–GAY RIGHTS POSITIONS

Another way to track the gay rights movement is to follow the newsmakers and opinion-makers who oppose gay rights. Columnist and presidential candidate Pat Buchanan and journalist George Will offer conservative opinions in a variety of newspaper op-ed pages. Buchanan regularly publishes in the *New York Post*, and Will frequently appears in the *Washington Post*. The following activists can be tracked in database searches of news stories or as authors of op-ed and opinion pieces: Jerry Falwell of the Liberty Alliance; Pat Robertson of the 700 Club; Ralph Reed of the Christian Coalition; Gary Bauer of the Family Research Council and a presidential candidate in 2000; James Dobson of Focus on the Family; Will Perkins of Colorado for Family Values, who was a leader of the Amendment 2 movement; and Reverend Fred Phelps, leader of the antigay protests around Matthew Shepard's death and around the funerals of people who died from AIDS complications and maintainer of a web site called "God Hates Fags" (http://www.godhatesfags.com).

CHAPTER 8

ANNOTATED BIBLIOGRAPHY

The following bibliography contains three major sections: books, articles, and web sites.

The books section is by no means a comprehensive listing of all the books on this wide-ranging topic; rather, it is a selection of the most important and representative volumes that a beginning researcher might find useful. It includes those books considered "classics" as well as a broad sampling of key books on major topics in gay rights.

The articles were drawn primarily from daily newspapers around the United States, as well as from some specialized publications such as the *Nation*. The intention was to include a wide variety of newspapers so that researchers would have access to the spectrum of opinion across the nation and to focus primarily on sources that would be available in most libraries. Thus, for more specialized gay/lesbian sources and more scholarly periodical resources, the researcher is advised to consult the specialized periodicals described in the previous chapter.

Articles are organized according to the following topics: adoption, AIDS activism, AIDS discrimination, ballot measures, civic organizations, court decisions, culture/media, custody, domestic partnerships, education, hate crimes legislation, history and analysis of the movement, housing rights, immigration laws, international, marriage, military, politics, religion, sodomy laws, transgender issues, and workplace issues.

The web sites listed here likewise do not represent the virtual universe of available Internet resources. They do, however, constitute a good starting place for the beginning researcher, along with an assurance that with these listings, the researcher can easily keep up with major political and legal events in the ever-changing field of gay rights.

BOOKS

Adam, Barry D. *The Rise of a Gay and Lesbian Movement.* Boston: Twayne, 1987. Adam thoroughly reviews the early gay and lesbian rights movements in Germany and the United States along with the reactions they provoked among the heterosexual majority. He also provides encapsulations of changes taking place in Canada, Mexico, and Europe.

Bawer, Bruce. *A Place at the Table: The Gay Individual in American Society.* New York: Touchstone Books, 1994. Bawer, a gay, conservative Christian, posits that the media-dominated gay centers of New York, Los Angeles, and San Francisco are out of touch with the kinds of lives most gay men are living in the heartland of the country. He believes these men constitute a virtual gay silent majority who have been silenced by the political and sexual radicals of the gay "elite." In his opinion, the excesses and self-destructiveness of gay culture must be addressed before the community has any hope of achieving real political equality.

Berubé, Allan. *Coming Out under Fire: The History of Gay Men and Women in World War Two.* New York: Free Press, 1990. This is a comprehensive and scholarly study of the role played by lesbians and gay men in World War II, along with the military's policies and attitudes about homosexuality. It provides an excellent context for any discussion of the "don't ask, don't tell" controversy that has dominated gay political discourse in the 1990s.

Blasius, Mark, and Shane Phelan, eds. *We Are Everywhere: A Historical Sourcebook of Gay and Lesbian Politics.* New York: Routledge, 1997. Blasius and Phelan have compiled a volume of primary source material that will help both the academic historian as well as the common reader. Manuscripts range from 18th-century legal documents to contemporary essays and analysis. The book charts how life has changed for gay people as well as how gay people themselves have created change.

Boswell, John. *Same-Sex Unions in Premodern Europe.* New York: Vintage, 1995. In this landmark book, Boswell traces the history of same-sex marriages in the early Christian church throughout Europe and the Mediterranean world. He makes a very strong case that these unions existed and were even officially sanctioned. Boswell takes great pains to distinguish the sexual presumptions about marriage among our premodern ancestors from those held by our postmodern society.

Bryant, Anita. *The Anita Bryant Story: The Survival of Our Nation's Families and the Threat of Militant Homosexuality.* Old Tappan, N.J.: Revell, 1977. The Stonewall riots of 1969 may have signaled the "coming out" of the gay liberation movement, but Anita Bryant's campaign to overturn a gay rights ordinance in Dade County, Florida marked the beginnings of the religious right backlash that continues to this day. It also proved that the gay community could effectively organize nationally to combat homophobia. Bryant tells her side of the story in her own words.

Bunch, Charlotte. *Passionate Politics.* New York: St. Martin's Press, 1986. A collection of essays by one of the leading theorists of the lesbian-feminist movement, this book includes an extensive section detailing Bunch's early experience and involvement in the gay and lesbian rights movement.

Chauncey, George. *Gay New York: Gender, Urban Culture, and the Making of the Gay Male World, 1890–1940.* New York: Basic Books, 1994. Chauncey has had much to do with altering perceptions about gay and lesbian history. In this book he reveals that the New York of the early 20th century had a thriving gay culture that, contrary to popular perception, was quite open about its existence and which supported clubs, restaurants, and bathhouses. The sexual suppression during the middle part of the century virtually erased this history. This book is a powerful reminder that cultural acceptance does not equal political empowerment.

Clendinen, Dudley, and Adam Nagourney. *Out for Good: The Struggle to Build a Gay Rights Movement.* New York: Simon & Schuster, 1999. This comprehensive look at the political, reformist wing of the modern gay rights movement is based on interviews with 330 gay rights activists directly involved in everything from the Stonewall riots of 1969 to ACT UP in 1987.

Comstock, David. *Violence against Lesbians and Gay Men.* New York: Columbia University Press, 1991. Comstock examines the history of violence against gay men and lesbians. He then speculates, based on sociological evidence, about why adolescent and young adult males are most likely to commit these crimes. An excellent background source for any discussion of the Matthew Shepard case.

Cruikshank, Margaret. *The Gay and Lesbian Liberation Movement.* New York: Routledge, Chapman & Hall, 1992. Cruikshank's book, part of the series "Revolutionary Thought/Radical Movements," divides the gay and lesbian movement into three distinct philosophical streams: a movement for sexual liberation, a civil rights movement, and an upsetting of hundreds of years of Western thought. She is particularly interested in the complex negotiations between gay men and lesbians.

D'Emilio, John. *Making Trouble.* New York: Routledge, Chapman & Hall, 1992. D'Emilio's book contains a collection of his essays on a wide variety of topics that affect the gay and lesbian community, from capitalism to higher learning and from sodomy statutes to effective strategies for building a movement.

———. *Sexual Politics, Sexual Communities: The Making of a Homosexual Minority in the United States, 1940–1970.* Chicago: University of Chicago Press, 1983. D'Emilio fills in the history of the gay and lesbian rights movement in the country before Stonewall. He presents an examination of such groups as the Mattachine Society and the Daughters of Bilitis, as well as other early "homophile" organizations.

Duberman, Martin. *About Time: Exploring the Gay Past.* New York: Meridian, 1991. Duberman, one of the country's foremost gay historians and political theorists, collects many of his essays into this volume, as well as a selection of historical documents dating to the 19th century.

———. *Midlife Queer: Autobiography of a Decade, 1971–1981.* Madison: University of Wisconsin Press, 1998. Duberman continues his examination of the gay rights movement with this examination of the urban gay culture of the post-Stonewall 1970s. He refracts this history through the multiple prisms of radical politics, fledgling gay studies programs, alternative psychiatric therapies, and the sexual social scene of the pre-AIDS generation.

———. *Stonewall.* New York: Dutton, 1993. Well-written account of the events of June 27 and 28, 1969, commonly referred to as the Stonewall riots. Duberman provides an excellent historical context for what is generally recognized as the birth of modern gay liberation by recounting the lives of six individuals who experienced the event.

Duberman, Martin, Martha Vicinus, and George Chauncey, Jr., eds. *Hidden from History: Reclaiming the Gay and Lesbian Past.* New York: New American Library, 1989. The three editors, all leading scholars in the field of gay and lesbian studies, have collected essays tracing the history of same-sex relationships and desire from preindustrial societies through the 19th century and into the postmodern era.

Editors of the *Harvard Law Review. Sexual Orientation and the Law.* Cambridge, Mass.: Harvard University Press, 1990. This book is a reprint of the May 1989 issue of the *Harvard Law Review,* which examined the legal problems faced by gay men and lesbians. Most of the major topics are covered, including employment, education, domestic partnerships, and adoption and custody battles.

Faderman, Lillian. *Odd Girls and Twilight Lovers: A History of Lesbian Life in Twentieth-Century America.* New York: Columbia University Press, 1991. Faderman tells the compelling story of lesbian life in the 20th century, from the "Boston marriages" of the early 1900s to the "lipstick lesbians" of today. Using journals, unpublished manuscripts, songs, news accounts, novels, medical literature, and numerous interviews, she relates an often surprising narrative of lesbian life.

———. *Surpassing the Love of Men: Romantic Friendship and Love Between Women from the Renaissance to the Present.* New York: Morrow, 1981. Springing from an examination of Emily Dickinson's passionate friendship and private correspondence with her sister-in-law, Sue Gilbert, Faderman's exploration of the history of female same-sex relationships in Western culture is a classic of lesbian feminist scholarship.

———. *To Believe in Women: What Lesbians Have Done for America—A History.* New York: Houghton Mifflin, 1999. Faderman continues the work she began in *Surpassing the Love of Men,* chronicling the stories of the women who, while fighting for suffrage, higher education, and women's entrance into "male" professions, also "lived in committed relationships with other women."

Fricke, Aaron. *Reflections of a Rock Lobster: A Story about Growing Up Gay.* Boston: Alyson Publications, 1981. Fricke recounts the story of his legal battle to be allowed to take another boy to his senior prom.

Gibson, Gifford Guy, with Mary Jo Risher. *By Her Own Admission: A Lesbian Mother's Fight to Keep Her Son.* Garden City, N.Y.: Doubleday, 1977. In 1976, a Texas jury declared Mary Jo Risher an "unfit mother" because she was a lesbian. Her son, Richard, was taken from her and awarded to her former husband. This book recounts the story of the long court battles surrounding that event.

Harris, Daniel. *The Rise and Fall of Gay Culture.* New York: Hyperion, 1997. In this collection of interconnected essays, Harris argues that the social gains gay men have won in the past 30 years have gradually robbed them of their unique cultural identity. Later essays include stinging critiques of more recent cultural phenomenon such as glossy gay magazines and AIDS memorabilia.

Hippler, Mike. *Matlovich: The Good Soldier.* Boston: Alyson Publications, 1989. This book chronicles the life and struggles of the first gay man to come out while still in the military. His five-year dispute with the air force would foreshadow much of the controversy that has dogged the armed services during the 1990s.

Hunter, Nan D., Sherryl Michaelson, and Tom Stoddard. *The Rights of Lesbians and Gay Men: The Basic ACLU Guide to a Gay Person's Rights.* Carbondale: Southern Illinois University Press, 1992. One of the American Civil Liberties Union's handbooks on the rights of individuals, this book is a complete review of the rights of gay men and lesbians. It covers speech, association and organization, employment, housing and public accommodation, the armed services, families, criminal law, and HIV discrimination.

Jay, Karla, and Allen Young. *After You're Out.* New York: Links Books, 1975. This collection offers several dozen personal essays describing the profound changes the early gay liberation movement made in individual lives. The book is divided into three main sections: "Identity and Lifestyles," "Survival in a Hostile World," and "Creating Community and Helping Ourselves."

———. *Out of the Closets.* New York: Douglas Books, 1972. This is one of the essential documents of the early radical culture that gave birth to the gay liberation movement. Topics covered include health care, the Cuban revolution, and sexual politics.

Katz, Jonathan. *Gay American History: Lesbian and Gay Men in the U.S.A.* New York: Thomas Y. Crowell, 1976. A scholarly compendium of almost

200 source documents chronicling homosexual practice in America from 1566 to the mid-1970s; the chapter "Resistance: 1859–1972" contains much material on the early gay rights movement.

Keen, Lisa, and Suzanne Goldberg. *Strangers to the Law: Gay People on Trial.* Ann Arbor: University of Michigan Press, 1998. Keen and Goldberg chronicle the background, strategies, proceedings, and arguments of the case against Colorado's Amendment 2 that became known as *Romer v. Evans.*

Kramer, Larry. *Reports from the Holocaust: The Story of an AIDS Activist.* New York: St. Martin's Press, 1989. Kramer is a cofounder of Gay Men's Health Crisis (now GMHC) and ACT UP (AIDS Coalition to Unleash Power); he is also the author of the controversial novel *Faggots* and the play *The Normal Heart.* In this book he has created a memoir of his frontline work in the battle against AIDS.

Leupp, Gary P. *Male Colors: The Construction of Homosexuality in Tokugawa Japan.* Berkeley: University of California Press, 1996. Leupp examines male-male sex in early modern Japan, where it was not only tolerated but celebrated, much as in ancient Athens. He finds an explanation for its unusual prevalence in social factors such as the absence of women from monasteries and their scarcity in samurai society and the cities, the culture surrounding Kabuki theater, and the world of male prostitutes.

Marcus, Eric. *Making History: The Struggle for Gay and Lesbian Equal Rights, 1945–1990: An Oral History.* New York: Columbia University Press, 1992. Approximately 45 individuals, mostly gay and lesbian but some heterosexual, talk about the gay and lesbian rights movement, especially their own roles in regard to that movement.

McGarry, Molly, and Fred Wasserman. *Becoming Visible.* New York: Penguin Putnam, 1998. A pictorial history of gay and lesbian life in New York City that documents the landmark exhibit of the same name at the New York Public Library. The book illustrates the intersecting worlds of sex, politics, and cultural life that have created what is now generally thought of as the gay community.

Murray, Stephen O. *Latin American Male Homosexualities.* Albuquerque: University of New Mexico Press, 1995. This book explores the multiple viewpoints of gay men of Latino descent.

Murray, Stephen O., and Will Roscoe, eds. *Boy-Wives and Female Husbands: Studies of African Homosexualities.* New York: St. Martin's Press, 1998. Among the many myths created about Africa, the myth that homosexuality is absent or incidental is one of the oldest and most enduring. The editors challenge this misperception in the essays collected here, which date from the colonial period to the present and cover the major regions of black Africa. Evidence of same-sex marriages, cross-dressing, role reversal, and premarital peer homosexuality is presented within a context of many societies' politically motivated denial of the reality of same-sex desire.

Owens, Robert E. *Queer Kids: The Challenges and Promise for Lesbian, Gay, and Bisexual Youth.* Binghamton, N.Y.: Haworth Press, 1998. In this book Owens advocates for the concerns of gay teens. Observing what he considers to be the benign neglect of society at large in providing support and vital information for queer kids, Owens focuses on counselors, parents, and adolescents; discusses stereotypes and prejudices; and seeks to provide viable solutions to the challenges facing young people coming of age in a heterosexual-dominant culture. His book serves as an excellent reference guide to gay community resources across the United States and includes interviews with teen activists from across the country.

Rector, Frank. *The Nazi Extermination of Homosexuals.* New York: Stein and Day, 1981. Rector provides a historical discussion of gays and lesbians who suffered during the Holocaust and presents the personal accounts of gay men who survived the camps.

Robson, Ruthann. *Sappho Goes to Law School: Fragments in Lesbian Legal Theory.* New York: Columbia University Press, 1998. Robson applies post-structural analysis, queer theory, and a feminism rooted in everyday concerns to a wide range of legal problems and possibilities facing the lesbian community. Topics explored include lesbians and criminal justice, same-sex marriage, and child custody cases. Beyond politics, Robson theorizes a radical overturn of Socratic pedagogy, the basis of much of Western thought processes, to be replaced by a system of learning based on Sapphic lyric models.

Rotello, Gabriel. *Sexual Ecology: AIDS and the Destiny of Gay Men.* New York: Dutton, 1997. Rotello's chronicle follows the growth of promiscuity among homosexual men through its promotion by bathhouse owners and the gay media. He views this cultural phenomenon as the biological precondition that allowed the AIDS virus to explode in the gay male population. He warns against a return to past sexual mistakes, as a generation comes of age who did not witness firsthand the devastation of AIDS. Rotello's book was highly controversial when first published and remains an interesting attempt to link scientific and sociological methodologies.

Russo, Vito. *The Celluloid Closet: Homosexuality in the Movies.* New York: Harper & Row, 1987. In this groundbreaking book, Russo deconstructs 70 years of Hollywood cinematic practice and representation. He unearths hitherto buried images of homosexuality and gender variance in Hollywood films from the 1920s to the present, thus tracing a history of how gay men and lesbians have been erased or demonized in movies and, indeed, in all of American culture.

Schulman, Sarah, and Urvashi Vaid. *My American History: Lesbian and Gay Life During the Reagan/Bush Years.* New York: Routledge, Chapman and Hall,

1994. A compilation of editorials, news articles, speeches, and book excerpts published in gay and feminist publications that chronicles the growth of the gay and lesbian coalition, ACT UP, and the Lesbian Avengers between 1981 and 1993. Included are examinations of early AIDS activism; battles against the Moral Majority and antigay violence; the dispute over gay and lesbian books in the New York City public schools; the growth of federal AIDS initiatives and funding; and the rise of basketball star Earvin "Magic" Johnson as the ideal AIDS poster boy. To some of the pieces Schulman appends brief commentaries that update the development of the issues discussed and that place them in greater perspective.

Shilts, Randy. *And the Band Played On: Politics, People, and the AIDS Epidemic.* New York: St. Martin's Press, 1987. In the first major book on AIDS, *San Francisco Chronicle* reporter Randy Shilts examines the making of an epidemic. His work is critical of the medical and scientific communities' initial response and particularly harsh on the Reagan Administration, but he also turns a similarly critical eye on the gay community. He wonders why gay men were so reluctant to mobilize as so many around them were dying. This book is indispensable for any discussion of the early days of the AIDS crisis.

———. *Conduct Unbecoming.* New York: St. Martin's Press, 1993. Shilts has written an accessible history of U.S. military policies regarding gays and lesbians in the armed forces. He focused particularly on the "don't ask, don't tell" controversy in the early days of the administration of President Clinton and the often contradictory positions held both by the military and its spokespeople.

———. *The Mayor of Castro Street: The Life and Times of Harvey Milk.* New York: St. Martin's Press, 1982. This is considered a classic of gay biography, written by one of America's best-known gay journalists. Milk was the first openly gay man in history to be elected to the city government of a major American city. He was subsequently assassinated, along with the city's progay mayor, George Moscone, by a disgruntled fellow politician. Shilts contextualizes Milk's life within the immense social and political changes that were occurring in the United States in the 1970s.

Signorile, Michelangelo. *Queer in America: Sex, the Media, and the Closets of Power.* New York: Random House, 1993. In this memoir, the provocateur of "outing" discusses his history of publicly exposing the homosexuality of celebrities and government officials. Among the people that Signorile revealed as gay in his weekly magazine column were billionaire publisher Malcolm Forbes and assistant secretary of defense Pete Williams. Signorile defends outing as a powerful tool that eliminates the refuge of the closet for hypocritical enemies of gay rights, an argument that raises serious legal, ethical, and psychological issues.

Simpson, Ruth. *From the Closet to the Courts: The Lesbian Transition.* New York: Richard Seaver/Viking Press, 1976. A very personal view of the early years of the gay rights movement by a lesbian whose involvement in the movement began in 1969.

Smith, Barbara, ed. *Home Girls: A Black Feminist Anthology.* New York: Kitchen Table: Women of Color Press, 1983. Smith has collected writings from the country's leading African-American feminists, including many in the lesbian-feminist movement. Smith released an updated paperback edition of the book in October 1999.

Smith, Charles Michael. *Fighting Words: Personal Essays by Black Gay Men.* New York: Avon Books, 1999. Collecting almost 30 essays into one collection, Smith presents the range of issues African-American gay men face in the United States. Battling racism in the gay community and homophobia in the black community, these men explore with honesty the demands of often conflicting identities.

Sullivan, Andrew. *Virtually Normal: An Argument About Homosexuality.* New York: Knopf, 1995. From the standpoint of many activists in the gay rights movement, Sullivan has a decidedly conservative take on the issues facing the gay community. A practicing Catholic and onetime editor of the centrist magazine *New Republic,* Sullivan eschews radical "identity politics" and believes that winning marital rights is the key to gay people's dream of full participation in the political and cultural life of this country. This book is considered essential reading by gay rights advocates for any discussion of the same-sex marriage controversy that has dominated gay discourse in the 1990s.

Timmons, Stuart. *The Trouble with Harry Hay: Founder of the Gay Movement.* Boston: Alyson Publications, 1990. This biography of one of the most important figures of the early gay rights movement in the United States follows Hay's career from the 1950s to the 1980s.

Tobin, Kay, and Randy Wicker. *The Gay Crusaders.* New York: Paperback Library, 1972. The authors present biographical sketches of 15 men and women active in the early stages of the gay and lesbian rights movement.

Vaid, Urvashi. *Virtual Equality: The Mainstreaming of Gay and Lesbian Liberation.* New York: Anchor/Doubleday, 1995. The title of Vaid's book refers to her belief that the gay community has access to power but no real civil rights protection and has visibility while remaining vulnerable to discrimination and violence. Vaid challenges the gay community to face the forces that divide it and begin the work necessary to achieve genuine equality with the rest of America.

Warner, Michael. *The Trouble With Normal: Sex, Politics and the Ethics of Queer Life.* New York: Free Press, 1999. Warner adds a provocative view to the debate on gay marriage, suggesting that rather than trying to assimilate into the world of "normality," gay men and lesbians make common cause with other groups that are excluded from the definition of normality. He is particularly concerned about the tendency for gay men and lesbians to see marriage as a means to become "normal"; in Warner's view, marriage is inappropriate to the sexual relationships of many people, both gay and straight, and is unethical in its arbitrary denial of rights to unmarried people.

White, Edmund. *States of Desire: Travels in Gay America.* New York: Simon & Schuster, 1991. In this collection of essays, noted gay novelist White interviews gay men living in towns, cities, and rural communities across the United States.

ARTICLES

ADOPTION

Editorial. "Gay Couples and Adoption." *Washington Post*, December 20, 1997, p. A20. Puts the New Jersey adoption case that awarded joint parental rights to two gay men into legal perspective. Editorial comes out in favor of gay adoption if it is in the best interests of the child, although it's unclear how the writer(s) would make that determination.

Goldman, John J. "N.J. Settlement OKs Adoptions by Gay Couples." *Los Angeles Times*, October 23, 1997, p. 1. Reports on the settlement of a case in which New Jersey becomes the first state to allow homosexual or unmarried heterosexual couples to jointly adopt children. The case focused on the efforts of Jon Holden and Michael Galluccio to adopt their two-year-old foster son Adam.

Moss, J. J. "Focus on the Family." *Out*, August 1997, pp. 74–75, 104–105. This article provides an overview of the adoption issue with regard to the rights of gay men and lesbians. Efforts of gay and lesbian couples who either have adopted children or are trying to adopt children are discussed.

Reyes, David. "Adoption Proposal Sparks Sharp Debate." *Los Angeles Times*, September 6, 1996, p. 3. Report on California governor Pete Wilson's plan to strengthen existing regulations barring adoptions by unmarried couples. Activists attack the plan as an attempt to keep gays and lesbians from becoming adoptive parents.

Smith, Rhonda. "Moms Navigate The Legal System: In 'Gayby Boom,' Parents More Savvy and More Burdened." *Washington Blade*, vol. 30:8, 1999, p. 1, 12. Legal issues facing lesbian couples who have children together are discussed. Smith pays particular attention to disputes that arise when lesbian couples separate, and the biological mother tries to deny custody or visitation rights to her former partner.

Wilson, Yumi. "Governor's Decision On Adoption Causes Ire." *San Francisco Chronicle*, March 14, 1995, p. A4. Report on California governor Pete Wilson's decision to rescind an order allowing unmarried couples to adopt children.

AIDS ACTIVISM

Bull, Chris. "Still Angry After All These Years." *The Advocate*, issue 791–792, August 17, 1999. Discusses the AIDS Coalition to Unleash Power (ACT UP) and their continued activism, despite a sharp reduction in membership. According to this report, its old fire still smolders.

Gallagher, John. "Are Gay Men Listening?" *The Advocate*, issue 750/751, 1998, p. 44. Profiles of seven gay men from across the country, including members of the radical organization Sex Panic who are confronting issues of maintaining negative HIV status while not abandoning the gay liberation ideal of sexual freedom.

Levy, Dan. "A Decade of AIDS Activism Changed America—and ACT UP." *San Francisco Chronicle*, March 22, 1997, p. A1. On the 10th anniversary of its first demonstration, Levy examines the decline of ACT UP's influence in the gay community. In many ways, he explains, the organization is a victim of its own successes.

Minton, Torri. "S.F. Maintains Regulation of Gay Sex Clubs." *San Francisco Chronicle*, June 13, 1997, p. 21. Over the objections of members of San Francisco's gay community, the city's human rights commission votes to uphold rules requiring sex clubs to be monitored at all times. The city claims that the need to slow the spread of disease outweighs privacy considerations.

Morales, Jorge. "Curtains for New York Sex Clubs?" *The Advocate*, issue 677, March 21, 1995. p. 20. Report on the increased use of sex clubs in New York City. Patrons are ignoring posted signs from the health department specifying allowable behavior, prompting action from both AIDS activists and the city government.

Oppenheimer, Joshua. "Unforgiving Errors." *Gay Community News*, vol. 23:1, Summer 1997, pp. 40–45. In this review, Oppenheimer lacerates Gabriel Rotello's book *Sexual Ecology*, describing it as one of the "most destructive volumes . . . to emerge from the (AIDS) epidemic." He refutes most of the major points in the book.

Schoofs, Mark. "Beds, Baths, and Beyond." *The Village Voice*, vol. 40:13, March 28, 1995, p. 13. Schoofs profiles a New York City group called Gay and Lesbian HIV Prevention Activists, which is pressuring the city government to regulate local gay bathhouses and sex clubs.

Stolberg, Sheryl Gay. "Gay Culture Weighs Sense and Sexuality." *New York Times*, November 23, 1997, section 4, p. 1. Report on the controversy over Sex Panic, a New York prosex AIDS prevention group, which is battling the city and conservative members of the gay community over regulation of public sex.

AIDS DISCRIMINATION

Bayles, Fred. "Disability Law Covers People with AIDS Virus." *USA Today*, June 26, 1998, p. 3A. In *Bragdon v. Abbot*, a case involving an HIV-positive Maine woman whose dentist refused to fill a cavity, the Supreme Court rules that the Americans with Disabilities Act, which outlaws discrimination against disabled people in public accommodation, also applies to people with HIV/AIDS.

Cimons, Marlene. "Probe Is Urged of White House Incident Seen as Insulting to Gays." *Los Angeles Times*, June 15, 1995, p. 24. Report that members of the uniformed division of the Secret Service donned rubber gloves before shaking hands with gay elected leaders who were attending a meeting at the White House.

Editorial. "Who's Being Disgusting on AIDS?" *New York City*, July 9, 1995, p. 414. An editorial criticizes Senator Jesse Helms for seeking to inflame passions over AIDS by slowing action on a federal funding bill for the care and treatment of people with AIDS.

McDonald, Greg, and William E. Clayton. "President Fires Back at Helms/Senator's Rhetoric on Gays, AIDS Funding Draws Response." *Washington Post*, July 7, 1995, p. 1. Report on President Clinton's call for Congress to reauthorize the Ryan White Act, a federal program that provides AIDS services, after Senator Jesse Helms made disparaging remarks about gay people and people with AIDS.

Mintz, John. "Reversal on Military HIV Issue Is Rare Hill Victory for Gay Rights Activists." *Washington Post*, April 26, 1996, p. A9. Report on compromise between the White House and Congress killing a regulation enacted by Congress in the previous year; the regulation would have discharged 1,049 military service members with HIV, the virus that causes AIDS, thus denying them medical benefits.

O'Hare, Thomas, Cynthia L. Williams, and Alan Ezoviski. "Fear of AIDS and Homophobia: Implications for Direct Practice and Advocacy." *Social Work*, vol. 41:1, January 1996, p. 51. The relationship between homophobia and the fear of AIDS is examined in this study of undergraduates at a Rhode Island college. Respondents who were more liberal endorsed rights for gay men and lesbians, were less homophobic, and had less fear of AIDS.

Rankin, Bill. "Gay Group Backs HIV-Positive Dental Hygienist's Suit Over Lost Job." *Atlanta Journal-Constitution*, January 29, 1999, p. B1. Rankin reports on a lawsuit (*Bragdon v. Abbot*) that will test the Supreme Court's

June 1998 ruling that the Americans with Disabilities Act applies to people with HIV/AIDS.

Sadownick, Doug and Bruce Mirken. "The Great American Insurance Scam." *The Advocate*, issue 607, July 14, 1992, p. 36. Widespread discrimination in the health insurance industry, particularly against gay men, is discussed, and the high cost of AIDS care is addressed.

Seelye, Katharine Q. "Helms Puts the Brakes to a Bill Financing AIDS Treatment." *New York Times*, July 5, 1995, p. A12. Senator Jesse Helms, a Republican from North Carolina who has vigorously fought homosexual rights, wants to reduce the amount of federal money spent on people with AIDS. The Seelye interview reveals the senator's most extreme antigay positions.

BALLOT MEASURES

"Ground Zero: Fear and Renewal in Colorado." *The Village Voice*, vol. 38: 3, January 19, 1993, p. 30. In the wake of Colorado's Amendment 2, which voided the state's gay rights laws, the gay community has been split by the boycott drive. Ground Zero, a gay group formed in response to the vote, is profiled, and the rise of antigay violence is discussed.

Biskupic, Joan. "Court Allows Ban on Gay Rights Laws." *Washington Post*, October 14, 1998, p. A1. Report on Supreme Court's refusal to hear arguments in the case brought against Cincinnati voters' repeal of the addition of sexual orientation to that city's antidiscrimination ordinance. The Court's action appears to contradict its earlier ruling in *Romer v. Evans*, in which Colorado's Amendment 2 was struck down.

———. "Gay Rights Case Closely Watched At High Court." *Washington Post*, October 10, 1995, p. A1. Biskupic profiles the main players in *Romer v. Evans* as the Supreme Court prepares to hear oral arguments in the case. Richard Evans, who initiated the lawsuit blocking Colorado's Amendment 2 from taking effect, and Kevin Tebedo, executive director of Colorado for Family Values, the group that sponsored the amendment, are interviewed.

Booth, Michael. "Gay-Rights Ban Narrowly Winning." *Denver Post*, November 4, 1992, p. A14. Colorado voters narrowly approve Amendment 2, which outlaws discrimination protection for homosexuals. A table listing election results is given.

———. "Tea Tempest Brews Doubts About Ban." *Denver Post*, February 14, 1993, p. C7. The debate among gay rights groups about whether a boycott is an effective way to combat Colorado's anti–gay rights law is discussed in the wake of the failed boycott of Boulder, Colorado's Celestial Seasonings tea company.

Boxall, Bettina. "Battle Lines Drawn Over Oregon's Anti-Gay Measure." *Los Angeles Times*, October 22, 1992, p. A1. Measure 9 is discussed; this ballot initiative in Oregon would write into the Oregon constitution a moral condemnation of homosexuality and require state and local government agencies to discourage it.

Dawidoff, Robert. "Gays Won't Take Clinton's Betrayal Lightly." *Los Angeles Times*, June 11, 1995, p. M5. Dawidoff criticizes the Clinton administration's decision not to file a friend-of-the-court brief to the Supreme Court concerning Colorado's Amendment 2 and says gays will unite politically to be heard.

Dunlap, David W. "After Bitter Debate on Gay Rights, Maine Will Vote in Referendum on Discrimination." *New York Times*, November 5, 1995, p. 130. After a rancorous debate, Maine voters prepare to decide Question 1, which asks whether civil rights safeguards should be conferred solely on the basis of certain characteristics. Sexual orientation is explicitly excluded from that list.

———. "Court Upholds Anti-Homosexual Initiative." *New York Times*, May 14, 1995, p. 118. The Sixth Circuit U.S. Court of Appeals upholds the right of Cincinnati voters to deprive gays and lesbians of specific legal protections. The court declares constitutional a charter amendment that bars the city council from adopting any measure that creates a "protected status" on the basis of sexual orientation.

Epstein, Aaron. "High Court Hearing Set on 'Family Values' vs. 'Gay Rights.'" *Houston Chronicle*, October 7, 1995, p. 21. Epstein profiles Will Perkins, a car dealer, and Angela Romero, a police officer, two people on opposite sides of the Colorado debate over gay rights.

Ford, Royal. "Bid to End Gay Rights Protection Defeated Amid Voter Signup Flap." *Boston Globe*, November 8, 1995, p. 22. Report on defeat of Maine voter referendum that would have limited civil rights protections to certain specified groups. Gays and lesbians would have been excluded from the list of those deemed needing protection, and any existing gay rights ordinances would have been nullified.

Knight, Al. "60 Seconds." *Denver Post*, January 30, 1993, p. B7. Knight raises questions concerning the January 1993 injunction against Colorado's anti–gay rights Amendment 2, including the question of whether the judges who issued the injunction had the right to do so.

Maupin, Armistead. "Boycott Colorado." *New York Times*, November 21, 1992, p. A19. Famed gay novelist Maupin comments on Amendment 2, asserting that the measure violates human rights and that the state should be boycotted until the law is repealed.

Pankratz, Howard. "Amendment 2 Blocked." *Denver Post*, January 16, 1993, p. A1. A Denver district judge orders a preliminary injunction against Colorado's anti–gay rights Amendment 2, saying the measure's opponents have shown that the law could allow state-sanctioned discrimination against homosexuals.

———. "Ohio Issue Stokes Debate." *Denver Post*, September 24, 1995, p. A10. Gay rights advocates say that it is imperative courts consider their "sexual orientation," not their sexual conduct. Both state and federal courts in Denver and Cincinnati have viewed orientation and conduct as the same in their rulings on antigay measures passed by local electorates.

Perkins, Will. "Drive for Homosexual Rights Undermines Family Values." *Denver Post*, May 23, 1992, p. B7. Perkins, the executive board chairman of Colorado for Family Values, criticizes the movement for homosexual rights and denounces homosexuality. His organization is responsible for putting Amendment 2 on the state ballot.

Pursley, Sara. "Gay Politics in the Heartland: With the Lesbian Avengers in Idaho." *The Nation*, vol. 260:3, January 23, 1995, p. 90. The Lesbian Avengers, a New York–based activist group, supported grassroots, proleslesbian, and progay efforts in northern Idaho in response to Proposition One. The proposition against gays and lesbian rights was defeated with a 51 percent "no" vote.

Savage, David G. "Government to Stay out of Legal Battle Over Gay Rights." *Los Angeles Times*, June 9, 1995, p. A36. The Clinton administration has announced that it will stay out of the Supreme Court battle over gay rights and will not take a legal position in the *Romer v. Evans* case, which challenges Colorado's anti–gay rights initiative.

Signorile, Michelangelo. "Behind the Hate in Oregon." *New York Times*, September 3, 1992, p. A23. Signorile criticizes the Oregon Citizens Alliance for its campaign against homosexuals, alleging that the organization's strategies include mass mailings of misleading and false statistics.

Sipchen, Bob. "Maine Voters Reject Rights Referendum." *Los Angeles Times*, November 8, 1995, p. 12. Report on defeat of statewide referendum that would have blocked new laws and repealed existing local ordinances that extend civil rights protection to people not already covered by Maine's Human Rights Act. That law bars many types of discrimination, but not discrimination based on sexual preference.

Smith, Kimberly Jean. "Maine Won't Discriminate: Won't Go Away!" *Gay Community News*, vol. 24:2, 1998, pp. 22–27. Smith discusses the community's responses to Maine Won't Discriminate's recent civil rights campaigns. Many activists fear it is now more concerned with courting the goodwill of politicians than with improving the lives of gay men and lesbians living in Maine.

Solomon, Alisa. "The Maine Event: Why Gay Rights Went Down in a Liberal State." *The Village Voice*, vol. 43:9, March 3, 1998, p. 48. Analysis of reasons why Maine voters repealed a gay rights law for their state even though advance polls showed two-thirds of the population supporting the existing legislation.

————. "Up the Maine Stream." *The Village Voice*, vol. 40:45, November 7, 1995, p. 41. Maine voters will soon decide on a referendum that eliminates sexual orientation from human rights legislation. Solomon investigates this increasingly organized assault on gay rights.

Wiessler, Judy, and Gretchen Parker. "Court Leery of Anti-Gay Rights Issue." *Houston Chronicle*, October 11, 1995, p. 1. Report on the presentation of legal arguments before the Supreme Court on Colorado's Amendment 2. The article goes into great detail about the justices' questions for plaintiff and defense attorneys.

Zia, Helen. "Woman of the Year: Donna Red Wing." *The Advocate*, issue 619, December 29, 1992, p. 42. Gay rights activist Donna Red Wing is profiled. Red Wing's most recent battle for gay rights occurred in Oregon, where she lead a successful effort to defeat an antigay proposal.

CIVIC ORGANIZATIONS

Aguilar, Louis. "Activists Say Problem Is Largely Homophobia." *Washington Post*, June 20, 1995, p. A8. Aguilar gauges the reaction from various gay rights leaders to the Supreme Court's ruling against the Gay, Lesbian and Bisexual Group of Boston's suit to be allowed to march in a local St. Patrick's Day parade.

Daly, Christopher B. "'Southie' Residents: Savoring a Victory, Defending a Way of Life." *Washington Post*, June 23, 1995, p. A3. Residents of South Boston, a neighborhood known as Southie, defended their way of life and savored a Supreme Court ruling that states gay rights activists can be legally barred from their annual St. Patrick's Day parade.

Greenhouse, Linda. "Supreme Court Backs Boy Scouts in Ban of Gays from Membership." *New York Times*, June 29, 2000, p. 1. The Supreme Court rules that the Boy Scouts' First Amendment protection of freedom of association outweighs the state of New Jersey's law against discrimination in public accommodations. The case involved James Dale, a New Jersey scoutmaster, who had been dismissed from the Scouts after publicly revealing his homosexuality.

Harrison, Eric. "Showcase City of the South Rebels at Anti-Gay Arts Vote." *Los Angeles Times*, April 20, 1997, p. A1. After a controversial production of Tony Kushner's gay-themed Pulitzer Prize–winning play, *Angels in America*, at Charlotte (North Carolina) Repertory Company, local religious conservatives pass a law forbidding funding to anything promoting "perverted forms of sexuality." Article reports on efforts to resist the law.

MacDonald, Heather. "Boy Scout Battle Pits Gay Activists vs. Minority Kids." *Wall Street Journal*, July 6, 2000, p. A26. In this editorial, MacDonald suggests that the white gay elite will try to pressure corporations and philanthropic organizations to stop funding the Boy Scouts after the Suptreme Court ruling allowing them to forbid openly gay scoutmasters. She predicts this will deprive thousands of poor inner-city youth of valuable character-building experiences.

Norbury, Christopher. "Molding Faulty Model Citizens." *Washington Post*, July 3, 2000, p. A19. Editorial by a gay man who in his youth was a Boy Scout. Norbury expresses his concern that the Boy Scouts' determination to exclude gay scouts will foster bigotry in young people.

Ribadeneira, Diego. "Boy Scouts, Church Spar on Gay Issue." *Boston Globe*, July 21, 1998. Report on conflict between Boy Scouts of America and the Unitarian Universalist church. The Scouts want the church to stop awarding religious badges to Unitarian scouts because the church is supportive of gay rights and has been publicly critical of the scouts' antigay stance.

Rivera, Elaine. "All for a Scout's Honor." *Time*, vol. 154, issue 7, August 16, 1999, p. 33. New Jersey Supreme Court chooses to uphold James Dale's membership in the Boy Scouts after he was expelled from the organization for "coming out."

Savage, David G. "Court Rules Gays Can Be Kept out of Boston Parade." *Los Angeles Times*, June 20, 1995, p. A1. The Supreme Court declares that the private organizers of an annual city parade may exclude gay marchers, ruling unanimously that the parade sponsors' right to free speech outweighs state civil rights laws.

Sincere, Richard E., Jr. "Pro-gay Ruling in New Jersey Hurts Gay Rights." *Wall Street Journal*, August 11, 1999, p. A18. Conservative gay rights supporter argues against New Jersey Supreme Court ruling against Boy Scouts of America, which retroactively expelled former Eagle Scout James Dale for being openly gay. Writer argues against the ruling on First Amendment grounds.

Supreme Court. "Excerpts from the Supreme Court's Ruling on Gays and the Boy Scouts." *New York Times*, June 29, 2000, p. 28. The partial text of the ruling in *Boy Scouts of America v. Dale* that upheld the scouts' right to exclude gay members.

Torpy, Bill. "Moral Battleground: Gay Rights Debate Rages in Carrollton." *Atlanta Journal-Constitution*, September 8, 1996, p. G3. Carrollton, Georgia has become a battlefront over morals and lifestyle concerning the rights and acceptance of homosexuals, ever since the *Carrollton Times-Georgian* ran an article about local gays starting a support group.

Will, George F. "Boy Scouts: On to the High Court." *Washington Post*, August 15, 1999, p. B7. Conservative commentator Will weighs in with his opinion why the New Jersey Boy Scout decision is bad for democracy. The decision had reinstated Eagle Scout James Dale after he was expelled from the Boy Scouts for coming out.

Yeoman, Barry. "Southern Discomfort." *The Advocate*, issue 755, 1998, pp. 34–36. Report on the Mecklenburg County board of commissioners that voted to cut arts funding to any Charlotte, North Carolina group that, in its view, promotes homosexuality.

COURT DECISIONS

Biskupic, Joan. "Court Declares Gays Not Legally Different." *Washington Post*, May 22, 1996, p. A1. Biskupic interprets the Supreme Court's decision in *Romer v. Evans* as an affirmation of the notion that there is no good reason why gays and lesbians should be discriminated against or treated differently under the law.

———. "In Terms of Moral Indignation, Justice Scalia Is a Majority of One." *Washington Post*, June 30, 1996, p. A3. Profile of conservative Supreme Court justice Antonin Scalia. Biskupic analyzes the language of several of his recent decisions, with particular emphasis on his vehement dissent in the landmark gay rights case *Romer v. Evans*.

Booth, Michael and Jim Mallory. "Gay-Rights Arena Wide Open." *Denver Post*, May 21, 1996, p. A1. Coloradans on both sides of the gay rights issue weigh their options after the Supreme Court strikes down the state's Amendment 2. The general consensus is that the field is wide open for anything, pro- or antigay.

———. "$2 Million to Fight Gay Rights Battle Amendment 2 Tab Could Still Grow." *Denver Post*, May 22, 1996, p. B1. The cost to Colorado taxpayers for the state attorney general's defense of antigay Amendment 2 in the courts is documented. Although not the most expensive litigation facing the state, the price tag will still be substantial.

Dionne, E. J., Jr. "Not Always Local." *Washington Post*, June 4, 1996, p. A17. An editorial critical of Supreme Court justice Antonin Scalia's dissent from the majority opinion in *Romer v. Evans*.

Editorial. "Rethinking Equality." *Wall Street Journal*, May 22, 1996, p. A22. Editorial discussing the Supreme Court's decision in *Romer v. Evans* that strikes down Colorado's Amendment 2. The editorial lauds the decision, saying the decision sends a message that all Americans should be treated equally before the law.

Goldstein, Richard. "Half Frec." *The Village Voice*, vol. 41:23, June 4, 1996, p. 21. Goldstein discusses the ambiguities surrounding the Supreme Court's decision in *Romer v. Evans*, striking down Colorado's antigay Amendment 2. He argues that President Clinton's public announcement against gay marriages that same week shows that, for gays, the battle is only beginning.

Greenhouse, Linda. "Gay Rights Laws Can't Be Banned, High Court Rules." *New York Times*, May 21, 1996, p. A1. Report on the Supreme Court's decision in *Romer v. Evans* to strike down Colorado's Amendment 2.

Hetter, Katia. "The New Civil Rights Battle." *U.S. News and World Report*, vol. 120:22, June 3, 1996, p. 28. In light of the Supreme Court decision overturning Colorado's antigay Amendment 2, Hetter examines other issues facing the gay community in a thorough overview of the contemporary concerns of many activists.

Holding, Reynolds, and David Tuller. "High Court Upholds Gay Rights." *San Francisco Chronicle*, May 21, 1996, p. A1. Report on the Supreme Court's decision in *Romer v. Evans* to strike down Colorado's Amendment 2.

Kmiec, Douglas W. "Irrationality Prevails in Gay Rights Ruling." *Los Angeles Times*, May 22, 1996, p. 9. Kmiec interprets Colorado's Amendment 2 as an effort on the part of the state's citizens to remain legally neutral on the issue of homosexuality. In his opinion the Supreme Court's decision in *Romer v. Evans* upends this very rational objective.

Maguire, Gilbert S. "The Most Politically Significant Supreme Court Case of 1996." *American Prospect*, vol. 7:1, January 1996, p. 53. Maguire discusses *Romer v. Evans*. He believes the gay rights case concerning Colorado's Amendment 2 could undermine the Supreme Court's credibility if the Court grants "suspect-class" protection on homosexuals.

Moss, J. Jennings. "Bigotry on Trial." *The Advocate*, issue 694, November 14, 1995, p. 27. The U.S. Supreme Court is looking at Colorado's Amendment 2 as voters in Maine get ready to vote on an antigay ballot measure. Some gay rights supporters are confident that the Supreme Court will overturn Amendment 2.

Nagourney, Adam. "Affirmed by the Supreme Court." *New York Times*, May 26, 1996, section 4, p. 4. Nagourney writes about the U.S. Supreme Court striking down Colorado's Amendment 2 in *Romer v. Evans*, contending that the ruling represents a high point in the history of the gay rights movement.

Norton, Gale A. "Reflections on Amendment 2." *Denver Post*, June 22, 1996, p. B7. Norton, attorney general of Colorado, discusses the implications of the Supreme Court's Amendment 2 decision concerning gay rights and says the court's opinion is disappointing in its failure to provide useful guidance.

Perkins, Will. "Ruling Attacks Our Sovereignty." *Denver Post*, May 22, 1996, p. B7. Perkins, the head of the aggressive antigay organization Colorado for Family Values, editorializes against the Supreme Court decision in *Romer v. Evans* as "a kick in the teeth" to all of the Coloradans who voted for Amendment 2.

Price, Deb. "Ruling Sets Precedent for Fighting Anti-gay Laws." *Detroit News*, May 21, 1996, p. A4. Price describes the Supreme Court's decision in *Romer v. Evans*, striking down Colorado's antigay Amendment 2, as "the most important victory in the history of the gay rights movement." She views the ruling as a break with the Court's own antigay past.

Rabey, Steve. "Court Strikes Down Homosexual Rights Ban." *Christianity Today*, vol. 40:7, June 17, 1996, p. 68. Reporting from a Christian perspective, Rabey discusses the Supreme Court's ruling in *Romer v. Evans*, overturning Colorado's Amendment 2.

Rosen, Jeffrey. "Disoriented." *The New Republic*, vol. 213:17, October 23, 1995, p. 24. Colorado and Ohio rulings against gay rights initiatives are being sent up to the Supreme Court, and Rosen believes the Supreme Court is not likely to agree that the initiatives violate the Constitution. A discussion of the situation in Colorado and the constitutionality of the decision is included.

Stowell, Collis. "Opponents of Gays Search for New Weapons." *New Orleans Times-Picayune*, June 16, 1996, p. A20. Report on the efforts of conservative groups in the aftermath of the Supreme Court's ruling in *Romer v. Evans*, which struck down Amendment 2; conservatives are now trying to craft antigay legislation that will withstand judicial review. Their model is Question 1, a defeated Maine voter referendum, that would have limited state civil rights protection to certain groups.

Vobejda, Barbara. "Gay Rights Ruling Highlights Society's Fault Line." *Washington Post*, May 22, 1996, p. A13. Vobejda examines the ways in which the seemingly simple question of whether or not Americans approve of homosexuality opens up a host of complex controversies.

Will, George. "Challenging High Court's Reasoning on Gay Rights." *New Orleans Times-Picayune*, May 23, 1996, p. B7. Conservative commentator Will weighs in on the Supreme Court's decision in *Romer v. Evans*. He maintains that the majority opinion is a grievous misreading of the Constitution and violates the rights of Colorado's citizens.

CULTURE/MEDIA

Biskupic, Joan. "Decency Can Be Weighed In Arts Agency's Funding." *Washington Post*, June 26, 1998, p. A1. Report on the Supreme Court decision in *NEA v. Finley*, a controversy over National Endowment for the Arts (NEA) withdrawal of funding to artists deemed "obscene." The court upholds the federal government's right to consider general standards of decency in deciding whether arts projects should receive grants. Codefendants were straight performance artist Karen Finley and three other performance artist who are gay.

Bray, Hiawatha. "Gay Rights Group Urges Members to Quit CompuServe." *Boston Globe*, January 7, 1996, p. 57. In late December, CompuServe began to block access to about 200 newsgroups (bulletin board services) on a portion of the Internet called Usenet. A number of the newsgroups featured discussions of gay and lesbian issues.

Bumiller, Elisabeth. "The Wenner Story's Out; An Uneasy Press Finally Breaks the Silence." *Washington Post*, March 6, 1995, p. D1. Bumiller examines the public disclosure that *Rolling Stone* publisher Jann Wenner has left his wife for a man. Amid accusations of "outing," gay journalists argue that withholding stories like Wenner's implies a confused discomfort at best and hypocrisy at worst.

Che, Cathay. "Offending Catholics." *The Advocate*, issue 763, 1998, p. 49. This article discusses the controversy surrounding the production of Terrence McNally's play *Corpus Christi*, which reimagines the Christ story as that of a gay man and his friends in Texas. The Catholic League attempted to pressure the play's producer into closing it (attempts that were eventually unsuccessful).

"CompuServe Said to Act Alone on Ban." *Washington Post*, January 3, 1996, p. C3. Report on the U.S. Internet service provider CompuServe's decision to block access to what it considers to be sexually explicit web sites, many of which are targeted at gay men. CompuServe claims it is doing so because of German legal requirements.

Dawidoff, Robert. "TV-H: Hazardous to Your Hypocrisy." *Los Angeles Times*, October 19, 1997, p. M5. Dawidoff ridicules ABC-TV's decision to put a parental warning label on its sitcom *Ellen* (which features an openly lesbian leading character) when, he contends, other programs in the network's lineup have far more graphic sexual content.

Dickerson, Marla. "Christian Group Escalates Boycott Against Disney." *Los Angeles Times*, July 2, 1996, p. 1. Report on the vociferously antigay American Family Association throwing its considerable organizational muscle behind the Southern Baptist boycott of Disney. These Christian groups perceive Disney as promoting the "gay lifestyle."

Egan, Timothy. "Gay Reporter Wants to Be Activist." *New York Times*, August 10, 1996, section 1, p. 8. Sandy Nelson, a journalist in Tacoma, Washington was removed from her reporting duties and reassigned to the copy desk after she led an unsuccessful campaign to protect gay rights in Tacoma. The implications of her case for gay rights, free speech, and journalistic ethics are discussed.

Feinstein, Howard. "Quel Drag!" *The Village Voice*, vol. 41:33, August 13, 1996, p. 66. Nigel Finch's film *Stonewall* is designed to right some of the injustices endured by drag queens and portray them as the true revolutionaries in the gay rights movements, but Feinstein argues that this is an oversimplification of history.

Friess, Steve. "Are Gays Really Rich?" *The Advocate*, issue 758, 1998, pp. 37–39. The popular image of luxury, economic and social contentment, and health and leisure among the gay and lesbian population is examined and found to be misleading.

Gallagher, Maggie. "Opposition to Gay Rights Is Not Evidence of Bigotry." *St. Louis Post-Dispatch*, October 31, 1996, p. B7. Gallagher defends her position that gays and lesbians are not entitled to any special civil rights protections because in her view homosexuality is sinful, and the government would have to tyrannically reeducate people like her to realistically enforce such laws.

Gamarekian, Barbara. "Arts Agency Denies 4 Grants Suggested by Advisory Panel." *New York Times*, June 30, 1990, p. A1. The National Endowment for the Arts has rejected 4 of 18 grants recommended by the agency's theater panel. The four artists refused the grants are Karen Finley, Holly Hughes, John Fleck, and Tim Miller, the latter three of whom are homosexual.

Gowen, Annie. "Holy Hell; Fred Phelps, Clergyman, Is on a Crusade." *Washington Post*, November 12, 1995, p. F1. Profile of Fred Phelps of Topeka, Kansas. The avowedly antigay minister and disbarred lawyer has become an increasing presence in the national media because of his and his family's angry protests against gay rights.

Graff, E. J. "'Pride' and Prejudice." *Boston Globe*, June 16, 1996, p. 65. Graff examines the tensions in Boston's gay and lesbian community over how its presents itself in an era of stereotypes following the uproar over lewd acts in the 1996 Gay and Lesbian Pride parade.

Green, Chuck. "Causes of 'Gayness' Unsolved by Debate." *Denver Post*, May 26, 1996, p. C1. Green talks to teachers of young children to test the theory that evidence of homosexual orientation can be manifest at an early age. He believes that if it can be proven that sexual orientation is innate, the gay community will make huge political strides.

Innes, Charlotte. "To Assimilate or Not to Assimilate?" *Los Angeles Times*, July 20, 1997, p. E12. This article examines the controversy over *Sexual Ecology: AIDS and the Destiny of Gay Men*, by Gabriel Rotello, and *The Rise and Fall of Gay Culture*, by Daniel Harris, books that explore the role of sexuality in gay culture and the way sexuality influences assimilation into the larger culture.

Kennicott, Philip. "Changing TV Landscape: DeGeneres Comes Out for Real and on Her Sitcom." *St. Louis Post-Dispatch*, April 27, 1997, p. C3. Opinion piece alleges that Ellen DeGeneres's coming out is of more significance for straight, "mainstream" culture than it is for gay culture, arguing that the coming out is an event that has been carefully staged and controlled, and therefore given meaning, by heterosexual institutions.

Kirp, David L. "How Gays Lost It at the Movies." *Dissent*, vol. 43: 1, Winter 1996. Kirp contrasts the gay audiences' 1995 acceptance of the release of *Cruising*, a 1980 Al Pacino film about a serial killer in New York's gay underground, with the huge gay protests that first greeted the film. He sees this as devolution in gay political consciousness.

Lassell, Michael. "NEA Four Survive a Year of Uproar." *The Advocate*, issue 591, December 3, 1991, p. 76. The National Endowment for the Arts announces that grants have been awarded to several homosexual performance artists in the wake of controversy over the "NEA Four," four performance artists (three of whom were gay) whose funding was withdrawn. The controversy faced by the NEA and its gay recipients is discussed.

Lowry, Brian. "ABC Won't Renew 'Ellen.'" *Washington Post*, April 24, 1998, p. B2. Report on the decision of ABC-TV to cancel *Ellen*, the first sitcom with an openly homosexual lead character, after protests and declining ratings.

Maggenti, Maria. "Cinema Verité." *The Advocate*, issue 690, September 19, 1995, p. 18. Maggenti, director of the lesbian-themed film *The Incredibly True Adventure of Two Girls in Love*, examines the ways that gay films are expected to measure the status of gays and lesbians in the culture at large. She maintains that movies alone cannot liberate gays and lesbians, only they can do that for themselves.

Minkowitz, Donna. "The NEA Hurricaine." *The Advocate*, issue 607, July 14, 1992, p. 44. Minkowitz discusses the appointment of open lesbian and political conservative Anne-Imelda Radice as acting chair of the National Endowment for the Arts, which has been embroiled in controversy for funding homoerotic art. Minkowitz views Radice's appointment as a divide-and-conquer strategy by the Bush administration.

Myerson, Allen R. "A Texas Paper in a Dispute over Gay Editor." *New York Times*, January 29, 1996, p. D1. After one reader complained, the *Fort Worth Star-Telegram* transferred Todd Camp, an openly gay editor of a weekly children's section, and apologized for allowing him to edit the section despite Camp's contributions to a weekly gay newspaper, the *Texas Triangle*.

Sadownick, Doug. "Frohnmayer Faces Gay and Lesbian Critics." *The Advocate*, issue 572, March 12, 1991, p. 50. The controversy surrounding National Endowment for the Arts chairman John Frohnmayer and the gay and lesbian arts community is discussed in the wake of the NEA's withdrawal of funding from four controversial performance artists, three of whom are gay. Frohnmayer refuses to take responsibility for the agency's defunding of gay and lesbian artists.

Shister, Gail. "TV Producers Decry 'HC' Label for Homosexual Content." *Buffalo News*, March 16, 1999, p. C4. Quotes from Hollywood figures ridiculing the Christian Action Network's call for all TV programs with gay characters or situations to receive a parental warning label.

Simons, John. "Gay-Rights Groups Cause AOL to Halt Online Thesaurus." *Wall Street Journal*, January 18, 1999, B7. Simons reports on the successful protest against an online version of Merriam-Webster's *Colle-*

giate Thesaurus that included several derogatory words for gay men as synonyms for "homosexual."

Smith, Barbara. "The Fight Is for Social, Political and Economic Justice." *Gay Community News*, vol. 23:4, 1998, pp. 40–41. Barbara Smith, a well-known figure in the lesbian-feminist movement, explains her criticisms of the proposed Millennium March on Washington planned for 2000: In her view, the march organizers are ignoring the needs of people of color and those living outside the accepted norms and sexual behavior.

St. George, Donna. "How the Tide Was Turned." *Washington Post*, August 29, 1999, p. W6. St. George profiles the town of Rehoboth Beach, Delaware, a major gay summer resort destination. Ten years ago the residents of the town were opposed to the influx of gay residents and visitors. Now neighbors live in harmony.

Suris, Oscar. "Saugatuck Attracts Many Gay Tourists, but There Is Friction." *Wall Street Journal*, August 22, 1995, p. A1. Saugatuck, Michigan's reaction to the notion of a "gay-friendly" statute is examined. The community is popular with both gay and straight vacationers, but has become mired in controversy over an ordinance that would ban discrimination based on sexual orientation.

Thomas, Cal. "Bigotry Accusation Suppresses Truth." *Buffalo News*, September 4, 1999, p. C3. Conservative editorial attacks critics of radio talk show host and psychologist Dr. Laura Schlessinger's assertion that homosexuality is a curable pathology.

———. "Denying the Freedom to Change." *Denver Post*, August 9, 1995, p. B7. Thomas editorializes against an American Psychological Association resolution that would discourage mental health professionals from offering therapies designed to change their patients' sexual orientations. He sees this as part of a gay rights agenda to normalize homosexuality in the culture.

Tuller, David. "New Wave of Outings in Politics." *San Francisco Chronicle*, October 26, 1996, p. 1A. Confronted with the Republican Party's aggressively antigay platform, gay activists and journalists have responded with a spate of "outings"—the most concentrated cluster since 1991. The implications of the practice are discussed.

United States Supreme Court. "Excerpts From Ruling to Uphold Decency Tests for Awarding Federal Arts Grants." *New York Times*, June 26, 1998, A17. Edited text of the Supreme Court's ruling in *NEA v. Finley*, which declares as constitutional the U.S. government's policy of placing content restrictions on federally funded works of art.

Warner, Michael. "Media Gays: A New Stone Wall." *The Nation*, vol. 265:2, July 14, 1997, pp. 15–19. Warner takes the gay neoconservative movement to task for having coopted all of the mainstream media attention at the expense of more radical voices in the gay rights movement. He argues that the neoconservative position can lead to repressive social policy.

Waxman, Sharon. "Gay Groups Object to 'Dr. Laura.'" *Washington Post,* January 12, 2000, p. C1. Report on gay rights groups' responses to syndicated radio talk show host and psychologist Laura Schlessinger. Schlessinger has called homosexuality "deviant" and "a biological error."

Wilstein, Steve. "The Gay Emergence in Sport/Barriers Are Slow to Crumble." *San Francisco Chronicle,* June 21, 1995, p. E1. Wilstein examines the phenomenon of gays and lesbians at the highest echelons in American sports and speculates on what their coming out would mean for the culture as a whole.

Wright, Kai. "'You're Thinking About Your Friends Next Door.'" *Washington Blade,* vol. 30:7, 1999, p. 10. The journey of Pulitzer Prize–winning columnist William Raspberry from opposing gay adoption to championship gay rights is chronicled. Raspberry describes how his beliefs have changed over the years about the civil rights that gays deserve.

Zahra, Tara. "The Myth of Gay Affluence." *American Prospect,* issue 46, September/October 1999, p. 14. Opinion piece debunking popular perception that gays and lesbians are better off financially than other Americans.

CUSTODY OF CHILDREN

Associated Press. "Virginia Lesbian Denied Custody of Son." *San Francisco Chronicle,* April 22, 1995, p. A3. Report on the decision of the Virginia Supreme Court to deny custody to Sharon Bottoms of her three-year-old son in favor of the boy's grandmother, Bottoms's mother. The court reasoned that Bottoms's lesbian relationship could stigmatize the child.

Gallagher, John. "Raw Deal." *The Advocate,* November 2, 1993, p. 24. Discusses the interstate battle between a California man who was awarded custody of a girl to whom he has no genetic ties and the girl's biological mother. The case involves Kevin Thomas, a 43-year-old man from Van Nuys, California, who successfully sued for custody of five-year-old Courtney Thomas when his platonic relationship with the child's biological mother, Catherine Thomas, ended.

Gover, Tzivia, and Sally Clark. "Fighting for Our Children." *The Advocate,* November 26, 1996, p. 22. The battle fought by Sharon Bottoms for her son Tyler Doustou is discussed. Bottoms lost custody of her son because she is a lesbian. The case of Fred Smith, a gay man who lost his sons after raising them from birth, is also discussed.

Halbfinger, David M. "Rights of Gays as Parents Are Widened by Court." *New York Times,* April 7, 2000, p. 5. Significantly expanding the parental rights of gay and lesbian people in New Jersey, the state supreme court rules that a woman who had helped raise her former partner's twins deserved visitation rights after the couple's breakup. Gay rights advocates called the decision the clearest ruling yet that "psychological" parents should be treated the same as biological parents in custody disputes.

McNair, Jean. "Lesbian in Virginia Abandons 3-Year Custody Battle for Son." *Boston Globe*, August 16, 1996, p. A3. Associated Press story on the decision by Sharon Bottoms to shift her attention from getting her son back from her mother to receiving expanded visitation rights. Bottoms's mother sued for custody after Sharon came out as a lesbian.

Peres, Judy. "Sperm-Donor's Case Challenging Old Laws." *Chicago Tribune*, August 12, 1997, p. 1. Report on the dispute between a gay man and a lesbian couple over parental rights to the 11-month-old baby he fathered through donated sperm.

Pfeiffer, Sacha. "Ruling Affirms 'De Facto' Parent, SJC Gives Lesbian Visitation Rights." *Boston Globe*, June 30, 1999, p. B1. In a groundbreaking ruling that expands parental rights for gay men and lesbians, the state's highest court rules that a woman who helped raise her female partner's biological son was entitled to visitation rights after the couple split up.

Polikoff, Nancy. "The Limits of Visibility: Queer Parenting Under Fire. A History of Legal Battles." *Gay Community News*, vol. 24:3–4, 1999, pp. 38–48. Polikoff discusses various legal battles since the 1970s regarding gay parents. The state-by-state nature of family law has always produced a checkered legal and political climate for lesbian and gay parents.

Price, Deb. "In Custody Cases, Bigotry Is Used All Too Often to Tear Families Apart." *Detroit News*, April 28, 1995, p. C1. Deb Price comments on the mixed-race and same-sex child custody cases, respectively, of Linda Palmore in Florida and Sharon Bottoms in Virginia.

"Sex with Boyfriend Costs Gay Man Custody." *New York Times*, July 31, 1998, p. A10. Report on the finding of the North Carolina Supreme Court that Fred Smith, a gay father who admitted to having sex with his boyfriend in their home, cannot retain custody of his two sons. The article contends that, while of obvious interest to gays and lesbians in North Carolina, the ruling could affect unmarried heterosexual couples as well.

DOMESTIC PARTNERSHIPS

Anand, Geeta. "Health-care OK'd for the Partners of City Workers." *Boston Globe*, March 14, 1996, p. 21. In a major victory for gay rights, the Boston City Council votes to extend health care benefits to the partners of unmarried city employees. The legislation does not define "domestic partners," leaving that up to the city to decide.

Brooke, James. "Gay Rights Landmark/Denver Offers Health Benefits to Partners." *Houston Chronicle*, September 18, 1996, p. 18. Four years after Coloradans approved Amendment 2, which forbade any municipality from passing progay legislation, Denver's major signs an ordinance extending health coverage to the same-sex partners of city employees.

Croft, Jay. "Domestic Partner Benefits Fight Ends." *Atlanta Journal-Constitution*, October 26, 1999, p. A1. Croft reports on the city of Atlanta's successful dispute with Georgia State Insurance Commissioner John Oxendine over his opposition to its plan to extend health care benefits to the domestic partners of city employees.

Davis, Patricia. "Court Finds Arlington's Benefits Policy Illegal." *Washington Post*, March 5, 1999, p. B1. Report of judge's ruling on legal grounds that Arlington, Virginia's policy of granting health benefits to unmarried couples violates state law. However, the judge hopes that the law will be reconsidered on appeal.

Editorial. "Friendly Skies Clouding Over." *San Francisco Chronicle*, January 21, 1997, p. A18. Editorial praising the San Francisco Board of Supervisors commitment to enforcing its domestic partnership law by demanding that one of the city's biggest tenants, United Airlines, extend domestic partnership benefits to all its employees. The *Chronicle* objects, however, to the manner in which the city has made its demands.

Hodges, Arthur, and Michael Booth. "Health Aid to Partners of Gay, Lesbian Workers to Cost City $150,000." *Denver Post*, August 28, 1996, p. B3. A report on the Denver city council debate over extending health benefits to same-sex partners of city employees reveals how economic considerations are often used as a basis for discrimination.

Holding, Reynolds. "S.F. Partners Law Under Fire Again." *San Francisco Chronicle*, June 18, 1997, p. A14. Report on a lawsuit challenging San Francisco's domestic partners ordinance, filed by the American Center for Law and Justice (ACLJ), a law firm founded by Pat Robertson. The law to which the ACLJ objects requires all city contractors to offer benefits to the same-sex partners of their employees.

Jochnowitz, Jay. "Lawyer Battles Registry of Domestic Partners." *Albany (New York) Times Union*, June 25, 1996, p. B1. Report on attorney James Brunner's filing of an action to stop the city of Albany from licensing unmarried couples, including same-sex couples, in a domestic partner registry. This is the first legal challenge of its kind in the state.

Lattin, Don. "A Compromise in the Battle for Gay Rights." *San Francisco Chronicle*, February 23, 1997, p. S3. Report on the compromise reached between the city of San Francisco and its Catholic archdiocese regarding the city's new domestic partner law. Millions of dollars in city funds for Catholic Charities was at stake. Article includes extensive excepts from interview with Archbishop William Levada.

———. "Church, S.F. Clash Over Partners Law." *San Francisco Chronicle*, January 28, 1997, p. A1. Catholic Charities of the Archdiocese of San Francisco has contracted with the city of San Francisco to open a new multimillion-dollar AIDS housing project. The city's recently passed domestic partner law, however, has jeopardized the arrangement, and the city's archbishop is threatening a lawsuit.

Lewin, Tamar. "Oregon's Gay Workers Given Benefits for Domestic Partners." *New York Times*, December 10, 1999, p. A20. Article on the first court ruling ever to declare it unconstitutional to deny benefits to the domestic partners of gay and lesbian public employees.

Pfeiffer, Sacha. "Domestic Partner Case Reaches SJC." *Boston Globe*, April 8, 1999, p. B1. The Massachusetts Supreme Judicial Court will decide the legality of a Boston policy granting health benefits to same-sex partners of city employees.

Price, Deb. "Copenhagen's Gay and Lesbian Couples Enjoy Rights That Remain a Distant Dream for American Same-Sex Couples." *Detroit News*, October 29, 1997, p. E1. Report on the status of domestic partnerships in Denmark, the first country to ever create a national registry for same-sex couples. Since the law went into effect in 1989, gay and lesbian couples have all of the same rights as married heterosexuals except those of a church blessing and adoption.

———. "San Francisco Values All People with Its Domestic-Partnership Law for City Contracts." *Detroit News*, February 21, 1997, p. E2. Deb Price praises San Francisco for sticking to its principles in its disputes with the Catholic Church and United Airlines over requirements that all entities doing business with the city must offer domestic partnership benefits to employees.

Shen, Fern. "Domestic Partner Plan Turns U-Md. into Battlefield." *Washington Post*, July 12, 1996, p. B5. A proposal to offer benefits to the unmarried domestic partners of University of Maryland employees has incurred the wrath of legislative leaders, drawn fire from the Catholic Church, and galvanized the Maryland gay community.

EDUCATION

Argetsinger, Amy. "Harassment Policy Under Attack." *Washington Post*, October 27, 1999, p. B9. Argetsinger focuses on the Maryland Board of Education, which is caught between gay rights groups and conservative organizations over its adoption of a policy protecting gay and lesbian students from harassment.

Babington, Charles. "Montgomery Rescinds Hiring Law Aimed at Keeping Gays from Children." *Washington Post*, May 25, 1994, p. D3. The Montgomery County (Maryland) Council votes to rescind a law that allowed employers to refuse to hire people who were gay or bisexual if the employee would be working with children of his or her own sex.

Daly, Gavin. "Students Rally for Gay-Straight March." *Boston Globe*, May 21, 1995, p. 34. Report on the nation's first Gay-Straight Youth Pride March in Boston. Students from about 100 Massachusetts high schools participated with the support of older gays and lesbians who remembered their own struggles as teenagers.

DeGette, Cara. "Students Lose Bid for Gay Club at School." *Denver Post*, February 5, 1999, p. B-3. Report on attempts of students at Palmer High School in Colorado Springs to form a gay/straight student club. Principal is denying a charter on the grounds that it would allegedly open the door for devil worshipers and Nazi sympathizers to demand similar accommodation.

Freiberg, Peter. "Teachers Learning Some Hard Lessons." *New York Blade*, February 19, 1999, p. 10. Freiberg examines the efforts of activists across the country to eliminate employment discrimination against out gay and lesbian teachers. Lawsuits in Utah, California, Ohio, and Wisconsin are highlighted.

Goldberg, Carey. "Colleges Feel Cost of Shunning Recuiters Over Gay Rights Issue." *New York Times*, April 19, 1996, p. A22. The City College of San Francisco must consider whether to lift its ban on military recruitment on its campuses because of the Pentagon's antigay policies or risk losing Defense Department grants. A new federal law cuts off all Defense Department grant money to public and private institutions that bar military recruiters.

Hart, Jordana. "For Gay Students, School Bullies Abound Despite Law." *Boston Globe*, May 20, 1995, p. 1. Hart examines how, some two years later, a 1993 gay and lesbian students rights bill passed in Massachusetts has done little to quell student harassment of other students perceived as "queer."

Herscher, Elaine. "Coming Out at School/Even in the Bay Area, Gay Teachers Are Taking a Risk." *San Francisco Chronicle*, March 11, 1998, p. A13. Report on the risks public school teachers take with their careers when they decide to be open about their sexuality with students.

Illescas, Carlos. "DPS Meeting Weighs Gay Rights." *Denver Post*, January 8, 1999, p. B-1. Denver Public School Board of Education hears testimony over a proposal to prohibit antigay discrimination in hiring and educational practices.

Moulton, Kristen. "Gay Rights at Issues as Students Protest Ban on Clubs." *Buffalo News*, February 24, 1996, p. A5. Report on a high school student protest in Salt Lake City, Utah over a ban on all nonacademic extracurricular activity, after the Utah state legislature passes a law aimed at preventing gay and lesbian student groups.

Neff, Lisa. "PBS Broadcasts Prompt Demonstrations." *Windy City Times*, vol. 14:45, 1999, p. 8. Report on controversy surrounding *It's Elementary*, a documentary designed to help teachers discuss the lives of gay people with their students. Demonstrations for and against the film are held in San Antonio and Seattle the night it airs on PBS.

Ness, Carol. "Gay Youth Learn the Activist Ropes." *San Francisco Chronicle*, August 20, 1995, p. C1. Report on the first-ever national gay youth leadership training institute at Walker Ranch in Marin, California, sponsored by the National Gay and Lesbian Task Force.

Olinger, David. "School Gay Rights Group Sues/Unequal Treatment Claimed." *Denver Post*, January 23, 1998, p. C1. A high school club promoting gay/straight student dialogue becomes the first such organization to file a lawsuit against its school district, claiming that it has the same constitutional rights as any other club.

Ribadeneira, Diego. "Film Sparks New Clash in War over Gays." *Boston Globe*, June 1, 1999, p. B1. Report on the controversy around the documentary *It's Elementary*, which is designed as a tool for teachers to introduce the subject of homophobia into the classroom.

Rotello, Gabriel. "Trickle-down Liberation." *The Advocate*, issue 701, February 20, 1996, p. 72. Rotello discusses the lives of gay and lesbian youth, arguing that the gay rights movement has improved the lives of most gays and lesbians, but has also made life harder for many teenagers by stripping away their "cover."

Rothman, Clifford. "A Stand for Human Worth." *Los Angeles Times*, February 26, 1997, p. E3. An in-depth profile of Jamie Nabozny, a Wisconsin teenager who successfully sued his high school principal and two other school officials for failing to protect him from antigay physical abuse at the hands of classmates.

Shecter, Jennifer. "Conservative Legislators Try to Punish Colleges That Back Gay Rights." *Chronicle of Higher Education*, vol. 42:33, April 26, 1996, p. A28. Many state lawmakers around the United States are stepping up efforts to limit the activities of gay students and faculty members on college campuses. Tactics include trying to bar colleges from providing money for gay causes and seeking to evict gay student groups from campus buildings.

Smith, Doug. "L.A. Unified OKs Benefits for Partners." *Los Angeles Times*, June 3, 1997, p. B1. After a contentious debate, a divided Los Angeles school board votes to extend health benefits to the domestic partners of unmarried employees. Some board members fear that the added cost to the district would take money away from academic activities.

Williams, Dick. "Gay Activists Say Tolerance Isn't Enough." *Atlanta Journal-Constitution*, September 6, 1997, p. A20. Conservative editorial critical of any effort on the part of gay rights advocates to introduce gay-positive curriculum into schools.

HATE CRIMES LEGISLATION

Associated Press. "2 Charged in Alabama Gay Slaying." *Houston Chronicle*, March 5, 1999, p. 17. Article reporting facts on rural Alabama slaying of gay man by two acquaintances after he sexually propositioned them.

Babington, Charles. "Wielding Veto, President Presses Hate Crimes Issue." *Washington Post*, October 27, 1999, p. A2. Babington discusses President Clinton's battle with Congress over the inclusion of sexual orientation in the budget appropriations financing enforcement of the federal "hate crimes" law.

Chandrasekaran, Rajiv. "Gay Group Seeks Hate Crime Probe in Hikers' Killings." *Washington Post*, June 8, 1996, p. B1. Report on the National Gay and Lesbian Task Force's request that the FBI investigate the slayings of two young female hikers in Shenandoah National Park as a possible antilesbian hate crime.

Clines, Francis X. "Slaying of Gay Black Spurs Call for Justice." *New York Times*, July 13, 2000, p. 16. Report on the brutal beating death of an openly gay African-American man by two teenage white boys in a small West Virginia town. Local authorities refuse to classify the murder as a bias crime.

Coleman, Cornelius. "Gay Student Dies 5 Days After Beating." *Denver Post*, October 13, 1998, p. A1. Article about the death of Matthew Shepard, the University of Wyoming student whose murder intensified the debate around hate crimes legislation.

Clymer, Adam. "Senate Expands Hate Crimes Law to Include Gays." *New York Times*, June 21, 2000, p. A1. Report on U.S. Senate vote that would make hate attacks on gays and lesbians a federal crime. This is the first time that either house of Congress has backed such protection.

Davis, Marcia. "Crime Trends Disturb Gay Community." *Washington Post*, July 25, 1996, p. DC2. Nearly 40 gays and lesbians met with police, fire, and rescue officials in Washington, D.C., over concerns that muggings and hate crimes are on the rise.

Denizet-Lewis, Benoit. "Advocates Reflect on Mixed Year." *San Francisco Chronicle*, October 12, 1999, p. A17. This piece provides an overview of gay rights progress in California during 1999, especially for gay and lesbian youth.

Foskett, Ken. "Atlanta Bombings: Looking for Answers." *Atlanta Journal-Constitution*, February 25, 1997, p. A16. In a test of the Justice Department's commitment to combating hate crimes based on sexual orientation, gay rights groups urge Attorney General Janet Reno to treat the bombing of an Atlanta lesbian bar as a hate crime. She refuses.

Harrison, Eric. "Mississippi Slayings Ignite Suspicions of Gay Activists." *Los Angeles Times*, January 29, 1995, p. 1. Harrison surveys the complex nexus of class, race, and sexuality in the double murders of Robert Walters and Joseph Shoemake in Laurel, Mississippi. Marvin McClendon, an African-American youth, stands charged with their killing.

————. "Youth Gets Life for Murder of 2 Gay Men in Mississippi." *Los Angeles Times*, February 10, 1995, p. 13. In a case closely watched by gay rights activists, a jury rejects defense claims that the killing of two white gay men by an African-American teenager was justified because the victims were "sexual predators."

Holleran, Scott. "We Must Not Think Bad Thoughts." *San Francisco Chronicle*, April 7, 1999, p. A21. Editorial arguing that hate crimes legislation is a form of thought control.

Janofsky, Michael. "Judge Rejects 'Gay Panic' as Defense in Murder Case." *New York Times*, November 2, 1999, p. A14. In the context of the Matthew Shepard murder trial, the article explains what the "panic defense" is and how it has been used by defense lawyers in various cases. Includes a quote from a gay activist who disagrees with the judge's decision not to listen to the "gay panic" defense.

Kee, Lorraine. "A Year Later, Leaders of Lesbian and Gay Groups Assess Effects of Matthew Shepard's Murder." *St. Louis Post-Dispatch*, October 16, 1999, p. 18. Kee offers a Missouri perspective on the aftermath of the Matthew Shepard murder, including the hate crimes law passed by the Missouri state legislature.

King, Loren. "More Gay Groups Come Out Against Death Penalty." *Bay Windows*, vol. 17:9, 1999, pp. 3, 20. One month before the first of two accused killers of Matthew Shepard goes on trial in Wyoming, gay activists urge opposition to the death penalty. Various comments in support of this view are offered.

Murphy, Kim. "No Place to Rest." *Los Angeles Times*, December 20, 1995, p. E1. Report on the murders of Roxanne Ellis and Michelle Abdill, a lesbian couple from a small town in Oregon who had been active in the fights against that state's antigay ballot initiatives. The connection between hate crimes and such initiatives is examined.

Neff, Lisa. "Hate Crime Initiatives Launched." *Windy City Times*, vol. 14:32, 1999, pp. 1, 14. Article announcing President Clinton's three-part plan to promote safety and tolerance for gay and lesbian students. He proposes passing the Hate Crimes Prevention Act, educating middle-school students about sexual diversity, and collecting hate crimes data from public schools and universities.

————. "NYPD Hit with Brutality Charges: Gay Activists Demand Federal Investigation." *Windy City Times*, vol. 14:16, 1998, pp. 1, 5. Report on members of the October 9th Coalition, a lesbian and gay rights activists group, filing for a federal investigation into alleged police brutality in New York City at a memorial for murdered Wyoming college student Matthew Shepard.

Perez-Pena, Richard. "State Senate to Pass Bill on Hate Crime." *New York Times,* June 7, 2000, p. B1. After blocking it for 11 years, the Republican-controlled New York State Senate passes a hate crimes bill that includes sexual orientation among its protected categories.

Roth, Bennett. "Gay Leaders Criticize Bush Over Stance on Hate Crimes." *Houston Chronicle,* March 24, 1999, p. 1. Republican Presidential candidate George W. Bush is taken to task for remarks he made against adding sexual orientation to Texas's James Byrd Jr. Hate Crimes Act, as well as for opposing unrelated Texas legislation concerning gay adoption.

Scheer, Robert. "Hate Rhetoric Opened Door for a Murder." *Los Angeles Times,* October 13, 1998, p. 7. Editorial taking the religious right to task for what the writer sees as its culpability in fostering an atmosphere of hatred that helped lead to Matthew Shepard's murder.

Soraghan, Mike. "Activists, Anti-Gay Protesters Exchange Views Outside Church." *Denver Post,* October 17, 1998, p. A-16. Descriptions of events on the day of Matthew Shepard's funeral in Casper, Wyoming, which became the site of competing protests by both antigay and pro-gay demonstrators.

Sterngold, James. "Slaying of Gay Sailor Is Admitted." *New York Times,* May 4, 1993, p. A1. Terry M. Helvey of the U.S. Navy admits to beating to death Allen Schindler, a gay shipmate, in Japan in fall 1992. Gay rights advocates say the attack appears to have been a hate crime.

Trebay, Guy. "Overkill." *The Village Voice,* vol. 44:14, April 13, 1999, pp. 42–47. Trebay reports on the murder and beheading of Eddie Northington, a gay man who lived in Richmond, Virginia. The FBI and other officials are reluctant to declare his murder a hate crime, but locals believe that was what it was.

Wong, Doris Sue. "Senate Expands Hate-Crime Law." *Boston Globe,* June 21, 1996, p. 1. Report on the Massachusetts Senate approval of a landmark hate crimes bill that would impose stiffer penalties for crimes that cause personal injury committed against people because of their sexual orientation.

HISTORY/ANALYSIS OF THE MOVEMENT

Bawer, Bruce. "Radically Different." *New York Times Book Review,* November 5, 1995, p. 721. Gay conservative Bower unfavorably reviews gay radical Urvashi Vaid's book *Virtual Equality: The Mainstreaming of Gay and Lesbian Liberation.*

Brown, Rita Mae. "Reflections of a Lavender Menace." *Ms.,* vol. 6:1, July 1995, p. 40. Brown recalls her own experiences with the National Organization for Women and the national feminist group's policies regarding lesbians. In response to the alienation she felt, Brown organized the Lavender Menace to help lesbians have a voice in the women's movement.

Buring, D. "Gay Activism Behind the Magnolia Curtain: The Memphis Gay Coalition, 1979–1991." *Journal of Homosexuality*, vol. 32:1, 1996, pp. 113–135. The Memphis Gay Coalition was organized in 1979 but disbanded after 12 years. Buring examines the organizational problems and the forces of Southern culture that played roles in its disintegration.

Clark, Keith. "Family Values: The Gay and Lesbian 'Agenda' Rolls Along." *Out*, issue 116, pp. 14–16, 18. Discusses the gay rights movement's increasing focus and fight for lesbian and gay family-values issues, such as marriage, partnerships, children, schools, and religion.

Cusac, Anne-Marie. "Harry Hay." *The Progressive*, vol. 62:9, September 1998, pp. 19–23. Profile of the founder of the Mattachine Society and the Radical Faeries. The Mattachine Society, founded in 1950, was the first modern gay rights organization.

———. "Urvashi Vaid." *The Progressive*, vol. 60:3, March 1996, p. 34. In an interview, Vaid discusses her book, *Virtual Equality: The Mainstreaming of Gay and Lesbian Liberation;* her life of political activism; and the link between gays and lesbians and other cultural and social groups.

Duberman, Martin. "Uncloseted History." *The Nation*, vol. 268, issue 22, June 14, 1999, pp. 51–54. Radical historian Duberman critiques the liberal, centrist politics of *Out for Good*, the political history of the gay rights movement by Dudley Clendenin and Adam Nagourney; he also criticizes the book for not including more lesbian figures; however, he praises the inclusion of stories not included in other histories of the gay rights movement.

Fanshawe, Simon, and Peter Tatchell. "Come Right on Out: Head to Head: Does DIRECT ACTION Protest Advance the Gay Cause?" *Guardian*, April 18, 1998, p. 4. In a series of letters to each other, two veteran British gay rights activists engage in a spirited, and at times colorful, debate on the merits of disruptive civil disobedience versus quieter, behind-the-scenes politicking in advancing the cause of gay liberation.

Johnson, Dirk. "Gay-rights Movement Ventures Beyond Urban America." *New York Times*, January 21, 1996, p. 112. Johnson explores how gay life and culture, traditionally a province of major urban centers, is beginning to thrive in smaller cities, towns, and rural areas throughout the United States.

Kirp, David L. "Are You Now, or Have You Ever Been, a Homosexual?" *Tikkun*, vol. 11:1, January 1996, p. 91. Kirp reviews books by Bruce Bawer, John Preston, Urvashi Vaid, and Andrew Sullivan that cover the range of gay political perspectives—conservative to radical.

Lester, Will. "Anita Bryant Unwittingly Aided Gay Rights Movement 20 Years Ago." *Houston Chronicle*, February 2, 1997, p. 21. Twin profiles of Anita Bryant and Bob Kunst, adversaries 20 years earlier in the fight over the Dade County, Florida gay rights ordinance.

Lowe, Peggy. "Gay Activists Recall Long Fight for Rights." *Denver Post*, June 27, 1999, p. B1. A history of the gay rights movement from the perspective of retirement-age gays and lesbians in Denver.

Matthaei, Julie. "The Sexual Division of Labor, Sexuality, and Lesbian/Gay Liberation: Toward a Marxist-Feminist Analysis of Sexuality in U.S. Capitalism." *Review of Radical Political Economics*, vol. 27:2, June 1995, p. 1. Explores the way in which economic forces have contributed to the social construction of sexuality in the 19th and 20th centuries. The breakdown of the sexual division of labor is related to the rise of lesbian/gay and feminist movements.

Mendelsohn, Daniel. "The Day Harvey Milk Died." *George*, vol. 3:11, November 1998, pp. 122–125+. An affecting recreation of the events surrounding the assassination of Harvey Milk by the people who were in San Francisco when it happened. Includes a discussion of Milk's historical significance and legacy.

Miller, E. Ethelbert. "Essex Hemphill: Persecution Witness." *Washington Post*, November 12, 1995, p. G2. A eulogy for Essex Hemphill, the African-American poet, performance artist, essayist, editor, and gay cultural activist who died in November 1995.

Neely, Letta. "Talking with Barbara Smith: A Cross Generation." *Gay Community News*, vol. 24:3–4, 1999, pp. 20–29. In an interview, Barbara Smith, a radical black lesbian feminist activist, discusses whether she is marginalized as a writer, the importance of voting, and other issues.

Poindexter, C. C. "Sociopolitical Antecedents to Stonewall: Analysis of the Origins of the Gay Rights Movement in the United States." *Social Policy*, vol. 42:6, November 1997, pp. 607–15. This article examines three traditional organizational theories on social action movements for understanding the emergence of the modern U.S. gay civil rights movement. Poindexter asserts that change was only possible because there was decades-long organization already in place at the time of Stonewall.

Price, Deb. "And Justice for All." *Detroit News*, May 5, 1995, p. F1. Price details Coretta Scott King's work in securing rights for gays and lesbians. King is the widow of slain civil rights leader Martin Luther King.

———. "Goldwater's Vision of Gay Rights Will Be Missed." *Detroit News*, June 6, 1998, p. C3. Editorial eulogizing the late Arizona archconservative and onetime presidential nominee Barry Goldwater, who late in life enthusiastically "came out" for gay rights.

Reuben, Richard C. "Gay Rights Watershed?" *ABA Journal*, vol. 82, July 1996, p. 30. The U.S. Supreme Court's decision in *Romer v. Evans* to strike down Colorado's Amendment 2 is stirring controversy among legal professionals. They are debating whether past and future cases will be affected by the decision.

Rotello, Gabriel. "Gay and Lesbian Rights." *Social Policy*, vol. 28:3, Spring 1998, pp. 56–59. A longtime gay rights activist and former editor of *Outweek* magazine, Rotello offers an overview of the challenges facing the gay rights movement in the 1990s and predicts the direction in which the movement is headed.

Signorile, Michelangelo. "Reagan, the Right, and Us." *The Advocate*, issue 800, December 7, 1999, pp. 24–26. Signorile argues that Ronald Reagan's alliance with the Christian Right in the early 1980s helped push a complacent gay community to an unprecedented level of radical activism.

Smith, Barbara. "Whose American History?" *Gay Community News*, vol. 20:4, Winter 1995, p. 9. Smith reviews *My American History* by Sarah Schulman and *Memoirs of a Race Traitor* by Mab Segrest.

Vaid, Urvashi. "Status Quo or Queer." *The Advocate*, issue 755, 1998, p. 72. Vaid draws parallels between the gay rights and feminist movements and sees both civil rights struggles as rooted in a commitment to dismantling patriarchal societal structures.

White, Edmund. "Activism and Its Discontents." *The Village Voice*, vol. 41:23, June 4, 1996, p. 13. The noted gay author Edmund White reviews *Midlife Queer*, an autobiography of noted gay historian Martin Duberman, which focuses on the gay rights movement in the 1970s.

Wingert, Pat, and Steven Waldman. "Did Washington Hate Gays?" *Newsweek*, vol. 126:16, October 16, 1995, p. 81. Gay rights advocates are trying to make October Lesbian, Gay, and Bisexual History month. They want schools to acknowledge the homosexuality of such people as Julius Caesar and Michelangelo and to teach students about the history of homosexual persecution.

HOUSING RIGHTS

Abrams, Garry. "A Tenant Tempest." *Los Angeles Times*, October 27, 1992, p. E1. Report on a civil suit by a heterosexual couple against their Hollywood, California landlord charging sexual discrimination. The couple maintains that the owner plans to turn their apartment building into an all-gay enclave, and they are being pressured to leave.

Dalton, Katherine. "Privacy and the 'Lesbian Roommate' Case." *Wall Street Journal*, July 20, 1992, p. A14. Dalton discusses what became known as "the lesbian roommate case" in Madison, Wisconsin, in which the privacy rights of two women came into conflict with the housing rights of a third woman who had answered their ad seeking a roommate.

Dewar, Helen. "Senate Votes to Confirm Achtenberg." *Washington Post*, May 25, 1993, p. A7. Report on the U.S. Senate vote to approve President Clinton's nomination of gay rights activist Roberta Achtenberg as a

Housing and Urban Development assistant secretary in charge of fair housing and equal opportunity. Achtenberg is the first openly homosexual person to be appointed to a high federal post.

Editorial. "Bill and Roberta." *Wall Street Journal*, May 26, 1993, p. A18. Editorial critical of President Clinton's appointment of openly lesbian Roberta Achtenberg as assistant secretary of Housing and Urban Development. She is attacked for her opposition to the Boy Scouts's refusal to allow openly gay scouts in their organization.

Girardet, Evelyne. "Methodist Camp Plans to Evict Family for Supporting Gay Rights." *Houston Chronicle*, June 19, 1999, p. 8. After putting up signs supporting a gay couple evicted from a vacation community, a heterosexual family finds itself also under fire from neighbors.

Honan, William H. "A.C.L.U. Sues Yeshiva U. on Housing for Gay Couples." *New York Times*, June 25, 1998, p. B6. In one of the first lawsuits of its kind, the American Civil Liberties Union's Lesbian and Gay Rights Project files suit against Yeshiva University for denying lesbian and gay graduate students the opportunity to live with their domestic partners in campus housing.

Nakashima, Ellen. "Va. Housing Board Votes to Bar Loans To Unmarried and Homosexual Couples." *Washington Post*, December 20, 1995, p. D6. The Virginia Housing Development Authority votes 6-1 to support restricting loans for first-time low- and moderate-income home buyers to people related by blood, marriage, or adoption.

Perry, Tony. "Gays Recruited to Save Neighborhood." *Los Angeles Times*, July 26, 1993, p. A3. The neighborhood of Azalea Park in San Diego is featured for its attempts to recruit gay men and lesbians to buy in the area to help save the declining neighborhood.

IMMIGRATION LAWS AND POLITICAL ASYLUM

Breslauer, Jan. "Love Knows No Boundaries." *Los Angeles Times*, February 6, 2000, p. 3. Interview with performance artist Tim Miller, who is fighting the U.S. Immigration and Naturalization Service to allow his Australian lover to stay in the United States. This battle is the subject of Miller's new solo performance piece, *Glory Box*.

Epstein, Jack. "Why Brazil's Homosexuals Find Asylum in the U.S.: Rio, a Magnet for Gay Tourists, Is Also Tolerant of Anti-homosexual Violence." *Christian Science Monitor*, December 7, 1998, p. 7. Epstein discusses the granting of political asylum to an openly gay Brazilian writer who had to flee that country after writing a book on homosexuals in the Brazilian military. Includes information on issues and prejudices facing gays and lesbians in Brazil.

McKim, Jenifer. "Asylum Law Tested by Fearful Gay Dominican." *Boston Globe*, August 20, 1996, p. B1. Discusses the case of Luis Villalona-Perez, a gay man from the Dominican Republic, who is one of the first aliens to apply for political asylum under revised Department of Justice regulations. Villalona-Perez claims he will be murdered if he returns to his country because he is gay.

Park, Jin S. "Pink Asylum: Political Asylum Eligibility of Gay Men and Lesbians Under U.S. Immigration Policy." *UCLA Law Review*, vol. 42:4, April 1995, p. 1115. Park argues that the U.S. should be able to grant asylum to gay men and lesbians as a social group when they are subject to a well-founded fear of persecution in their native country. The challenge for gay rights activists is to prove that such fears are legitimate.

Solomon, Alisa. "Lesbian, Gay, and Binational." *Village Voice*, February 29, 2000, pp. 44–45. Report on New York representative Jerrold Nadler's introduction of the Permanent Partners Immigration Act of 2000 into the U.S. Congress. The bill, if made into law, would insert the words "permanent partner" into the sections of immigration law that address legally married couples.

INTERNATIONAL GAY RIGHTS ISSUES*

Bacchetta, Pauola. "New Campaign for Lesbian Rights in India." *off our backs*, vol. 29:4, April 1999, p. 6. A number of lesbian groups in India have organized themselves into a coalition called "Campaign for Lesbian Rights."

Brummer, Stefaans. "South Africa OKs Gays in Its Military." *Christian Science Monitor*, May 29, 1996, p. 6. Report on South Africa's decision to end discrimination against gays in its military, thereby becoming one of the few nations in the world to allow homosexuals to serve openly.

Duke, Lynne. "Mugabe Makes Homosexuals Public Enemies." *Washington Post*, September 9, 1995, p. A19. Robert Mugabe, the president of Zimbabwe, hurled antigay epithets as he prohibited GALZ—Gays and Lesbians of Zimbabwe—from setting up an exhibit at the Zimbabwe International Book Fair. Duke explores the complex racial and class resentments behind Mugabe's statements.

Dwyer, Victor. "A Tortuous Road." *Maclean's*, vol. 109:20, May 13, 1996, p. 24. Dwyer examines Bill C-33, which would amend the Canadian Human Rights Act to prohibit discrimination based on sexual orientation in Canadian federal institutions.

---

*As there are a multitude of issues involved in international gay rights, this list of documents is just a sample of articles detailing the most significant of late 20th-century and early 21st-century events.

Gay Rights

Faul, Michelle. "'Paradise' Can Be an Ordeal for Gays." *St. Louis Post-Dispatch*, June 13, 1999, p. T8. Faul examines discrimination faced by gays and lesbians, both tourists and locals, in the Caribbean, particularly Jamaica.

Gallagher, John. "Counterattack." *The Advocate*, issue 694, November 14, 1995, p. 30. Gay activists and the U.S. government have been working to prevent an escalation of antigay sentiment in southern Africa. Antigay statements made by President Robert Mugabe of Zimbabwe are discussed.

Haller, Vera. "Intolerance of Homosexuals in Italy Underscored by Tragedy." *Washington Post*, February 15, 1998, p. A28. Article on challenges facing gay men in Italy, a predominantly Catholic nation. Haller focuses on a series of murders of older gay men in Rome over the past seven years.

Meldrum, Andrew. "Gays Challenge Mugabe's Ban." *The Guardian*, July 31, 1996, p. 111. Gays and Lesbians of Zimbabwe (GALZ) is taking President Robert Mugabe's government to court for blocking GALZ's participation in the Zimbabwe International Book Fair.

Patton, Susannah. "French Gay Rights Bill Stirs Furor." *Houston Chronicle*, December 12, 1998, p. 31. Report on controversy surrounding the French bill that would grant unmarried couples certain legal economic rights such as inheritance and joint tax return filings. The bill's significance for the rest of Europe is discussed.

Price, Deb. "Irish Leader Uses Continental Unity Issue to Expand Freedoms at Home." *Detroit News*, October 30, 1997, p. E4. Article examines the strategies that David Norris, a popular Irish MP (member of Parliament), has used to move Ireland from being one of the most repressive countries for gay people to one of the most liberal. Ireland now has more legal protections for homosexuals than the United States.

Sly, Liz. "S. Africa's Gays Have Much to Celebrate." *Chicago Tribune*, October 5, 1994, p. 14. The new South African constitution prohibits discrimination not only on the basis of race and gender, but also on the basis of "sexual orientation," making it the only constitution in the world that specifically protects homosexuals.

Smith, Miriam. "Social Movements and Equality Seeking: The Case of Gay Liberation in Canada." *Canadian Journal of Political Science*, vol. 31:2, June 1998, pp. 285–309. This article examines the impact of the Canadian Charter of Rights and Freedoms on social movement politics in Canada, using the case of the gay liberation movement as an example.

Swardson, Anne. "Canada Approves Gay Rights; Controversial Vote Reveals Political Rifts." *Washington Post*, May 10, 1996, p. A29. Report on passage of the Canadian bill by Parliament, granting full civil rights protections to gays and lesbians. With this bill, Canada now grants more rights to gay people than the United States does.

Tate, Richard. "Driving with Mr. Mandela." *The Advocate*, issue 798, November 9, 1999, pp. 83–84. Profile of Cecil Williams, a gay man who worked for black and gay rights in South Africa and was a friend of Nelson Mandela.

Ward, Lucy. "Crisis as Lords Veto Gay Law." *The Guardian*, July 23, 1998, p. 1. Report on the British House of Lords vote that rejected a bill equalizing the age of consent in Great Britain for heterosexuals and gay men to 16 years of age. Currently gay sex is illegal in England for anyone under the age of 18.

MARRIAGE

Bauer, Gary. "It's Hardly 'Bigotry' to Defend Marriage." *Houston Chronicle*, September 15, 1996, p. C5. Bauer discusses the institution of marriage in the light of a lawsuit filed in Hawaii by homosexual activists, asserting that "counterfeit marriage" would undermine legal and cultural support for all marriages and jeopardize many basic freedoms.

Beyers, Dan. "Montgomery Students Push for Discussion of Gay Issues." *Washington Post*, December 8, 1996, p. B1. Although Montgomery County, Maryland school officials pulled the plug on an attempt by students to broadcast a discussion on the pros and cons of same-sex marriage, the students have insisted that the program be aired.

Biskupic, Joan. "Gay Marriage Is Allowed by Hawaii Court." *Washington Post*, December 4, 1996, p. A1. A judge in Hawaii ruled on December 3, 1996 that the state may not prohibit same-sex marriages, the first legal decision in American history allowing men to marry men and women to marry women.

Black, Chris. "Gay Unions: Frank, Studds Speak." *Boston Globe*, July 12, 1996, p. 3. Barney Frank and Gerry Studds, Massachusetts's two gay representatives, transform a routine debate on the House floor over the Defense of Marriage Act into a deeply personal testament, citing their relationships and their experiences.

Cohen, Cathy. "The Price of Inclusion in the Marriage Club." *Gay Community News*, vol. 21:3–4, Winter 1996, p. 27. The marriage campaign in the gay community is an ill-fated strategy, according to Cohen, who thinks the institution of marriage cannot be separated from its roots in patriarchy, class exploitation, and white supremacy.

Dally Johnston, Michelle. "Gays Vow to Fight Ban Bill." *Denver Post*, February 13, 1997, p. A18. Report on Colorado state representative Marilyn Musgrave's introduction of a bill banning gay marriages in that state. The legislature had earlier in the year killed two unrelated measures that would have strengthened gay rights.

Dart, John. "15 Ministers Reject Ban on Rites for Gays." *Los Angeles Times*, January 18, 1997, p. B4. Dissenting from the position of their 8.6

million–member church, which forbids ministers from officiating at same-sex commitment ceremonies, United Methodist Church clergy sign a public statement disagreeing with this rule.

Dunlap, David W. "Some Gay Rights Advocates Question Drive to Defend Same-Sex Marriage." *New York Times*, June 7, 1996, p. 12. Dunlap examines the fear among some gay activists that a political battle over gay marriage rights will divert attention from what they regard as more critical issues.

Elie, Lolis Eric. "Senate Bill Isn't Logical." *New Orleans Times-Picayune*, February 19, 1997, p. B1. Editorial critical of pending Louisiana legislation that would ban same-sex marriage. Elie attacks the notion that allowing gay marriage would somehow weaken its heterosexual counterpart.

Ettelbrick, Paula L. "Marriage Must Not Eclipse Other Family Organizing." *Gay Community News*, vol. 21:3–4, Winter 1996, p. 25. Ettelbrick discusses the "marriage strategy" among gays and lesbians, arguing that a victory on this issue is no more or less worthy of preservation than the other family gains that have been made for gays and lesbians.

Ettelbrick, Paula L., Don Feder, and Robert Knight. "Q: Would Vermont's Civil Union Law Be Good for Other States?" *Insight on the News*, vol. 16:23, June 19, 2000, pp. 40–43. Ettelbrick answers this question with a resounding "yes," detailing the societal good such a same-sex marriage statute would do. In two sidebars, Feder and Knight answer the question with an equally resounding "no," basing their objections on traditional notions of morality.

Frank, Thomas. "Same Sex Ban Vetoed—Romer Strives to Find Some Middle Ground." *Denver Post*, March 26, 1996, p. A1. Report on Colorado governor Roy Romer's veto of a bill that would have barred the state from recognizing same-sex marriages performed in other states. Calling the bill "mean-spirited and unnecessary," Romer nonetheless affirmed his personal belief that marriage is only between one man and one woman.

Frum, David. "The Courts, Gay Marriage, and the Popular Will." *Wall Street Journal*, vol. 2:3, September 30, 1996, p. 30. Frum argues that the courts are going against the will of the American electorate when they sanction gay marriage and that laws prohibiting gay marriage are indeed constitutional.

Galst, Liz. "The Complicated World of Andrew Sullivan." *Boston Globe*, October 18, 1998, p. K5. A critique of the gay conservative's book *Love Undetectable: Notes on Friendship, Sex, and Survival*; the review points out the many inconsistencies in Sullivan's positions on issues ranging from AIDS to legalizing same-sex marriages.

Giordano, Scott A. "Phelpses Feel the Power of Gays in Vermont." *Bay Windows*, vol. 17:33, 1999, pp. 3, 25. Article on the Reverend Fred Phelps, one of the nation's most militant and controversial antigay activists, who has gone to Vermont to protest same-sex marriage. Article also chronicles the efforts of Vermont's gay activists to counteract Phelps's messages.

Goldberg, Carey. "Vermont High Court Backs Rights of Same-Sex Couples." *New York Times*, December 21, 1999, p. 1. Report on the landmark ruling of Vermont's Supreme Court, which found that same-sex couples cannot be denied the same rights and privileges as their married, heterosexual counterparts. The state legislature is now required to remedy inequality through legislation.

Goldstein, Richard. "The Great Gay Marriage Debate: Ready or Not, Here It Comes." *The Village Voice*, vol. 41:2, January 9, 1996, p. 24. Goldstein argues that marriage, a political issue that has simmered on the back burner of gay rights movements for years, is about to become red-hot. He contends that it is time for society to legally justify the love between two gays or lesbians.

Graff, E. J. "Marriage a la Mode." *Boston Globe*, June 13, 1999, p. 11. Graff offers an excellent encapsulated history of marriage in Western Europe and North America, while building a case for the legal recognition of same-sex relationships.

————. "What Is Marriage?" *Boston Globe*, July 21, 1996, p. C1. Graff comments on the nature of marriage and its import for the debate over the legality of same-sex unions, observing that the definition of marriage over centuries of human history has been altered to fit the social conditions of the day.

————. "When Heather's Mommies Marry." *Boston Globe*, January 5, 1997, p. F1. Graff comments on the ways in which the 1996 Hawaii Supreme Court ruling allowing same-sex marriage offers benefits to the children of gay and lesbian citizens.

Gutierrez, Eric. "French Connections." *The Advocate*, issue 806, February 29, 2000, p. 42. The everything-but-marriage approach to same-sex partnership proposed in Vermont became law last year in France. A look at how one Catholic country got behind gay unions is presented.

Ha, Julie. "Gay Couples Tie Knots in Symbolic Ceremony." *Los Angeles Times*, February 13, 1999, p. 5. Ha discusses action in West Hollywood to commemorate National Freedom to Marry Day and to protest the Knight Initiative, which would prevent California from recognizing same-sex marriages performed in any nation or any other state.

Hanania, Joseph. "The Debate Over Gay Marriages: No Unity." *Los Angeles Times*, June 13, 1996, p. E1. An examination of the debate over whether the struggle to legalize gay marriage is a battle that merely fits into Republican election strategy or a sudden mobilization of the gay community.

Harris, John F. "Small Protest Greets President; Gay Rights Advocates Demonstrate During Clinton Political Trip in West." *Washington Post*,

June 10, 1996, p. A10. Report on the outcome of President Clinton's controversial trip to San Francisco following his endorsement of the Defense of Marriage Act. The small number of protestors who actually showed up to greet the president leads to speculation on the political motives behind the controversy.

Harris, Scott. "Just Your Normal Life with 2 Fathers." *Los Angeles Times*, July 11, 1996, p. B5. Scott Harris discusses the marriagelike relationship between two men in California's San Fernando Valley and considers the progress that the gay rights movement has made on the issue of same-sex marriage.

Herscher, Elaine. "Petitions Seek Vote on Banning Gay Marriages/675,000 Signatures Submitted." *San Francisco Chronicle*, September 22, 1998, p. A15. A report on the latest attempt by California citizens to ban gay marriage.

———. "Same-Sex Marriage Suffers Setback." *San Francisco Chronicle*, November 5, 1998, p. A2. Voters in Hawaii and Alaska approve amendments to their state constitutions limiting marriage to one man and one woman. The Hawaii vote is of particular importance because it was in that state that the push to legalize same-sex marriage began.

Hill-Holtzman, Nancy. "Foe of Gay Marriages Says His Son Is Homosexual." *Los Angeles Times*, September 11, 1996, p. B3. Republican assemblyman William Knight, author of the Knight Initiative, acknowledges that one of his sons is gay. Knight also admits that his younger brother, now deceased, was gay.

Hirshman, Linda R. "Against the Possibility of Equality." *Los Angeles Times*, September 25, 1996, p. B9. Hirshman contends that the aversion to the concept of gay marriages in the United States is actually based on the assumption that marriage cannot be the joining of two equals, but must remain the union of a dominant man and a submissive woman.

Hubler, Shawn. "Public Shows Ambivalence About Same-Sex Marriages." *Los Angeles Times*, July 10, 1996, p. 1. A series of interviews with various residents of Los Angeles shows the range of views regarding same-sex marriage that are held by many heterosexuals.

Jones, Alan. "What's Behind the Gay Marriage Vote." *San Francisco Chronicle*, September 16, 1999, p. A27. Editorial critical of religious conservatives' support of the Knight Initiative.

Kersch, Ken I. "Gay Rights: A Process of Evolution." *Washington Post*, June 10, 1996, p. A19. Kersch, a gay rights supporter, analyzes the Defense of Marriage Act as a relatively moderate piece of legislation that could prove to be a blessing in disguise for the gay rights movement.

Kettle, Martin. "Bad to Be Gay: You Do? The Hell You Do!" *The Guardian*, August 4, 1998, p. T002. A British view of America, same-sex marriages, and other gay rights backlashes, including Senate Republican leader Trent Lott's comparison of homosexuality with kleptomania, as well as

Lott's attempt to block the appointment of James Hormel as ambassador to Luxembourg.

Knight, Al. "Same-Sex Marriage Loses Again." *Denver Post*, January 15, 1998, p. B7. Conservative editorial praising Georgia attorney general Mike Bowers's decision to rescind a job offer to Robin Shahar after he learned that she was a lesbian and was planning a commitment ceremony with her partner.

Kushner, Tony. "Of Gay Marriage and the Heartbreak Kid: Learning to Live with Normalization." *Los Angeles Times*, May 19, 1996, p. M1. Kushner, a noted gay playwright, weighs in with his perspective on the gay marriage debate.

Lambrecht, Bill. "Election Year Puts Political Spin on Gay Rights." *St. Louis Post-Dispatch*, May 20, 1996, p. A1. Lambrecht discusses the potential impact of Hawaii Supreme Court's ruling on gay marriage during an election year. Already, several states have passed laws barring same-sex marriage, and federal legislation against it is in the works.

Lattin, Don. "22 Pastors Want to Quit Methodist Church, Take Flocks." *San Francisco Chronicle*, May 1, 1998, p. A6. A report on the split in the Methodist Church over the issue of gay marriage. Conservative pastors want to leave the California-Nevada Annual Conference after it failed to discipline a minister who performed a lesbian marriage ceremony.

Link, David. "Gay Rights Not Just for Activists Anymore." *Los Angeles Times*, January 21, 1999, p. 9. Editorial supportive of holy union ceremony for a lesbian couple performed by 166 Methodist ministers in defiance of their church's prohibition against blessing same-sex relationships. The editorial makes the point that social change is no longer exclusively being fostered by big-city radicals.

Ly, Phuong. "Making a Public Declaration." *Washington Post*, April 30, 2000, p. C1. As part of the Millennium March on Washington for Equality, 3,000 gay and lesbian couples stage a mass commitment ceremony to protest the lack of nationwide recognition of same-sex marriages. Ly also details other events at the weekend-long gay rights gathering.

MacQuarrie, Brian. "Vt. House Approves Bill Allowing Same-Sex Unions." *Boston Globe*, April 26, 2000, p. A1. Despite overwhelming public opposition, the Vermont House of Representatives passes the historic law granting homosexual couples all of the legal rights accorded heterosexual couples. MacQuarrie details the often rancorous floor debate preceding the vote.

Marinucci, Carla, and Ed Epstein. "Sen. Hatch Blasts S.F. Supervisors." *San Francisco Chronicle*, October 5, 1999, p. A1. U.S. senator Orrin Hatch, a Mormon, of Utah, and San Francisco's liberal city board tangle over California's Knight Initiative, which would define marriage as exclusively between one man and one woman.

Mathis, Nancy. "Clinton to Honor Travel Vow." *Houston Chronicle*, June 8, 1996, p. 9. A report on the controversy surrounding a planned trip by Bill Clinton to the West Coast, after San Francisco mayor Willie Brown predicts that large protests will greet the president over his support of the Defense of Marriage Act.

———. "President Signs GOP Bill on Gay Marriages." *Houston Chronicle*, September 22, 1996, p. A2. President Clinton signs into law the Defense of Marriage Act, which allows states to ban gay marriages and bars gay couples from federal spousal benefits.

Matier, Phillip, and Andrew Ross. "How Brown, Clinton Both Won in Fracas Over Gay Marriage." *San Francisco Chronicle*, June 10, 1996, p. A17. Matier and Ross comment on the tug-of-war between the White House and Mayor Willie Brown over President Clinton's visit to San Francisco after Clinton came out strongly against same-sex marriages.

McIlroy, Anne. "Canada on Line for Gay Alimony." *The Guardian*, May 22, 1999, p. 19. The Canadian high court strikes down an Ontario law defining "spouse" as applying to heterosexual couples only.

Mehren, Elizabeth. "A Historic Day in Vermont as Civil Unions Become Legal." *Los Angeles Times*, July 1, 2000, p. 1. Mehren interviews several same-sex Vermont couples as they prepare to legalize their relationships in that state on the day civil unions become legal. Efforts on the part of state officials to implement the groundbreaking law are also detailed.

Milbouer, Stacy. "Taking Vows and Facing Criticism." *Boston Globe*, December 8, 1996, p. WKNH 1. The rough road faced by gay couples who have joined together in union ceremonies in New Hampshire is discussed.

Nickels, Jeff. "Equality Through Marriage." *Gay Community News*, vol. 21:3–4, Winter 1996, p. 25. Nickels contends that including gays in the institution of marriage would give marriage the fresh perspective it needs to benefit all people.

Polikoff, Nancy D. "Marriage as Choice? Since When?" *Gay Community News*, vol. 21:3–4, Winter 1996, p. 26. Polikoff comments that being given the choice to marry will take away what little is left of a vision of family units based on anything but a sexual dyad. Being given the right to marry would hurt gays and lesbians and remove the few rights they have.

Purdum, Todd S. "Gay Rights Groups Attack Clinton on Midnight Signing." *New York Times*, September 22, 1996, p. 22. Gay rights advocates criticize President Clinton for signing the Defense of Marriage Act, dismissing it as a "historical misjudgement" that endorses a "needless and mean-spirited bill."

———. "President Would Sign Legislation Striking at Homosexual Marriages." *New York Times*, May 23, 1996, p. A1. The White House says that if Congress passes a bill to deny federal recognition to same-sex marriages, President Clinton would sign it, although such unions are not legal in any state. The announcement infuriates gay rights groups.

Rosin, Hanna. "Same-Sex Couples Win Rights in Vermont." *Washington Post*, December 21, 1999, p. A1. A report on the landmark decision by the supreme court of Vermont mandating the state to extend the same benefits of matrimony to same-sex partnerships as it does to heterosexual marriages.

Safire, William. "Same-Sex Marriages? No. Domestic Partnerships? Yes." *St. Louis Post-Dispatch*, April 30, 1996, p. B11. Libertarian columnist William Safire examines the same-sex marriage vote in the Hawaii state legislature, arguing that the compromise rejected by the representatives (legalizing domestic partnerships but not marriage) was the better option.

Spayd, Liz, and Brigid Quinn. "The Gay Marriage Trap: We Fell into a Right-Wing Ambush." *Washington Post*, June 16, 1996, p. C1. Spayd and Quinn relate how conservatives made same-sex marriage a cause célèbre by foisting the issue onto the political agenda during an election year, crediting President Clinton's signing of the Defense of Marriage Act as a way of saving the gay movement's broader civil rights agenda.

Stammer, Larry. "Defying Their Church's Stance on Gays." *Los Angeles Times*, January 16, 1999, p. 2. A report on the protest by Methodist ministers, who are blessing a lesbian couple in defiance of the church's Judicial Council forbidding such acts.

Teicher, Stacey A. "Debate Heats up over Same-Sex Marriages in New England." *Christian Science Monitor*, July 19, 1999, p. 2. Teicher analyzes court cases in New England involving insurance and parental rights that have bearing on the same-sex marriage debate.

Times Wire Service. "Hawaii's High Court Rules Gay Marriage Issue Closed." *Los Angeles Times*, December 11, 1999, p. 17. Wire report on ruling by Hawaii's highest court that the 1998 amendment to the state constitution banning same-sex marriage, which was voted in by the citizenry, settles the matter as to whether or not heterosexual-only marriage is unconstitutional.

Tuller, David. "Making Waves." *San Francisco Chronicle*, June 23, 1996, p. S1. The same-sex marriage controversy in Hawaii is examined as the Hawaiian Supreme Court prepares to take up the issue, even as island residents have mixed feelings.

Unz, Ron. "Gay Marriages Today, Polygamy Tomorrow?" *San Francisco Chronicle*, October 8, 1999, p. A25. A unique conservative take on the gay marriage issue grounded in historical argument.

Vaillancourt, Meg. "Weld: Mass. Would Honor Out-of-State Gay Unions." *Boston Globe*, December 5, 1996, p. A1. Massachusetts governor William Weld declares that if a Hawaiian law recognizing gay marriages is upheld by the state's supreme court, Massachusetts will be forced to recognize those bonds as legal.

Wardlaw, Jack. "Same-Sex Marriage Ban Denounced." *New Orleans Times-Picayune*, February 20, 1997, p. A3. Report on proposed amendment to the Louisiana state constitution that would ban same-sex marriages even though the state already defines marriage as only between one man and one woman.

Wardle, Lynn D. "It's Church's Role to Tackle Moral Issues." *Los Angeles Times*, July 15, 1999, p. 9. A strongly worded opinion against gay marriage from a professor of law at Mormon-affiliated Brigham Young University.

Warren, Jenifer. "Gays Gaining Acceptance in State, Poll Finds." *Los Angeles Times*, June 14, 2000, p. A3. Contrary to expectations, a poll cosponsored by two gay rights groups finds that Californians have become more sympathetic, rather than more antagonistic, to the concerns of the gay community after that state passed the anti–gay marriage Proposition 22.

———. "Proposition 22: Gays Differ Sharply Over Their Next Steps." *Los Angeles Times*, March 9, 2000, p. A3. Warren reports on the response of California's gay and lesbian community to the passage in that state of a ballot measure defining marriage as only between one man and one woman.

Waxman, Sharon. "Out in Hollywood, But Not For Clinton." *Washington Post*, June 12, 1996, p. C1. Report on the reaction of one group of gay activists to the announcement by President Clinton that he will sign the Defense of Marriage Act. Out There, a film industry group, debates whether or not to support Clinton's reelection bid.

White, Gayle. "Clergy Give Gay Marriages Mixed Reception." *Atlanta Constitution*, September 13, 1996, p. C5. An examination of the attitudes of Atlanta clergy toward the Defense of Marriage Act, which seeks to define marriage as a union between "one man and one woman."

Williams, Dick. "Just What Does 'Marriage' Mean in Georgia?" *Atlanta Journal*, February 20, 1996, p. A8. Williams supports a Georgia bill defining marriage as an act between a man and a woman, claiming the bill is important in light of Hawaii's move to allow same-sex marriages.

Wilson, James Q. "Against Homosexual Marriage." *Canadian Journal of Political Science*, vol. 101:3, March 1996, p. 34. In this review of Andrew Sullivan's book *Virtually Normal*, Wilson focuses on Sullivan's arguments for gay marriage, criticizing them on several fronts.

Yang, John E. "House Bill to Stop Gay Marriages Has Stormy Start." *Washington Post*, June 13, 1996, p. A8. The House Judiciary Committee approves election-year legislation intended to blunt efforts to legalize gay marriages, which the bill's backers said would threaten the nation's social structure.

———. "House Votes to Curb Gay Marriages." *Washington Post*, July 13, 1996, p. A1. The House overwhelmingly approved legislation on July 12, 1996 that would seek to prevent gay marriages by defining marriage in federal law for the first time as the union of a man and a woman.

Yardley, Jonathan. "The March of Time." *Washington Post*, December 9, 1996, p. E2. Jonathan Yardley urges people to discuss the issues of same-sex marriages calmly and without hysterics, asserting that a word fraught with fewer connotations than *marriage* should be adopted.

MILITARY

"Then There Was Nunn." *Time*, vol. 142:4, July 26, 1993, p. 40. Sam Nunn's introduction of the "don't ask, don't tell, don't pursue" legislation is discussed.

Birnbaum, Jeffrey H. "Clinton Adopts Policy to Ease Military Gay Ban." *Wall Street Journal*, July 20, 1993, p. A2. President Clinton's endorsement of a "don't ask, don't tell" rule toward homosexuals in the military is discussed.

Boxall, Bettina. "Some Hoots, a Few Hurrahs Greet Clinton Policy on Gays in Military." *Los Angeles Times*, July 20, 1993, p. A14. The public reaction to President Clinton's announcement of his "don't ask, don't tell" policy on gays in the military is examined. Some believe Clinton took a step forward with the issue, while others feel Clinton backed down from his principles.

Carroll, James. "At Stake in the Battle Over Gays in the Military." *Boston Globe*, January 11, 2000, p. A15. Carroll argues that a democratic civil society is threatened if its military apparatus develops a "martial elite" that considers itself morally superior to the civilians it is charged with defending. He sees the military's resistance to admitting gays as a manifestation of this danger.

Clark, Keith. "ROTC Recruiters: Military Recruiters Still a Problem on Campuses." *Out*, May 1999, pp. 21–23. Discussion of activities and policies instituted by universities and colleges around the country to accommodate the presence of Reserve Officers' Training Corps (ROTC) recruiters on their campuses, often in direct violation of state and local or the school's own antidiscrimination policy.

Clines, Francis X. "Killer's Trial Shows Gay Soldier's Anguish." *New York Times*, December 9, 1999, p. 18. Account of the conviction of U.S. Army Private Calvin Glover in the baseball bat bludgeoning of Private Barry Winchell in Kentucky. Detailed quotations from court testimony show the specific ways in which verbal instances of homophobia can escalate into physical violence, as well as the culpability of military officers in doing nothing to stop the harassment.

Cordes, Colleen. "Showdown Over Military Recruiting and Gay Rights." *Chronicle of Higher Education*, April 24, 1998, pp. A43–44. Article on a federal law that would deny funding to any school that does not allow the U.S. military to recruit directly on its campus. Many colleges and all law schools had barred ROTC programs because of the Pentagon's refusal to allow openly gay and lesbian service members.

DeSmet, Kate. "Military Gay Policy Shot Down." *Detroit News*, March 31, 1995, p. A1. In the first judicial ruling on "don't ask, don't tell" in the military, a Brooklyn, New York federal judge declares the policy unconstitutional. Gay activists urge the Clinton administration not to appeal the ruling.

Editorial. "Light in the Closet." *The New Republic*, vol. 209:6, August 9, 1993, p. 7. The *New Republic* argues that "don't ask, don't tell," while morally and intellectually contemptible, is a real advance for civil rights.

Finder, Alan. "Court Backs the Pentagon on Gay Rights." *New York Times*, September 24, 1998, p. A12. The U.S. Second Court of Appeals let stand the military's "don't ask, don't tell" policy, stating that such constitutional issues as equal protection do not necessarily apply to the armed services.

Frank, Nathaniel. "Military Coup." *The New Republic*, vol. 222:1/2, January 4–11, 1999, pp. 14–15. Lengthy opinion piece critical of military's opposition to full inclusion of gay and lesbian service personnel as fundamentally undemocratic.

Gladwell, Malcolm. "U.S. Court Rejects Pentagon Policy on Gays." *Washington Post*, March 31, 1995, p. A1. Report on a federal court declaration that the core of the Pentagon's "don't ask, don't tell" policy is unconstitutional, violating both the free speech and equal protection clauses of the Constitution.

Goodman, Ellen. "A Double-Take on Gays." *Boston Globe*, November 7, 1993, p. A7. Goodman criticizes the "don't ask, don't tell, don't pursue" policy that the Clinton administration is following on the issue of gays in the military.

Gordon, Michael R. "Pentagon Spells Out Rules for Ousting Homosexuals." *New York Times*, December 23, 1993, p. A1. The Pentagon issues new rules intended to put into practice its new "don't ask, don't tell, don't pursue" policy for homosexuals in the military.

Graham, Bradley. "Reinforcing 'Don't Ask.'" *Washington Post*, August 14, 1999, p. A2. Graham concisely breaks down the revisions in Pentagon policy regarding gays in the military.

Holding, Reynolds. "New Policy on Gay GIs Can Begin." *San Francisco Chronicle*, October 30, 1993, p. A1. The U.S. Supreme Court rules that the Defense Department can implement its new "don't ask, don't tell" policy on gays and lesbians in the military.

————. "Supreme Court Silent On Gays in the Military." *San Francisco Chronicle*, October 22, 1996, p. A1. In its first opportunity to review "don't ask, don't tell," the Supreme Court refuses to hear a case involving a naval lieutenant who came out to his commanding officer, the man in charge of implementing the policy in the navy.

Ireland, Doug. "Search and Destroy." *The Nation*, vol. 271:6, July 10, 2000, pp. 11–16. In-depth article focusing on the status of gays and lesbians in the armed forces six months after President Clinton orders a review of the "don't ask, don't tell" policy.

Keen, Lisa. "Deferring to Congress: Federal Panel Finds U.S. Policy of 'Don't Ask, Don't Tell' Constitutional." *Washington Blade*, vol. 29:39, 1998, pp. 1, 20. Reporting from a progay perspective on the 2nd Circuit U.S. Court of Appeals ruling that Congress and the military had justified the gays-in-the-military policy adequately by suggesting that it "promotes unit cohesion, enhances privacy and reduces sexual tension."

Kempster, Noman. "Discharges Up After 'Don't Ask, Don't Tell.'" *Los Angeles Times*, February 27, 1997, p. A18. A report issued on the first three years of the "don't ask, don't tell" policy governing gays and lesbians in the armed forces shows that discharges for homosexual behavior have actually increased under the policy.

Lancaster, John, and Ann Devroy. "Aspin Backs a 'Don't Ask, Don't Tell' Policy on Gays." *Washington Post*, June 23, 1993, p. A1. Defense Secretary Les Aspin has thrown his support behind a compromise proposal that would allow gays to serve in the military as long as they keep their sexual orientation private.

Marinucci, Carla. "End 'Don't Ask, Don't Tell,' Gore Insists." *San Francisco Chronicle*, December 14, 1999, p. A1. This article indicates how far the debate over gay rights has come since 1992, as three major Democratic political candidates, First Lady and New York senatorial candidate Hillary Clinton and presidential candidates Al Gore and former senator Bill Bradley scramble to assume the most progay position on gay armed service members in the 2000 elections.

Matier, Phillip, and Andrew Ross. "New Effort to Disband S.F. Schools' Troubled ROTC Program." *San Francisco Chronicle*, June 12, 1995, p. A13. Matier and Ross comment on the fight to dump the city's high school ROTC program in response to the federal ban on gays in the military.

Pear, Robert. "President Admits 'Don't Ask,' Policy Has Been Failure." *New York Times*, December 12, 1999, p. 1. Report on a radio interview in which President Clinton acknowledges that his policy on gays in the military has not worked and needs to be reexamined. His remarks come in the wake of the murder conviction of Private Barry Winchell's killer.

Pressley, Sue Ann. "Hate May Have Triggered Fatal Barracks Beating." *Washington Post*, August 11, 1999, p. A1. Profile of U.S. Army Private First Class Barry Winchell, who was bludgeoned to death at Fort Campbell, Kentucky, allegedly because he was gay.

Rosenberg, Eric. "Group Says Military Violated Gay Policy in Record Numbers." *Houston Chronicle*, February 19, 1998, p. 4. Report on the findings of the Servicemembers Legal Defense Network, an advocacy group for gay and lesbian military personnel that has discovered that the Pentagon's "don't ask, don't tell" policy has led to an increase, rather than a decrease, in antigay harassment in the armed services.

Schmitt, Eric. "Gay Rights Advocates Plan to Press Clinton to Undo Policy of 'Don't Ask, Don't Tell.'" *New York Times*, December 25, 1999, p. 20. Sensing new possibilities in the political climate, gay rights advocates are pressing the Clinton administration to combat harassment against homosexuals in the armed forces while laying the groundwork to overturn the military's "don't ask, don't tell" policy.

Shenon, Philip. "Sailor Victorious in Gay Case of On-Line Privacy." *New York Times*, June 12, 1998, p. A1. Article reporting on the settlement reached between Timothy McVeigh, America Online (AOL), and the U.S. Navy. McVeigh had been investigated by the navy after he identified himself as gay in his AOL member profile.

Tuller, David. "Gays Criticize Military Shift on 'Don't Ask.'" *San Francisco Chronicle*, August 14, 1999, p. A1. Overview of military's revisions to the "don't ask, don't tell" policy after the murder of an army private, Barry Winchell, in Kentucky. The article includes quotes from gay activists who feel the Pentagon delayed too long in making those revisions.

Weinstein, Henry. "Appeals Court Backs Military Policy, Upholds Discharge of Two Gay Men." *Los Angeles Times*, September 6, 1997, p. A25. The Ninth Circuit Court of Appeals in San Francisco upholds the discharge of two servicemen for admitting to superior officers that they were homosexuals. Although no actual evidence of homosexual activity was produced, the justices ruled that the Pentagon's actions and its overall "don't ask, don't tell" policy were "rational."

Zuniga, Joseph. "'Don't Ask, Don't Tell' Won't Do." *Washington Post*, May 18, 1993, p. A21. Joseph Zuniga, who is being honorably discharged from the U.S. Army because of his homosexuality, says that the Senate Armed Services Committee's proposal to institute "don't ask, don't tell" won't work.

POLITICS

Arkes, Hadley. "Fear and Loathing in L.A." *Wall Street Journal*, November 20, 1999, p. W17. A conservative editorial by a professor of jurisprudence at Amherst who is critical of tactics used by gay rights activists protesting a psychiatric convention.

Associated Press. "California Moves to Extend Gay Rights with New Laws." *New York Times*, October 4, 1999, p. 18. Overview of three California gay rights laws that establish domestic partnerships, outlaw harassment of gay and lesbian students and teachers, and criminalize housing and job discrimination based on sexual orientation.

———. "Democratic Leaders Reject Call by Bradley to Expand Gay Rights." *St. Louis Post-Dispatch*, September 25, 1999, p. 15. African-American liberals criticize presidential candidate Bill Bradley's gay rights strategy as ill-advised.

———. "Hormel Named Luxembourg Envoy." *Washington Post*, June 5, 1999, p. A10. Report on resolution to President Clinton's long-running battle with the Senate to appoint first gay ambassador James Hormel.

Bawer, Bruce. "Up (with) the Establishment." *The Advocate*, issue 698–699, January 23, 1996, p. 112. Gay conservative commentator Bawer believes that gay rights groups should seek help from gay and gay-friendly people within establishment institutions; he believes that this could lead to the acceleration of positive change.

Bernstein, Alan. "Dole's Denial Puts Spotlight on Gay Group." *Houston Chronicle*, September 5, 1995, p. 17. Profile of the Log Cabin Republicans, a group dedicated to educating the Republican Party about gays and lesbians from the inside. The 1996 presidential candidate Bob Dole recently returned to them a $1,000 contribution they had attempted to make to his campaign.

Bernstein, Andrea. "The Silence of the Pols." *The Village Voice*, vol. 42:26, July 1, 1997, p. 46. A look at the gay political scene in New York City as more and more "out" candidates compete for elected office while, in Bernstein's view, very little of substance actually gets accomplished for the gay community.

Biskupic, Joan. "For Gays, Tolerance Translates to Rights." *Washington Post*, November 5, 1999. Biskupic provides an overview of gains in the gay rights movement in the late 1990s, linking them to changes in public perceptions of homosexuality.

Bono, Chastity. "Sonny & Chas." *The Advocate*, issue 698–699, January 23, 1996, p. 28. In an interview with his daughter, Representative Sonny Bono discusses her lesbianism, his feelings toward gay rights, and gays in the military. Sonny Bono, now deceased, was a famous television personality before becoming a lawmaker.

Borgman, Anna. "Lesbians Ponder Ways to Counter Attacks by Right." *Washington Post*, February 12, 1995, p. B1. Discusses a gathering of 650 lesbians in College Park, Maryland for an annual conference; focuses on the activists at a political workshop who urge the women to actively promote their own values to battle the religious right.

Brownstein, Ronald. "Reed's Testament Is a Complicated Mix of Prayer, Passion and Politics." *Los Angeles Times*, April 28, 1997, p. A5. On the occasion of Ralph Reed's resignation as executive director of the rabidly antigay Christian Coalition, Brownstein surveys his accomplishments and examines how Reed helped move fundamentalist politics from the fringes to the center of American political discourse.

Bull, Chris. "Bill Bradley Wants You!" *The Advocate*, issue 796, October 12, 1999, pp. 26–35. In an interview, presidential candidate Bill Bradley discusses several proposals that would benefit the gay and lesbian community, including combating antigay harassment and discrimination in public schools.

———. "Here They Go Again." *The Advocate*, issue 675, February 21, 1995, p. 26. U.S. senator Jesse Helms has rushed two antigay bills to the Senate floor, while House Speaker Newt Gingrich has vowed to uncover what he views as progay school curricula. The status of gay rights in a Congress headed by Gingrich and Senator Bob Dole is discussed.

———. "His Brother's Keeper." *The Advocate*, issue 786, May 25, 1999, pp. 30–32. Profile of Parris Glendening, the governor of Maryland, who lost his brother to AIDS in 1992. When he was elected governor, he began working on a gay rights bill for the state in memory of his brother.

Burr, Chandler. "Historical Imperative: By 'Tolerating' Gays, Gingrich Denies Equality." *Los Angeles Times*, January 29, 1995, p. 2. Burr deconstructs Newt Gingrich's use of the word "tolerance" in regard to the gay community and shows that, historically, the word "equality" is the only one that matters.

Califia, Pat. "For Richer or for Poorer." *Out*, issue 72, November 1999, p. 66. Califia takes the gay mainstream press to task for focusing on the moneyed gay elite. She sees real political change coming from activists in the working class.

Campbell, Duncan. "Leading US Cities Could Vote in Gay Mayors." *The Guardian*, November 19, 1999, p. 17. Duncan offers a British perspective on the Los Angeles and San Francisco mayoral races. In Los Angeles, longtime conservative city councillor Joel Wachs comes out as he prepares to run for mayor; in San Francisco, gay rights activist Tom Ammiano forces a runoff election after a successful write-in campaign.

Coggan, Roger. "If They Unite to Fight, Minorities Can Be a Majority." *Los Angeles Times*, January 8, 1996, p. 5. Member of excluded groups, including gays and lesbians, have the opportunity to form the core constituency of a new majority coalition, Coggan argues; but, he says, this will happen only when each of the groups acknowledges the uniqueness of the others as they collectively organize around common values.

Conniff, Ruth. "Tammy Baldwin." *The Progressive*, vol. 63:1, January 1999, pp. 64–68. Representative Tammy Baldwin, Democrat from Wisconsin, the first open lesbian ever to be elected to Congress, is interviewed about her political career, gay rights, and hate crimes.

Cotton, Terri. "Anti-Gay Rights Push Fails." *Denver Post*, January 26, 1999, p. B-4. Colorado for Family Values, the organization behind Amendment 2, tries once again to exclude homosexuality from an existing antidiscrimination law, this time in Colorado Springs.

Dyer, R. A. "Christian Groups and Gay Activists Agree on Little." *Houston Chronicle*, August 16, 1996, p. A19. Across the city of San Diego, sometimes in unruly anti-AIDS protests or during blockades of abortion clinics, Christian and gay activists confront each other during the 1996 Republican National Convention.

Editorial. "Gay Rights in California." *New York Times*, October 9, 1999, p. 16. A mainstream liberal opinion praises California governor Gray Davis for signing three gay rights measures into law.

Ewegan, Bob. "Attitudes Are More Important Than Laws." *Denver Post*, April 19, 1999, p. B7. This editorial proposes that the very existence of civilized debate over gay rights legislation is in itself progress, even if the legislation is defeated.

Feinstein, Dianne, and Robert G. Torricelli. "Sexual Orientation Is Not a Job Qualification." *Los Angeles Times*, June 4, 1998, p. 9. Two liberal members of the Senate, who have led the fight to bring the nomination of James Hormel as ambassador to Luxembourg to a floor vote, call for his confirmation.

Freedland, Jonathan. "Don't Ask, Don't Tell, Don't Worry, United States." *The Guardian*, June 24, 1995, p. 16. Freedland surveys the landscape of gay rights in the United States from a British perspective. He focuses on the Supreme Court's decision to allow Boston's St. Patrick's Day parade to exclude gay groups, as well as discussing the Clinton White House's recent gay controversies.

Gallagher, John. "Are We Really Asking for Special Rights?" *The Advocate*, issue 757, April 14, 1998, pp. 24–37. Gallagher examines the belief that nondiscrimination protections for gays amount to an unfair advantage that is denied to other people.

Gingrich, Candace. "Gay, Proud . . . and Gingrich." *Washington Post*, September 24, 1995, p. C2. Gingrich, a lesbian whose brother is Newt Gingrich, discusses the way her life has been changed since her brother became Speaker of the House and comments on her tour with the Human Rights Campaign Fund.

Goldstein, Richard. "The Trojan Elephant." *The Village Voice*, vol. 44:36, September 14, 1999, pp. 61–63. Goldstein examines the Republican Party's relationship to the gay community through its history of antigay policies.

———. "Virtual Reality." *The Village Voice*, vol. 40:38, September 19, 1995, p. 85. Goldstein reviews *Virtually Normal* by Andrew Sullivan and *Virtual Equality* by Urvashi Vaid.

Gonnerman, Jennifer. "Is There a Lesbian in the House?" *The Village Voice*, vol. 41:24, June 11, 1996, p. 22. Report on Dale McCormick's quest to become the first open lesbian in Congress. She is facing increasing homophobia, however, as she campaigns to be the representative from Maine's 1st congressional district.

Goodheart, Adam. "Gay Rights: Wrong Strategy." *Washington Post*, November 21, 1995, p. E2. Goodheart reviews Urvashi Vaid's book *Virtual Equality*, agreeing with her premise that this is the best of times and the worst of times for gay America: The nation is increasingly dotted with homophobic enclaves, while many out gays choose to insulate themselves in middle-class urban enclaves.

Goodman, Ellen. "The Real Issue Is Civil Rights, Not Gay Rights." *Houston Chronicle*, July 26, 1998, p. 6. Editorial critical of the religious right's insistence that, when it comes to gay issues, they are the ones who are being silenced and discriminated against.

Heaton, Paul. "Lessons from Ypsilanti." *The Advocate*, issue 763, 1998, p. 11. Article uses the experiences of gay rights activists in Ypsilanti, Michigan, who successfully led the defeat of an antigay initiative, as an example of how coalition-building across communities can be an effective strategy for combating homophobic legislation.

Hibbard, Susan. "Reading Between the Lines: Race and Sexuality in Right-wing (and Gay) Campaigns." *Gay Community News*, vol. 20:4, Winter 1995, p. 7. Gay messages have supported the formulation of rights as a scarce commodity that must be rationed carefully to deserving victims. The use of race and gender in the campaigns of the right wing and the responses by gay rights groups are discussed.

Hohler, Bob, and Jayson T. Blair. "Gay Rights Movement Finds Agenda in Peril." *Boston Globe*, July 8, 1996, p. 1. Analysis of the dilemma faced by the gay community in the 1996 presidential election: Gays and lesbians are at odds with Republican candidate Bob Dole but have been disheartened by the Democratic candidate, President Bill Clinton.

Holder, Ann. "Queer Organizing in Kentucky: An Interview with Carla Wallace." *Gay Community News*, vol. 22:1, Summer 1996, p. 6. In this interview, Wallace discusses how lesbian- and gay-identified groups can form alliances within their communities. Her Fairness Campaign has created and sustained a broad-based educational effort around issues of sexual orientation.

Holmes, Steven A. "Check from Gays Still Issue for Dole." *Houston Chronicle*, October 19, 1995, p. 10. The continuing flap over a $1,000 donation to 1996 Republican presidential candidate Bob Dole from the gay political group Log Cabin Republicans is examined. After apologizing to the group for rejecting their contribution, Dole comes under the fire from the right wing of his party.

————. "Civil Rights Dance Lesson: The Tiny Step Forward." *New York Times*, September 15, 1996, section 4, p. 5. The public's ambivalence presents tricky questions of strategy for the gay rights movement. Its leaders say battles have to be chosen cautiously, tactics planned carefully.

Humm, Andy. "Guess Who's Coming to Dinner?" *The Village Voice*, vol. 41:40, October 1, 1996, pp. 11, 14. The article examines the controversy in the New York gay and lesbian community over the invitation extended to New York City mayor Rudy Giuliani by the Empire State Pride Agenda to speak at their annual dinner.

Ireland, Doug. "Gay Politics: Moving in a New Direction—Rebuilding the Gay Movement." *The Nation*, vol. 269/issue 2, July 12, 1999, pp. 11–18. In-depth look at how local gay groups are successfully building coalitions with labor and other minority groups while eschewing the single-issue politics of Washington-based "gaycrats."

Khan, Surina. "Tracking Gay Conservatives." *Gay Community News*, vol. 22: 1, Summer 1996, p. 7. The number of openly gay conservatives in the Republican Party is now larger than it ever has been. This article takes a closer look at the roles they play within the GOP and suggests that their successes have been mixed at best.

Kuehl, Sheila. "I Do, Therefore I Am." *The Advocate*, issue 791–792, August 17, 1999, p. 128. Kuehl discusses her life as an activist for the gay and lesbian rights movement, beginning when she attended a meeting of women students at UCLA.

Kurtz, Howard. "Clinton Ad Touting Defense of Marriage Is Pulled." *Washington Post*, October 17, 1996, p. A18. After receiving protests from gay rights organizations, President Bill Clinton's campaign withdraws a radio ad boasting that he had signed a law aimed at preventing same-sex marriages.

Lawrence, Jill. "The Politics of Gay Rights." *Atlanta Journal-Constitution*, June 23, 1996, p. A8. Gay activism and religious conservatives help make gay rights an important but tricky issue for both parties, forcing politicians into difficult balancing acts. The politics of gay rights are explored.

Makeig, John. "Lawyers in Murder Trial Accused of Anti-Gay Bias." *Houston Chronicle*, February 22, 1995, p. 13. Makeig reports on the case of a gay man sentenced to death by the state of Texas for murdering his lover and the homophobic statement made by the prosecution during his trial.

Moore, Teresa. "King's Niece Slams Gay Rights." *San Francisco Chronicle*, August 20, 1997, p. A17. Comments of an African-American civil rights

leader reveal a split between some on the left as to whether or not gay
rights is a desirable, or even necessary, goal worth fighting for.

Moss, J. Jennings. "Good-bye, Mr. Studds." *The Advocate*, issue 695, November 28, 1995, p. 20. Report on Representative Gerry Studds, Democrat from Massachusetts, and his decision not to run for a 13th term in
Congress. As the first openly gay member of Congress, he was an influential voice for gay rights.

Nagourney, Adam. "A Movement Divided Between Push and Shove." *New
York Times*, October 25, 1998, section 4, p. 3. Writer contrasts two con-
temporaneous events: a protest march held in New York commemorating
Matthew Shepard's murder, and the Human Rights Campaign's endorse-
ment of the conservative Alfonse D'Amato for reelection as senator from
New York.

Navarro, Mireya. "2 Decades On, Miami Endorses Gay Rights." *New York
Times*, December 2, 1998, p. A1. In an implicit rebuke 22 years after
Anita Bryant's anti–gay rights campaign, Dade County commissioners
passed an ordinance adding sexual orientation to its antidiscrimination
policy. This article focuses on the changes in Miami that led to the vote.

Price, Deb. "As Dole's Likely Successor in Senate, Lott Is a Real Worry for
Gay Americans." *Detroit News*, March 22, 1996, p. E1. Price deconstructs Republican Senate majority-leader-to-be Trent Lott over his antigay voting record, as well as his history of personal animosity toward the
gay and lesbian community.

———. "California Leads the Way on Gay Rights." *Detroit News*, October 11,
1999, A9. An unabashedly progay piece praising California governor Gray
Davis's signing into law three significant legislative advances for gay rights.

———. "Clinton Has to Take Off the Rubber Gloves When He Handles
Gay Rights Issues." *Detroit News*, November 8, 1996, p. E3. Deb Price
looks at the gains for the gay rights movement in the 1996 elections.

———. "Election '96 Brings Many Gains for the Gay-Rights Movement,
with Just a Few Losses." *Detroit News*, November 8, 1996, p. E3. Price
looks at the gains for the gay rights movement in the 1996 elections, such
as Clinton's reelection as the first gay-friendly president.

———. "Equality for Gays Progresses Faster Than Some May Realize."
Detroit News, March 8, 1999, p. A9. Optimistic editorial surveying the
accelerated pace of change in favor of gay rights in the 1990s.

———. "Gays Need Democrats to Win 2000 Election." *Detroit News*, November 1, 1999, p. A7. Editorial linking the fortunes of the gay rights
movement directly to the Democratic Party's prospects in the 2000 elections, especially at the congressional level.

———. "GOP Congressman Is Proof That Education Can Reverse Gay
Bias." *Detroit News*, April 5, 1996, p. E1. Price profiles Massachusetts

representative Peter Torkildsen and his evolution from a staunch enemy of the gay rights movement to one of its most loyal Republican allies in Congress.

————. "Inroads in Public Office Pave Way to Gay Rights." *Detroit News*, June 6, 1997, p. C2. In this column, Price argues for the election of more openly gay and lesbian candidates as one very effective tool to achieving greater civil rights protections.

————. "Rep. Kolbe's Admission Will Free Him to Be a Voice for Gay Rights." *Detroit News*, August 9, 1996, p. E1. Price praises the decision of Arizona congressman Jim Kolbe to come out as gay after the House passes the Defense of Marriage Act.

Ratcliffe, R. G. "Gay Republicans Win Lawsuit Against GOP." *Houston Chronicle*, June 15, 1996, p. 1. Report on a Texas judge's ruling that the Texas Republican Party violated the free speech rights of the Log Cabin Republicans, an intraparty gay group, by refusing them a booth and program advertising at the state convention.

Rios, Delia M. "GOP Still Gives Cold Shoulder to Gay Republicans." *New Orleans Times-Picayune*, March 24, 1996, p. A22. Gay Republicans might have looked to the 1996 election as the year they secured the right to participate among the party ranks without being scorned. But the relationship this election year has more often been characterized by anger and resentment and remains tenuous at best.

Robison, Clay. "Gay GOP Group Gearing Up." *Houston Chronicle*, June 19, 1996, p. A19. Report on the suit of Log Cabin Republicans against Texas GOP leaders' efforts to ban a gay rights booth from the state convention. The Log Cabin Republicans has also asked the state party to remove anti-gay language from its platform.

Rosenfeld, Megan. "Across the Great Divide." *Washington Post*, May 22, 1996, p. C1. Profile of Human Rights Campaign head Elizabeth Birch, one of the country's leading mainstream gay activists. While celebrating the Supreme Court's decision in *Romer v. Evans*, she must also prepare to battle the Defense of Marriage Act.

Rosin, Hanna. "Newly Elected Gay Congresswoman Is Taking Historic Role in Stride." *Washington Post*, December 26, 1998, p. A12. Profile of Tammy Baldwin, the first openly gay candidate to be elected to the U.S. Congress.

Rothman, Clifford. "David Mixner." *Los Angeles Times*, September 3, 1995, p. M3. In an interview, gay activist David Mixner discusses the political power of the gay and lesbian vote and its implications on the 1996 presidential election.

Rothschild, Matthew. "Get Up, Stand Up." *The Progressive*, vol. 60:5, May 1996, p. 4. Rothschild discusses the importance of the left in standing up for gay and lesbian rights. He relates the story of Paul Soglin, the heterosexual mayor of Madison, Wisconsin, who received threats after he criticized a city employee for distributing antigay literature.

Sack, Kevin. "Gay Issues Return in Rematch for Senate Seat." *New York Times,* October 7, 1996, p. B6. Senator Jesse Helms has mounted an advertising blitz that attempts to link his election opponent for the North Carolina senate seat, former Charlotte, North Carolina mayor Harvey Gantt, to a variety of homosexual causes.

———. "Gay Rights Movement Meets Big Resistance in S. Carolina." *New York Times,* July 7, 1998, p. A1. Report on efforts of gay rights activists to make inroads in South Carolina despite the state's deep-seated religious fundamentalism, political conservativeness, and history of prejudice.

Sandalow, Marc. "Gay Officials Meet at the White House." *San Francisco Chronicle,* June 14, 1995, p. A1. In an unprecedented meeting at the White House, 45 gay and lesbian elected officials urged Clinton administration officials to take a more forceful role on issues ranging from job discrimination to AIDS.

Scales, Ann. "President Takes Stand on Gay Rights." *Boston Globe,* November 9, 1997, p. A1. Report on a historic first—President Clinton becomes the first sitting U.S. president to address a political gathering of gays and lesbians at the annual dinner of the Human Rights Campaign.

Schmitt, Eric. "Senators Reject Both Job-Bias Ban and Gay Marriage." *New York Times,* September 11, 1996, p. A1. The Senate votes to deny federal benefits to married people of the same sex and to permit states to ignore such marriages sanctioned in other states. The Senate also defeats by a single vote a separate bill that for the first time would have banned discrimination against homosexuals in the workplace.

Shea, Lois R. "Analysts Cautious on Gay-Rights Defeat/Repeal of Maine Antidiscrimination Law Not Seen as Start of National Trend." *Boston Globe,* February 12, 1998, p. B16. Report on the Maine referendum repealing that state's gay rights law. Maine is the first state ever to void an existing piece of legislation of that kind.

Simmons, Todd. "The End: Has the Gay Movement Met Its Match?" *The Advocate,* January 24, 1995, p. 28. The deeply conservative political terrain on Capitol Hill may make it difficult for the Human Rights Campaign Fund and the National Gay and Lesbian Task Force to be effective. Problems within both organizations are noted.

Skelton, George. "A Remarkable Floor Debate on Gay Rights." *Los Angeles Times,* June 5, 1997, p. A31. Excerpts from a debate on the floor of the California State Assembly over a bill introduced by openly lesbian assemblywoman Sheila Kuehl that would have protected California public school students from discrimination on the basis of sexual orientation.

Smolowe, Jill. "The Unmarrying Kind." *Time*, vol. 147:18, April 29, 1996, p. 68. Focusing on local targets, religious conservatives are waging a fervent campaign to stomp out gay rights. Religious conservatives' crusades against gay marriages and gays in the classroom are discussed.

Solomon, Alisa. "Back to the Streets." *The Village Voice*, vol. 43:44, November 3, 1998, p. 34. Writer sympathetic to the cause of gay rights reports on aftermath of the Matthew Shepard protest march in New York City that was violently broken up by police and wonders if this signals a resurgence in gay radical activism.

———. "Good for the Gays?" *The Village Voice*, vol. 43:43, October 27, 1998, pp. 58–61. Piece exploring rationale for the Human Rights Campaign's endorsement of conservative Republican Alfonse D'Amato for re-election as U.S. senator from New York and questioning the wisdom of that choice.

Stan, Adele M. "Candace Gingrich." *Ms.*, vol. 6:4, January 1996, p. 44. Profile of gay rights activist Candace Gingrich, half-sister of the Republican Speaker of the House, Newt Gringrich, a legislator notoriously hostile to gay and lesbian rights.

Stanhope, Victoria. "More Mayhem About the Millennium March." *off our backs*, vol. 29: 6, June 1999, pp. 6–8. Stanhope reveals the conflicts behind planning a major gay rights protest, referring to a report on the National Organization for Women Lesbian Rights Summit.

Swanson, K. C. "A Pragmatic Push for Gay Rights." *National Journal*, vol. 28:12, March 23, 1996, p. 659. Elizabeth M. Birch, executive director of the Human Rights Campaign, is profiled. The goal of Birch and her group is to defeat Senator Jesse Helms of North Carolina on Election Day in 1996.

Tanui, Jemeli. "Frank: Political Path Best for Gay Rights." *Syracuse Post-Standard*, December 16, 1999, p. B1. Account of speech given by openly gay Massachusetts representative Barney Frank to a Syracuse, New York gay rights group. Frank proposes that the best way to achieve further gains for the movement is through lobbying and letter-writing rather than through civil disobedience.

Thurman, Skip. "Clinton to Openly Advocate Gay Rights." *Christian Science Monitor*, November 7, 1997, p. 4:2. Thurman places President Clinton's historic address before the Human Rights Campaign's annual dinner in the context of his support for ENDA, the House bill that would allow discrimination cases to be brought against employers on the basis of sexual orientation.

Trebay, Guy. "Full Court Press." *The Village Voice*, vol. 41:23, June 4, 1996, p. 18. Trebay asserts that the Supreme Court ruling in *Romer v. Evans*, which strikes down Colorado's antigay Amendment 2 and President

Clinton's stance against same-sex marriages, both serve to energize the gay rights community, albeit for different reasons.

Tuller, David. "Gays Plan San Diego Protests." *San Francisco Chronicle*, August 9, 1996, p. A1. A report on the plans of gays and lesbians to express their anger over what they say is the Republican party's antigay stance during its convention in San Diego.

Wieder, Judy. "Kramer vs. Kushner." *The Advocate*, issue 791–792, August 17, 1999, pp. 90–95. Wieder interviews political playwrights Larry Kramer and Tony Kushner, who discuss art as activism—their attempts to transform the world through art because the "smell of injustice" is too intolerable.

Wright, Kai, Rhonda Smith, and Bill Roundy. "Legislative Activity Percolates Across the Nation." *Washington Blade*, vol. 30:17, 1999, p. 20. An update of the progress of gay rights–related bills in state legislatures around the country in 1999.

Yang, John E. "Gays in a Conservative Closet." *Washington Post*, November 7, 1997, p. A23. Yang profiles the closeted aides of several antigay Republican congressmen.

RELIGION

Boudreaux, Richard. "Vatican's Stance on Gays Makes It a Protest Target." *Los Angeles Times*, July 8, 2000, p. 2. Report on the Catholic Church's response to the international gay rights protest, World Pride, held in Rome during the Church's jubilee year. The changing attitudes of many Italian Catholics towards gays and lesbians is discussed.

Carlin, David R. "The Gay Movement and Aggressive Secularism." *America*, vol. 173:8, September 23, 1995, p. 12. Writing from the position that the gay rights movement is not just an effort to legitimize the actions of homosexuals but part of a larger effort to force secularism into society, Carlin discusses why Catholics generally underestimate its significance.

Culver, Virginia. "Religions Still Wrangle." *Denver Post*, May 21, 1996, p. A11. Culver discusses how *Romer v. Evans* may settle the issue of gay rights in Colorado from a legal perspective, but for many Colorado churches, the debate rages on.

Dart, John. "Southern Baptist Delegates OK Disney Boycott." *Los Angeles Times*, June 19, 1997, p. A1. Report on the Southern Baptist convention, the largest Protestant domination in the United States, which has called for a boycott of all Walt Disney products, movies, and theme parks because of the company's perceived progay bias.

Dorning, Mike. "Episcopal Heresy Trial Tests Gay Clergy Issue." *Chicago Tribune*, February 28, 1996, p. 14. At St. John's Cathedral in Wilmington, Delaware, for only the second time in the history of the Episcopal

Church in America, a bishop goes on trial for heresy: Walter Righter is charged with ordaining an openly gay man as a church deacon.

Dunlap, David W. "Minister Brings Anti-Gay Message to the Spotlight." *New York Times,* December 19, 1994, p. A16. A report on the tireless crusade of Louis P. Sheldon, a Presbyterian minister and the chairman of the Traditional Values Coalition, against rules and regulations that confer equality on homosexuals.

French, Ron. "Pastor Welcomes Gay 'Sinners.'" *Detroit News,* November 18, 1996, p. A1. A report on the outcome of a dispute between a Congregational minister and a gay churchgoer who was asked not to attend the church anymore after his picture appeared in a local newspaper as a gay rights activist.

Gelertner, David. "Gay Rights and Wrongs." *Wall Street Journal,* August 13, 1998, p. A14. A conservative editorial proposing a return to what the author refers to as "classical liberalism" as a solution to the "issue of homosexuality"—gays and lesbians would not be discriminated against, and in return they would conduct their lives discreetly.

Hollandsworth, Skip. "Mel White." *Texas Monthly,* vol. 23:9, September 1995, p. 123. Former ghostwriter for the religious right, pastor, and recently proclaimed gay, White is now rallying for equality for all human beings. His efforts to further the gay rights movement and his history with Christian leaders are discussed.

Kennedy, Lisa. "The Quiet American Hero." *Out,* issue 72, November 1999, p. 92. Kennedy profiles the Reverend Jimmy Creach, a Methodist minister from Raleigh, North Carolina, who has continually defied his church by performing commitment ceremonies for gays and lesbians across the country.

Leland, John, and Mark Miller. "Can Gays 'Convert'?" *Newsweek,* vol. 132:7, August 17, 1998, pp. 46–50. In-depth examination of the ex-gay movement, focusing on Exodus International, a conservative Christian ministry that claims homosexuality can be "cured."

Leonard, Mary. "Activists Applaud Report on Gay Churches." *Boston Globe,* August 12, 1999, p. A5. Gay activists interpret a report chronicling the conflicts over gay rights within America's churches as ultimately good for the movement.

Mendoza, Martha. "Presbyterian Church Panel Proposes Ordination of Chaste Gays." *Washington Post,* July 5, 1996, p. A4. Gays who abstain from sex could be ordained in the nation's largest Presbyterian church organization under a proposal from church leaders. One longtime Presbyterian gay rights activist is leaving the church because of the proposal.

Murphy, Carlyle. "Mutual Apology for Hateful Speech." *Washington Post,* October 24, 1999, p. C3. Murphy documents the public meeting of Moral

Majority founder Reverend Jerry Falwell and gay minister Mel White's Soulforce organization at Falwell's Thomas Road Baptist Church.

Niebuhr, Gustav. "Religious Coalition Plans Gay Rights Strategy." *New York Times*, August 24, 1999, p. 10. Niebuhr reports on multidenominational progay groups who are organizing against the influence of conservative religious organizations.

Olivo, Antonio, and Joseph Trevino. "Foes Find Common Cause Against Gay Rights." *Los Angeles Times*, August 17, 1999, p. 1. Olivo explores phenomenon of Latino Pentecostal churches in California joining with former adversaries to fight gay rights legislation.

Ribadeneira, Diego. "Breach of Faith: The Struggle by Gays and Lesbians to Find a Spiritual Home Is Dividing Congregations Across America." *Boston Globe*, March 22, 1998, p. 10. Thorough overview of the efforts of many gays and lesbians to find acceptance in various Catholic, Protestant, and Jewish faith communities. Ribadeneira emphasizes the work of those congregations who welcome homosexuals.

Rosin, Hanna. "Vatican Intervenes Against Gay Ministry." *Washington Post*, July 14, 1999, p. A1. Rosin discusses in much depth the outreach work and subsequent punishment by the Vatican of progay Catholic clergy Reverend Robert Nugent and Sister Jeannine Grannick.

Sennott, Charles M. "Christian Right Woos Catholics." *Boston Globe*, December 10, 1995, p. 41. Report on conservative activist Ralph Reed's national launch of the Catholic Alliance, a spin-off of the Christian Coalition, which he heads, at a gathering in Boston. Reed hopes to unite Catholics and evangelical Protestants to turn back gains in abortion and gay rights.

Stanley, Alessandra. "Pope Declares His 'Bitterness' Over Gay Event." *New York Times*, July 10, 2000, p. 11. Pope John Paul II speaks out against the week-long World Pride event held in Rome, world headquarters of the Catholic Church. This is in keeping with his long-standing opposition to gay rights.

Toolan, David S. "In Defense of Gay Politics: Confessions of a Pastoralist." *America*, vol. 173:8, September 23, 1995, p. 18. Toolan investigates whether social ostracism of openly homosexual men and women is the only way for Catholics to deal with gays and lesbians. He believes the gay rights movement is not subversive, but rather an effort to serve and contribute to the common good without pretense and hypocrisy.

Vara, Richard. "The Lambeth Conference/In Faith and Practice." *Houston Chronicle*, August 15, 1998, p. 1. A report on the split along conservative/liberal lines and between the First and Third Worlds that led the Anglican communion to declare homosexuality "incompatible with scripture."

Waller, James. "The Ties That Bind." *Lambda Book Report*, vol. 7:7, February 1999, pp. 25–27. Review of three books dealing with gays and lesbians and mainstream religion: *The Lesbian and Gay Christian Movement: Campaigning for Justice, Truth and Love*, edited by Sean Gill; *Coming Out as Sacrament*, by Chris Glaser; and *Sexual Orientation and Human Rights in American Religious Discourse*, edited by Saul M. Olyan and Martha C. Nussbaum.

SODOMY LAWS

Aarons, Leroy F. "A Once-Pariah Nation Declares for Gay Rights." *San Francisco Chronicle*, November 13, 1998, p. A29. Editorial praising the decision of South Africa's highest court to overturn that country's 300-year-old sodomy law. Includes text of the judge's decision in which he directly links oppression of gay men to the statute.

Brewer, Steve. "Sodomy Law Overturned." *Houston Chronicle*, June 9, 2000, p. 1. Basing its decision on Texas's Equal Rights Amendment, a Texas appeals court throws out that state's law making homosexual sodomy illegal. Heterosexual sodomy has been legal in the state since 1973.

Copeland, Larry. "Georgia's Sodomy Law Overturned." *USA Today*, November 24, 1998, p. 1A. The overturning of the Georgia law was symbolically important to gay rights activists, since it was this statute that was upheld by the Supreme Court in *Bowers v. Hardwick* in 1986—a ruling that has since been used in many cases to justify discrimination.

Coyle, Pamela. "Second State Court Overturns Sodomy Law." *New Orleans Times-Picayune*, March 18, 1999, p. A1. In a case involving heterosexual rape, a Civil District Court judge strikes down Louisiana's law outlawing oral and anal sex. Gay activists interviewed praise the ruling, since the law is disproportionately enforced against homosexuals.

Duggan, Paul. "Texas Sodomy Arrest Opens Legal Battle for Gay Activists." *Washington Post*, November 29, 1998, p. A3. Reports on the arrest of John Lawrence and Tyrone Gardner, who were caught having sex in Lawrence's bedroom in Houston by a Harris County sheriff responding to a spurious complaint about a man with a gun.

Foley, Dorothy. "Sodomy Laws and You." *The Advocate*, issue 755, 1998, p. 9. Foley, an attorney for the United States Department of Justice, explains why gay men and lesbians should advocate for the repeal of state sodomy laws, even though they are rarely enforced.

Shumate, Richard. "Setting the Record Straight." *The Advocate*, issue 675, February 21, 1995, p. 33. Profile of Georgia attorney general Michael Bowers. Critics claim he is a bigot who attacks gay rights in the name of justice, but Bowers claims he is just doing his job. Bowers's disagreement with the gay and lesbian community is detailed.

Walker, Martin. "Montana Wants Gays to Register." *The Guardian*, March 24, 1995, p. 118. Stunned gay activists have appealed to the governor of Montana to veto the first law in the country that would require homosexuals to register with their local police, along with convicted felons and sex criminals. The protest was triggered when the state senate approved the measure.

Ward, David. "Gays Hail Bolton 7 'Victory'/Consenting Males Convicted Over Private Group Sex Are Spared Jail." *The Guardian*, February 21, 1998, p. 4. A British report on a group of gay men who had videotaped their private sex parties and who were subsequently arrested and charged under the 1967 Sexual Offences Act, which prohibits sex between more than two men at a time. The same law does not apply to heterosexuals.

Zuckoff, Mitchell. "Gay Rights Battlefield: State Laws on Sodomy." *Boston Globe*, December 5, 1998, p. A1. Excellent overview of 1998 efforts in many U.S. states to repeal statutory prohibitions against certain sexual practices. Zuckoff focuses particular attention on a lawsuit filed in Arkansas on behalf of seven gay and lesbian plaintiffs.

Transgender Issues

Califia, Pat. "Love Me Gender." *POZ*, October 1999, pp. 64–67. Califia profiles Veronika Cauley, San Francisco commissioner of veterans affairs and a transgender activist deeply involved in helping the African-American, HIV-positive transgendered community in her city. The majority of San Francisco's male-to-female transsexuals are infected with the virus.

Colapinto, John. "The True Story of John/Joan." *Rolling Stone*, issue 775, December 11, 1997, pp. 54–73. The story of John/Joan Thiessen, who was born a boy but turned into a girl by doctors at Johns Hopkins Hospital after a botched circumcision, is presented. For 25 years, it was considered a medical triumph—proof that a child's gender identity could be changed—and thousands of sex reassignments were performed based on this example. Colapinto proposes, however, that the surgery was in fact a colossal failure, because in his teens, John chose to reassert his masculine identity.

Davis, Lennard J. "Gaining a Daughter: A Father's Transgendered Tale." *The Chronicle of Higher Education*, vol. 46:29, March 24, 2000, pp. B4–B6. Highly personal account of one father's coming to terms with his son's identity as a transgendered heterosexual. Even though he is a progressive academic, he is deeply ambivalent about his son's decision to "come out," a decision which forces him to reevaluate his own theoretical positions on gender and sexuality.

Gagne, Patricia, and Richard Tewksbury. "Knowledge and Power, Body and Self: An Analysis of Knowledge Systems and the Transgendered Self." *Sociological Quarterly*, vol. 40:1, Winter 1999, pp. 59–83. The authors examine the relationship between the body and the self and the ways in which systems of power impact upon both.

Annotated Bibliography

Helvie, Sherri. "Willa Cather and Brandon Teena: The Politics of Passing." *Women and Language*, vol. 20:1, Spring 1997. Using a comparison of the lives of Willa Cather, the early 20th-century lesbian novelist, and Brandon Teena, a transsexual Nebraskan murdered in 1993, as an organizing theme, Helvie discusses the inadequacies of language in describing human sexuality.

Jefferson, Margo. "When Art Digests Life and Disgorges Its Poison." *New York Times*, February 21, 2000, p. E2. Noted arts critic Jefferson compares two films on the life of Brandon Teena, one a documentary (*The Brandon Teena Story*), the other a fictional feature film (*Boys Don't Cry*). She finds that each on its own is an integral work; seen together they are revelatory.

Maltz, Robin. "Real Butch: The Performance/Performativity of Male Impersonation, Drag Kings, Passing as Male, and Stone Butch Realness." *Journal of Gender Studies*, vol. 7:3, November 1998, pp. 273–286. Maltz examines the issue of "queer" female masculinity in an essay encompassing theatrical male impersonators from the 1940s to 1960s, contemporary drag king performers, women who pass as male in everyday life, and lesbians who eroticize masculinity.

Minkowitz, Donna. "Lovehurts." *The Village Voice*, vol. 39:16, April 19, 1994, p. 24. Teena Brandon, who lived life as Brandon Teena, a man, is profiled. Brandon fooled many women, including one who was engaged to Brandon for three months. S/he was raped and murdered by two male acquaintances when the charade was revealed.

Moulton III, John L., and Carolyn E. Adams-Price. "Homosexuality, Heterosexuality, and Cross-dressing: Perceptions of Gender Discordant Behavior." *Sex Roles*, vol. 37:5/6, September 1997, pp. 441–450. A sociological study examining the attitudes of both gay and straight men toward heterosexual and homosexual transvestites.

Price, Deb. "Nonconformist Challenges Gay Leaders." *Detroit News*, September 7, 1999, p. A9. Profile of Kerry Lobel, head of the National Gay and Lesbian Task Force, and her efforts to include protection for transgendered workers in the federal gay civil rights act.

Rafferty, Carole. "Gender Identity Problems/Gays Angered About Doctors Forcing Issue." *Houston Chronicle*, August 2, 1995, p. 3. Rafferty examines the controversy surrounding "gender identity disorder," a diagnosis used by the psychiatric community to categorize young people who dress in ways and exhibit behavior that are associated with the opposite sex. Gay activists see the diagnosis as a tool for homophobic parental control.

Wheeler, Linda. "Fire Chief Apologizes for Paramedic's Slur." *Washington Post*, August 19, 1995, p. B2. Washington, D.C.'s fire chief apologizes for a derogatory comment made by a paramedic about a transvestite who was being treated at the scene of a car accident. The man, Tyrone Michael Hunter, later died from his injuries.

Wheelwright, Julie. "The Boyfriend." *The Guardian*, February 20, 1996, p. T6. Wheelwright reports on the aftermath of the murder of Brandon Teena at the hands of John Lotter and Marvin Nissen. The Nebraska men became enraged when they discovered Teena wasn't a man, then abducted and raped him, later killing him.

WORKPLACE ISSUES

Associated Press. "Gays No Longer Regarded As Risks by U.S. Agencies." *San Francisco Chronicle*, March 25, 1995, p. A2. Release of General Accounting Office report that shows federal agencies no longer consider sexual orientation as a basis for denying security clearance to a worker.

———. "Landmark Ruling for Gay Rights/Canada's High Court Says Homosexuals Are Protected Under Code." *Houston Chronicle*, April 3, 1998, p. 32. In a case involving a gay man fired from a job at a Christian university in Alberta, the Canadian Supreme Court rules that Alberta's civil rights code must be amended to include protection against discrimination based on sexual orientation.

Boxall, Bettina. "City Settles Police Brutality Suit Over Incident at Gay Rights Protest." *Los Angeles Times*, February 7, 1997, p. B3. Activists protesting California governor Pete Wilson's veto of legislation prohibiting discrimination in the workplace are awarded damages after being beaten by the police.

———. "Few Gays Using Law That Bars Job Bias." *Los Angeles Times*, November 24, 1995, p. 3. Boxall examines the realities of antigay job bias. Proving on-the-job discrimination is often difficult, and, even with legal protection in California, employees are reluctant to come forward. The case of three workers in Sacramento is detailed.

Chandrasekaran, Rajiv. "Same-Sex Partners Win IBM Coverage." *Washington Post*, September 20, 1996, p. A1. IBM, with 110,000 employees, becomes the largest U.S. company to extend health and other benefits to same-sex partners of its employees. Gay rights activists hail this as "a monumental step forward."

Christian, Nichole M. "At Chrysler, Debate Grows on Gay Rights." *Wall Street Journal*, October 28, 1996, p. B1. Report on the efforts of the United Auto Workers (UAW) to pressure the Chrysler corporation to add sexual orientation to its employee nondiscrimination policy. The article includes accounts of instances of antigay harassment.

Coffee, John C. Jr. "Blocking Bias Via Proxy." *Wall Street Journal*, February 2, 1993, p. A14. A report on the Securities and Exchange Commission's decision to deny shareholders the right to use their corporation's proxy statement to challenge discriminatory corporate employment practices after a controversy erupted over the decision by Cracker Barrel, a restaurant chain, to fire all of its openly gay employees.

Croft, Jay. "High Court Won't Hear Case of Gay Lawyer." *Atlanta Journal-Constitution*, January 13, 1998, p. C1. Supreme Court decides not to review the case of Robin Shahar, who lost a position with Georgia attorney general Mike Bowers after he learned that she had taken part in a commitment ceremony with another woman.

Dunlap, David W. "Case Cited as Example of Need for Gay Rights." *New York Times*, January 15, 1995, p. 117. The Pennsylvania Superior Court has upheld the right of a business owner to dismiss an employee on the grounds of homosexuality and then collect damages from the employee for opening a competing business.

Editorial. "Gay Rights Issue Won't Go Away." *Los Angeles Times*, September 12, 1996, p. B8. An editorial comments on the defeat of the Employment Non-Discrimination Act (ENDA) in the Senate and says it would be a mistake to consider the bill dead; ENDA would prohibit job discrimination on the basis of sexual orientation.

Elie, Lolis Eric. "Gay-rights Bills Facing Tests." *New Orleans Times-Picayune*, April 5, 1999, p. B1. Report on two bills introduced into Louisiana legislature to outlaw job discrimination against gays and lesbians.

Fay, Charles. "Boeing Extends Health Plan to Gays." *Los Angeles Times*, October 24, 1999, p. 10. This article provides a rich selection of quotes from people on all sides of the issue of domestic partnerships.

Herscher, Elaine. "S.F. Partner's Law Echoes Throughout U.S." *San Francisco Chronicle*, September 10, 1999, p. A4. Herscher documents the dramatic increase between 1997 and 1999 of U.S. companies extending benefits to the same-sex partners of their employees as a direct result of San Francisco law that requires all businesses transacting with that city to provide domestic partner benefits to their employees.

Holmes, Steven A. "Helms Bill That Targets Federal Gay Workers." *San Francisco Chronicle*, February 3, 1995, p. A1. Senator Jesse Helms of North Carolina introduces legislation that could limit the ability of gays and lesbians who work for the federal government to form employee associations.

Karkabi, Barbara. "Families and Friends Lobby for Gay Rights." *Houston Chronicle*, March 25, 1996, p. 1. Profile on the Houston chapter of PFLAG (Parents and Friends of Gays and Lesbians), a group that is participating in an event known as "Mom and Dad Go to Washington" to lobby Congress to pass the Employment Non-Discrimination Act (ENDA).

Kindred, Dave. "Young Attorney Fights for Beliefs." *Atlanta Constitution*, January 17, 1996, p. B4. Kindred comments on lesbian lawyer Robin Brown Shahar's lawsuit against Georgia attorney general Mike Bowers for withdrawing the state's offer of a job when the office learned of a commitment ceremony between Shahar and Francine Greenfield.

Kraul, Chris. "Workplace is Key to Push for Lesbian, Gay Rights, Activists Say." *Los Angeles Times*, October 16, 1995, p. D1. A report on "Progress," the Professional Gay Lesbian & Bisexual Related Employee Support Summit. This meeting represents the first ever statewide gathering of leaders of gay and lesbian employee groups in California.

Leeds, Jeff. "Exxon Mobil Halts Health Benefits to Domestic Partners." *Los Angeles Times*, December 7, 1999, p. 1. This article examines the recent decision of the newly formed Exxon Mobil Corporation to suspend further health benefits to the partners of its gay and lesbian employees. Those employees already under the Mobil plan from before the merger would continue to receive the benefits.

Lewis, Gregory B. "Lifting the Ban on Gays in the Civil Service." *Public Administration Review*, vol. 7:5, September/October 1997, pp. 387–395. In-depth history of the obstacles gays and lesbians have overcome to become accepted members of the U.S. civil service.

Mathis, Nancy. "Clinton Backs Ban on Job Bias Against Gays and Lesbians." *Houston Chronicle*, April 25, 1997, p. A2. Report on President Bill Clinton's official reaffirmation of his support for ENDA. Clinton makes his announcement after the Human Rights Campaign releases a survey indicating that a majority of Americans support the legislation.

Meers, Erik. "Good Cop, Gay Cop." *The Advocate*, issue 754, 1998, pp. 26–34. This article chronicles the struggles and advances of gays and lesbians in law enforcement as police departments across the country open their ranks to homosexuals. Workplace discrimination litigation has driven many changes in policy.

Oppel, Richard A. Jr. "When Corporate Worlds Collide: Exxon's Decision on Benefits." *New York Times*, December 8, 1999, p. 12. A report on the recent merger of Mobil and Exxon's differing corporate cultures and on the merger's impact on the new company's gay and lesbian employees. The company becomes the second major U.S. corporation to rescind a domestic partnership program already in place.

Phillips, Dave. "Automakers' Recognition of Gay Groups Signals Major Shift." *Detroit News*, July 20, 1997, p. C1. Article on the Detroit "Big 3" automakers' recognition of gay employee organizations. This is of particular importance to homosexual blue-collar workers who, up to this point, have had little protection from on-the-job harassment.

Price, Deb. "Anti-discrimination Vote Shows Senate May Not Be so Chilly Toward Gay Rights." *Detroit News*, September 13, 1996, p. E1. Deb Price comments on the Senate's decision to pass both the Defense of Marriage Act (DOMA), banning same-sex marriages, and the Employment Non-Discrimination Act (ENDA), outlawing job discrimination based on sexual orientation.

———. "Gay Workers' Rights Make Gains in House." *Detroit News*, September 14, 1998, p. A11. Analysis of reasons why Republican-controlled House of Representatives was willing to let stand President Bill Clinton's executive order barring discrimination of gays and lesbians in federal employment.

———. "Supreme Court Shows Its Progress by Not Treating Gay Issues as Dynamite." *Detroit News*, December 5, 1997, p. E2. Price praises the Supreme Court for what she sees as its newfound sophistication in dealing with gay issues in this editorial on the case of a straight oil rig worker who was sexually harassed by his male coworkers.

Purdum, Todd. "Clinton Ends Ban on Security Clearance for Gay Workers." *New York Times*, August 5, 1995, p. A9. President Clinton ends decades of common Cold War practice by signing an executive order barring the federal government from denying security clearances to homosexuals on the basis of their sexual orientation.

Rankin, Bill. "Lesbian's Claims Rejected; Bowers Backed." *Atlanta Journal-Constitution*, May 31, 1997, p. D1. An account of the reasoning behind the appeals court decision to allow Georgia attorney general Mike Bowers to legally renege on a job for an out lesbian, Robin Shahar. The justices stated that Shahar's presence on Bowers's legal staff would impinge on the attorney general's ability to enforce certain laws, especially that state's sodomy prohibition—given that the state sodomy law would define Shahar's lesbian activity as criminal.

Smith, Rhonda. "Education Union Issues Call For Gay Protections." *Washington Blade*, vol. 29:34, 1998, p. 12. A report on the Second World Congress of Educators' resolution calling for the protection of gay and lesbian teachers worldwide. Comments for and against the resolution are presented.

Stewart, James B. "Coming Out at Chrysler." *The New Yorker*, July 21, 1997, p. 38. Stewart profiles Ron Woods, an electrician and member of the United Auto Workers labor union at the Chrysler plant in Detroit, who fought back against physical and verbal harassment on the job. Woods's efforts led to the formation of a gay employees' group at the company.

Stout, Hilary. "Clinton Backs Gay-Rights Bill to Ban Job Bias." *Wall Street Journal*, October 23, 1995, p. B10. President Bill Clinton has decided to endorse legislation that would bar employers from discriminating against gay employees and job applicants. While the bill has little chance of passing the Republican-controlled Congress, it may help the president's relations with gay groups.

Swisher, Kara. "Coming Out for Gay Rights: Some Companies Are Beating Congress to the Punch on Workplace Protections." *Washington Post*, June

16, 1995, p. D1. ENDA, the federal gay employment antidiscrimination law, has little chance of passing while Republicans control Congress. But even without federal laws in place, a growing number of corporations nationwide, including IBM and Lotus Development Corporation, are doing it on their own.

Weisberg, Louis. "Did Somebody Say 'Gay'?: McDonald's Adds Orientation to Anti-Bias Policy." *Windy City Times*, vol. 14:32, 1999, p. 4. Report from a Chicago-based weekly on McDonald's adding sexual orientation to its nondiscrimination policy after a shareholder's resolution made possible by the Securities and Exchange Commission's overturning of a 1992 decision that allowed the Cracker Barrel company to block such proposals.

Wheeler, Linda. "D.C. Fire Department Accused of Gay Bias." *Washington Post*, August 29, 1996, p. D5. A gay rights group has released a report accusing Washington, D.C. fire chief Otis Latin of tolerating homophobic attitudes among rescue personnel and refusing to implement sensitivity training.

WEB SITES

ACT UP: AIDS Coalition to Unleash Power. Available Online. URL: http://www.actupny.org. Downloaded on July 19, 2000. The web site for the New York branch of ACT UP, the AIDS Coalition to Unleash Power. A current issues index on the home page offers the latest information on AIDS activism, while a listing of crucial links offers further data on AIDS treatment, research, and politics. The site also provides a wide variety of documents and essays on ACT UP's history and current activities.

The Data Lounge. Available Online. URL: http://www.datalounge.com. Downloaded on July 19, 2000. An online magazine that offers continuously updated political analysis and news, with a focus on gay rights. The home page offers a link called "issues" that allows researchers to get past and current Data Lounge articles on AIDS, antigay initiatives, antigay violence, culture and the media, education, family and child care, gay origins, gay vote, government and sodomy laws, marriage and domestic partnerships, military service, perspectives in Africa, religion, sexual expression, workplace issues, and bias laws and initiatives. An excellent way to get a quick snapshot of the latest developments on any issue.

Gay Rights Info. Available Online. URL: http://www.gayrightsinfo.com. Downloaded on July 19, 2000. A comprehensive listing of legal rights issues for gay men and lesbians. This outstanding source of information lists the latest on congressional voting records, federal departmental policy, state and local legislation, Supreme Court decisions, sodomy laws, antidiscrimination law, domestic partnership, hate crime/bias crime law, and corporate policy on gays and lesbians.

Gayscape.com—The Gay Internet. Available Online. URL: http://www. gayscape.com. Downloaded on July 19, 2000. A gay directory. The subcategory called "Pride" includes listings for gay rights; activist groups; antiviolence; gays and lesbians in the military; and gay, lesbian, and bisexual youth.

Human Rights Campaign Web Site. Available Online. URL: http/www.hrc. org. Downloaded on July 19, 2000. The web site of the Human Rights Campaign (HRC), the major national gay rights lobbying group. In addition to offering information on HRC and its current activities, the home page offers links to information on HIV/AIDS, workplace, antigay/hate, marriage, lesbian health, and transgender issues, as well as specific information on three of HRC's major legislative efforts: the Hate Crimes Prevention Act, the Religious Liberty Protection Act, and the Employment Non-Discrimination Act. A link to "Coming Out Resources" provides a resource guide on that issue, as well as a listing of various national organizations and a suggested bibliography linked to an online bookstore.

LAMBDA: GLBT Community Services Web Site. Available Online. URL: http://www.lambda.org. Downloaded on July 19, 2000. A nonprofit gay/lesbian/bisexual/transgender agency based in El Paso, Texas. This excellent, youth-oriented web site provides information on a wide range of issues, including hate crimes, domestic violence among gay/lesbian families, health issues, and a special section on "youth OUTreach." A unique feature of this site is its interest in providing the materials of other gay/lesbian organizations; thus, PFLAG's hate crime report and the National Coalition of Anti-Violence Programs' bias reports and domestic violence reports are available here.

LAMBDA Legal Defense and Education Fund Web Site. Available Online. URL: http://www.lambdalegal.org. Downloaded on July 19, 2000. The web site for the LAMBDA Legal Defense and Education Fund, the oldest and largest U.S. group working for the civil rights of lesbians, gay men, and people wth HIV/AIDS. The home page offers news of LAMBDA's latest cases; one recent sampling, for example, offered reports ranging from a challenge to the Arkansas sodomy law to a high school student group's efforts to form a Gay-Straight Alliance. Links to information on gay marriage, "documents every lesbian and gay man needs," and "The Lambda Update" (a comprehensive report on LAMBDA's activities) were also available.

National Center for Lesbian Rights Home Page. Available Online. URL: http://www.nclrights.org. Downloaded on July 19, 2000. The web site for the National Committee on Lesbian Rights. The home page offers links to information on recent decisions and legal cases that affect lesbian rights.

National Gay and Lesbian Task Force Online. Available Online. URL: http://www.ngltf.org. Downloaded on July 19, 2000. The web site for the National Gay and Lesbian Task Force, one of the major U.S. gay political organizations. Researchers can find news and legislative updates in this comprehensive online newsletter, as well as access to recent state legislative databases and links to other key organizations: national gay/lesbian groups, state organizations, fraternities and sororities, and potential allies (such as People for the American Way).

NOW and Lesbian Rights. Available Online. URL: http://www.now.org/issues/lgbi/index.html. Downloaded on July 19, 2000. Lesbian rights page on the web site of the National Organization for Women (NOW). The site offers information on lesbian rights actions that NOW is involved in, as well as information on key issues of the past several years, such as same-sex marriage and Colorado's Amendment 2.

Oasis Magazine. Available Online. URL: http://www.oasismag.com. Downloaded on July 19, 2000. A self-described "online Webzine written by, about and for queer and questioning youth." Listings on a recent visit to the site included voter analysis, a poll on gays in the military, an article about a gay student's suit against a school, the Supreme Court's Boy Scout case, LAMBDA's suit against the Los Angeles Police Department, and a call for a more multicultural gay men's health movement. Also archives information from previous issues.

!OutProud! Available Online. URL: http://www.outproud.org. Downloaded on July 19, 2000. The web site for !Outproud!, the National Coalition of Gay, Lesbian, Bisexual, & Transgendered Youth. The web site offers youth-oriented resources on a wide variety of topics, with a focus on coming out. Gay rights researchers will be particularly interested in links to "queer sites on the World Wide Web" and daily updates from "Channel Q," a gay/lesbian news organization. A list of recommended books is also available.

Queer Resources Directory. Available Online. URL: http://www.qrd.org. Downloaded on July 19, 2000. The web site of the Queer Resources Directory, which as of July 19, 2000 described itself as offering "25,382 files about everything queer." Subject headings include families; youth; religion; health; electronic resources; media; events; culture and history; international information; business; legal; workplace; and politics, political news, and activism. Organizations, directories, and newsletters can also be accessed.

CHAPTER 9

ORGANIZATIONS
AND AGENCIES

This chapter lists all of the major organizations concerning gay rights, including both those groups who favor gay rights and those who oppose them. The chapter begins with a listing of the major progay rights groups—the national organizations set up to promote the legal, political, and cultural rights of lesbians and gay men. It goes on to list lesbian and gay groups that focus on legal issues, lesbian and gay youth groups, and some other significant gay rights groups, particularly those representing lesbians and gay men of color. The pro–gay rights section concludes with a listing of the various lesbian and gay archives around the country, which contain historical material and, occasionally, legal documents.

The final section of this chapter includes a listing of the major national anti–gay rights groups, as well as some nationally significant local organizations, such as the ones in Oregon and Colorado, which became nationally known for their work in promoting statewide anti–gay rights referendums in 1993. The Oregon and Colorado measures became models for other groups, who went on to get other anti–gay rights bills on the ballots in several other states.

PRO–GAY RIGHTS GROUPS

Note: *The Gay Almanac* and *The Lesbian Almanac* (see Books, Chapter 8) have extensive listings of gay and lesbian organizations, community centers, AIDS groups, and other resources.

MAJOR NATIONAL GAY AND LESBIAN ORGANIZATIONS

AIDS Coalition to Unleash Power (ACT UP)—New York
322 Bleecker Street, Suite 65
New York, NY 10014
Phone: (212) 966-4873
Email: actupny@panix.com
URL: http://www.actupny.org
Engages in AIDS activism; has some access to research. Although this listing is New York City–specific, the New York chapter maintains information sources relevant to all other chapters.

American Civil Liberties Union Lesbian and Gay Rights Project
132 West 43rd Street
New York, NY 10036
Phone: (212) 844-9800
Does research on legal issues and takes cases.

Gay and Lesbian Alliance Against Defamation (GLAAD)
150 West 26th Street
New York, NY 10001
Phone: (212) 807-1700
Research and action on portrayals of lesbians and gay men in the media and popular culture.

Gay Men's Health Crisis (GMHC)
129 West 20th Street
New York, NY 10011
Phone: (212) 807-6664
Hot line: (212) 807-6655

An AIDS activist organization whose mission statement is "to provide compassionate care to people with AIDS; educate to keep people healthy; and advocate for fair and effective public policies." The Lesbian AIDS Project can be contacted at the same address, at (212) 337-3532.

Human Rights Campaign Fund
1012 14th Street, Northwest, #607
Washington, DC 20005
Phone: (202) 628-4160
URL: http://www.hrc.org/
Lobbies Congress; engages in political action, grassroots organizing.

Lambda Legal Defense and Education Fund
666 Broadway, 12th Floor
New York, NY 10012
Phone: (212) 995-8585
URL: http://www.lambdalegal.org/
Does legal research and takes on cases; also has an AIDS project.

Lesbian Avengers
c/o Lesbian and Gay Community Services Center
208 West 13th Street
New York, NY 10011
Phone: (212) 967-7711 extension 3204
Young, militant group best known for going to Idaho and bringing about the surprising defeat of an anti–gay rights bill there.

National Gay and Lesbian Task Force
1734 14th Street, Northwest
Washington, DC 20009
Phone: (202) 332-6483
URL: http://www.ngltf.org
Lobbying, political action, grass-roots organizing, legal research; also has a campus project and a "military freedom" project.

Parents, Families and Friends of Lesbians and Gays (PFLAG)
1012 14th Street, Northwest, #700
Washington, DC 20005
OR
Box 27605
Washington, DC 20038
Phone: (202) 638-0243
Activist group representing gay-friendly straight people.

Queer Nation
c/o Lesbian and Gay Community Services Center
208 West 13th Street
New York, NY 10011
Phone: (212) 260-6156
A militant group that came out of ACT UP.

Senior Action in a Gay Environment (SAGE)
305 Seventh Avenue
New York, NY 10001
Phone: (212) 741-2247
Activist group for gay senior citizens.

OTHER GAY AND LESBIAN LEGAL PROJECTS

Gay and Lesbian Advocates and Defenders (GLAD)
P.O. Box 218
Boston, MA 02112
Phone: (617) 426-1350

LeGaL: Lesbian and Gay Law Association
799 Broadway #340
New York, NY 10003
Membership: (212) 353-9118
Fax: (212) 353-2970
Referral Service: (212) 459-4873
Email: le-gal@interport.net

National Center for Lesbian Rights (NCLR)
1663 Mission Street, 5th Floor
San Francisco, CA 94103
Phone: (415) 392-6257
URL: http://www.nclrights.org

National Lesbian and Gay Law Association
Box 77130, National Capitol Station
Washington, DC 20014
Phone: (202) 389-0161

ORGANIZATIONS THAT FOCUS ON LESBIAN AND GAY YOUTH

American Institute for Teen AIDS Prevention
P.O. Box 136113
Fort Worth, TX 76136
Phone: (817) 237-0230

Center Kids: The Family
    Project
Lesbian and Gay Community
    Services Center
208 West 13th Street
New York, NY 10011
Phone: (212) 260-7310
Fax: (212) 260-2657

Coalition for Lesbian and Gay
    Student Groups
Box 190712
Dallas, TX 75219
Phone: (214) 621-6705
Fax: (214) 528-8436

Gay Lesbian Student Educational
    Network (GLSEN)
121 West 27th Street, Suite 804
New York, NY 10001
Phone: (212) 727-0135
Fax: (212) 727-0254
Email: glsen@glsen.org
URL: http://www.glsen.org

Hetrick-Martin Institute for
    Lesbian and Gay Youth
2 Astor Place
New York, NY 10003
Phone: (212) 674-2400
Fax: (212) 674-8650

National Youth Advocacy
    Coalition
1638 R Street, Northwest,
    Suite 300
Washington, DC 20009
Phone: (202) 319-7596
Fax: (202) 319-7365
Email: nyac@nyacyouth.org
URL: http://www.nyacyouth.org

OTHER POSSIBLE SOURCES FOR PRO–GAY RIGHTS INFORMATION

African American Lesbian and
    Gay Alliance
P.O. Box 50374
Atlanta, GA 30302

AIDS Action Council
1875 Connecticut Avenue,
    Northwest, #700
Washington, DC 20009

American Federation of Teachers
National Gay and Lesbian
    Caucus
P.O. Box 19586
Cincinnati, OH 45219

American Federation of Veterans
Veterans Hall
346 Broadway, Suite 811
New York, NY 10013
Phone: (212) 349-3455

American Foundation for AIDS
    Research (AmFAR)
733 Third Avenue
New York, NY 10017
Phone: (212) 682-7440

Asian Pacific Lesbian and
    Bisexual Network
P.O. Box 460778
San Francisco, CA 94146-0778
Phone: (510) 814-2422

Association of Lesbian and Gay
    Psychiatrists
1439 Pineville Road
New Hope, PA 18938

Black Lesbian and Gay
  Leadership Forum
1219 South La Brea Avenue
Los Angeles, CA 90019
Phone: (213) 964-7820

Canadian AIDS Society
170 Laurier Avenue West, #1101
Ottawa, Ontario K1P 5V5
Fax: (613) 563-4998

Center for Lesbian and Gay
  Studies (CLAGS)
Graduate Center of the City
  University of New York
33 West 42nd Street, Room
  404N
New York, NY 10036
Phone: (212) 642-2924

Committee on Gay and Lesbian
  Concerns
American Psychological
  Association
1200 17th Street, Northwest
Washington, DC 20036
Phone: (202) 336-5500

Gay and Lesbian Medical
  Association
273 Church Street
San Francisco, CA 94114
Phone: (415) 255-4547

Gay Teachers Caucus of the
  National Education
  Association
32 Bridge Street
Hackensack, NJ 07606
Phone: (201) 489-2458

International Gay and Lesbian
  Human Rights Commission
540 Castro Street
San Francisco, CA 94114
Phone: (415) 255-8680

Lesbian and Gay Labor Network:
  Coalition of Labor Union
  Activists
P.O. Box 1159
Peter Stuyvesant Station
New York, NY 10009
Phone: (212) 923-8690

Lesbian Teachers Network
P.O. Box 301
East Lansing, MI 48826

Mobilization Against AIDS
584-B Castro Street
San Francisco, CA 94114
Phone: (415) 863-4676

National Coalition of Black
  Lesbians and Gays
P.O. Box 19248
Washington, DC 20036

National Latino/a Lesbian and
  Gay Organization
P.O. Box 44483
Washington, DC 20026

National Leadership Coalition
  on AIDS
1730 M Street, Northwest,
  Suite 905
Washington, DC 20036
Phone: (202) 429-0930

National Lesbian Forum/Alliance
  Nationale des Lesbiennes
P.O. Box 482
Regina, SK, Canada S4P 3A2

National Minority AIDS
 Council (NMAC)
300 I Street, Northeast,
 Suite 400
Washington, DC 20002
Phone: (202) 544-1076

Network Linking Asian Lesbians
 in Asia and the Diaspora
P.O. Box 2594
Daly City, CA 94017-2594
Phone: (415) 476-8180
Fax: (415) 476-8887

Society for the Psychological
 Study of Gay and Lesbian
 Issues
American Psychological
 Association
1200 17th Street, Northwest
Washington, DC 20036
Phone: (202) 336-5500

Trikone [for gay and lesbian
 South Asians]
P.O. Box 21354
San Jose, CA 95151
Phone: (408) 270-8776

ARCHIVES AND LIBRARIES

Archives Gaies du Québec
4067 St.-Laurent, Suite 202
Montreal, Québec
Canada H2W 1Y7C
Phone: (514) 289-9987

Blanche Baker Memorial Library
 and Archives/ONE, Inc.
3340 Country Club Drive
Los Angeles, CA 90019
Phone: (213) 735-5252

Canadian Gay Archives
P.O. Box 639, Station A
Toronto, Ontario
Canada M5W 1G2

Dallas Gay and Lesbian Historic
 Archives
2701 Reagan
Dallas, TX 75219
Phone: (214) 528-4233

Douglas County Gay Archives
P.O. Box 942
Dillard, OR 97432-0942
Phone: (503) 679-0013

Gay and Lesbian Archives of
 Washington, DC
P.O. Box 4218
Falls Church, VA 22044
Phone: (703) 671-3930

Gay and Lesbian Historical
 Society of Northern
 California
P.O. Box 424280
San Francisco, CA 94142
Phone: (415) 626-0980

Henry Gerber/Pearl M. Hart
 Library and Archives
Midwest Lesbian/Gay Resource
 Center
3352 N. Paulina Street
Chicago, IL 60657
Phone: (312) 883-3003

Homosexual Information
 Center
115 Monroe Street
Bossier City, LA 71111

International Gay and Lesbian
  Archives
P.O. Box 38100
Los Angeles, CA 90038-0100

June Mazer Lesbian Collection
626 North Robertson Boulevard
West Hollywood, CA 90069
Phone: (310) 659-2478

Lesbian and Gay Historical
  Society of San Diego
P.O. Box 40389
San Diego, CA 92615
Phone: (619) 260-1522

Lesbian Herstory Archives
P.O. Box 1258
New York, NY 10116
Phone: (718) 768-DYKE

National Museum and Archive
  of Lesbian and Gay History
Lesbian and Gay Community
  Services Center
208 West 13th Street
New York, NY 10011
Phone: (212) 620-7310

New York Public Library
Division of Humanities, Social
  Sciences, and Special
  Collections
Fifth Avenue and 42nd Street
New York, NY 10018
Phone: (212) 930-0584

Pat Parker/Vito Russo Center
  Library
Lesbian and Gay Community
  Services Center
208 West 13th Street

New York, NY 10011
Phone: (212) 620-7310

Southeastern Lesbian Archives
Box 5502
Atlanta, GA 30307

Stonewall Library and Archives
330 SW 27th Street
Fort Lauderdale, FL 33315

ANTI–GAY RIGHTS GROUPS

The Christian Broadcasting
  Network
977 Centerville Turnpike
Virginia Beach, VA 23463
Phone: (757) 226-7000
Founded by Reverend Pat Robert-
son; sponsors *The 700 Club* TV
show.

The Christian Coalition
1801 Sarah Drive, Suite L
Chesapeake, VA 23320
Phone: (804) 424-2630
Headed by Ralph Reed.

Colorado for Family Values
  (CFV)
228 North Cascade, Suite 102
P.O. Box 190
Colorado Springs, CO 80903-
  1323
Phone: (719) 577-4916
Fax: (719) 577-4805
Headed by Will Perkins; founded
to promote Colorado's Amendment

2, which barred all Colorado local governments from passing laws against discrimination on the basis of sexual orientation.

Family Research Council
801 G Street, Northwest
Washington, DC 20001
Phone: (202) 393-2100
Fax: (202) 393-2134
Headed by Gary Bauer.

Focus on the Family
Colorado Springs, CO 80995
Phone: (800) A-FAMILY
URL: http://www.family.org
Headed by Dr. James Dobson; their mission statement is "To cooperate with the Holy Spirit in disseminating the Gospel of Jesus Christ to as many people as possible, and, specifically, to accomplish that objective by helping to preserve traditional values and the institution of the family."

Liberty Council
P.O. Box 540774
Orlando, FL 32854
Phone: (407) 875-2100
Fax: (407) 875-0220
Email: liberty@lc.org
URL: http://www.lc.org
Founded by Reverend Jerry Falwell; nationwide nonprofit religious civil liberties education and legal defense organization dedicated to preserve religious freedom.

Oregon Citizens Alliance (OCA)
P.O. Box 407
Wilsonville, OR 97070-0407
Phone: (503) 682-0653
Founded to promote Oregon's Proposition 9, a statewide anti–gay rights measure.

PART III

APPENDICES

APPENDIX A

————————————

EXCERPTS FROM COURT DECISIONS

SUPREME COURT

BOWERS V. HARDWICK, 106 S. CT. 2841 (1986)

This landmark Supreme Court decision upheld the constitutionality of Georgia's sodomy law—and, by extension, affirmed the rights of individual states to outlaw sodomy. For background on this case, see Chapter 2. Justice Byron White wrote the majority opinion, joined by Chief Justice Warren Burger and Justices Lewis Powell, William Rehnquist, and Sandra Day O'Connor. Justice Harry Blackmun wrote a dissenting opinion, joined by Justices Brennan, Marshall, and Stevens. Following is White's majority opinion.

This case does not require a judgment on whether laws against sodomy between consenting adults in general, or between homosexuals in particular, are wise or desirable. It raises no question about the right or propriety of state legislative decisions to repeal their laws that criminalize homosexual sodomy, or of state-court decisions invalidating those laws on state constitutional grounds. The issue presented is whether the Federal Constitution confers a fundamental right upon homosexuals to engage in sodomy and hence invalidates the laws of the many States that still make such conduct illegal and have done so for a very long time. The case also calls for some judgment about the limits of the Court's role in carrying out its constitutional mandate. . . .

Accepting the decisions in [other] cases and the . . . description of them, we think it evident that none of the rights announced in those cases bears any resemblance to the claimed constitutional right of homosexuals to engage in acts of sodomy that is asserted in this case. No connection between family, marriage, or procreation on the one hand and homosexual activity on the other has been demonstrated, either by the Court of Appeals or by respondent. Moreover, any claim that these cases nevertheless stand for the proposition that any kind of private sexual conduct between consenting adults is constitutionally insulated from state proscription is unsupportable. . . .

Precedent aside, however, respondent would have us announce, as the Court of Appeals did, a fundamental right to engage in homosexual sodomy. This we are quite unwilling to do. It is true that despite the language of the Due Process Clauses of the Fifth and Fourteenth Amendments, which appears to focus only on the processes by which life, liberty, or property is taken, the cases are legion in which those Clauses have been interpreted to have substantive content, subsuming rights that to a great extent are immune from federal or state regulation or proscription. Among such cases are those recognizing rights that have little or no textual support in the constitutional language. . . .

Striving to assure itself and the public that announcing rights not readily identifiable in the Constitution's text involves much more than the imposition of the Justices' own choice of values on the States and the Federal Government, the Court has sought to identify the nature of the rights qualifying for heightened judicial protection. In *Palko v. Connecticut*, 326 (1937), it was said that this category includes those fundamental liberties that are "implicit in the concept of ordered liberty," such that "neither liberty nor justice would exist if [they] were sacrificed." A different description of fundamental liberties appeared in *Moore v. East Cleveland*, (1977), where they are characterized as those liberties that are "deeply rooted in this Nation's history and tradition." See also *Griswold v. Connecticut.*

It is obvious to us that neither of these formulations would extend a fundamental right to homosexuals to engage in acts of consensual sodomy. Proscriptions against that conduct have ancient roots. See generally Survey on the Constitutional Right to Privacy in the Context of Homosexual Activity, 40 U. Miami L. Rev. 521, 525 (1986). Sodomy was a criminal offense at common law and was forbidden by the laws of the original 13 States when they ratified the Bill of Rights. In 1868, when the Fourteenth Amendment was ratified, all but 5 of the 37 States in the Union had criminal sodomy laws. In fact, until 1961, all 50 States outlawed sodomy, and today, 24 States and the District of Columbia continue to provide criminal penalties for sodomy performed in private and between consenting adults. . . . Against this background, to claim that a right to engage in such conduct is "deeply rooted in this Nation's history and tradition" or "implicit in the concept of ordered liberty" is, at best, facetious. . . .

Respondent, however, asserts that the result should be different where the homosexual conduct occurs in the privacy of the home. He relies on

Stanley v. Georgia, (1969), where the Court held that the First Amendment prevents conviction for possessing and reading obscene material in the privacy of one's home: "If the First Amendment means anything, it means that a State has no business telling a man, sitting alone in his house, what books he may read or what films he may watch.". . .

Stanley did protect conduct that would not have been protected outside the home, and it partially prevented the enforcement of state obscenity laws; but the decision was firmly grounded in the First Amendment. The right pressed upon us here has no similar support in the text of the Constitution, and it does not qualify for recognition under the prevailing principles for construing the Fourteenth Amendment. Its limits are also difficult to discern. Plainly enough, otherwise illegal conduct is not always immunized whenever it occurs in the home. Victimless crimes, such as the possession and use of illegal drugs, do not escape the law where they are committed at home. Stanley itself recognized that its holding offered no protection for the possession in the home of drugs, firearms, or stolen goods. . . . And if respondent's submission is limited to the voluntary sexual conduct between consenting adults, it would be difficult, except by fiat, to limit the claimed right to homosexual conduct while leaving exposed to prosecution adultery, incest, and other sexual crimes even though they are committed in the home. We are unwilling to start down that road.

Even if the conduct at issue here is not a fundamental right, respondent asserts that there must be a rational basis for the law and that there is none in this case other than the presumed belief of a majority of the electorate in Georgia that homosexual sodomy is immoral and unacceptable. This is said to be an inadequate rationale to support the law. The law, however, is constantly based on notions of morality, and if all laws representing essentially moral choices are to be invalidated under the Due Process Clause, the courts will be very busy indeed. Even respondent makes no such claim, but insists that majority sentiments about the morality of homosexuality should be declared inadequate. We do not agree, and are unpersuaded that the sodomy laws of some 25 States should be invalidated on this basis.

ROMER V. EVANS, 517 U.S. 620 (1996)

This decision found that Colorado's Amendment 2 was unconstitutional. Amendment 2 prevented Colorado local governments from passing laws banning discrimination on the basis of sexual orientation. Justice Kennedy wrote the majority opinion, joined by Stevens, O'Connor, Souter, Ginsburg, and Breyer, with Justice Scalia filing a dissenting opinion, joined by Chief Justice Rehnquist and Justice Thomas. For more background on Romer v. Evans, *see Chapter 2.*

Gay Rights

Majority Opinion

[The opinion begins by defining Amendment 2 as the statewide law that would repeal certain local antidiscrimination laws.]

Yet Amendment 2, in explicit terms, does more than repeal or rescind these provisions. It prohibits all legislative, executive or judicial action at any level of state or local government designed to protect the named class, a class we shall refer to as homosexual persons or gays and lesbians. The amendment reads:

> *"No Protected Status Based on Homosexual, Lesbian, or Bisexual Orientation. Neither the State of Colorado, through any of its branches or departments, nor any of its agencies, political subdivisions, municipalities or school districts, shall enact, adopt or enforce any statute, regulation, ordinance or policy whereby homosexual, lesbian or bisexual orientation, conduct, practices or relationships shall constitute or otherwise be the basis of or entitle any person or class of persons to have or claim any minority status, quota preferences, protected status or claim of discrimination. This Section of the Constitution shall be in all respects self-executing."*

Soon after Amendment 2 was adopted, this litigation to declare its invalidity and enjoin its enforcement was commenced in the District Court for the City and County of Denver. Among the plaintiffs . . . were homosexual persons, some of them government employees. They alleged that enforcement of Amendment 2 would subject them to immediate and substantial risk of discrimination on the basis of their sexual orientation. Other plaintiffs . . . included the three municipalities whose ordinances we have cited and certain other governmental entities which had acted earlier to protect homosexuals from discrimination but would be prevented by Amendment 2 from continuing to do so. . . .

The State's principal argument in defense of Amendment 2 is that it puts gays and lesbians in the same position as all other persons. So, the State says, the measure does no more than deny homosexuals special rights. This reading of the amendment's language is implausible. . . .

Homosexuals, by state decree, are put in a solitary class with respect to transactions and relations in both the private and governmental spheres. The amendment withdraws from homosexuals, but no others, specific legal protection from the injuries caused by discrimination, and it forbids reinstatement of these laws and policies.

The change that Amendment 2 works in the legal status of gays and lesbians in the private sphere is far-reaching, both on its own terms and when considered in light of the structure and operation of modern anti-discrimination laws. . . .

Appendix A

Amendment 2 bars homosexuals from securing protection against the injuries that . . . public-accommodations laws address. That in itself is a severe consequence, but there is more. Amendment 2, in addition, nullifies specific legal protections for this targeted class in all transactions in housing, sale of real estate, insurance, health and welfare services, private education, and employment. . . .

Not confined to the private sphere, Amendment 2 also operates to repeal and forbid all laws or policies providing specific protection for gays or lesbians from discrimination by every level of Colorado government. . . .

Amendment 2's reach may not be limited to specific laws passed for the benefit of gays and lesbians. It is a fair, if not necessary, inference from the broad language of the amendment that it deprives gays and lesbians even of the protection of general laws and policies that prohibit arbitrary discrimination in governmental and private settings. . . . At some point in the systematic administration of [existing anti-discrimination] laws, an official must determine whether homosexuality is an arbitrary and thus forbidden basis for decision. Yet a decision to that effect would itself amount to a policy prohibiting discrimination on the basis of homosexuality, and so would appear to be no more valid under Amendment 2 than the specific prohibitions against discrimination the state court held invalid. . . .

In any event, even if, as we doubt, homosexuals could find some safe harbor in laws of general application, we cannot accept the view that Amendment 2's prohibition on specific legal protections does no more than deprive homosexuals of special rights. To the contrary, the amendment imposes a special disability upon those persons alone. Homosexuals are forbidden the safeguards that others enjoy or may seek without constraint. They can obtain specific protection against discrimination only by enlisting the citizenry of Colorado to amend the state constitution or perhaps, on the State's view, by trying to pass helpful laws of general applicability. This is so no matter how local or discrete the harm, no matter how public and widespread the injury. We find nothing special in the protections Amendment 2 withholds. These are protections taken for granted by most people either because they already have them or do not need them; these are protections against exclusion from an almost limitless number of transactions and endeavors that constitute ordinary civic life in a free society. . . .

We cannot say that Amendment 2 is directed to any identifiable legitimate purpose or discrete objective. It is a status-based enactment divorced from any factual context from which we could discern a relationship to legitimate state interests; it is a classification of persons undertaken for its own sake, something the Equal Protection Clause does not permit. "[C]lass legislation . . . [is] obnoxious to the prohibitions of the Fourteenth Amendment. . . ." Civil Rights Cases, 109 U.S., at 24.

We must conclude that Amendment 2 classifies homosexuals not to further a proper legislative end but to make them unequal to everyone else. This Colorado cannot do. A State cannot so deem a class of persons a stranger to its laws. Amendment 2 violates the Equal Protection Clause, and the judgment of the Supreme Court of Colorado is affirmed.

It is so ordered.

Minority Opinion

[The dissenting opinion argues that homosexuals are just another political class: they have the right to argue for special protection, and the public has the right to deny them that protection. For more detail on the dissenting opinion, see Chapter 2.]

The Court's opinion contains grim, disapproving hints that Coloradans have been guilty of "animus" or "animosity" toward homosexuality, as though that has been established as Unamerican. Of course it is our moral heritage that one should not hate any human being or class of human beings. But I had thought that one could consider certain conduct reprehensible—murder, for example, or polygamy, or cruelty to animals—and could exhibit even "animus" toward such conduct. Surely that is the only sort of "animus" at issue here: moral disapproval of homosexual conduct, the same sort of moral disapproval that produced the centuries-old criminal laws that we held constitutional in *Bowers*. The Colorado amendment does not, to speak entirely precisely, prohibit giving favored status to people who are homosexuals; they can be favored for many reasons—for example, because they are senior citizens or members of racial minorities. But it prohibits giving them favored status because of their homosexual conduct—that is, it prohibits favored status for homosexuality.

But though Coloradans are, as I say, entitled to be hostile toward homosexual conduct, the fact is that the degree of hostility reflected by Amendment 2 is the smallest conceivable. The Court's portrayal of Coloradans as a society fallen victim to pointless, hate-filled "gay-bashing" is so false as to be comical. Colorado not only is one of the 25 States that have repealed their antisodomy laws, but was among the first to do so. . . . But the society that eliminates criminal punishment for homosexual acts does not necessarily abandon the view that homosexuality is morally wrong and socially harmful; often, abolition simply reflects the view that enforcement of such criminal laws involves unseemly intrusion into the intimate lives of citizens. . . .

There is a problem, however, which arises when criminal sanction of homosexuality is eliminated but moral and social disapprobation of homosexuality is meant to be retained. The Court cannot be unaware of that problem; it is evident in many cities of the country, and occasionally bubbles to the surface of the news, in heated political disputes over such matters as the introduction into local schools of books teaching that homosexuality is an optional and fully acceptable "alternate life style." The problem (a problem, that is, for those who wish to retain social disapprobation of homosexuality) is that, because those who engage in homosexual conduct tend to reside in disproportionate numbers in certain communities; . . . have high disposable income, . . . and of course care about homosexual-rights issues much more ardently than the public at large, they possess political power much greater than their numbers, both locally and statewide. Quite understandably, they devote this political power to achieving not merely a grudging social toleration, but full social acceptance, of homosexuality. . . .

That is where Amendment 2 came in. It sought to counter both the geographic concentration and the disproportionate political power of homosexuals by (1) resolving the controversy at the statewide level, and (2) making the election a single-issue contest for both sides. It put directly, to all the citizens of the State, the question: Should homosexuality be given special protection? They answered no. The Court today asserts that this most democratic of procedures is unconstitutional. Lacking any cases to establish that facially absurd proposition, it simply asserts that it must be unconstitutional, because it has never happened before.

STATE COURT

NORTON V. MACY, 417 F2d 1161 (1969)

When a National Aeronautics and Space Administration (NASA) employee was arrested for soliciting another man, he was fired from his job. The employee sued to regain his job, and the U.S. Court of Appeals eventually upheld his suit, ruling that federal employees could not be fired for "immoral behaviors" that did not affect their work performance. As the court described it:

Appellant's dismissal grew out of his arrest for a traffic violation. In the early morning of October 22, 1963, he was driving his car in the vicinity of Lafayette Square. He pulled over to the curb, picked up one Madison Monroe Procter, drove him once around the Square, and dropped him off at the starting point. The two men then drove off in separate cars. Two Morals Squad officers, having observed this sequence of events, gave chase, traveling at speeds of up to 45 miles per hour. In the parking lot of appellant's Southwest Washington apartment building, Procter told the police that appellant had felt his leg during their brief circuit of Lafayette Square and then invited him to appellant's apartment for a drink. The officers arrested both men and took them "to the Morals Office to issue a traffic violation notice."

. . . Meanwhile, pursuant to an arrangement, the head of the Morals Squad telephoned NASA Security Chief Fugler, who arrived on the scene at 3:00 A.M. in time to hear the last of the interrogation. . . .

[Subsequently] NASA concluded that appellant did in fact make a homosexual advance on October 22, and that this act amounted to "immoral, indecent, and disgraceful conduct." It also determined that, on the basis of his own admissions to Fugler, even as subsequently clarified, appellant possesses "traits of character and personality which render [him] unsuitable for further Government employment." A Civil Service Appeals Examiner and the Board of Appeals and Review upheld these conclusions. . . .

[The Court then outlines the two bases on which appellant's discharge could be justified.]

We are not prepared to say that the [Civil Service] Commission could not reasonably find appellant's homosexual advance to be "immoral," "indecent," or "notoriously disgraceful" under dominant conventional norms. But the notion that it could be an appropriate function of the federal bureaucracy to enforce the majority's conventional codes of conduct in the private lives of its employees is at war with elementary concepts of liberty, privacy, and diversity. And whatever we may think of the Government's qualifications to act *in loco parentis* in this way, the statute precludes it from discharging protected employees except for a reason related to the efficiency of the service. Accordingly, a finding that an employee had done something immoral or indecent could support a dismissal without further inquiry only if all immoral or indecent acts of any employee have some ascertainable deleterious effect on the efficiency of the service. The range of conduct which might be said to affront prevailing mores is so broad and varied that we can hardly arrive at any such conclusion without reference to specific conduct. Thus, we think the sufficiency of the charges against appellant must be evaluated in terms of the effects on the service of what in particular he has done or has been shown to be likely to do. . . .

[or, failing this test]

. . . appellee is now obliged to rely solely on this possibility of embarrassment to the agency to justify appellant's dismissal. . . .

[the Court then concludes that]

Lest there be any doubt, we emphasize that we do not hold that homosexual conduct may never be cause for dismissal of a protected federal employee. Nor do we even conclude that potential embarrassment from an employee's private conduct may in no circumstances affect the efficiency of the service. What we do say is that, if the statute is to have any force, an agency cannot support a dismissal as promoting of the efficiency of the service merely by turning its head and crying "shame."

Since we conclude that appellant's discharge cannot be sustained on the grounds relied on by the Commission, the judgment of the District Court may be Reversed.

GAY STUDENTS ORGANIZATION OF THE UNIVERSITY OF NEW HAMPSHIRE V. BONNER, 367 F. SUPP. 1088 (1974)

A group of gay students at the University of New Hampshire sued the university for equal access to facilities that would have been allowed to nongay students—a plea that was upheld in 1974 by the New Hampshire Supreme Court. As the court found:

This civil rights action arises out of the denial by the University of New Hampshire officials of the right of the Gay Students Organization (hereinafter GSO), a homosexual organization, to hold "social functions." . . .

The GSO was organized and officially recognized as a student organization in May of 1973. The normal recognition procedure was followed. . . . On November 9, 1973, the GSO sponsored a dance on campus. This function was held without incident. . . . After the dance, there was criticism by the Governor of New Hampshire, who complained to the University about the propriety of allowing such a "spectacle." . . .

Thereafter, the GSO asked for permission to sponsor an on-campus play on December 7, 1973, and to have a social function following the play. The GSO was granted the right to put on the play, but permission for a social function following the play was denied. . . .

The play was presented on December 7th as scheduled. Although the play itself caused little comment, there was some reaction to "Fag Rag Five" and "Fag Rag VI," two "extremist homosexual" publications which were distributed sometime during the evening. . . .

After the play, the Governor of New Hampshire wrote an open letter to the Board of Trustees, wherein he stated:

> *Therefore, after very careful consideration, I must inform you the trustees and administration that indecency and moral filth will no longer be allowed on our campuses.*

Either you take firm, fair and positive action to rid your campuses of socially abhorrent activities or I, as governor, will stand solidly against the expenditure of one more cent of taxpayers' money for your institutions. . . .

Shortly thereafter, on December 17, 1973, Dr. Bonner, President of the University, issued a public statement which condemned the distribution of the Fag Rag literature, ordered an "immediate investigation" to establish responsibility for the distribution, and declared:

. . . I have ordered that the current Trustee ban on GSO social functions be interpreted more strictly by administrative authorities than had been the case before December 7, 1973.

[The Court's summary of its findings concludes that:]

In essence, this case is quite simple. The First Amendment guarantees all individuals, including university students, the right to organize and associate "to further their personal beliefs." . . . Absent the attendance of well-defined circumstances, a university must recognize any bona fide student organization and grant to that organization the rights and privileges which normally flow from such recognition. . . . From this, it follows that the GSO has the same right to be recognized, to use campus facilities, and to hold functions, social or otherwise, as every other organization on the University of New Hampshire campus.

University officials must understand that *[quoting from a previous case:]*

mere disagreement . . . with the group's philosophy affords no reason to deny it recognition. . . . The [University], acting here as the instrumentality of the State, may not restrict speech or association simply because it finds the views expressed by any group to be abhorrent. . . .

For the foregoing reasons, the defendants are herewith enjoined from prohibiting or restricting the sponsorship of social functions or use of University facilities for such functions by the Gay Students Organization. Defendants are further enjoined from treating the Gay Students Organization differently than other University study organizations.

So ordered.

FRICKE V. LYNCH, 491 F. SUPP. 381 (1980)

Aaron Fricke wanted to take a male date to his high school senior prom—and when the school said he could not, Fricke sued. Eventually, a U.S. District Court ruled that same-sex couples had to be allowed to attend a high school senior reception:

This year, during or after an assembly in April in which senior class events were discussed, Aaron Fricke, a senior at Cumberland High School, decided that he wanted to attend the senior reception with a male companion. . . .

Aaron asked principal Lynch for permission to bring a male escort, which Lynch denied. . . . Lynch gave Aaron written reasons for his action; his prime reason was the fear that a disruption would occur and Aaron or, especially, Paul [his intended companion] would be hurt. He indicated in court that he would allow Aaron to bring a male escort if there were no threat of violence. . . .

After considerable thought and research, I [the judge] have concluded that even a legitimate interest in school discipline does not outweigh a student's right to peacefully express his views in an appropriate time, place, and manner. To rule otherwise would completely subvert free speech in the schools by granting other students a "heckler's veto," allowing them to decide—through prohibited and violent methods—what speech will be heard. The first amendment does not tolerate mob rule by unruly school children.

This conclusion is bolstered by the fact that any disturbance here, however great, would not interfere with the main business of school—education. No classes or school work would be affected; at the very worst an optional social event, conducted by the students for their own enjoyment, would be marred. In such a context, the school does have an obligation to take reasonable measures to protect and foster free speech, not to stand helpless before unauthorized student violence.

BRASCHI V. STAHL ASSOCIATES CO., 74 N.Y.2D 201, 544, N.Y.S. 2D 784, 543 N.R. 2ND 49 (1989)

When Miguel Braschi's life partner died, Braschi was in danger of being evicted from his rent-controlled apartment, for only his partner's name was on the lease. A married widow or widower would have had the legal right to stay in the apartment—and Braschi sued for the same right. In 1989, the New York Court of Appeals ruled that unmarried domestic partners have the same housing rights available to married couples:

Appellant, Miguel Braschi, was living with Leslie Blanchard in a rent-controlled apartment located at 405 East 54th Street from the summer of 1975 until Blanchard's death in September of 1986. In November of 1986, respondent, Stahl Associates Company, the owner of the apartment building, served a Notice to Cure on appellant contending that he was a mere licensee with no right to occupy the apartment since only Blanchard was the tenant of record. In December of 1986 respondent served appellant with a Notice to Terminate, informing appellant that he had one month to vacate the apartment and that, if the apartment was not vacated, respondent would commence summary proceedings to evict him. . . .

[The Court then summarizes the history of the New York State housing law.]

Contrary to all of these arguments, we conclude that the term family, as used in 9 NYCRR §2204.6(d), should not be rigidly restricted to those people who have formalized their relationship by obtaining, for instance, a marriage certificate or an adoption order. The intended protection against sudden eviction should not rest on fictitious legal distinctions or genetic history, but instead should find its foundation in the reality of family life. In the context of eviction, a more realistic, and certainly equally valid, view of a family includes two adult lifetime partners whose relationship is long-term and characterized by an emotional and financial commitment and interdependence. This view comports both with our society's traditional concept of "family" and with the expectations of individuals who live in such nuclear units. . . .

[In reaching its final decision, the Court concludes that:]

Appellant and Blanchard lived together as permanent life partners for more than ten years. They regarded one another, and were regarded by friends and family, as spouses. The two men's families were award of the nature of the relationship, and they regularly visited each other's families and attended family functions together, as a couple. Even today, appellant continues to maintain a relationship with Blanchard's niece, who considers him an uncle.

In addition to their interwoven social lives, appellant clearly considered the apartment his home. He lists the apartment as his address on his driver's license and passport, and receives all his mail at the apartment address. Moreover, appellant's tenancy was known to the building's superintendent and doormen, who viewed the two men as a couple.

Financially, the two men shared all obligations including a household budget. The two were authorized signatories of three safe deposit boxes, they maintained joint checking and savings accounts, and joint credit cards. In fact, rent was often paid with a check from their joint checking account. Additionally, Blanchard executed a power of attorney in appellant's favor so that appellant could make necessary decisions—financial, medical and per-

sonal—for him during his illness. Finally, appellant was the named beneficiary of Blanchard's life insurance policy, as well as the primary legatee and
so-executor of Blanchard's estate. Hence, a court examining these facts could
reasonably conclude that these men were much more than mere roommates.

*[Based on the Court's decision in this case, the New York State Housing Agency an-
nounced a new and broader definition of family that includes unmarried same-sex
couples.]*

In the Matter of Alison D. (Anonymous) v. Virginia M. (Anonymous), 77 N.Y. 2d 651, 572, N.E. 2d 27, 569 N.Y.S. 2d 586 (1991)

*This case concerned a lesbian couple that had separated. At issue was the question of
whether the nonbiological parent had visitation rights with the child that they had
raised together. The court decision describes the facts of the case, goes on to give the
minority opinion, which would deny the nonbiological parent any visitation rights
whatsoever, and then gives the dissenting opinion by Judge Judith Kaye, who argued for the nonbiological parent's right to visit the child she had helped to raise.*

Decision

At issue in this case is whether plaintiff, a biological stranger to a child who
is properly in the custody of his biological mother, has standing to seek visitation with the child under Domestic Relations Law § 70. Plaintiff relies on
both her established relationship with the child and her alleged agreement
with the biological mother to support her claim that she has standing. We
agree with the Appellate Division that, although plaintiff apparently nur-
tured a close and loving relationship with the child, she is not a parent within
the meaning of Domestic Relations Law § 70. Accordingly, we affirm.

I

Petitioner Alison D. and respondent Virginia M. established a relationship
in September 1977 and began living together in March 1978. In March
1980, they decided to have a child and agreed that respondent would be ar-
tificially inseminated. Together, they planned for the conception and birth
of the child and agreed to share jointly all rights and responsibilities of
child-rearing. In July 1981, respondent gave birth to a baby boy, A.D.M.,
who was given petitioner's last name as his middle name and respondent's
last name became his last name. Respondent shared in all birthing expenses

and, after A.D.M.'s birth, continued to provide for his support. During A.D.M.'s first two years, petitioner and respondent jointly cared for and made decisions regarding the child.

In November 1983, when the child was 2 years and 4 months old, petitioner and respondent terminated their relationship and petitioner moved out of the home they jointly owned. Petitioner and respondent agreed to a visitation schedule whereby petitioner continued to see the child a few times a week. Petitioner also agreed to continue to pay one-half of the mortgage and major household expenses. By this time, the child had referred to both respondent and petitioner as "mommy". Petitioner's visitation with the child continued until 1986, at which time respondent bought out petitioner's interest in the house and then began to restrict petitioner's visitation with the child. In 1987 petitioner moved to Ireland to pursue career opportunities, but continued her attempts to communicate with the child. Thereafter, respondent terminated all contact between respondent and the child, returning all of petitioner's gifts and letters. No dispute exists that respondent is a fit parent. Petitioner commenced this proceeding seeking visitation rights pursuant to Domestic Relations Law § 70.

Supreme Court dismissed the proceeding concluding that petitioner is not a parent under Domestic Relations Law § 70 and, given the concession that respondent is a fit parent, petitioner is not entitled to seek visitation pursuant to section 70. The Appellate Division affirmed, with one justice dissenting, and granted leave to appeal to our court. . . .

II

Petitioner concedes that she is not the child's "parent"; that is, she is not the biological mother of the child nor is she a legal parent by virtue of an adoption. Rather she claims to have acted as a "de facto" parent or that she should be viewed as a parent "by estoppel". Therefore, she claims she has standing to seek visitation rights. These claims, however, are insufficient under section 70. Traditionally, in this State it is the child's mother and father who, assuming fitness, have the right to the care and custody of their child, even in situations where the nonparent has exercised some control over the child with the parents' consent. . . . To allow the courts to award visitation—a limited form of custody—to a third person would necessarily impair the parents' right to custody and control. Petitioner concedes that respondent is a fit parent. Therefore she has no right to petition the court to displace the choice made by this fit parent in deciding what is in the child's best interests. . . .

While one may dispute in an individual case whether it would be beneficial to a child to have continued contact with a nonparent, the Legislature did not in section 70 give such nonparent the opportunity to compel a fit parent to allow them to do so. . . .

Accordingly, the order of the Appellate Division should be affirmed, with costs.

Judge Kaye's Dissenting Opinion

The Court's decision, fixing biology as the key to visitation rights, has impact far beyond this particular controversy, one that may affect a wide spectrum of relationships—including those of long-time heterosexual stepparents, "common law" and non-heterosexual partners such as involved here, and even participants in scientific reproduction procedures. Estimates that more than 15.5 million children do not live with two biological parents, and that as many as eight to ten million children are born into families with a gay or lesbian parent, suggest just how widespread the impact may be. . . .

But the impact of today's decision falls hardest on the children of those relationships, limiting their opportunity to maintain bonds that may be crucial to their development. The majority's retreat from the courts' proper role—its tightening of rules that should in visitation petitions, above all, retain the capacity to take the children's interests into account—compels this dissent. . . .

Most significantly, Virginia M. agrees that, after long cohabitation with Alison D. and before A.D.M.'s conception, it was "explicitly planned that the child would be theirs to raise together." It is also uncontested that the two shared "financial and emotional preparations" for the birth, and that for several years Alison D. actually filled the role of co-parent to A.D.M., both tangibly and intangibly. In all, a parent-child relationship—encouraged or at least condoned by Virginia M.—apparently existed between A.D.M. and Alison D. during the first six years of the child's life.

While acknowledging that relationship, the Court nonetheless proclaims powerlessness to consider the child's interest at all, because the word "parent" in the statute imposes an absolute barrier to Alison D.'s petition for visitation. That same conclusion would follow, as the Appellate Division dissenter noted, were the co-parenting relationship one of ten or more years, and irrespective of how close or deep the emotional ties might be between petitioner and child, or how devastating isolation might be to the child. I cannot agree that such a result is mandated by section 70, or any other law. . . .

CITY OF DALLAS AND MACK VINES V. MICA ENGLAND, 846 S. W. 2D 957 (TEX. 1993)

Mica England, a lesbian, was refused the right to apply for a job with the Dallas police force on the grounds that the state's sodomy laws made lesbianism illegal.

As a result, the Texas Court of Appeals ruled that the state's sodomy laws were unconstitutional:

Mica England, appellee, sued the State of Texas, the City of Dallas, and Mack Vines, challenging the constitutionality of the Texas statute criminalizing private sexual relations between consenting adults of the same sex, Tex. Penal Code Ann. §21.06 (West 1989), and seeking to enjoin the Dallas Police Department's policy of not hiring lesbians and gay men because they violate this criminal statute. . . . The trial court now held the statute unconstitutional and enjoined the City of Dallas and its police chief both from enforcing the statute and from denying employment in the police department to lesbians and gay men solely because they violate the statute. . . .

Background

England applied for a position with the Dallas Police Department in 1989. She was invited to interview for the position and, when asked about her sexual orientation, she responded truthfully that she was a lesbian. The interviewer then informed England that under the police department's hiring policy her homosexuality made her ineligible for employment. England sued the police department, Vines (the police chief under whose tenure she was denied employment) and the State, challenging the constitutionality of the hiring policy and the criminal statute underlying the hiring policy. She also sought injunctive relief, damages, and attorney's fees. . . .

After granting the State's plea to the jurisdiction, the trial court granted partial summary judgment, declaring section 21.06 of the Penal Code unconstitutional, and enjoining the police department and its police chief from enforcing the statute and from denying employment in the police department based solely on an applicant's admission of violating section 21.06 or of being homosexual. . . .

The State as sovereign is immune from suit absent its consent. E.g., *Missouri Pac. R.R. v. Brownsville Navigation Dist.*, 453 S.W.2D 812, 813 (Tex. 1970). However, actions of a state official that are unconstitutional, illegal, wrongful, or beyond statutory authority are not immunized by government immunity and a suit seeking relief from the official's conduct is not one against the state. . . .

Conclusion

We affirm the trial court's judgment in all respects.

Appendix A

BAEHR, ET AL. V. LEWIN, 93, C.D.O.S. 3657

In this famous Hawaii case, a group of same-sex couples filed suit demanding the right to engage in same-sex marriages. The Hawaii State Supreme Court ruled that the state constitution did not guarantee this right, while also pointing out that the state's ban on same-sex marriage might be illegal, because it violated the state's constitutional protection against discrimination on the basis of sex. The court decision remained pending while the state legislature revised the state constitution to make the court case moot. Following is an excerpt from the original court decision:

Background

On May 1, 1991, the plaintiffs filed a complaint for injunctive and declaratory relief in the Circuit Court of the First Circuit, State of Hawaii, seeking, *inter alia:* (1) a declaration that Hawaii Revised Statutes (HRS) §572-1 (1985)—the section of the Hawaii Marriage Law enumerating the requisites of [a] valid marriage contract [sic]—is unconstitutional insofar as it is construed and applied by the DOH [Department of Health] to justify refusing to issue a marriage license on the *sole* basis that the applicant couple is of the same sex; and (2) preliminary and permanent injunctions prohibiting the future withholding of marriage licenses on that sole basis.

[The Court then reviews the facts of the case, namely that three same-sex couples (the "applicant couples") filed applications for marriage licenses, but were denied by the DOH even though they qualified for such licenses on all criteria except that they were of the same sex. The Court then summarizes the defendant's arguments, essentially that there is no protection for same-sex marriages in Hawaii under either the state or federal constitution. The Court responds first to this point:]

Applying the foregoing standards to the present case, we do not believe that a right to same-sex marriage is so rooted in the traditions and collective conscience of our people that failure to recognize it would violate the fundamental principles of liberty and justice that lie at the base of our civil and political institutions. Neither do we believe that a right to same-sex marriage is implicit in the concept of ordered liberty, such that neither liberty nor justice would exist if it were sacrificed. Accordingly, we hold that the applicant couples do not have a fundamental constitutional right to same-sex marriage arising out of the right to privacy or otherwise.

[The Court then opens a new line of discussion, one that was never raised by the applicants themselves.]

269

Our holding, however, does not leave the applicant couples without a potential remedy in this case. As we will discuss below, the applicant couples are free to press their equal protection claim. If they are successful, the State of Hawaii will no longer be permitted to refuse marriage licenses to couples merely on the basis that they are of the same sex. But there is no fundamental right to marriage for same-sex couples under Article I, section 6 of the Hawaii Constitution.

[The Court then outlines reasons that the applicant couple may have good cause to continue pressing their case:]

The applicant couples correctly contend that the DOH's refusal to allow them to marry on the basis that they are members of the same sex deprives them of access to a multiplicity of rights and benefits that are contingent upon that status. Although it is unnecessary in this opinion to engage in an encyclopedic recitation of all of them, a number of the most salient marital rights and benefits are worthy of note. They include (1) a variety of state income tax advantages, including deductions, credits, rates, exemptions, and estimates, under HRS chapter 235 (1985 and Supp. 1992); (2) public assistance from and exemptions relating to the Department of Human Services under HRS chapter 346 (1985 and Supp. 1992); (3) control, division, acquisition, and disposition of community property under HRS chapter 510 (1985); (4) rights relating to dower, courtesy, and inheritance under HRS chapter 533 (1985 and Supp. 1992); (5) rights to notice, protection, benefits and inheritance under the Uniform Probate Code, HRS chapter 560 (1985 and Supp. 1992); (6) award of child custody and support payments in divorce proceedings under HRS 571 (1985 and Supp. 1992); (7) the right to spousal support pursuant to HRS §572-24 (1985); (8) the right to enter into premarital agreements under HRS chapter 572D (Supp. 1992); (9) the right to change of name pursuant to HRS §574-5(a)(3) (Supp. 1992); (10) the right to file a nonsupport action under HRS chapter 575 (1985 and Supp. 1992); (11) post-divorce rights relating to support and property division under HRS chapter 580 (1985 and Supp. 1992); (12) the benefit of the spousal privilege and confidential marital communications pursuant to Rule 505 of the Hawaii Rules of Evidence (1985); (13) the benefit of the exemption of real property from attachment or execution under HRS chapter 651 (1985); and (14) the right to bring a wrongful death action under HRS chapter 663 (1985 and Supp. 1992). For present purpose, it is not disputed that the applicant couples would be entitled to all of these marital rights and benefits, but for the fact that they are denied access to the state-conferred legal status of marriage.

Appendix A

[The Court then outlines the basis for a different challenge to same-sex marriages in Hawaii:]

The equal protection clauses of the United States and Hawaii Constitutions are not mirror images of one another. The fourteenth amendment to the United States Constitution somewhat concisely provides, in relevant part, that a state may not "deny to any person within its jurisdiction the equal protection of the laws." Hawaii's counterpart is more elaborate. Article I, section 5 of the Hawaii Constitution provides in relevant part that "no person shall . . . be denied the equal protection of the laws, *nor be denied the enjoyment of the person's civil rights or be discriminated against in the exercise thereof because of* race, religion, *sex,* or ancestry." (Emphasis added.) Thus, by plain language, the Hawaii Constitution prohibits its state-sanctioned discrimination against any person in the exercise of his or her civil rights on the basis of sex.

[Finally, the Court renders its conclusion and decision.]

Because, for the reasons stated in this opinion, one circuit court erroneously granted Lewin's [Director of DOH] motion for judgment on the pleadings and dismissed the plaintiff's complaint, we vacate the circuit court's order and judgment and remand this matter for further proceedings consistent with this opinion. On remand, in accordance with the "strict scrutiny" standard, the burden will rest on Lewin to overcome the presumption that HRS §572-1 [the state marriage license law] is unconstitutional by demonstrating that it furthers compelling state interests and is narrowly drawn to avoid unnecessary abridgments of constitutional rights.

APPENDIX B

EXCERPTS FROM
STATEMENTS OF
GOVERNMENT POLICY AND
LEGISLATION

POLICY ON HOMOSEXUAL
CONDUCT IN THE
ARMED FORCES

As of press time, for this book, the U.S. Armed Forces policy on homosexuality was under review. Following is a summary of the policy in force during most of President Bill Clinton's time in office, taken from a Secretary of Defense Memorandum of July 19, 1993, outlining the policy known as "don't ask, don't tell."

The Department of Defense has long held that, as a general rule, homosexuality is incompatible with military service because it interferes with the factors critical to combat effectiveness, including unit morale, unit cohesion and individual privacy. Nevertheless, the Department of Defense also recognizes that individuals with a homosexual orientation have served with distinction in the armed services of the United States.

Therefore, it is the policy of the Department of Defense to judge the suitability of persons to serve in the armed forces on the basis of their conduct. Homosexual conduct will be grounds for separation from the military services. Sexual orientation is considered a personal and private matter, and homosexual orientation is not a bar to service entry or to continued service unless manifested by homosexual conduct. . . .

Appendix B

Policy Guidelines on Homosexual Conduct in the Armed Forces

Summary of Policy

Accession Policy Applicants for military service will no longer be asked or required to reveal if they are homosexual or bisexual, but applicants will be informed of the conduct that is proscribed for members of the armed forces, including homosexual conduct.

Discharge Policy Sexual orientation will not be a bar to service unless manifested by homosexual conduct. The military will discharge members who engage in homosexual conduct, which is defined as a homosexual act, a statement that the member is homosexual or bisexual, or a marriage or attempted marriage to someone of the same gender.

Investigation Policy No investigations or inquiries will be conducted solely to determine a service member's sexual orientation. Commanders will initiate inquiries or investigations when there is credible information that a basis for discharge or disciplinary action exists. Sexual orientation, absent credible information that a crime has been committed, will not be the subject of a criminal investigation. An allegation or statement by another that a service member is a homosexual, alone, is not grounds for either a criminal investigation or a commander's inquiry.

HATE CRIMES STATISTICS ACT

The only existing federal legislation that explicitly makes gay men and lesbians a protected group is the Hate Crimes Statistics Act of 1993. However, the act is specifically restricted to gathering statistics. Following is its complete text:

That
(a) this Act may be cited as the 'Hate Crime Statistics Act.'
(b)(1) Under the authority of section 534 of title 28, United States Code [this section] the Attorney General shall acquire data, for the calendar year 1990 and each of the succeeding 4 calendar years, about crimes that manifest evidence of prejudice based on race, religion, sexual orientation, or ethnicity, including where appropriate the crimes of murder, non-negligent manslaughter; forcible rape; aggravated assault, simple assault, intimidation; arson; and destruction, damage or vandalism of property.

273

(2) The Attorney General shall establish guidelines for the collection of such data including the necessary evidence and criteria that must be present for a finding of manifest prejudice and procedures for carrying out the purposes of this section.

(3) Nothing in this section creates a cause of action or a right to bring an action, including an action based on discrimination due to sexual orientation. As used in this section, the term "sexual orientation" means consensual homosexuality or heterosexuality. This subsection does not limit any existing cause of action or right to bring an action, including any action under the Administrative Procedure Act or the All Writs Act.

(4) Data acquired under this section shall be used only for research or statistical purposes and may not contain any information that may reveal the identity of an individual victim of a crime.

(5) The Attorney General shall publish an annual summary of the data acquired under this section.

(c) There are authorized to be appropriated such sums as may be necessary to carry out the provisions of this section through fiscal year 1994.
Sec. 2.

(a) Congress finds that—

(1) the American family life is the foundation of American Society,

(2) Federal policy should encourage the well-being, financial security, and health of the American family,

(3) schools should not de-emphasize the critical value of American family life.

(b) Nothing in this Act [this note] shall be construed, nor shall any funds appropriated to carry out the purpose of the Act [this note] be used, to promote or encourage homosexuality.

DEFENSE OF MARRIAGE ACT (DOMA)

This act was passed by Congress in 1996 to preclude states from legalizing same-sex marriage, as Hawaii seemed poised to do. Due to the "Full Faith and Credit" clause of the U.S. Constitution, states are generally required to acknowledge contracts made in other states. DOMA—whose constitutionality has never been tested—would excuse states from recognizing same-sex marriages performed in other states.

No State, territory, or possession of the United States, or Indian tribe, shall be required to give effect to any public act, record, or judicial proceeding of any other State, territory, possession or tribe respecting a relationship between persons of the same sex that is treated as a marriage under the laws of such other State, territory, possession, or tribe, or a right or claim arising from such relationship.

APPENDIX C

EXCERPTS FROM HISTORICAL
DOCUMENTS

The following documents represent an attempt to convey the feeling of some of the major participants in the history of the U.S. gay rights debate by providing a handful of major speeches, manifestos, and other writings from a few key historical moments. This collection is by no means representative of either the gay rights movement or the anti–gay rights movement. These were all controversial writings in their time, and many people who seemed to be in the same political camp as the writer would have found much to disagree with. For reasons of space, each of these documents has been presented in excerpted form, but the flavor and content of the original has been preserved.

In this appendix, three excerpts representing various gay rights positions are offered: Martha Shelley's radical militant statement "Gay Is Good"; Harvey Milk's eloquent " The Hope Speech"; and Audre Lorde's argument for the importance of African Americans in the gay rights movement and in the feminist movement. These three excerpts were chosen for their three distinct approaches to the struggle for gay rights. Because the gay rights movement, as discussed in Chapter 1, is actually composed of hundreds of smaller movements, each with its own objectives and perspectives, these three arguments represent just a smattering of some of these views.

Also included in this appendix is a press release from Reverend Jerry Falwell. With the exception of a few extremist "hate" groups, there are very few organizations that are organized solely to fight against gay rights. As a result, the anti–gay rights movement is not as multilayered and is arguably far more focused than the pro–gay rights movements. Thus, only one excerpt representing and anti–gay rights position was chosen for this appendix. Neither this excerpt nor Reverend Falwell represent all anti–gay rights advocates. Yet, Reverend Falwell has been a prominent, respected, and eloquent leader for the anti–gay rights stance, and his arguments as presented in this press release focus on what is arguably the major basis for anti–gay rights arguments: religious tradition.

"GAY IS GOOD" (1970)
BY MARTHA SHELLEY

An early pioneer of the gay liberation movement, Martha Shelley's militant essay, "Gay is Good," was known for adopting a gay version of the Black Power slogan, "Black is Beautiful," as well as for its rejection of liberal tolerance in favor of radical activism.

Look out, straights. Here comes the Gay Liberation Front, springing up like warts all over the bland face of Amerika, causing shudders of indigestion in the delicately balanced bowels of the movement. . . .

We've got chapters in New York, San Francisco, San Jose, Los Angeles, Minneapolis, Philadephia, Wisconsin, Detroit and I hear maybe even in Dallas. We're gonna make our own revolution because we're sick of revolutionary posters which depict straight he-man types and earth mothers, with guns and babies. . . .

And I am personally sick of liberals who say they don't care who sleeps with whom, it's what you do outside of bed that counts. This is what homosexuals have been trying to get straights to understand for years. Well, it's too late for liberalism. Because what I do outside of bed may have nothing to do with what I do inside—but my consciousness is branded, is permeated with homosexuality. For years I have been branded with your label for me. The result is that when I am among gays or in bed with another woman, I am a person, not a lesbian. When I am observable to the straight world, I become gay. You are my litmus paper.

We want something more now, something more than the tolerance you never gave us. But to understand that, you must understand who we are.

We are the extrusions of your unconscious mind—your worst fears made flesh. From the beautiful boys at Cherry Grove to the aging queens in the uptown bars, the taxi-driving dykes to the lesbian fashion models, the hookers (male and female) on 42nd Street, the leather lovers . . . and the very ordinary very un-lurid gays . . . we are the sort of people everyone was taught to despise—and now we are shaking off the chains of self-hatred and marching on your citadels of repression.

Liberalism isn't good enough for us. And we are just beginning to discover it. Your friendly smile of acceptance—from the safe position of heterosexuality—isn't enough. As long as you cherish that secret belief that you are a little bit better because you sleep with the opposite sex, you are still asleep in your cradle and we will be the nightmare that awakens you.

We are women and men who, from the time of our earliest memories, have been in revolt against the sex-role structure and nuclear family structure. The roles we have played amongst ourselves, the self-deceit, the compromises and the subterfuges—these have never totally obscured the fact that we exist outside the traditional structure—and our existence threatens it.

Understand this—that the worst part of being a homosexual is having to keep it secret. Not the occasional murders by police or teenage queer-beaters, not the loss of jobs or expulsion from schools or dishonorable discharges—but the daily knowledge that what you are is so awful that it cannot be revealed. The violence against us is sporadic. Most of us are not affected. But the internal violence of being made to carry—or choosing to carry—the load of your straight society's unconscious guilt—this is what tears us apart, what makes us want to stand up in the offices, in the factories and schools and shout out our true identities. . . .

"THE HOPE SPEECH" (1978)
BY HARVEY MILK

Gay politician Harvey Milk was known for making inspiring speeches urging gay and lesbian voters to seize political power through the electoral process. Following are excerpts from one of Milk's well-known speeches.

. . . So let's look at 1977 and see if there was indeed a move to the right. In 1977, gay people had their rights taken away from them in Miami. But you must remember that in the week before Miami and the week after that, the word homosexual or gay appeared in every single newspaper in this nation in articles both pro and con. In every radio station, in every TV station and every household. For the first time in the history of the world, everybody was talking about it, good or bad. Unless you have dialogue, unless you open the walls of dialogue, you can never reach to change people's opinion. In those two weeks, more good and bad, but *more* about the word homosexual and gay was written than probably in the history of mankind. Once you have dialogue starting, you know you can break down the prejudice. In 1977 we saw a dialogue start. In 1977, we saw a gay person elected in San Francisco. In 1977 we saw the state of Mississippi decriminalize marijuana. In 1977, we saw the convention of conventions in Houston. And I want to know where the movement to the right is happening. . . .

Appendix C

I know we are pressed for time so I'm going to cover just one more little point. That is to understand why it is important that gay people run for office and that gay people get elected. I know there are many people in this room who are running for central committee who are gay. I encourage you. There's a major reason why. If my non-gay friends and supporters in this room understand it, they'll probably understand why I've run so often before I finally made it. Y'see right now, there's a controversy going on in this convention about the governor. Is he speaking out enough? Is he strong enough for gay rights? And there is a controversy and for us to say it is not would be foolish. Some people are satisfied and some people are not.

You see there is a major difference—and it remains a vital difference—between a friend and a gay person, a friend in office and a gay person in office. Gay people have been slandered nationwide. We've been tarred and we've been brushed with the picture of pornography. In Dade County, we were accused of child molestation. It's not enough anymore just to have friends represent us. No matter how good that friend may be.

The black community made up its mind to that a long time ago. That the myths against blacks can only be dispelled by electing black leaders, so the black community could be judged by the leaders and not by the myths or black criminals. The Spanish community must not be judged by Latin criminals or myths. The Asian community must not be judged by Asian criminals or myths. The Italian community should not be judged by the mafia, myths. And the time has come when the gay community must not be judged by our criminals and myths.

Like every other group, we must be judged by our leaders and by those who are themselves gay, those who are visible. For invisible, we remain in limbo—a myth, a person with no parents, no brothers, no sisters, no friends who are straight, no important positions in employment. A tenth of a nation supposedly composed of stereotypes and would-be seducers of children—and no offense meant to the stereotypes. But today, the black community is not judged by its friends, but by its black legislators and leaders. And we must give people the chance to judge us by our leaders and legislators. A gay person in office can set a tone, can command respect not only from the larger community, but from the young people in our own community who need both examples and hope.

The first gay people we elect must be strong. They must not be content to sit in the back of the bus. They must not be content to accept pablum. They must be above wheeling and dealing. They must be—for the good of all of us—independent, unbought. The anger and the frustrations that some of us feel is because we are misunderstood, and friends can't feel that anger and frustration. They can sense it in us, but they can't feel it. Because a friend has never gone through what is known as coming out. I will never forget what it was like coming out and having nobody to look up toward. I remember the lack of hope—and our friends can't fulfill that. . . .

"I AM YOUR SISTER: BLACK WOMEN ORGANIZING ACROSS SEXUALITIES" (1980) BY AUDRE LORDE

African-American lesbian-feminist Audre Lorde was a pioneer in calling for the recognition of race and class issues within both the women's and the lesbian-feminist movement. In this excerpt from her famous speech, she identifies homophobia as something that divides black women in their efforts to win liberation.

. . . Because I feel it is urgent that we not waste each other's resources, that we recognize each sister on her own terms so that we may better work together toward our mutual survival, I speak here about heterosexism and homophobia, two grave barriers to organizing among Black women. And so that we have a common language between us, I would like to define some of the terms I use: *Heterosexism*—a belief in the inherent superiority of one form of loving over all others and thereby the right to dominance; *Homophobia*—a terror surrounding feelings of love for members of the same sex and thereby a hatred of those feelings in others.

In the 1960s, when liberal white people decided that they didn't want to appear racist, they wore dashikis, and danced Black, and ate Black, and even married Black, but they did not want to feel Black or think Black, so they never even questioned the textures of their daily living (why should flesh-colored Band-Aids always be pink?) and then they wondered, "Why are those Black folks always taking offense so easily at the least little thing? Some of our best friends are Black . . ."

Well, it is not necessary for some of your best friends to be Lesbian, although some of them probably are, no doubt. But it is necessary for you to stop oppressing me through false judgment. I do not want you to ignore my identity, nor do I want you to make it an insurmountable barrier between our sharing of strengths.

When I say I am a Black feminist, I mean I recognize that my power as well as my primary oppressions come as a result of my Blackness as well as my womanness, and therefore my struggles on both these fronts are inseparable.

When I say I am a Black Lesbian, I mean I am a woman whose primary focus of loving, physical as well as emotional, is directed to women. It does not mean I hate men. Far from it. The harshest attacks I have ever heard against Black men come from those women who are intimately bound to them and cannot free themselves from a subservient and silent position. I would never presume to speak about Black men the way I have heard some of my straight sisters talk about the men they are attached to. And of course that concerns me, because it reflects a situation of noncommunication in the heterosexual Black community that is far more truly threatening than the existence of Black Lesbians. . . .

And I am not alone.

When you read the words of Langston Hughes you are reading the words of a Black Gay man. When you read the words of Alice Dunbar-Nelson and Angelina Weld Grimké, poets of the Harlem Renaissance, you are reading the words of Black Lesbians. When you listen to the life-affirming voices of Bessie Smith and Ma Rainey, you are hearing Black Lesbian women. When you see the plays and read the words of Lorraine Hansberry, you are reading the words of a woman who loved women deeply. . . .

Homophobia and heterosexism mean you allow yourselves to be robbed of the sisterhood and strength of Black Lesbian women because you are afraid of being called a Lesbian yourself. Yet we share so many concerns as Black women, so much work to be done. The urgency of the destruction of our Black children and the theft of young Black minds are joint urgencies. Black children shot down or doped up on the streets of our cities are priorities for all of us. The fact of Black women's blood flowing with grim regularity in the streets and living rooms of Black communities is not a Black Lesbian rumor. It is sad statistical truth. The fact that there is widening and dangerous lack of communication around our differences between Black women and men is not a Black Lesbian plot. It is a reality that is starkly clarified as we see our young people becoming more and more uncaring of each other. Young Black boys believing that they can define their manhood between a sixth-grade girl's legs, growing up believing that Black women and girls are the fitting target for their justifiable furies rather than the racist structures grinding us all into dust, these are not Black Lesbian myths. These are sad realities of Black communities today and of immediate concern to us all. We cannot afford to waste each other's energies in our common battles. . . . I do not want to be tolerated, nor misnamed. I want to be recognized.

I am a Black Lesbian, and I *am* your sister.

"WHY DID I DO IT?" (1999)
BY REV. JERRY FALWELL

One of the most influential antigay leaders in the United States has been the Reverend Jerry Falwell, whose Liberty Alliance (formerly the Moral Majority) made headlines when Falwell hosted an "antiviolence summit" with Reverend Mel White, a former Falwell associate and current leader of a gay evangelical group. In the following press release, which was released on October 23, 1999, Falwell explains why he sponsored the historic meeting.

Why did I do it?

This past weekend in Lynchburg, Va., my ministry hosted an anti-violence summit with about 200 homosexual-rights advocates and 200 conservative Christians in attendance. The purpose of this assembly was to design a dual strategy, within both constituencies, calling for an end to the epidemic of violence in our nation. The Rev. Mel White, co-chair of Soulforce and my friend for more than 15 years, organized the assemblage of religious homosexuals, while I directed the conservative-Christian branch.

During the press conference that followed the anti-violence forum, I shared a personal story with more than 100 media persons from around the country. I told how I was once asked by a reporter, "Rev. Falwell, what would you do if one of your sons told you, 'Dad, I'm gay'?" (My children were still at home when I was asked this question. They are now parents themselves.)

I responded, "There is absolutely nothing one of my three children could say or do that would cause me to expel them from my love or from my home." If my son told me he was gay, I would tell him, "While I do not approve of the lifestyle you have chosen, I love you unconditionally; this is still your home. And while I pray that I can lead you back to normalcy, nothing has changed in our relationship."

As most people know, my position on homosexuality is founded in the Bible. I believe the Bible—God's infallible Word—prohibits all sexual activity outside the traditional bonds of marriage between a man and woman. I Thessalonians 4:3 tells us to "abstain from fornication." I Peter 2:11 further teaches us to "abstain from fleshly lusts, which war against the soul."

Romans 1:26-27 informs us of an earlier time when sexual immorality and self-worship brought great consequence to those involved. "For this cause God gave them up unto vile affections: for even their women did change the natural use into that which is against nature: And likewise also the men, leaving the natural use of the woman, burned in their lust one toward another; men with men working that which is unseemly, and receiving in themselves that recompense of their error which was meet." Other similar verses abound.

With 200 homosexuals staring me in the face last Saturday, I accentuated the biblical position that homosexuality is sin. I also cautioned everyone attending that meeting that my position would never falter. I will never presume to counter God's Law.

However, I believe that the Bible also calls me (and all Christians, for that matter) to be a minister of God's Truth. That means that I am to love all people—no matter how much I may disagree with them. The anti-violence forum was therefore designed to not only join forces with the homosexual community in reducing the strident rhetoric, on both sides of this debate, but to build a bridge of love and communication to the millions of gays and lesbians in our culture.

CAN WE LOVE GOD AND NOT OUR BROTHER?

Nevertheless, while Christians cannot condone homosexuality, there is no biblical mandate that we must viciously rebuke those who embrace that lifestyle. The Rev. Fred Phelps of Topeka, Kan., who protested our summit along with a handful of supporters, takes a radically different approach.

Phelps and his entourage spat out venomous taunts at homosexuals attending the summit, as well as thousands of my church members on Sunday morning. I believe Phelps and his ilk are dangerous because their noxious words are motivated by hatred. I believe there is a distinct likelihood that their words can coerce violence. That is not how my Bible tells me we are to conduct our lives.

Matthew 5:44 instructs us to, "Love your enemies, bless them that curse you, do good to them that hate you, and pray for them which despitefully use you, and persecute you." By loving those who oppose us, we stand on the high ground and gain an ability to clearly communicate the gospel of Christ. No one pays any heed to the message of Fred Phelps because it offers no hope of redemption—only retribution.

I challenge Rev. Phelps to explain how he can justify his actions when the Bible cautions against such endeavors. "Beloved, if God so loved us, we ought also to love one another" (I John 4:11). I remind Rev. Phelps of another verse, I John 4:20: "If a man say, I love God, and hateth his brother, he is a liar; for he that loveth not his brother whom he hath seen, how can he love God whom he hath not seen?"

I truly believe that the Bible compels Christians to humbly reach out with the message of the gospel. God saved me out of a life of sin, and He can do it for anyone. Anyone! Carrying signs that reflect alarming messages such as "Fags Burn In Hell," strikingly contrasts the biblical command to "preach the gospel to every creature" (Mark 16:15).

That is one of the verses that prompted me to agree to host the anti-violence summit. My hope is that many more people will now openly listen to my message because I have clarified that my impetus for preaching the gospel of Christ is His perfect love. There is no hate motivating my message and I am going to be ever cautious to ensure that my position is always motivated in this regard.

"New Creatures" in Christ

One need look no further than the electrifying testimony of Michael Johnston to see how God is not limited in whom He can reach. Michael, who joined us in Lynchburg over the weekend, was consumed by the homosexual lifestyle for many years. As a tragic result, he now carries the AIDS virus.

But God is gloriously using Michael as he courageously shares Christ's love and redemptive power with many people that may otherwise never hear the gospel message. Of course, he is paying a price for this effort as the homosexual community bitterly attacks his labors. Michael's full reward will not come in this world; but in a greater world that lies ahead.

It is important to note that when Michael fully gave his life to Christ, he became a "new creature" in Him. God accepts us where we are, but He immediately draws us to Him and calls us to a life of transformation in Him. "Therefore if any man be in Christ, he is a new creature: old things are passed away; behold, all things are become new" (II Corinthians 5:17). To disregard this verse is to be blinded by one's own desires.

Great Christian theologian A. W. Tozer described salvation as "the restoration of a right relation between man and his Creator." He continued by saying that "a satisfactory spiritual life will begin with a complete change in relation between God and the sinner; not a judicial change merely, but a conscious and experienced change affecting the sinner's whole nature."

I am committed to helping Michael Johnston and thousands of other "ex-gays" declare their message of godly deliverance because I continue to believe that many homosexuals are hungering for an escape from their lifestyle. Furthermore, I agree with Robert Knight of the Family Research Council who said last week, "Pretending darkness is light does not turn sin into virtue."

There would be no value to my message if I ignored the transformation of the Christian that is mandated by Christ.

Opposition to the Summit

I realize that many will continue to stridently oppose my message. Bob Kunst, leader of the homosexual-rights group known as the Oral Majority, is one such person. Bob also protested our anti-violence summit, saying that I should stay out of homosexuals' business. He also believes that my insistence in calling homosexuality sin is, in itself, a precarious insult to homosexuals.

Nevertheless, I cannot turn a blind eye to Romans, Chapter 1, and several other biblical passages simply because Bob Kunst doesn't like the message that his actions are sinful and dangerous. My objective is not to challenge Bob's right to conduct his life as he pleases—within the bounds of law that we all must observe. My intent is rather to challenge the homosexual agenda which, I believe, not only counters the Bible, but also contradicts the Judeo-Christian values set forth by our nation's Founding Fathers.

I not only have a right to challenge him, I believe I have a biblical mandate to confront the culture—as did the Apostle Paul—with the Truth of Christ.

OUR AGE OF VIOLENCE

Will this summit thwart the death of a homosexual young person at the hand of a brutal attacker? Will this summit avert Christian young people from being slaughtered in their schools and churches by crazed gunmen? I can only hope that it will have a positive impact in saving lives or averting assaults.

All people in our nation deserve the right to pursue their lives in a safe environment. Any Christian who lifts a hand against a homosexual does so without the approval of God. While I will preach homosexuality as sin until the day I die, I will also condemn the bitter anger that occasionally rears its head by those claiming to be Christians. In addition, the homosexual community must stop their assaults on Christians.

I repeat that I am committed to upholding the biblical message of Christ's redemptive power. It is my sincere hope that, through this meeting, we will positively affect this violent culture in which we live. It is also my fervent hope that we can affect eternity. I pray that, through the high visibility of this summit, many individuals will soon come to know the peace "which passeth all understanding" that Paul described in Philippians 4:7.

CREDITS

---

articles *(continued)*
  on hate crimes
    legislation 199–202
  on history and
    analysis of gay
    rights movement
    202–205
  on housing rights
    205–206
  on immigration laws
    and political asylum
    206–207
  on international gay
    rights issues
    207–209
  on marriage 209–217
  on military 217–220
  on politics 220–230
  on religion 230–233
  on sodomy laws
    233–234
  on transgender issues
    234–236
  on workplace issues
    236–240
assimilationism 8–10
auto workers 53

B
backlash 3–4, 11, 38–40,
  72, 92, 102, 126, 133
Badgett, M. V. Lee 102
Baehr, et al., v. Lewin
  61–62, 63, 79
  excerpt from
  269–271
Baker, Jack 136, 145
Balaban, Evan 14
Baldwin, Tammy 136
ballot measures, articles
  on 182–185
Baptists 117–118
Barnes and Noble
  120–121
Barnett, Jeanne 115

Barrie, Dennis 103
bars and clubs 33–34,
  35–36
  Snake Pit 37
  Stonewall 23, 24, 35,
    36–38, 57, 71, 90,
    124
bathhouses 40–41
Bauman, Robert 136
Bawer, Bruce 9, 167
Becoming Visible
  (McGarry and
  Wasserman) 60, 163
Bell, Arthur 136
Ben, Lisa 136
bibliography 170–242
  articles. *See* articles
  books 170–179
  web sites 240–242
biographical listing
  135–151
Birch, Elizabeth 78–79,
  136, 155–156
bisexuals 17, 153
Biskupic, Joan 84,
  94–95, 166
Blackmun, Harry A. 90
Black Panthers 23, 24
Blanchard, Leslie
  98–100
Bonauto, Mary 94
books 105–106, 113,
  163–165
  in bibliography
  170–179
  on history of gay
  rights 31–32, 164
Boozer, Melvin 136–137
Boston 7, 45, 132
Boswell, John 32, 47, 48
Bottini, Ivy 137
bottom 153
Bottoms, Pamela Kay
  66
Bottoms, Sharon 66

Bottoms v. Bottoms 66
Bower, B. 119–120
Bowers, Michael J. 77,
  89, 137, 149
Bowers v. Hardwick 50,
  51, 52, 77, 86, 88–92,
  109, 128, 133, 137,
  151, 161
  excerpt from
  253–255
Boy George 106
Boy Scouts of America
  (BSA) 7, 95, 119, 133,
  134, 139
*Boy-Wives and Female
  Husbands* (Murray and
  Roscoe, eds.) 32
Bragdon, Randon 76
Bragdon v. Abbott 76
Braschi, Miguel 98–100,
  129
*Braschi v. Stahl Associates
  Co.* 88, 98–100, 129
  excerpt from
  263–265
Briggs, John V. 39, 137,
  153
Briggs Initiative
  (Proposition 6) 39, 72,
  109, 126, 137, 153
Broberg, William "Bro"
  16
Brown, Howard 137
Brown, Rita Mae 125,
  137
Bryant, Anita 11, 38–39,
  72, 126, 137–138
Buchanan, Patrick 43,
  169
Buckley, William F. 41
Buehrens, John 119
buggery 49
Burke, Fred G. 108
Buseck, Gary 76
Bush, George 130

butch 35, 153
Byton High 110–111,
    127

C

Califia, Pat (Patrick) 17,
    22, 102, 112, 138
California 82–83,
    109–110
    Proposition 6 (Briggs
        Initiative) in 39, 72,
        109, 126, 137, 153
    Proposition 22
        (Knight Initiative)
        in 70, 79–80, 117,
        133, 134, 156
Callen, Michael 138
Cammermeyer,
    Margarethe 138
Campbell, Jack 138
Carey, Rea 111
Carter, Jimmy 138
Catholic Church 7, 113,
    114, 142, 143, 147
Cervantes, Madolin 138
Charlton, Ellie 115
Chicoine, Lisa 65, 66
Chicoine v. Chicoine 65–66
children 21
    adoption of 6, 28,
        67–69, 82–84, 132
    articles on
        179–180
    custody of 6, 18, 21,
        28, 29, 31, 46,
        64–68, 153
    articles on
        194–195
    visitation rights and
        158
Christian Action
    Network 104–105
Christian Broadcasting
    Network, news release
    from 281–282

Christian Coalition 14,
    81, 83, 153
*Christianity, Social
    Tolerance, and
    Homosexuality* (Boswell)
    47
Christian right 153, 154
Christians, Christianity
    7, 14, 113
    sodomy laws and
        46–49
    See also religion
Christopher Street West
    parade 19
Church of Jesus Christ of
    Latter-Day Saints
    116–117
*City of Dallas and Mack
    Vines v. Mica England*
    52
    excerpt from
        267–268
civic organizations,
    articles on 185–187
Civil Service
    Commission, U.S. 57,
    73, 97
civil service jobs 56–57,
    72–74
civil unions 28, 63, 80,
    134
    See also marriage, gay
Clark, Karen 138
class 24, 25, 84
Clausen, Jan 16
Clendinen, Dudley 163
Cliff, Michelle 138
Clinton, Bill 74, 78, 85,
    117, 133, 136, 143, 146
    and gays in the
        military 43, 74–75,
        131, 134, 138–139,
        147, 151
Clinton, Hillary 75
closet 14, 156

clubs and bars 33–34,
    35–36
    Snake Pit 37
    Stonewall 23, 24, 35,
        36–38, 57, 71, 90,
        124
Cochran, Susan 119
Cock-a-pillar 19
Cohen, William 75, 134
Cohn, Roy 139
Colorado, Amendment 2
    in 42–43, 55, 58, 92,
    93, 131, 132, 149,
    152–153, 255–259
Combahee River
    Collective 125
Come Out! 19, 37, 107
coming out 14, 111, 153
communism 57, 87, 123
"Compulsory
    Heterosexuality and
    the Lesbian
    Continuum" (Rich)
    11–12, 148
Comstock Law (1873)
    59, 60
Connors v. City of Boston
    81
consenting adults 71,
    153
Cordova, Jeanne 139
court cases 45, 87–100
    articles on 187–189
    excerpts from
        253–271
    federal 95–97
    Internet sources of
        information on
        168–169
    state 97–100
        excerpts from
            259–271
    Supreme Court. *See*
        Supreme Court,
        U.S.

gay rights *(continued)*
  international, articles
    on 207–209
  legal aspects of. *See*
    legal issues
  marriage and. *See*
    marriage, gay
  in 1990s 42–44
  organizations and
    agencies 243–250
  queer theory and
    26–27
  researching 161–169.
    See also
    bibliography
  Stonewall uprising
    23, 24, 35, 36–38,
    57, 71, 90, 124
  and tensions between
    gay men and
    lesbians 17–23
  and theories of
    homosexuality
    10–17
  types of issues in 5–8
*Gay Students Organization
of the University of New
Hampshire v. Bonner*
  57–58, 97–98
  excerpt from
    261–262
gender 16–17, 26–27
  antidiscrimination
    laws and 54–55
genetics 14, 15
Georgetown University
  58
Georgia 51, 77, 88–89,
  92, 133
Gilbert, Arthur 49
Ginsberg, Ruth Bader 55
Gish, John 108
Gittings, Barbara 35,
  141
Glick, Deborah 42
glossary 152–158

GMHC 25, 26, 41, 120,
  127, 141, 143, 155
Goldberg, Suzanne 82
Goldstein, Richard 167
Goldwater, Barry 141
Gomez, Jewelle 141–142
Goodstein, David 142
Gore, Al 75, 134
government jobs 56–57,
  72–74
government legislation.
  See legislation
Graff, E. J. 29, 30, 31
Grannick, Jeannine 114,
  142, 147
GRID (Gay-Related
  Immune Deficiency)
  40, 127, 152
Grier, Barbara 142
Griswold v. Connecticut 71

H
harassment
  in military 75, 151
  sexual 53, 54
  of students 111–112,
    146–147
  in workplace 53–55
Hardwick, Michael
  88–89, 90, 92, 137
Harmon, Linda 58
Harris, Daniel 9
Harris, Elise 167
Harvey Milk School
  111, 127
hate crimes 6, 84–87,
  130, 134, 155
  articles on 199–202
  Hate Crimes
    Prevention Act
    (HCPA) 85
  Hate Crimes
    Statistics Act (1990)
    84–85, 130, 155
    excerpt from
    273–274

Hawaii 61–62, 63, 79,
  80, 112, 131, 132,
  133
Hay, Harry 34–35, 123,
  142, 156
Heche, Anne 104
Helms, Jesse 85, 103,
  104, 129, 142, 145
Helvey, Terry 130
heterosexism 155
history of gay rights 18,
  31–44, 162
  articles on 202–205
  books on 31–32,
    164
  chronology
    122–134
  excerpts from
    historical
    documents
    276–285
HIV (human
  immunodeficiency
  virus) 130, 155, 166
  disability law and 42,
    76, 133
  rates of infection with
    120
  See also AIDS
Holden, Jon 69, 83, 84,
  132, 142
Hollibaugh, Amber
  142–143
homoerotic 155
homophile 34, 155
homophobia 155
Homosexual-
  Heterosexual Alliance
  Reaching for Tolerance
  (HHART) 58
homosexuality
  and assimilationism
    vs. cultural identity
    8–10
  conversion and
    14–15, 154–155

debates on nature of
10–17
history of 32–33
See also gay men; gay
rights; lesbians,
lesbianism
"Hope Speech, The"
(Milk) 277–279
Hormel, James 117, 133,
143, 144
housing 31, 88, 98–100
articles on 205–206
disability law and 42,
76, 130
Hudson, Rock 41, 128
Hughes, Holly 103, 130
Hull, Bob 123
Human Rights
Campaign (HRC) 24,
78, 86, 136, 139,
155–156
web site for 241

I

"I Am Your Sister"
(Lorde) 279–281
Idaho 71, 125
Illinois 50, 70–71, 123
immigration laws 87,
123, 130
articles on 206–207
income 21, 102
Indigo Girls 107
initiatives 70
In re ZJH (Sporleder v.
Hermes) 67–68
Integrity 7, 113
Internal Security Act
(McCarran-Walters
Act) (1950) 37, 87,
123, 124
international gay rights
issues, articles on
207–209
Internet 167–169
in the closet 14, 156

In the Matter of Alison D.
(Anonymous) v. Virginia
M. (Anonymous)
265–267
Ireland, Doug 111, 167
Islam 116

J

Jackson, Jesse 143
James, Michele 118
Jennings, Dale 35
Jennings, Kevin 110,
112
Jews, Judaism 7, 46–48,
49, 113, 116, 134
job issues. *See*
employment
John, Elton 106
Johnston, Jill 143
journals 166

K

Kameny, Franklin 143
Kansas 109
Kaplan, Lisa 16
Katz, Jonathan 33, 50
Kaye, Judith 67
Keen, Lisa 67
Kendall 32
Kendell, Kate 83
Kendrick, Benjamin 81
Kennedy, Anthony M.
93
Kennedy, Lisa 115, 118,
167
Kight, Morris 143
Kim, Richard 86
Knight, John 133, 156
Knight, Pete (William J.
"Pete") 79–80
Knight Initiative
(Proposition 22) 70,
79–80, 117, 133, 134,
156
Knights of the Clock 34
Koch, Edward 143

Kowalski, Sharon 60–61
Kozachenko, Kathy 38,
125
Kramer, Larry 22, 26,
41, 127, 143–144, 155
Kushner, Tony 9, 103,
139, 144, 167

L

Ladder 35, 60, 123
Lahusen, Kay Tobin 141
Land, Richard 117–118
lang, k.d. 107
Lapidus, Lenora M. 83
Lawrence, John 52
legal issues 3, 5–6,
44–69, 70–100
AIDS and disability
law 42, 76, 130,
133
articles on ballot
measures 182–185
employment. *See*
employment
family. *See* family
issues
free speech and
assembly 57–60,
73, 97–98, 102–108
gay marriage. *See*
marriage, gay
hate crimes. *See* hate
crimes
housing 31, 88,
98–100
articles on
205–206
disability law and
42, 76, 130
and illegal vs.
extralegal activities
44–45
immigration 87, 123,
130
articles on
206–207

Phelps, Fred 148, 169, 283–284
Philadelphia 42
physicians 56
political asylum, articles on 206–207
politics 8, 10, 21, 24, 25, 26, 38, 44, 45
   articles on 220–230
   queer theory and 27
pornography 59
postgay 156
Post Office, U.S. 59–60
Powell, Anthony 51
Powell, Colin 74–75
Powell v. State of Georgia 51
POZ 108, 120–121, 166
Presbyterian Church 118
Price, Deb 55, 78, 121, 166
Proctor, Madison Monroe 95–96
Proposition 6 (Briggs Initiative) 39, 72, 109, 126, 137, 153
Proposition 9 92, 93, 131
Proposition 22 (Knight Initiative) 70, 79–80, 117, 133, 134, 156
psychology 10–11, 15–16
publishers 105–106, 108, 142, 143
Puerto Rican Day parade 45, 46

Q

Quakers 118–119
queer 107, 156, 157
Queer Nation 130, 157
queer theory 8, 16–17, 26–27
Quinn, James 53–54

R

race 24, 25
Rainbow Curriculum 112–113, 131
rational nexus 68, 97
Ray, Amy 107
Raymer, Jim 115
Reagan, Ronald 39, 40, 41, 148
referendums 70
Rehnquist, William 55, 93
religion 7, 10, 11, 43, 113–119
   articles on 230–233
   same-sex marriages and 29
   sodomy laws and 46–49
religious right 153, 154
Religious Society of Friends 118–119
Remafedi, Gary 120
reporters 166
Republicans 43, 131
researching gay rights 161–169. *See also* bibliography
   helpful sources for 163–169
Rich, Adrienne 11–12, 138, 148
Risch, Neil 15
Rise and Fall of Gay Culture, The (Harris) 9
Rivera, Sylvia 148
Robertson, Pat 153
Robson, Ruthann 9, 30–31, 46, 61, 62, 84
Rodwell, Craig 36, 148
Romer, Richard 92
Romer v. Evans 43, 55, 58, 92–95, 132, 149, 152, 161
   excerpt from 255–259
Roos, Don 105

Rotello, Gabriel 30, 167
Rowland, Chuck 123

S

sadomasochism 157
St. Patrick's Day parades 7, 45–46, 132
Saliers, Emily 107
Same-Sex Unions in Premodern Europe (Boswell) 32
San Francisco Chronicle 165–166
Sappho Goes to Law School (Robson) 30–31, 46, 62
Sarria, Jose 149
Savage, Dan 167
Scalia, Antonin 55, 93–94, 149
Schindler, Allen 130
Schoofs, Mark 167
schools 44–45, 108–113, 131, 146–147
   articles on education issues 197–199
   curriculum in 7, 112–113
   free speech and assembly in 57–60
   students in 44, 57–58, 97–98, 110–112, 131
   teachers in 7, 39, 44, 108–110, 126, 137, 153
Schubert, Walter 56
Schumer, Charles 136, 156
Science News 119–120
Sedgwick, Eve Kosofsky 27
Seomin, Scott 105
separatism 20, 25, 157
sexual discrimination, 54–55, 61–62, 79

Sexual Ecology (Rotello) 30, 167
sexual freedom 8, 17, 19
  AIDS and 20, 30, 40–41, 142
  marriage and 29, 30
sexual harassment 53, 54
sexual identity 8, 16, 19, 33, 52
sexuality 16–17, 26–27.
  See also homosexuality
sexual minorities 157
Shahar, Robin 77, 137, 149
Shelley, Martha 276–277
Shepard, Judy 149
Shepard, Matthew 6, 85, 133, 144, 148, 149, 169
Shilts, Randy 146, 149
Signorile, Michelangelo 14, 22–23, 56, 107, 156, 167
Smith, Barbara 144, 149–150
Smoky Hill High School 58
Snake Pit 37
Socarides, Charles 150
society, participation in 7
Society for Individual Rights v. Hampton 73
Sodom 46–47
sodomy 157
sodomy laws 5–6, 46–52, 70–72, 86, 87, 125, 129, 134
  American history of 49–50
  articles on 233–234
  background of 46–49
  Bowers v. Hardwick 50, 51, 52, 77, 86, 88–92, 128, 133, 137, 151, 161

excerpt from 253–255
  child custody and 18, 46, 64
  repeal of 50, 71–72, 88, 91, 124, 125
sources 163–169
South Carolina, University of 58
Southern Baptist Convention (SBC) 117–118
Spear, Allan 38
Sporleder v. Hermes (In re ZJH) 67–68
Stachelberg, Winnie 78, 86
Stoddard, Tom 92
Stonewall uprising 23, 24, 35, 36–38, 57, 71, 90, 124
Studds, Gerry 129, 150
students 44, 57–58, 97–98, 110–112, 131
  See also schools
suicide 119–120
Sullivan, Andrew 9, 30, 44, 150, 167
Sullivan, Mark 120
Supreme Court, U.S. 43, 50, 57, 71, 73, 76, 87, 88–95, 124, 125
  Bowers v. Hardwick 50, 51, 52, 77, 86, 88–92, 109, 128, 133, 137, 161
    excerpt from 253–255
  Gay Students Organization of the University of New Hampshire v. Bonner 57–58
    excerpt from 261–262

Oncale v. Sundowner Offshore Services Inc. 55

T

teachers 7, 39, 44, 108–110, 126, 137, 153
Teena, Brandon 150
television shows 22, 104–105, 117, 126, 132
tenants movement 42, 100
Texas 51–52, 134
Thomas, Clarence 93
Thompson, Karen 60–61
top 157
transgendered 157
transgender issues, articles on 234–236
transsexual 157
transvestite 158
Trask Amendment 58
Tribe, Laurence 89
Troche, Rose 105
Tyler, Robin 150–151

U

Unitarian Universalist Association (UUA) 119
United Church of Christ (UCC) 118
United Methodist Church 115, 139
universities 57–58
Utah 82, 109

V

Vaid, Urvashi 151
Vanity Fair 107
Van Ooteghem v. Gray 73
Vermont 63, 80, 133, 134
Village Voice 37, 166, 167
Vinales, Diego 37

DE 06 '04			
DE 08 '04			
DE 16 '04			
NO 15 '05			
JA 18 '06			
JA 19 '06			
FE 06 '06			
FE 23 '06			
MY 04 '06			
AP 12 '07			
MY 03 '0			

South Campus
White Bear Lake Area High School
3551 McKnight Road
White Bear Lake, MN 55110